The Literary Imagination
in Jewish Antiquity

The Literary Imagination in Jewish Antiquity

EVA MROCZEK

OXFORD
UNIVERSITY PRESS

OXFORD
UNIVERSITY PRESS

Oxford University Press is a department of the University of Oxford.
It furthers the University's objective of excellence in research, scholarship,
and education by publishing worldwide. Oxford is a registered trade mark of
Oxford University Press in the UK and in certain other countries

Published in the United States of America by Oxford University Press
198 Madison Avenue, New York, NY 10016, United States of America

First issued as an Oxford University Press paperback, 2018

Library of Congress Cataloging-in-Publication Data
Mroczek, Eva, author.
The literary imagination in Jewish antiquity / Eva Mroczek.
pages   cm
Includes bibliographical references and index.
ISBN 978-0-19-027983-7 (cloth : alk. paper); 978-0-19-088608-0 (paperback : alk. paper)
1. Bible. Old Testament—Criticism, interpretation, etc.
2. Jews—History—70-638.
3. Judaism—History—Post-exilic period, 586 B.C.–210 A.D.   I. Title.
BS1171.3.M76   2015
221.6—dc23   2015031602

In memory of my grandmothers
Hanna Dmochowska-Mroczek (1930–1991)
and
Genowefa Rafałowicz (1935–2010)

CONTENTS

ACKNOWLEDGMENTS

The image on the cover of this book is by Montreal artist Guy Laramée, whose carved book sculptures speak of the containment and shaping of written knowledge. In Laramée's works, discarded dictionaries, encyclopedias, and even Bibles are no longer vessels for verbal communication: they are shaped into landscapes made of hidden words. In this piece, five stacked volumes, their spines still intact, have become a stark rock face dotted with caves. To the scholar of early Judaism, the landscape evokes the hills of Qumran, which, for two thousand years, concealed the Dead Sea Scrolls. As the hills revealed their secrets, we came face to face with textual forms and literary landscapes vastly different from our own.

Carving up books seems sacrilegious to bibliophiles. But the accumulation, erosion, and reshaping of knowledge that we see in Laramée's work reflects our own dynamically changing textual history. That history moves more slowly than Laramée's power tools, but both the physical forms of writing and the way people have conceptualized literary worlds and religious texts continue to take new shapes. This book takes up these questions from the perspective of Second Temple Jewish literature, asking how it appeared to its creators and earliest audiences—before the concepts of "book" and "Bible," which structure our own literary imagination, were available to think with. I thank Guy Laramée and his representation, Jayne Baum of JHB Gallery, New York, for permission to use this image. Even more, I thank him for creating work that insists we undo our assumptions about how writing is supposed to look.

My own thinking about the contours of early Jewish literature began in graduate school at the University of Toronto. Parts of this book originate in my PhD dissertation, completed there in 2012. My doctoral supervisor, Hindy Najman, drew me into the field with her inimitable energy and imagination, and showed me how to listen to ancient texts on their own terms. But she also helped me find—and trust—my own voice as a scholar. She continues to be my mentor, and I am grateful to have had a teacher who models such generosity and intellectual energy.

My path to ancient Judaism was by way of modern Jewish thought, and I owe a debt of gratitude to David Novak for teaching me how to think comparatively across texts and time. Judith Newman and Sarianna Metso taught me to place Qumran in a larger network of early Jewish practices. John Marshall and John Kloppenborg showed me the interconnectedness of religious texts in a broader ancient Mediterranean cultural world. I had the good fortune to study Hebrew with Robert Holmstedt; his patience and rigor gave me the confidence to do this work. Amir Harrak and Tirzah Meacham taught me to revel in the diversity and surprises of Aramaic texts. Harry Fox illuminated the world of rabbinic midrash with an eye for the aesthetic and the transgressive, which still inspires the questions I ask of ancient literature. I also thank James Kugel, who, during a semester in Toronto, taught me to examine the threads from which texts are woven and modeled the literary sensitivity and clarity that can make our field so exciting.

A large part of this book was written at Indiana University. I was lucky to count Bert Harrill and David Brakke as colleagues for a short time, but as trusted mentors for far longer. Winnifred Sullivan and Mark Roseman provided exemplary support to junior faculty in the Departments of Religious Studies and Jewish Studies. I thank Amali Ibrahim, Shaul Magid, Jason Mokhtarian, Jeremy Schott, and Stephen Selka for friendship and support, and all my colleagues at IU for being part of a culture that encouraged big ideas and intellectual risks. Two extraordinary graduate students—Matthew Brittingham and Brian Hillman—read and helped improve early drafts. Above all, I thank my dear friend Sarah Imhoff, who became my family shortly after I arrived in Bloomington, for her loyal support and a friendship that I know can survive geography.

Several mentors encouraged me as this project expanded beyond its more modest beginnings. My enormous thanks go to Benjamin G. Wright III, who patiently listened to my ideas before they were any good: he is an exemplary teacher, mentor, and friend. I am grateful for all I have learned from the work of Florentino García Martínez, Annette Yoshiko Reed, John Reeves, Eileen Schuller, Loren Stuckenbruck, Eugene Ulrich, and Steven Weitzman, and for their interest in engaging the work of younger scholars.

Many colleagues and friends have proven that intellectual exchange can be both challenging and humane. Sonja Anderson, Brennan Breed, Thomas Bolin, Tim Langille, Liv I. Lied, Ellen Muehlberger, and Stephen Young took time to read parts of the project, and showed me how our work is always better when it emerges in dialogue. Michael Press believed in the book from early on, and offered invaluable help in shaping it. Carla Sulzbach read and edited the entire manuscript with unwavering humor and insight. Jacqueline Vayntrub read drafts and started an exciting conversation about ancient text production that renewed my own belief in this project. Timothy Michael Law first inspired me with his vision for the study of ancient religious cultures in the academy and beyond; now, I am grateful that the intellectual spaces he creates can also foster deep friendships, and I thank him for his.

I finished writing *The Literary Imagination* as a member of the Religious Studies Department at the University of California, Davis. My new colleagues, especially David Biale, Catherine Chin, Naomi Janowitz, and Flagg Miller, responded to earlier versions of parts of this book and invited me to join them in a conversation about the creation and transmission of religious knowledge across time and media. I look forward to continuing it for many years.

I thank Cynthia Read and her team at OUP, especially Glenn Ramirez and Gwen Colvin, for shepherding the book through publication. Kristel Clayville's thoughtful editing gave my writing clarity. I am grateful for Robert Milks's sharp and judicious copy editing and for James Tucker's careful work on the index.

Parts of this book originated in different forms in "The Hegemony of the Biblical in the Study of Second Temple Jewish Literature," *Journal of Ancient Judaism* 6 (2015): 2–35, and "The End of the Psalms in the Dead Sea Scrolls, Greek Codices, and Syriac Manuscripts," *Snapshots of Evolving Traditions: Textual Fluidity, Manuscript Culture and New Philology*, ed. L.I. Lied and H. Lundhaug (Berlin: de Gruyter). I thank the publishers for permission to reproduce some of that material here. Translations of biblical texts are adapted from the NRSV; translations used for other primary texts are indicated in the notes.

I am grateful to my parents, who taught me my first foreign language—English—and instilled a curiosity about the cultures and languages of the world by traveling with me halfway around it; and my sister Julia, who has been my proudest supporter since before she could talk.

The shape of this book was only beginning to emerge from the shadows when I first described it to Seth Sanders on a ski lift in the Catskill Mountains. Since then, neither books nor landscapes have ever looked quite the same: they have taken on sharper contours and bolder colors. I think this book, too, became bolder and brighter in conversation with him. So has life in general. I am grateful to him for challenging me and imagining with me every day.

The Literary Imagination
in Jewish Antiquity

Introduction

Beyond Bible and Book

"A Fire Which Burns and Inflames My Bones"

In about 800 CE, Timothy I, patriarch of the Nestorian Church in Baghdad, heard a stunning report from Jerusalem. An Arab hunter and his dog had discovered several Hebrew manuscripts "in a chamber within a mountain" near Jericho.[1] Among these manuscripts, Timothy reports, were texts "completely missing from the Old Testament, both in our Christian one and their Jewish one." The cache must contain untold secrets, a profusion of unread writing—including, Timothy's informant said, more than two hundred psalms of David.

For the patriarch—who vividly speculates that the precious manuscripts must have been hidden by the prophet Jeremiah or his scribe Baruch, as Babylonian troops were burning Jerusalem to the ground—this discovery opened up a world of ancient writings far beyond what he knew as Scripture. But Timothy received no further response to his inquiries about the manuscripts, and his textual desires remained unfulfilled. "This," he lamented, "is in my heart like a fire which burns and inflames my bones."

Timothy had only a secondhand glimpse of an ancient scriptural world, but we have more to go on when we tell the story of early Jewish texts. The Dead Sea Scrolls, discovered in the Judean desert over a millennium after Timothy's report, along with renewed interest in the Apocrypha and Pseudepigrapha from Hellenistic and Roman times, have transformed our picture of early Jewish literature.[2] The discovery of the Dead Sea Scrolls has revolutionized the study of the Bible, showing that the text forms of biblical books were not fixed but still in flux, and variant editions of texts like Jeremiah and Exodus existed side by side.[3]

But the discoveries in the Judean desert gave us far more than information about the textual history of biblical books. Indeed, like the report that reached Timothy, they opened a window into a larger textual world that the categories of "Bible" and "book" cannot contain. In the Second Temple period, the "Bible" was not yet a unified textual entity, a specific selection of texts collected into a defined corpus. Instead, we see a rich culture where literary production flourished, there was no fixed canon, and claims to divine inspiration and authority continued in important nonbiblical traditions: the books of *Enoch*, *Jubilees*, and— like Timothy's two hundred psalms of David—a variety of psalm collections of diverse inventories and scopes that do not entirely overlap with the biblical.

What did this literary world seem like to Second Temple writers? How did they imagine it from their own, precanonical perspective? We are lucky to have clues from ancient writers themselves, who were often self-conscious about the writtenness of their creations and frequently reflected on the origins and history of their literary heritage as they understood it. From the clues Second Temple Jewish writers have left us in the Dead Sea Scrolls and other literature from the Hellenistic and early Roman period, we can glimpse an imagined world of divinely inspired writing that did not inhabit a single corpus or location, but was ancient, multiform—and never fully accessible. From the perspective of early Jewish scribes, the history of written revelation stretches back long before Moses received the tablets of the law on Mount Sinai. The revelation of written texts is part of the lore about Israel's patriarchs and kings: these heroes come to be remembered as great writers, and serve as models for the producers of new literature. Scribes recognize the authority and divine inspiration of texts like the Enochic corpus and the revelations to other ancient ancestors, which present themselves not as derivative of or dependent on material we now call biblical, but indeed, prior to it.

But the study of early Jewish texts continues to be constrained by two kinds of anachronism: a religious one—"Bible"—and a bibliographic one—"book." Scholars laud the vibrancy of nonbiblical traditions, and many now agree these texts were produced before the biblical canon was fixed—indeed, before it was even imagined. But for the most part, nonbiblical early Jewish texts have been treated as handmaids to the study of the Bible, rather than as part of a body of ancient literature that was often conferred the same kind of status as and used alongside texts that are now biblical. And important recent research on the scribal and educational contexts in which ancient writings emerged, such as the work of David Carr and Karel van der Toorn, has shown that our sources have been poorly served by modern categories of text, authorship, and publication.[4] Yet while we recognize the anachronism of such concepts, little alternative language exists for how texts were conceptualized and classified in antiquity. Pioneering scholars—like John Barton, Florentino García Martínez, Robert Kraft, Hindy Najman, Annette Reed, John Reeves, and Michael Stone—have proposed sophisticated approaches to precanonical textual culture, particularly ancient ideas of attribution, authority, and authenticity; and they have argued that the biblical canon should no longer dictate the study of early Jewish literature. But the implications of their work have not yet been integrated into the field, and the Bible still sets the agenda for the questions we ask.[5]

But what would it mean to take seriously what the Dead Sea Scrolls and recent scholarship on Pseudepigrapha have taught us—that is, that there was no fixed canon until well into the Common Era; that religious inspiration was not exclusively confined to what would become biblical text; and that concepts of authorship and textual identity were different in the ancient world? If—as T. Michael Law bluntly puts it—"before the Bible, there was no Bible,"[6] what was possible to imagine about sacred literature?

This book is a study of the literary imagination in early Judaism that offers one way into these questions. Without pretensions to comprehensiveness, I use a selection of Second Temple Jewish textual traditions to ask what the literary world might have looked like to their producers and earliest audiences, before the categories of "Bible" and "books" were available concepts.

I would like to be clear that in suggesting an alternative to thinking in terms of "Bible" and "book," I am not proposing an oral model of early Jewish literature. Oral contexts are key to the way texts were produced and used, and much excellent work has been done on orality and processes of textualization in the development of biblical literature.[7] But I focus here specifically on writing, on the role of written texts and writing figures in the ancient imagination. The corrective to anachronistic biblical and bookish categories is not only to be found in a turn to orality: the focus of my study is that aspect of early Jewish culture that is deeply, self-consciously textual, but shaped differently from our own. Indeed, the major purpose of this study is to show that it is possible—with attention to the words of ancient writers themselves—to imagine the expressly *literary* aspects of early Jewish culture without presupposing the Bible.[8]

Presuppositions about the Bible's textual centrality, then, can be challenged from a variety of methodological perspectives. From the standpoint of social history, it matters who had access to texts and what group interests they represented. Michael Satlow has argued that well into the Common Era, biblical texts had little influence beyond elite scribal circles, and they were considered authoritative only in specific and limited ways.[9] Texts might be used to inspire new writings, for example, or read as sources of divine messages to be decoded. But the idea that they should be normative for human behavior and religious practice was a late development. Satlow situates the emergence of biblical texts' normative authority and its spread beyond the rarified elites in the context of power struggles between competing Jewish groups in the late Second Temple period.[10]

I am sympathetic to this deconstruction of anachronistic presuppositions about biblical centrality before there was a Bible as such.[11] But while Satlow considers how textual authority functioned and developed in the early Jewish social world at large, I take a different approach. My focus here is more immanent, focusing on native literary theories—what we can decode from the texts themselves about how their elite producers understood their own literary world.

From this perspective, however, the idea of different kinds of textual authority also highlights something important about how to approach a written repertoire that was not yet gathered into a single collection. Texts were important for different reasons, because they were not conceived as one iconic corpus with a fixed set of cultural meanings, but inhabited a developing and multiform literary culture.

Through this immanent approach to early Jewish textual concepts, I describe ways that writings could be culturally meaningful in an earlier conceptual and material context, even before they had solidified into a Bible as such, or into its specific, fixed books. Of particular interest to me is a case study: the transmission of psalms and traditions about the ideal psalmist, David. I begin my study with psalms at Qumran and early Judaism more broadly: we do not see a "book of Psalms," but diverse psalm collections that vary widely in both size and inventory. I focus especially on the Great Psalms Scroll from Qumran, which contains both biblical and nonbiblical compositions in a radically different order from the biblical Psalter, and lauds David as a scribe and sage who wrote a staggering 4,050 songs. As well as considering the psalmic materials and Davidic traditions, I pay particular attention to the book of Ben Sira and the book of *Jubilees*, illuminating how these texts have been poorly served by biblical and bibliographic categories of analysis, and proposing new ways to approach them. Before authorial property, widespread literacy, and a fixed idea of Scripture, how did ancient people think about and organize their own literature? And can we emerge from our own cultural constraints—the mental architecture that structures the way our sources have been published, and the way we conceptualize their identities and hierarchies—to imagine our way into a different literary world?

At the end of the book, I return to the psalmic case study with a comparative look at a much later context in which psalms, both biblical and apocryphal, are recollected: the Syriac Christian tradition of Bishop Timothy and his successors. Timothy lived centuries after the canon was closed, yet he was still able to imagine inspired ancient texts that were not in the Bible. And medieval Syriac psalms manuscripts also show that not everything that was considered inspired and authentic could be found within biblical boundaries.

Nonbiblical Worlds

My starting point for a reconfiguration of the Jewish textual landscape is to recognize the persistence of the Bible as an anachronistic structuring principle for the study of this period. Fewer and fewer scholars would now argue that "Bible" and "canon" were operative ideas in Second Temple Judaism. And yet the biblical still dictates the way in which this rich literary culture is studied, serving as a powerful conceptual magnet that arranges all cultural products around itself. Despite our caveats about anachronism, the biblical returns as the default way by which texts are classified, and sets the agenda for the questions we ask.[12] Texts we call apocryphal or pseudepigraphic are called this only because they are not part of the Protestant canon of the Old Testament, not for any internal reason, and studied largely for how they relate to that canon. Two major questions dominate the field, both of them about the biblical: the nature of biblical interpretation and the development of the canon. As a result, most of these texts are read not as literary products in their own right, but mined for biblical allusions and taken as witnesses to early biblical interpretation, or combed through for clues about the views of Scripture and canonicity its authors held. When the Bible is the central text, everything else recedes into paratext, auxiliary material whose purpose is to contextualize and illuminate the biblical.

The desire to mine the Second Temple period for information about the Bible is not surprising. We want to know about the origins of the normative present, to tell evolutionary stories about how the Bible—and its uses and meaning in Judaism or Christianity—came to be. Beyond our desire to tell teleological stories, tracing biblical threads through the Second Temple period has deep roots in the history of theology. The emergence of the scriptural canon and the development of biblical interpretation have long been central to the academic study of Judaism, often in dialectic with Christian anti-Jewish approaches to biblical studies. One major accomplishment of the twentieth century was to begin debunking the supersessionist model in which postexilic Judaism, what Wellhausen called "late Judaism" (*Spätjudentum*), was a dead tradition, where a living spirit of prophecy had given way to ossified legalism and scribalism. This period was a "dark ages" whose providential purpose was to set the stage for a new phase of religious development. With the influx of interest in the Apocrypha and Pseudepigrapha—invigorated through the discovery of the Dead Sea Scrolls— our picture of Second Temple Judaism has dramatically changed. Instead of stagnation, we see a rich culture where literary production flourished, and the Second Temple period is read as the crucible of Judaism's most salient features.

But for most of the field, the bulk of this era's cultural production essentially comprises the interpretation of Scripture. Judaism was "book religion," preoccupied with reading and interpreting "the Bible." For Shaye Cohen, for example, what is at stake is a sense of continuity that connects Second Temple Judaism with ancient Israel: early Jews, he writes, did not develop the "sense of newness" that Christians did, and knew they were living in a "post-classical world" in which the texts that would become the Tanakh were the undisputed classics that stood apart from all other literature, and were now only to be interpreted.[13] Michael Fishbane writes that in the Dead Sea Scrolls, the Bible is "the unique resource of past revelations, and the mediating source of all subsequent ones"; in his work on inner-biblical interpretation, Fishbane has traced this interpretive continuity back to some of the early phases of biblical composition.[14] Conversely, James Kugel speaks of an "interpretive revolution" in the Hellenistic period, when new methods of solving problems in biblical texts flourished and Scripture began to be understood as a unified and harmonious corpus. The literary activity of the period is—conceptually if not formally—a precursor to midrashic exegesis.[15] Despite their differing narratives about the development of interpretive practices, these models share a sense of biblical centrality, the Bible as a world unto itself—a holy world, homogenous and set apart.

How does this tendency manifest itself in scholarship? One example is the concept of "rewritten Bible," a popular topic of study in scholarship on the Second Temple period. Coined by Geza Vermes, the term "rewritten Bible" refers to those nonbiblical texts that seem to substantially "rewrite" already authoritative biblical material, incorporating interpretive harmonizations and embellishments.[16] Since Vermes, analyzing interpretive motifs and scriptural allusions in pseudepigraphic texts has formed a large portion of Second Temple studies, as scholars expend vigorous energy to trace exactly how Scripture is used in nonscriptural texts. Many current studies of rewritten Bible recognize the risk of anachronism in the name given to this genre: "rewritten Bible" presupposes that there *was* a Bible to rewrite that was conceptualized as different in kind from its rewritings. But the problem is acknowledged and often bracketed. Many scholars proceed as before, showing how pseudepigraphic texts relate to the Bible, even if intertextuality with what is now biblical is only one of a myriad of textual relationships and literary strategies of an ancient author. Texts like various parts of the Enochic corpus, *Jubilees*, the *Genesis Apocryphon*, and even the Qumran Psalms Scroll have been called and studied as "rewritten Bible" or "biblical interpretation," even though exegesis does not seem to be their primary concern, and shedding light on preexisting scriptures may have been only a part of their literary motivation. The semantic range of the word "interpretation" seems to have expanded beyond exegesis, becoming a broader umbrella term for the use of or allusion to tropes, characters, symbols, and expressions that also appear in biblical texts.

Considering practices of "scriptural interpretation" or "rewriting" reveals important aspects of Second Temple literary production, but risks obscuring other motivations and priorities. Early Jewish writers did use many of the same motifs, characters, and language that we find in earlier books now classified as canonical. But their work was not merely *rewriting* but also—simply—*writing*, since all cultural products draw on past utterances. Working to trace allusions to biblical texts is a worthwhile and important way of discerning how ancient scribes worked, but sometimes we miss seeing that these writings were not primarily imagined to flow out of and point to the Bible—as the solution to its problems, answers to its questions, and illumination of its meaning—but were intended and received as new literature, perhaps new authoritative Scripture, in their own right.

Thus, the scholarly momentum to rescue the Second Temple Period from obscurity has, paradoxically, reinscribed certain models that had once conferred the Christian term "inter-testamental period" on this era. In Jewish studies, this period has primarily been studied as a bridge between two normative bodies of *Jewish* religious discourse—the Bible and its rabbinic interpretation. The Second Temple period then becomes a "middle ages" that is meaningful only as a link between these canons.[17]

This, of course, is ahistorical; there was no canon of the Bible before the rabbinic period, so the "bridge" doubles back onto the same, rabbinic shore. And reducing the entire literary output of the Second Temple period to a satellite of the biblical not only risks reinscribing the old model of a derivative, in-between phase of Judaism; it also overlooks the motivations of ancient writers themselves. While early Jewish literature did draw on its older heritage—as all cultures do—it was not only derivative, interpretive, or otherwise exclusively sourced from and focused on Scripture. It is a vibrant period both for how it connects "biblical Israel" to rabbinic Judaism (or Christianity) and as a literary culture in its own right—a literary culture bourgeoning with newness.

The Bibliographic Imagination: Book as Metaphor

The dominance of the biblical at the expense of other ways of configuring the textual landscape is related to, and reinforced by, the dominance of the bibliographic. By this I mean concepts and principles by which texts are identified, delimited, and classified in modern scholarly practice—principles that do not necessarily fit ancient ways of conceptualizing literary production. Just as the category of "Bible" did not structure the way early Jews imagined writing because the concept was not available to them, they also did not follow modern categories of text, authorship, and publication.

Book historians like Roger Chartier have shown to what extent our bookish habits of organizing the written world—"inventorying titles, categorizing works, and attributing texts"—are historically contingent.[18] Warnings of anachronism abound, but these categories remain largely naturalized—for example, language about the "publication" of "biblical books" persists in the field. Further, the concerns of scholarly bibliography—establishing date, provenance, author, and authoritative text—drive the organization and study of these materials. Sources, then, are mined for bibliographic information: which biblical texts, exactly, did the writer possess? In what form? How did he understand biblical authorship? What view of Scripture did he hold? We ask questions that reflect modern desires to establish authoritative texts, trace authorial attribution, and define relationships and hierarchies between texts. We want to fill in the blanks in our own knowledge of these texts, and complete our own fragmentary bibliographies; but we also project these interests onto ancient people themselves.

Book historians have attempted to denaturalize the concept of "book" itself, showing that "books" are not inert containers for verbal meaning; rather, they are physical objects, textual artifacts, and cultural transactions, and both their physical forms and social meanings shape the way their content is created, transmitted, and received.[19] In the last two decades, the momentum to theorize digital text, which has given writing an entirely new morphology, has put this historical contingency into sharp relief. We have seen to what extent our most basic textual categories have been informed by assumptions specific to the print codex, and to what extent we can now see every kind of text with new eyes.[20] We are aware that the book as a concept emerges from a very specific history of the transmission of text in the modern West, and the very specific way in which we have become accustomed to accessing, reading, and organizing writing. Roger Chartier, for instance, argues that the "book" as we intuitively imagine it—as an entity that links a physical object, a text, and an author—is colored by the *libro unitario,* the practice of binding the work of a single author in one codex, a historical innovation of the fourteenth and fifteenth centuries.[21]

It seems obvious that ancient texts were not "books" in this sense, and to argue that the concept of "book" is an anachronism for early Judaism is old news. But I think there is more to be said about just how deeply and persistently this concept structures our thinking, even as we emphasize its inadequacy. Here, I would suggest that it is more generative to think of "book" not as an anachronism—a familiar, perhaps so familiar it is no longer audible, critique of scholarly method—but as a metaphor; indeed, as a *root* metaphor that provides the fundamental structure for our scholarly imagination.

In the simplest terms, to use a metaphor is to describe and understand one thing in terms of another. When we say "book," we are bringing in the entire history of the book as we know it, and its entire meaning in our lived experience—our own bibliographic temper: not only the codex, print, copyright, and widespread literacy but also scholarly editing and cataloging, our own anxieties about publishing, authorial book signings, the nineteenth-century novel, airport paperbacks, and the university library.

If such ideas, and many others, contribute to our sense of what the "book" is and means, then to call early Jewish texts "books" is to use a metaphor indeed. This is something different from an anachronism. Rather, to speak metaphorically—about one thing in terms of another—is to reveal and bring near some aspects of our subject, while at the same time obscuring and alienating others. Thus, to call ancient texts "books" is not to make a historically indefensible faux pas. It is to do the work of metaphor: to make them at home in our own imagination, and to ascribe to them the power, mystery, and anxiety that the "book" holds for us. But perhaps this metaphor's descriptive power has been exhausted, and now, rather than being satisfied with how it can help us speak about ancient texts, we are more conscious of and troubled by what it cannot help us describe.

What is the next step? Unlike a call to remove an anachronism—which implies that we can strip away our own contexts to uncover something authentic and objective—to recognize that our categories are metaphors, and to search out new ones, is both less arrogant, and a more fruitful way of discerning something meaningful about the ancient world. I propose that trying out new metaphors can help us find other corners of our imagination where these texts might also find a home—and ways of describing the sources that will illuminate those aspects of our ancient materials that have remained largely inconceivable.

Reconfiguring the Literary Landscape

While the modern study of early Jewish texts, then, is dominated by modern interests in the Bible and modern bibliographic concerns, these interests and concerns do not always dominate the ancient imagination. Their categories employed a different logic and a different poetics. And when literature is read primarily as a source of information about something else—in the service of telling another text's story—it becomes invisible as a text in its own right. What is pushed out are the literary interests and strategies of the authors, many of which do not converge around the Bible, its canonical status, and its interpretation.

This is not to downplay the importance of the texts that we call biblical in the Second Temple Jewish imagination. Instead, it is to reconfigure how we talk about their shapes and boundaries and their relationships with other texts in ways that do not presuppose modern biblical and bibliographic ideas, namely, a religious culture that converges around a book where the full revelation of the divine will is to be found.

To be sure, most of the texts treated as authoritative and extensively copied in the Second Temple period were quite close to the biblical books we now have. Among the Qumran manuscripts are texts that look very much like the Masoretic Text—the authorized text of biblical books in the rabbinic Bible—as well as the Hebrew texts that underlie the Septuagint—the Greek translation of the Hebrew Scriptures that was later used by early Christian communities.[22] Many of the texts now in the Bible had pervasive cultural influence, especially such texts as Genesis, Exodus, Deuteronomy, and Isaiah, which were widely copied and invoked in other writings. This is unmistakable. But the texts that are now biblical cannot be assumed to be the singular center of the literary imagination, or the source and touchstone of all other literary products, from the perspective of Second Temple writers and readers themselves.

Both the forms of the biblical texts and the shape of the biblical canon as it emerges in the rabbinic and patristic period have earlier roots. But it is not clear how a contained corpus of Scripture, with its specific list of books and a tripartite division into Torah, Prophets, and Writings, emerged from the more amorphous sense of revealed and authoritative literature that we see in Second Temple writings. References to the authority of the Torah abound, although this may not always be identical to our Pentateuch. Classic proof texts for the precursors of the canon include the translator's prologue to Ben Sira, which mentions that Ben Sira was learned in "the law and the prophets and the other books of our ancestors," but the reference is too vague to map clearly onto the tripartite division of the Jewish canon; and 2 Macc 13, which mentions a library founded by Nehemiah as well as Judah Maccabee's collection of books, but this tells us nothing about the idea of canon per se. The first references to a specific number of books come late in the first century CE—twenty-two books in Josephus and twenty-four in 4 Ezra—but, as we will see in the final chapter, they do not tell us which books they are, and the iconic number likely preceded the actual list of books that comprised it.

The turning point in the emergence of a bounded canon seems to be the destruction of the Jerusalem Temple in 70. At that point, the leadership of the Jewish community was consolidated in the hands of a specific group of scholars, conventionally called the rabbis. Many of the most popular writings, which had been copied, preserved, and interpreted for generations, continued to hold sway. Some texts that were once popular but, for instance, promoted the "wrong" calendar or transmitted knowledge deemed too esoteric, were no longer accepted for communal use.

This book, however, does not deal directly with the question of how the canon emerged. Instead, I treat the Judaism of the late Second Temple period, when "canon" was not an operative category, and when different possibilities existed for imagining the morphology of sacred literature. Beginning with questions about how our own normative corpora and concepts developed out of an earlier matrix risks sidelining those other possibilities, since they do not directly point to the answers we seek.

In seeking to describe a precanonical world on its own terms, then, I deliberately leave teleological questions in the margins. The very questions we ask can become magnets that attract certain kinds of sources to themselves, but leave others behind. We thus disrupt the shape of the literary world as it may have appeared to ancient people, who had no awareness of a canonical finish line.

How, then, can we integrate biblical and nonbiblical texts into a fuller picture of a literary imagination that was unaware of such categories? Outside the themes of "canon formation" and "biblical interpretation," and beyond the terms "pseudepigrapha" and "rewritten bible," little alternative language exists for describing early Jewish literary culture. But in this study, I suggest what a nonbiblicizing approach might look like—that is, how different our reading of the early Jewish cultural landscape might be if we took off the biblical—and bookish—spectacles. What would it look like if we put aside the driving interests of modern scholars in the origins and development of the Bible, and tried to imagine our way into the driving interests of ancient people, in their own context?

What emerges is a vibrant textual culture that was not necessarily centered on the biblical and not organized along modern bibliographic categories. In the absence of "Bible" as a structuring center, and long before modern scholarly anxieties about identifying texts, establishing authors, and completing bibliographies, ancient people had their own ways of imagining and classifying writing. In order to make these interests more visible, we might draw new metaphors both from our own scholarly imagination and from the images the ancient texts themselves employ. For instance, might thinking in terms of archives or databases, rather than books, help us rethink the relationships between early Jewish texts?[23] Might we take seriously, for example, Ben Sira's own characterization of his work as "a canal from a river" or as a "gleaner after the grape harvesters," or narratives in *Jubilees* about scribal heroes and imaginary texts, in our attempts to name and describe scribal products?

If we do, we see that different metaphors—both new and very old, gleaned from the texts themselves—lead to new possibilities for conceptualizing the literary imagination of these texts. We see the possibility that our sources inhabited a less defined textual world—one that was not constrained by a rigid concept of Scripture, and one that was not entirely within their reach. Rather than "authors" as figures that authorize and organize texts, we see generative literary characters who were known for the skill of writing; rather than "books," we have multigenerational projects that enabled their own expansion and were not necessarily intended or received as original or complete. We see that the very *idea* of a written text was sometimes more significant than any specific verbal content it communicated. The way ancient people conceptualized the totality of their literary inventory was often vague and undefined—characterized by a cultural receptivity to incompleteness, fragmentation, and possibility. More has been revealed than has ever been read; the world is full of secrets, and books—more books, better books!—are waiting to be discovered under every stone.

This book attempts to describe such a world on its own terms, not only as a way to answer modern questions about how the texts, canon, and exegesis of the Bible came to be. In our desire to fill in the gaps in this story, we often find it difficult to accept that sometimes, the sources we have are not in fact interested in our questions and do not follow our rules, but have different concerns and other anxieties. Our sources do not always supply data about the Bible; but while there is less information about the formation, interpretation, and canonization of specific biblical texts than we sometimes want, there is a wealth of material about the imaginative worlds of ancient writers, in which books—whether real or imagined, well known or lost, ancient or new, public or secret—were often the main characters.

Overview of Chapters

In this study of the ancient literary imagination, I use familiar sources to tell an unfamiliar story. One central example is the production and expansion of psalms (biblical and nonbiblical) in early Judaism, in both Hebrew and Greek, and their recollection in later materials, up to and including the Syriac Christian world of Bishop Timothy and his medieval successors. This was a continuous religious and aesthetic project connected to the creation of lore about the ideal psalmist and authorial figure, David, and spurred by the desire to propagate written heritage across the borders of language, canon, and religious identity. Along with Psalms, my two other major sources are the book of Ben Sira (also known as Sirach or Ecclesiasticus) and the book of *Jubilees*, seen in the context of other early Jewish texts. Using these sources, I present four chapters about how early Jews imagined their sacred literature in a pre-Bible, pre-book world. The fifth chapter looks ahead to when something like a canon begins to crystallize in Jewish and Christian materials of late antiquity, discussing the persistence of a broader, nonbiblically constrained literary imagination on both sides of the canonical and religious divide.

Many other sources, such as the visionary and scientific literature in Aramaic known only from the Dead Sea Scrolls, or works that survive only in Slavonic translations, can transform our sense of what early Jews were reading. Much important work is being done on recovering their place in literary and religious history.[24] But although these lesser-known texts make appearances in this book, they are not my primary focus. Rather, I have chosen my major sources because they have long been familiar to scholars, and seem to have a fairly firm and straightforward place in our conception of early Jewish literary history.

Psalms, Ben Sira, and *Jubilees* were all written in Hebrew, were translated into Greek and other languages, and enjoyed prominence and popularity in both Jewish and Christian circles. Each, in fact, is part of someone's Bible: the Psalms are shared across all traditions, Ben Sira counts among the Apocrypha but is scriptural for Catholics and Orthodox Christians, and *Jubilees* is included in Ethiopic canonical lists. While some of the Pseudepigrapha have come down to us only through Christian transmission in secondary or tertiary translations, and can more firmly be situated in Christian contexts of late antiquity and the Middle Ages,[25] my major sources can be more securely placed in the Second Temple Jewish milieu—although, for the sake of comparison and *Nachleben*, I discuss some of their patristic and rabbinic contexts as well.

But even more to the point of this book's theoretical interests, each of these sources seems easy to place in a straightforward bibliographic category. The Psalms are a biblical book, with a traditional author, David; Ben Sira is the first individually authored—not anonymous or pseudepigraphic—book in Jewish antiquity, which retells and celebrates Scripture; and *Jubilees* is our most prominent example of "rewritten Bible," giving an extended interpretation of Genesis and Exodus. But upon closer study, each of these traditions defies our biblical and bibliographic expectations.

Chapter 1, "The Mirage of the Bible: The Case of the Book of Psalms," shows how the Bible and its individual books set the agenda for the study of early Jewish literature, and how this can distort our reading of the ancient evidence. Through a study of psalmic texts and Davidic traditions, especially the material from Qumran, I illustrate how removing biblical lenses reveals a more vibrant picture of the resources and interests of early Jews. Conventional wisdom has it that the book of Psalms was the most popular book among the Dead Sea Scrolls and enjoyed great authority in early Judaism in general. But this mirage dissipates when we look at the material and literary evidence: no book of Psalms as such exists in early Judaism. Instead, there are a variety of collections that preserve psalms and psalmlike compositions, in various lengths and arrangements, for pedagogical, exorcistic, interpretive, and liturgical purposes. These compilations reveal practices of collecting and expanding texts that we cannot place on a linear timeline of "the making of the Bible." The conceptual force of the Bible creates illusory bibliographic unity not extant in the physical and literary evidence. Moving from the biblical to the bibliographic, the chapter argues that the psalms are not conceptualized as a "book" prior to the New Testament and rabbinic texts. Instead, they are imagined as an open genre, a heavenly archive that is only partially reflected in the extant texts. New metaphors suggested by theoretical work in book history—including efforts to describe the unbound textual world of the digital—can help reconceptualize a literary landscape not organized around books, but conceptualized in terms of textual clusters, mosaics of fragments, and expanding archives.

If there was no book of Psalms as such, how do we imagine its traditional author, David? The second chapter, "The Sweetest Voice: The Poetics of Attribution," uses David and the Psalms to rethink the phenomenon of pseudonymous attribution, and the idea of authors in early Jewish texts. What did it mean to say the psalms were "Davidic," and more broadly, why were Second Temple period texts so often pseudepigraphically connected with ancient figures? A common understanding of authorial attribution in antiquity is that there was a discomfort with anonymous texts—abhorrence of something unattributed and unplaced—which spurred a drive to pseudonymously attribute them to ancient authoritative figures. But I argue that rather than texts in search of authors, we sometimes have something like the opposite—characters in search of stories. That is, linking texts and figures was sometimes less about filling a bibliographic gap than about expanding lore about a popular cultural figure. The chapter traces the creation and reception of psalm headings, from the Septuagint through late antiquity, together with the development of David's character over time, from ancient king to cosmic angelic figure who is also known as a great writer and singer. Davidic attribution is not a piece of religious dogma that asserts the literal authorship of the book of Psalms, but an aesthetic, poetic, and honorific act that celebrates an ancient hero and lets him inhabit new literary homes. Reimagining the identity between text and figure in terms of a looser relationship of influence and narrative interest allows for a fuller understanding of pseudepigraphy as a variegated practice that is sometimes, but not always, motivated by authority and legitimation. Linking texts to figures is not merely a way of filling in a bibliographic gap in unattributed texts; rather, it is an opportunity to enrich stories about the characters—who come to inhabit more and more textual territories.

Chapter 3, "Like a Canal from a River: Scribal Products and Projects," continues the discussion of authorship, asking how we might conceptualize texts that do not appear to be the originary intellectual property of a single author but undergo development over time. Here, I focus on the book of Ben Sira, a second-century BCE text written in Hebrew. This text is always singled out in discussions of early Jewish textual concepts: unlike with the pseudepigraphic and anonymous texts that dominate the literary landscape, Ben Sira has used his own name. But although this has earned Ben Sira a reputation for being the first "authored book" in Judaism, I argue that he is in continuity with pseudepigraphic or anonymous authors in the way he understands his role as a channel of a tradition that is not coterminous with his life—that is neither original nor complete. This self-understanding can shed light on the dynamic compositional history of the text, which underwent several editions both during and after Ben Sira's life, and on its reception history in rabbinic literature: there, "Ben Sira" signifies neither an author nor a book, but an exemplary sagely *character*, or a looser, generic *tradition* of pedagogical lore. Based on the less rigid understanding of the figure of "author" and the textual variety of both psalms traditions and Ben Sira, I suggest new language for describing the textual production of ancient scribes as "projects"— open-ended and multigenerational—rather than "books." This takes seriously the literary images the ancient writer himself uses to describe his work as water, rays of light, and gleanings of a harvest, which all suggest a scribal task that is forward-moving, with neither clear origin nor fixed end. Not only the text-critical evidence for changing texts but also the imagery and metaphors the ancient writers used to describe their own work call for a less static way of naming their writings. Their own literary self-disclosures point to, even enable, the complex bibliographic histories of their texts.

The first three chapters, then, focus on specific case studies that disrupt the idea of "books" and "authors" in early Judaism. They reveal a picture of dynamic literary creation that is not meant to be contained or final, and of developing characters associated with the skill of writing. This idea of expanding archives, textual traditions found in multiple locations, and characters who are connected, but not isomorphic with them, comes through both in the physical manuscript evidence and in the self-conscious literary clues the writers have left in their work.

Chapter 4, "Shapes of Scriptures: The Nonbiblical Library of Early Judaism," takes a broader view, stepping back from specific books and authorial figures to consider more generally how early Jews imagined their "library." What texts were available, what writings were imagined, and what were the contours and hierarchies of this literary world? I read a variety of materials, especially from Qumran, that mention books and writing, and show that awareness of the literary inventory of the time did not presuppose the centrality of a scriptural collection. Many references to authoritative, divine writing refer to celestial texts, testamentary traditions handed down by the patriarchs, or revealed cosmological knowledge. The picture that emerges is of a large and not fully graspable literary landscape, never completely reflected in existing texts.

But this ancient library, of which the texts that are now biblical were a part but not always the center, has come to us filtered through a history of publication that has always grouped them as a separate corpus distinct from the Bible. I show how the framing of texts for modern readers, from the eighteenth century to today, has bolstered the Bible's unity and centrality, and has built a mental architecture that makes it difficult to approach the sources in any other way. Finally, I use the book of *Jubilees* as an example of how one text imagines its own literary heritage. While it is most commonly read as an interpretive rewriting of Genesis and Exodus, this text is, inside the world of its narrative, preoccupied with writings of different kinds: heavenly tablets, texts dictated by angels, and writings revealed to the patriarchs populate the story. I read *Jubilees* as a "native theory" of writing, a bibliographic history of written texts and their tradents from Enoch through Moses. The literary imagination as it is manifest in *Jubilees* has the history of writing, in multiple forms and revealed to multiple figures over the generations, tightly intertwined with the history of Israel. The first writer—Enoch— is also the last, as he continues his writing in heaven, still recording the deeds of humanity until the end of history itself.

This sacred literature exists in multiple locations, is perpetually unfinished, and has never been perfectly reflected in any scribal collection. Such a view is in stark contrast with the idea of a scriptural canon as a closed and complete corpus of revelation. While no concept of a scriptural canon existed before the Common Era, boundaries were drawn and texts were fixed in succeeding centuries in Jewish and Christian communities. And yet, even then, an ambiguity exists about the boundaries of sacred writings and the extent of human knowledge of or access to them. The fifth and final chapter, "Outside the Number: Counting, Canons, and the Boundaries of Revelation," discusses texts that do have a sense of boundaries, such as 4 Ezra, which mentions twenty-four public books (and seventy secret ones), and Josephus's Against Apion, which mentions twenty-two books, although neither of them are clear about which texts exactly are meant. The case study of Psalms continues with the Septuagint, which lists Ps 151 as Davidic but "outside the number," and Syriac manuscripts, which also preserve Pss 151–55 as authentic and Davidic, and yet not biblical. This tension between a bounded collection—limited by numbers—and a sense of authenticity outside its boundaries suggests something intriguing about the relationship between revelation and Scripture: "authentic" revealed text and existing scriptural collections were not necessarily imagined to be the same thing. Even as canons emerge, revealed writing remains a far wider concept, not imagined as coextensive with available scriptural text—a literary imagination, even a *religious* literary imagination, that is not biblically constrained. If not all authentic, divine texts are biblical, what *did* ensure a text's canonicity? Undoing the idea that canon and inspired writing are the same thing—and seeing them instead as overlapping, but not identical categories—forces us to ask difficult questions about what the boundaries of canon actually delineate, and what this says for our evolutionary narratives of the canonical process.

With our culturally constrained categories of "Bible" and "book" and our need to attribute texts and compile bibliographies, we have not yet appreciated these literary cultures in full. This book presents ways of describing ancient literary production that take seriously *both* what the ancient writers themselves tell us about their own concerns *and* the suppleness of our own scholarly imagination, which need no longer be constrained by canonical and bibliographic presuppositions. Rather than "books," writing was part of a heavenly archive never fully reflected in available texts: a perpetually evolving multigenerational work constantly adding new episodes. As their stories are retold over time, ancient heroes like David come to be known as great writers, and honored as legendary founders of growing textual traditions—not as dogma about the literal authorship of texts, but as poetic acts of attribution. An imagined library of patriarchal wisdom and celestial writings, never fully accessible, inspired Jewish scribes' literary creativity. The "Bible" does not structure literary culture. Rather, the sources give us a picture of a rich literary imagination whose horizons extend far beyond the available texts.

The Mirage of the Bible

The Case of the Book of Psalms

And David, son of Jesse, was wise,
and luminous like the light of the sun, and a scribe,
and discerning, and perfect in all his paths before God and men.
And YHWH gave him a discerning and enlightened spirit.
And he wrote psalms: three thousand six hundred;
and songs to be sung before the altar ...
The total was four thousand and fifty.
All these he spoke through prophecy
which had been given to him from before the Most High.

—11QPsalms^a, column 27

Introduction: Milton's Vial and the Uncontained Text

In his lecture "The Broken Phial: Non-book Texts," bibliographer D. F. McKenzie discusses the description of books in Milton's *Aeropagitica*. Books, says Milton, "preserve as in a viol the purest efficacie and extraction of that living intellect which bred them.... [A] good book is the pretious life-blood of a master-spirit, imbalm'd and treasur'd up on purpose to a life beyond life." Milton's image of a book as a vial (phial), McKenzie explains, "heightens the idea of enclosure, of the text as contained, determined, stable, of the author within, both clearly visible and enduringly present."[1] The book is a transparent container that preserves the sacred essence of an author's creation, and assures its stable afterlife.

But both book history—the study of books as physical, economic, and cultural objects—and literary theory have shattered Milton's vial. McKenzie writes: "The integrity of the author's text, its transparency, and the formal unity of the book which embodies it, implied in Milton's image of the phial, have been consistently broken down. Today, one reads rather of the *less*-than-sacred text, the destabilized, the indeterminate, the open text."[2]

In 1985, the idea of texts as open and unstable, a key theme in poststructuralist literary criticism, was already old news to McKenzie. Not even print books—whose textual instability in various editions, produced by authors, editors, and publishers over time, was vigorously studied by bibliographers—could any longer be seen as transparent and unreactive containers that preserve essential verbal meanings. How much more so when we consider texts that were not printed and bound as books? These might include maps, in McKenzie's example—and in mine, scraps and scrolls of inscribed parchment that contain various versions and recensions of ancient writings. For such nonbook texts that defy both material unity and textual stability over time, the vial metaphor breaks down completely.

So far, so obvious. But what strikes me most about McKenzie's description is that "the destabilized, the indeterminate, the open text" is identical with "the *less*-than-sacred text." To no longer see texts as "imbalm'd"—stable, contained, and enclosed—seems to go hand in hand with their disenchantment, with some loss of the text's sacred power. For how can a text that is contingent on its material form and community context, inconsistent and incomplete, also be *sacred*?

But this unlikely combination is just what we find in the literature of early Judaism. On the one hand, we see a religious culture that valued texts as authoritative and divinely revealed. On the other hand, the discovery of the Dead Sea Scrolls has broken the vial of the Bible as *the* sacred book, the contained and stable repository of religious authority and meaning. We have learned not only that scriptural texts existed in divergent and developing versions but also that no specific canon of sacred literature contained them in a unity.[3]

For modern readers, this seems impossibly dissonant. We intuitively identify sacred text with containment and stability, with a theologized idea of Bible as eternal word of God. As McKenzie's comment shows, this cluster of associations is culturally powerful, often regardless of a person's theological commitment. The icon of the "book," still intuitively understood in its Miltonian sense of a container of sacred essence, reinforces and is reinforced by the Bible, the most iconic sacred book of all.

This is a key reason why, I think, it has been so difficult for us to imagine the shape of early Jewish sacred writings at a time when they were neither stable nor contained—when neither text nor canon was fixed. Although we recognize these facts, much of our scholarship on these textual traditions feels like an attempt to fill a broken vial. The Bible still anachronistically structures the way we read and categorize this literature, and still remains the measure of how sacred texts should look. But before books and Bibles, Jewish sacred literature took different forms: acknowledging and decoupling the tight link between stability, containment, and sacredness can help them come into view.

In this chapter, I show what it might mean to approach the early Jewish sources without assuming a stable and contained Bible as an analytical category.[4] This is not the same thing as saying that early Jews had a wider literary corpus—that they were reading and writing more texts than just those that later became part of the biblical canon. Rather, it is to show how the idea of the Bible shapes the way we describe, identify, and evaluate texts of all kinds. It creates the mental architecture that structures the way we imagine textual hierarchies and boundaries. But before it existed as text and concept, it could not shape the way they were imagined in the ancient world.

My case study is the Psalms, a biblical tradition that is, nevertheless, poorly served by biblical categories. The Dead Sea Scrolls revealed a great diversity in the transmission of many biblical texts—famously, for example, differing versions of pentateuchal texts, especially Exodus, and a long and a short version of Jeremiah. But the varying contents, arrangements, and extents of the psalms manuscripts are one of the most striking examples of the fluidity and variety in scriptural traditions at Qumran. The psalms manuscripts, as I will show, illustrate the phenomenon of McKenzie's "broken vial" quite dramatically: they shatter our idea of a stable and contained "book of Psalms," and instead reveal a literary landscape of overlapping textual clusters and expanding archives.

But the case of the Psalms also shows how powerful the Bible and the book continue to be, as mutually reinforcing icons, in the scholarly imagination. Scholars have continued to use a later entity—the biblical book of Psalms—as a way of grouping and defining a far more complex diversity of psalm materials than such a concept suggests. The scholarly consensus has been that the many psalms manuscripts testify to the popularity and authority afforded to the book of Psalms in the Second Temple period, while also showing that it was not yet fully fixed.

But the physical manuscripts from Qumran and the literary evidence from other texts suggest something more: that the "book of Psalms" did not yet exist as a concept—it had not yet emerged as the dominant mode in which psalms traditions were conceived. Our interest in telling a teleological story of how a biblical book came to be has, in fact, imposed an illusory unity onto both manuscript and literary evidence, and obscured the way psalms traditions were imagined—as both sacred and uncontained, inhabiting multiple locations before the idea of a book of Psalms had emerged.

My argument for a nonteleological story about Jewish literature in this chapter is presented in three parts. First, I demonstrate the way in which the Bible persists as the lens through which we read both biblical and nonbiblical texts in the study of early Judaism. Second, I show, through the Psalms case study, how biblical and bibliographic categories have distorted our reading of physical and literary evidence, and how a new literary world emerges when we deliberately remove our biblical spectacles. While biblical scholars are primarily interested in the evidence that can fit into a narrative of biblical origins—the history of the development, canonization, and exegesis of Scripture—the categories and interests of the ancient writers were configured in other ways. Third, I suggest new ways of describing texts that do not depend on "book" language, but that take a cue from other nonbook textual traditions, including the digital, and from the ways the ancient writers themselves chose to describe their literary heritage. By deemphasizing the concept of a "book of Psalms," we can enable other ways of imagining psalm traditions through alternative metaphors, like a heavenly archive or revelatory project—illuminating aspects of the literary imagination that biblical interests and "book" language have kept obscure.

Biblical Spectacles

Warnings against structuring our scholarship around anachronistic biblical and bibliographic categories are not new. Robert Kraft has warned throughout his career against the "tyranny of canonical assumptions" and "textual myopia" in biblical studies—the tendencies to read our ancient evidence through the lenses of surviving canonical texts. To draw a clearer picture of the ancient literary imagination, scholars must resist "the temptation to impose on those ancients whom we study our modern ideas about what constituted 'scripture' and how it was viewed.... When they say 'scripture' (or the like—they don't say 'Bible'), they might refer to literature or traditions different from those we recognize."[5]

Already in the 1970s, Michael Stone critiqued the way in which our Bible sets the agenda for the study of ancient Judaism, and thus, actually hinders the study of biblical origins. He focuses on the books of *1 Enoch*, which come from roughly the same era as Chronicles, Ezra-Nehemiah, Daniel, Esther, Haggai, Malachi, and Zechariah, and are just as relevant for understanding the sacred literature and literary culture of the period. Yet for a long time, as Stone writes, literature like *1 Enoch* was either assimilated to biblical exegesis, marginalized as foreign, or neglected because its concerns seem different from those of the Bible[6]—defined, in any case, in relation to the biblical. But, Stone reminds us, the texts that would later become "the Bible" did not have cultural hegemony, but were part of a diverse, and not necessarily centralized, cultural landscape. He writes that it is specious "when faced by a third-century phenomenon, either to seek its roots in the Bible or to relegate it to foreign influence. Circles other than those transmitting the biblical books existed, or else those involved in transmitting the biblical books did not allow a considerable part of the intellectual culture of their day to be expressed in them."[7] Stone points out that the Bible was not the one container that held the essence of religious and intellectual culture, but that the sources and repositories of that culture were also found in other locations.

Kraft's and Stone's work invites scholars to envision the intellectual culture of early Judaism as multiform—not necessarily organized around our textual categories and hierarchies, or assimilable to the biblical. And a significant number of scholars have heeded their call, reconceptualizing common distinctions between canonical and noncanonical texts, and dominant and marginal traditions,[8] and reimagining how we might talk about sacred literature without projecting later categories of biblical unity and uniqueness.

But the field remains split in this respect, with the biblical still a dominant category of analysis. Shaye Cohen, for instance, writes that "Second Temple Judaism is a 'book religion.' At its heart lies the Bible, the book that Jews call Tanak."[9] Similarly, James Kugel writes that the Second Temple period was "a time when... the Bible had become *the* central focus of Israel's religion. Reading Scripture, and doing what it said, was now the very essence of Judaism."[10] Earlier, Michael Fishbane had offered a similar picture, in more theologized language, of the Bible as center and essence: "In the scrolls from Qumran... Mikra is the literary expression of Divine Truth; at once the unique resource of past revelations, and the mediating source of all subsequent ones.... Fatefully, the sectarians believed that outside their authoritative use and interpretation of Mikra there was no salvation."[11]

The Bible persists as an iconic book in the Miltonian sense: the vial of sacred truth, a vessel that contains the essence of divine revelation, gathering all of intellectual culture around itself as both its source and goal. While we recognize that the Dead Sea Scrolls themselves have broken the vial of the preserved and contained sacred text—that scriptures did not have a stable essence and did not inhabit one contained location—the later shape of the Bible as sacred book remains a powerful way to describe early Jewish textual culture.

Why might this be? Besides the difficulty of conceptualizing and redescribing sacred texts not bound in a Bible, the Bible is often the reason why we are interested in the literature of early Judaism in the first place. And indeed, the study of how the Bible came to be is also the study of early Jewish literary culture: it is in the Second Temple period that biblical texts took on their final editorial form and were compiled into scriptural collections. We must look to the literary culture of this era to understand how biblical texts were shaped, how the canon was formed, and how scriptural interpretation developed.

But when we begin with questions of biblical text and canon in mind, it is all too easy to read all our sources as part of the answer, and organize the much wider array of evidence according to our own priorities. As Stone writes,

> [S]cholars' contemporary cultural context determines what they perceive. Consequently, they tend to privilege the elements that are in focus through those particular "spectacles," even if other phenomena are present in the same data.[12] ... [Scholars] tend to study and emphasize those aspects of Judaism of the period of the Second Temple that

were important for the development of the later orthodoxies, Jewish or Christian, or for the exegesis of the Scriptures accepted by those later orthodoxies.[13]

Stone's references to both the *development* of the Bible and its *exegesis* highlight the different stages of the narratives of development that scholars tell: narratives in which what isn't "biblical" must be either "protobiblical" or "biblical interpretation"—where, in any case, the Bible remains the central character. We ask, "how did the Bible come to be?" "How did we arrive at Jewish and Christian modes of scriptural interpretation?" Such questions about origins and development are key to our field, but they also come with the risk of assimilating the diversity of early Jewish culture into an evolutionary story of biblical origins. It is as if, in the search for the origins of *Homo sapiens*, each found fossil were read as a phase of our evolution, without regard for the myriad species that have lived side by side, originated new species, or ceased to exist.

One striking example of such teleological thinking in biblical studies is the so-called Proto-Esther text from Qumran.[14] Since the prefix "proto" is used to mark a precursor or earlier version that developed into a later form, the nomenclature suggests that the text—named in 1957 by J. T. Milik—must be an early form of the biblical book of Esther. This would be significant because Esther is the only text in the Jewish canon that is not attested among the Dead Sea Scrolls.[15] And yet, this assumption would be incorrect: the only relationship Proto-Esther bears to Esther is that both take place in the Persian court. Not a single name or plot point from Esther appears in the fragment, and the text is in Aramaic, not in Hebrew. What the text tells us is not information about the origins of a biblical book, but that early Jewish writers continued to read and write Aramaic tales of court intrigue. But the impulse to find the origins of biblical books—and to fill the missing space in the "canon" at Qumran—was so powerful that this text was wedged into the role of both biblical precursor and canonical stopgap.

The naming of Proto-Esther, to be sure, belongs to an earlier time in biblical and Qumran studies. And yet the Bible retains its force. The example of Proto-Esther can serve as an analogy to many other scholarly moments of finding origins, ancestors, and moments of development on the way to the Bible in sources that may in fact reveal that ancient writers had other preoccupations than our own, and that demonstrate that ancient Jewish literature and culture do not necessarily align themselves around a biblical center. The sources do not only tell us about the prehistory of our Bible. They also invite us to reimagine what a world before the Bible would look like on its own terms—and how sacred texts might be imagined when they are not stable or contained.

Why There Was No "Book of Psalms" in the Second Temple Period: Manuscripts and the Imagination

How do we reimagine that world and tell its story through the Psalms?[16] Before the discovery of the Dead Sea Scrolls, our data for the book of Psalms was fairly uniform. The rabbinic Psalter, with 150 psalms, was not so different from the Septuagint Psalms, known from fourth- and fifth-century Christian manuscripts, which contained an additional Ps 151. Medieval Syriac codices sometimes added five additional apocryphal psalms at the end of the Psalter. But barring differences of division and counting, and the inclusion of different headings for the psalms, the book of Psalms was by and large the same book in the known ancient traditions. Scholars were aware of different chronological origins for separate psalms, since the dates of the individual compositions themselves have long been known to range from some of the earliest known Hebrew poetry through postexilic compositions. But by the Hellenistic period, it seemed to go without saying that the Psalter had long served as Israel's sacred prayer book, and was believed by the ancients to have been composed by King David as his own heartfelt expressions of prayer and praise.

But the discovery of the Dead Sea Scrolls revealed a different picture of psalms in the first century. Rather than a Miltonesque book where King David's purported revelatory words were contained and "imbalm'd," we have evidence that psalms existed in various arrangements, and that collections were continuing to expand. At the center of the discussion was 11QPsalms[a], one of the longest and best-preserved Dead Sea Scrolls, dated to the mid-first century. This text contains parts of about fifty compositions, most from what is now the last third of the Hebrew Psalter, but in an entirely different order from the biblical one. Not only this, but ten of the compositions are noncanonical texts, including Hebrew versions of the "additional" Greek Ps 151, two other psalms known only from medieval Syriac manuscripts, and a handful of other compositions unknown outside the Dead Sea Scrolls.

This unusual collection presented scholars with an obvious question: is this scroll a version of the scriptural Psalter, or is it another kind of text, such as a liturgical collection, that is secondary to and dependent on the biblical book of Psalms?[17] And does it represent an anomalous collection specific to the sectarians of Qumran, or can it tell us about the psalms in first-century Jewish culture more broadly? While the debate continues, the major scholarly consensus has become that 11QPsalms[a] does indeed represent a scriptural collection. It is not secondary to an already existing authoritative Psalter, because no one such text had yet been established. Instead, it represents a time when the order and contents of the book of Psalms had not yet been fixed, and—like the vast majority of the texts found at Qumran—it is not a strictly sectarian composition, but participates in a wider culture. These insights contributed to the history of the development of the Hebrew Psalter, which scholars now imagine happened gradually, perhaps in two distinct stages—the order and text of Pss 1–89 became stabilized first, with the latter half of the Psalter still in flux, and circulating in diverse versions as of the first century CE.

These were crucial insights for the study of the book of Psalms. Indeed, for the first century and earlier, it can no longer be thought of as a fixed book, but an indeterminate collection without a stable order, inventory, or boundaries. But, I will argue, our conclusions have not followed the evidence—neither the manuscripts from Qumran nor literary evidence in other sources—quite as far as it wants to take us. Even as this psalmic instability is common knowledge, the icon of Milton's vial and the mutually reinforcing icons of book and Bible continue to shape how psalms texts at Qumran, and in early Judaism in general, are described.

Qumran Psalms Manuscripts

The power of these icons comes through most clearly when the entire picture of psalms at Qumran is presented as a whole, in the context of the broader literary landscape of the Dead Sea Scrolls and early Judaism. Every beginning student of the Scrolls reads that the most highly attested book at Qumran is the book of Psalms. In thirty-six copies,[18] it is closely followed by Deuteronomy (twenty-six)[19] and Isaiah (about twenty-one).[20] This picture of a community's literary world is attractive, and confirms certain expectations: it corresponds with the most popular texts cited in the New Testament, and it presents us with a recognizable biblical curriculum that covers law, prophecy, and liturgical material. Indeed, it even falls neatly into a familiar arrangement, with each of Qumran's "top three" books representing one section of the tripartite canon of the Tanakh—Torah, Prophets, and Writings.

But the situation is not so simple, and the numbers that seem to attest to the Psalter's popularity are highly misleading. In fact, in the words of Mika Pajunen, they are a "statistical illusion."[21] Close attention to the Qumran psalms manuscripts reveals little evidence for the primacy of the book of Psalms—or in fact, for its very existence as a unified collection. The fragments included in the familiar list of thirty-six fragmented manuscripts (only a handful are actually "scrolls") are not copies of one work, and not one of them is a representation of the book of Psalms as such.[22] Instead, they represent several different genres, include different numbers of psalms, and attest to a variety of compilation principles on which psalmic texts were collected.

I now turn to a survey of the psalms manuscripts from Qumran. Table 1.1 lists all the manuscripts that have been counted among the well-known number of

Table 1.1 The Qumran manuscripts typically counted as Psalms scrolls do not represent multiple copies of the "book of Psalms." As this table shows, many are small fragments that contain a portion of only one psalm, while more extensive scrolls have significant differences in contents and organization from the biblical book of Psalms.

Manuscript	Only 1 Psalm (or Part of 1 Psalm) Represented[1]	Major Differences in Inventory from MT	Major Differences in Sequence from MT	Contents
1QPsᵃ				86, 92, 94–96, 119
1QPsᵇ				126, 127, 128 (*only Pss of Ascent, 120–134?*)
1QPsᶜ	x			44, unidentified frags.
2QPs				103, 104 (red ink)
3QPs	x			2:6–7
5QPs	x			119 only
pap6QPs	x			Words probably from 78:36–37
8QPs				17, 18
4QPsᵃ				19 pss from 5–71; 31 directly followed by 33; 38 by 71
4QPsᵇ				15 pss from Ps 91 to 118 (possibly final ps); 103 → 112
4QPsᶜ				15 ps represented, ranging from 16 to 53
4QPsᵈ			x	3 surviving pss in sequence of 106→147→104
4QPsᵉ			x	20 pss are represented, ranging from 76 to 146(?); sequence of 76→77; 115→116; 118→104 [+ 147]→ 105→ 146(?); 125→126 [+127 + 128]→129→130

[1] Three other manuscripts, likely from Qumran and now in the hands of collectors and institutions, also contain portions of single psalms: XPs A (Schøyen Collection; Ps 9:8–13), XPs B (Southwestern Baptist Theological Seminary; Ps 22:4–13); XPs C (Green Collection; Ps 11:1–4). On these fragments see P. W. Flint, "Unrolling the Dead Sea Psalms Scrolls," in *The Oxford Handbook of the Psalms* (ed. W. P. Brown; New York: Oxford University Press, 2014), 229–50, at 238–39.

Table 1.1 **Continued**

Manuscript	Only 1 Psalm (or Part of 1 Psalm) Represented[1]	Major Differences in Inventory from MT	Major Differences in Sequence from MT	Contents
4QPs^f		x		3 pss preserved: 22 (placement of frag. unknown), 107 (cols. I–IV), and 109 (cols. VI–VII); *Apostrophe to Zion; Eschatological Hymn; Apostrophe to Judah*
4QPs^g	X			119 only
4QPs^h	x			119 only
4QPs^j				48, 49, and 51
4QPs^k			x	2 pss preserved; sequence 135 [+one more comp?]→ 99
4QPs^l	x			Only 104 extant
4QPs^m				Portions of 93, 95, 97 and 98
4QPs^n			x	135 and 136; 135:11–12 is directly followed by 136:22–23
4QPs^o				Parts of 116–118
4QPs^p	x			Parts of 143:3–4, 6–8
4QPs^q			x	31→33, 34 (32 not present in expected place)
4QPs^r				Portions of 26, 27, 30
4QPs^s				5→6, 88
4QPs^t	x			2 words from 42:5
4QPs^u	x			2 words from 99:1
4QPs^v	x			Only part of 18 extant
4QPs89	x		x	Only 89; arrangement is vv. 20–22, 26, 23, 27–28, 31
4Q522	x	x		"Prophecy of Joshua"—text with place names and defeat of Canaanites + frags. of Ps 122

11QPsᵃ	x	x	Psalm 101→ 102→ 103; 118→ 104→
			147→105→ 146→ 148 [+ 120?] →
			121→ 122→ 123→ 124→ 125→126→
			127→ 128→ 129→ 130→ 131→
			132→ 119→ 135→ 136(+Catena) →
			145 → 154 +Plea for Deliverance
			→ 139→ 137→ 138→Sirach
			51→*Apostrophe to Zion*→93→
			141→133→144→Syriac Ps
			155→142→ 143→ 149→ 150→
			Hymn to Creator→David's Last
			Words→David's Compositions→
			140 → 134→ 151A→151B→
			blank col.
11QPsᵇ	x	x	77→78; Catena; 119; 118; Plea;
			Apostrophe to Zion;
			141→ 133→ 144
11QPsᶜ			Portions of 9 pss preserved, 2–25
11QPsᵈ			6; 9;18; 36→37; 39→40; 43; 45; 59;
			68; 78; 81; 86; 115→116;
			78:36–37?; 60:9?
11QPsApᵃ x	x		3 hymns of exorcism → 91 →
			end of scroll

This table was previously published in E. Mroczek, "The Hegemony of the Biblical in the Study of Second Temple Literature," Journal of Ancient Judaism 6 (2015): 2–35, at 34–35; printed here with permission from Vandenhoeck & Ruprecht.

thirty-six Psalms scrolls, as presented by Peter Flint.[23] Fourteen of the thirty-six manuscripts counted in his survey preserve merely (part of) a single psalm, sometimes only a word or two. Only six manuscripts preserve ten or more psalms.[24] By far the most extensive scroll is 11QPsalmsᵃ, which preserves thirty-nine canonical psalms, but here, as I have explained, both its order and its inventory are completely different from the canonical Psalter. Indeed, of those manuscripts that contain more than a scrap of a single psalm, five have significantly different inventories from the MT book of Psalms, and eight present the psalms in a distinctly different order.

While this variety of manuscript evidence does not point to the existence of a specific book of Psalms as such at Qumran, we can describe several other modalities. The fragmentary state of the manuscripts prevents us from drawing firm conclusions, but they do point to a variety of genres and scopes in which psalm compositions appeared. Of the fourteen fragments that preserve part of only a single biblical psalm, nothing suggests that any of them had originally belonged to a full Psalter—and in some cases, a very different context is clear.

For example, in 11Q11, Ps 91 closes a collection of four songs apparently meant for an exorcism ritual.[25] The motifs of divine refuge and protection from evil in Ps 91 fit well with the apotropaic themes of the other compositions. At least one of the texts has a Davidic heading, and the collection participates in a tradition that links David and exorcism, first evident in 1 Sam 16:13–23, where David's lyre playing rids Saul of an evil spirit. It is further developed in Pseudo-Philo's *Biblical Antiquities* 60:2–3, which provides the lyrics of the song he played—and which shares with 11Q11 a deep interest in the creation of darkness and light and a reference to Solomon. In 11Q11, then, we have a Davidic collection of ritual songs that, while it appears on our scholarly lists of "psalms scrolls," has little to do with the book of Psalms. Though it incorporates one of the same compositions, it has a very different genre, purpose, and shape, and forms part of a cluster of *non*biblical traditions that continue to be influential in late antiquity: for example, a fifth-century CE silver amulet from Tell el-Amarna and a Babylonian incantation bowl both preserve exorcistic texts attributed to David.[26]

Manuscript 4Q522, or 4QPs122, is a second example of an entirely different genre of literature in which a psalm appears—a Joshua apocryphon.[27] This text contains a discourse on place names in the campaigns of Joshua, the defeat of Canaanites, the promise of a secure Jerusalem with a temple planned by David and constructed by Solomon, and Ps 122, a Davidic song of ascents about the holy city of Jerusalem, which fits well with the triumphalist progression of the text.[28] The text is likely included in lists of "psalms scrolls" so it can be used specifically to do text criticism on Ps 122, and Flint acknowledges that it "does not qualify as a psalms scroll."[29] But it nevertheless appears on lists of the thirty-six psalm manuscripts, increasing the illusion of many copies of the book of Psalms.

A third example is 4QPs89,[30] one of the most curious—and perhaps the oldest[31]—texts on the list of Qumran "psalms scrolls." Parts of eight lines of a version of Ps 89 have been preserved on a "battered and isolated bit"[32] measuring 6 centimeters tall and 4.5 centimeters wide, written with unusual orthography, crowded letters, and text running into the margins. The text form of this psalm differs substantially from both the MT and the LXX, and the verses are in a different order. Based on the text squeezed in smaller letters in the top margin of the fragment, it seems that this text contained nothing more than part of Ps 89.[33] How do we explain this strange fragment? It has variously been called a "source" for the Psalter,[34] part of a "libretto of messianic testimonia,"[35] or a "practice page written from memory."[36] Here again, while we cannot precisely determine the purpose of this text, it represents a rather different modality of text production than its presence on a list of psalms scrolls may suggest.

Finally, three manuscripts contain only parts of the acrostic Ps 119 (4QPs[g], 4QPs[h], 5QPs), which indicates that this composition circulated independently.[37] Patrick Skehan, Eugene Ulrich, and Flint suggest that these texts were specially produced for private contemplative use.[38] Given its emphasis on wisdom, Torah, and the formation of the student,[39] considering the use of this psalm for private study at Qumran can enrich the picture of pedagogy we already have from other wisdom writings. It is perhaps better grouped with those texts than categorized as a psalms scroll.

These examples, then, illustrate four very different generic contexts in which psalms appeared: an exorcism ritual, a historical-prophetic composition related to Joshua literature, a possible practice text written from memory, and a single acrostic psalm for private contemplation. These texts have little in common with one another; they testify to a wide variety of genres in which psalmic texts appeared, rather than to the popularity or authority of a book of Psalms.

Besides these six manuscripts, another eight contain portions of one psalm only, sometimes preserving only a few words.[40] There is no reason to assume those fragments had originally belonged to larger psalm collections, to "Psalters"; perhaps, instead, they are remains of entirely different kinds of texts, quotations of psalms in other contexts, or smaller psalms collections.

What about those manuscripts, then, that *do* contain psalm collections? Here, too, the evidence testifies to a diversity of extents and contents, not copies or even versions of the same work. Physically, there is no way to be certain about the original size of the manuscripts, but it is unlikely that anything close to the scope of the book of Psalms had existed among the Scrolls. The most extensive scroll, 11QPsalms[a], contains about fifty compositions, all of which come from what is now roughly the last third of the biblical Psalter. It is unlikely that it had originally contained much more.[41] Even with only one-third of what is now the canonical psalter, this 5-meter scroll is by far the longest manuscript containing psalms, and among the longest scrolls found at Qumran.[42] A manuscript containing 150 psalms would be longer than any extant scroll.[43]

Thus, rather than Psalters, we have various shorter collections of psalms in different configurations, likely used for a variety of purposes. For example, the six fragments of 1QPs[b] contain parts of Pss 126–28, and perhaps represent a liturgical collection containing only the Psalms of Ascent.[44] 4QPsalms[b], among the most extensive manuscripts, preserves fifteen compositions in twenty-six extant columns, and likely ended with Ps 118.[45] Not only the scope but also the order is different from our book of Psalms. In the best-preserved scrolls, where the most physical joins between compositions are materially extant, the order often departs from the biblical sequence. Most famously, the order in 11QPs[a] is radically different: thirteen of the Psalms of Ascent, Pss 120–132, are in the same order as the MT,[46] but no other sequence of more than three psalms is the same.[47] Only five manuscripts include selections from both Pss 1–89 and 90–150,[48] and three of these display significant variations in order, non-MT contents, or both.[49]

Besides varying extents and arrangements, the diverse biblical and nonbiblical contents of the manuscripts do not justify the name of a single "work." All in all, sixteen non-MT compositions appear among five manuscripts classified as Psalms scrolls.[50] 11QPs[b] and 4QPs[f] both contain noncanonical hymns interspersed with biblical psalms. Again, the most famous example is 11QPs[a], which includes ten nonbiblical compositions. Some of these compositions imbue the collection with a distinct character, where liturgy and wisdom traditions are linked. For instance, the manuscript includes the Hymn to Wisdom also known from Ben Sira 51 (col. 21–22), which exalts personified Wisdom as the object of searching and contemplation; Ps 154, also known from Syriac manuscripts, which has Wisdom's heavenly voice teaching the community to praise (col. 18); and the prose piece "David's Compositions," which refers to calendrically arranged songs revealed prophetically to the enlightened sage, David. In this psalm collection, wisdom is divinely revealed, and praise is founded on cosmic principles.

The picture we have, then, is of a number of psalm collections, and collections containing psalms, that likely had very different genres and purposes. They are not copies of the same documents. They range from previously unknown works containing one psalm to fragments of single psalms, to collections of previously known psalms in previously unknown orders. In no case do they represent the same contents, order, or scope as our book of Psalms.

The way we imagine what people were reading and writing in the Second Temple period has not yet taken full stock of this shattered textual unity. It still seems natural to refer to the manuscript evidence to note the many copies of the book of Psalms, or the "importance of the Psalter for the Qumran community"[51]—even as that very manuscript data shows us that it was not Psalters that dominated the Qumran caves. To group the diverse scrolls and fragments into a list of thirty-six "representations," even "copies," of the "book of Psalms" at Qumran creates a mirage of bibliographic unity that the evidence does not support. More accurately, psalms are a popular genre of texts that exist in various collections that combine them in different ways,[52] but the "book of Psalms" as a unity is not attested at Qumran. And so the attractive biblical story of the top three books at Qumran—Psalms, Deuteronomy, and Isaiah—must be nuanced. In terms of a large number of copies of the *same document*, we need to look farther down the list of texts highly represented among the Qumran manuscripts, and consider the importance and prevalence of not only Exodus and Leviticus but also the nonbiblical texts, like *Jubilees*, the *Hodayot*, and the *Community Rule*.

For psalms, we must consider that they did not inhabit Psalters but traveled in various groups and different vehicles.

Finding the Book of Psalms in Early Judaism

The Qumran manuscripts, then, have broken the vial of the stable and contained "book," presenting us instead with multiformity, smaller textual clusters, and continuing rearrangement and expansion. But to say that no sense of a "book of Psalms" as a coherent and bounded work emerges is not only to make the chronological argument that the Psalter was still fluid, not fixed or closed, in the Second Temple period.[53] This observation is crucial to reconstructing the history of the book of Psalms, and to placing its precursors onto a timeline of how the Bible came to be. But to describe the evidence on its own terms—to imagine how the landscape might have looked to a person in the first century, who did not have access to such a timeline—we must make a stronger claim: the "book of Psalms" did not exist as a conceptual category in the Second Temple period.[54] This was not the way that psalms traditions were imaginatively construed.

A different picture from our unified, bounded idea of the book of Psalms emerges not only from the manuscripts, but from the literary evidence as well. The psalms are not referred to as a *sefer* in the Second Temple period; the term *sefer tehillim*, "book of Psalms," occurs in rabbinic literature,[55] but earlier evidence is lacking. Among the Qumran texts, a single reference to *sefer ha-tehillim* exists in a fragment about the eschatological battle in a *War Scroll* recension:[56]

> [2]...and to the whole army [...] [3] [...] *Blank* and after...[...] [4] [...]
> the Book of Psalms ([...]ספר התהלים), and aft[er...] [5] [...] and
> blessing. Thus shall they do to[wards...] [6] [...] for a burning [...] [7]
> [...] and a remn[ant...] [8] [...] like th[is...].[57]

But does this fragmentary reference really refer to the "book of Psalms"? Its first editor, Maurice Baillet, was already cautious: *if* it is really about the biblical book of Psalms, he wrote, this would be the oldest known attestation of its title.[58] His caution is warranted: besides our own interest in the Bible, there is little to indicate that it refers to the "book of Psalms" as such. In fact, references to "psalms" in other *War* texts suggest it is meant in a broader generic sense of eschatological songs. 1QM also makes reference to a תהלת המשוב ("hymn of return") in 14:2 and תהלת אל ("God's praise")[59] inscribed on a banner, one of the divine paraphernalia of the final war, in 4:14. García Martínez suggests that the reference does not refer to the "book of Psalms" but to songs and hymns to be sung at the eschatological battle.[60] Most recently, Kipp Davis has argued based on textual parallels that the reference is meant to refer to a collection of hymns similar to the *Hodayot*.[61] The burden of proof must be on the person who wishes to find the later meaning of the phrase as "book of Psalms" here, rather than to connect the phrase to the other kinds of hymns that seemed to interest the composers of the *War* texts.

Chronologically, "book of Psalms" first occurs in Greek in Luke 20:42 and Acts 1:20 (ἐν βίβλῳ Ψαλμῶν); the parallel texts in Matthew and Mark do not have it. Baillet also cites various Greek transliterations of the Hebrew ספר תהלים in Christian writings: a text attributed to Hippolytus, a gloss of a hexaplaric palimpsest, and Eusebius.[62] No earlier evidence exists.

What we *do* have in Jewish sources, instead, is a smattering of references to "psalms" that show they were imaginatively construed as a rather amorphous genre, not a specific, bounded collection. "David's Compositions"—a passage in col. 27 of 11QPsalms[a] to which I will return in detail—speaks of David, scribe and sage, prophetically writing 4,050 psalms and liturgical songs.[63] We do not find our "book of Psalms" here; instead, there are simply psalms, of various types and in great number, revealed and arranged according to cosmic, calendrical principles, but not identifiable with any specific collection. Josephus, writing in Greek, gives a similarly undefined picture of what psalms meant in the Hellenistic Jewish literary imagination, writing that David "composed songs and hymns to God in varied meters. Some he made in trimeters, and others in pentameters" (*Ant.* VII.305).[64] We have no mention of a βίβλος Ψαλμῶν, but a loose description of many compositions.[65]

Yet despite the lack of a "book of Psalms" both in the material remains and in the literary record, biblical categories remain. Flint, for instance, recognizes that the Qumran discoveries "emphasize the need for appropriate nomenclature in relation to 'biblical' texts, the 'Psalms,' and other terms."[66] But he concludes that the term "'Book of Psalms' seems very appropriate for the Qumran period, since this term is attested in the scrolls and because the Psalms as a collection were regarded as Scripture by the community."[67] Given that the one attestation of the term in the *War* fragment is without context or parallel in any contemporary text, evidence for the term's attestation with relation to the biblical book is unconvincing. But if the *title* of the book of Psalms is not attested, what do we make of Flint's second point—that "the Psalms as a collection were regarded as Scripture"?

Qumran *Pesharim* on Psalms

There is no question that psalms were copied and interpreted as authoritative Scripture; this is clear from three manuscripts containing *pesharim*, exegetical commentaries, on psalms that interpret them as prophetic for the community,[68] like the *pesharim* on the prophetic books. But what do these documents tell us about the conceptualization of the Psalms as a coherent or specific collection?

The most extensive *pesher*, 4Q171 (4QPesher Psalms[a]), contains commentary on Ps 37 and part of 45 and 60; the scraps of 4Q173 (4QPsalms Pesher[b]) deal

and nonbiblical, attested and imagined—related to liturgical practice. For both 2 Maccabees and 4QMMT, the context of the references and the texts' rhetorical interests strongly suggest that "David" refers not to psalms, but to other written Davidic traditions: in particular, the kind of Davidic liturgical ordinances that are mentioned in the book of Chronicles.

Let us look closely at the texts. 2 Macc 2 is a letter that instructs the Jews of Egypt to observe "the festival of the Jews," presenting Moses and Solomon, who prayed and sacrificed, as models. The letter says that

> [t]he same things are reported in the records and in the memoirs of Nehemiah, and also that he founded a library and collected the books about the kings and prophets, and of David (τὰ τοῦ δαυιδ), and letters of kings about votive offerings. In the same way Judas also collected all the books that had been lost on account of the war which had come upon us, and they are in our possession. So if you have need of them, send people to get them for you. Since, therefore, we are about to celebrate the purification, we write to you. Will you therefore please keep the days? It is God Who has saved all His people, and has returned the inheritance to all, and the kingship and priesthood and consecration, as He promised through the law. (vv. 13–18)

The fact that "books about the kings and prophets, and of David, and letters of kings about votive offerings" do not correspond to biblical categories has not dissuaded scholars from reading this as a text about the canon of the Bible. For example, Menahem Haran writes: "The division of the Bible into groups of books is here quite odd and vague. Whether this specification parallels the books of the Prophets and the Hagiographa in our Bible or whether it comprises less, we can only wonder at the confusion created by this scribe, in that there is no similarity between his terms and our Bible."[70] The standard presupposed here is "our Bible." If a scribe's terms do not correspond to our Bible, it must be because ancient people were confused about how to divide "the Bible," not because he had something else in mind.

But there are other texts that could have interested a Hellenistic writer besides canonical materials. As John Barton writes, the passage is about a "salvage operation on archival materials of all kinds,"[71] not about establishing a canon of Scripture. But although scholars have questioned the text's usefulness for telling the story of the canon, we have not challenged one biblical assumption: that the reference to "David" denotes the Psalms, and tells us something about their status in the second century BCE.

But when we stop isolating verse 13 as a proof text about biblical formation, new interpretive possibilities emerge that seem more appropriate to the text's own purposes. Its broader context is 2 Maccabees' letter about temple purification, which is concerned with "the kingship and priesthood and consecration, as [God] promised through the law" (2:17). Read in this way, the text shares a striking set of interests and references with the book of Chronicles. Like 2 Maccabees, Chronicles invokes writing associated with David. But these writings are not the book of Psalms or anything like it, but authoritative liturgical instructions—documents related to temple service that serve as a guide for future rulers. This includes the written Temple blueprint and instructions in 1 Chr 28:11–19, the "commandments" of Moses[72] and David for Solomon's temple service (2 Chr 8:13–15), and "the writing (כתב) of King David...and the document (מכתב) of his son Solomon" in the account of Josiah's Passover (2 Chr 35:4–6).

In Chronicles, then, David's legacy appears together with discourse about Moses's legal authority,[73] Solomon's sacrifice, and continuity with an ancient past that can be partially accessed through writing. Precisely the same themes and characters are central to 2 Macc 2. Given these shared concerns, and the interest in 2 Maccabees in presenting liturgical instructions based on ancient authorities, "those [writings] of David" most likely refer to the type of documents, lost or imagined, that the Chronicler invokes. The text has nothing to tell us about biblical psalms,[74] but testifies to interest in other writings—even texts the writer did not actually have.

The so-called Halakhic Letter, 4QMMT, presents parallel issues. It was probably composed in the second century BCE, and, like 2 Maccabees, it is also a letter about sacrificial matters—though in this case, from the Qumran sect to the Jerusalem priesthood.[75] And like 2 Macc 2, it is also ubiquitous in discussions about the shape of Scripture, based on one line that is reconstructed as

[כתב]נו אליכה שתבין בספר מוש[ה ו[בספר]י הנ[ביאים ובדוי[ד] [[11] [במעשי] דור ודור...[10]
[10] we have [written] to you so that you may study (carefully) the book of Moses and the books of the Prophets and [the writings of] Davi[d and the] [11] [events of] ages past. (4Q397 frag. 14–21)[76]

The reference to Moses, the Prophets, and David has been read as evidence for a canon of Torah, Prophets, and Writings.[77] "David" is not only taken for granted as a reference to the Psalms but also extended to signify the Ketuvim as a group.[78] But the notion of a tripartite canon in 4QMMT has been widely challenged in recent scholarship.[79] Eugene Ulrich has shown that the arrangement and reconstruction of the small fragments are tenuous,[80] and reading a tripartite canon in this text's lacunae is a function of biblical presuppositions.

But even if the reconstruction is accepted, a reference to the Psalms here does not fit the context as well as a reference to another kind of Davidic tradition. George Brooke and Timothy Lim both suggest that the text might refer to an account of David's deeds instead of to the Psalms[81]—and indeed, 4QMMT else-where presents David as an exemplar of piety,[82] and the deeds of righteous and wicked kings are offered as paradigms.[83] But in an exhortatory letter about cultic observance, perhaps it would be even more appropriate to refer to Davidic documents about liturgy, concrete or ideal, like those of Chronicles—the same way they might come to mind for the writer of 2 Maccabees, also writing a letter about liturgy and its precursors.

While it is attractive to see evidence here for the elusive history of the canon and specific biblical books, the imaginative world of early Jews cannot be assumed to be an inner-biblical one. Here again, the texts do not give us any plausible information about the status of the book of Psalms. As Robert Kraft has warned, when ancient writers cite texts, they do not always mean the same texts that have come down to us.[84] And sometimes ancient writers are interested in texts that even they did not possess.

Psalms without Psalters: Rethinking Psalms Traditions beyond "Bible" and "Book"

Psalms were being widely copied and used as revealed literature. But when we speak of a "book of Psalms," we are retrojecting an ideal category onto the evidence: this was not an operative concept in the Second Temple period. Common claims that the book of Psalms appears in more Qumran copies than any other book, and that the Psalter was considered scriptural and prophetic, turn out to be a trick of the light.[85]

If there was no book of Psalms, what was there instead? One difficulty in challenging anachronistic assumptions is that often there is no alternative to fill the void. There are two common reactions to critiques of anachronism in the field: one, that "we have to call it *something*"; and two, that even if our categories are imperfect, we cannot simply throw up our hands and give up.

While both statements may be true, there is more to be said. If we are asking questions that our sources cannot answer—indeed, questions whose very premises are foreign to our sources—perhaps it really is time to give up on them, and ask new ones instead. Thinking of "books," for example, has occasioned a fifty-year debate about the identity of the 11QPsalms[a] manuscript. The major question—is it really a book of Psalms?—was, for a long time, an obvious starting point for most scholarly work on the manuscript. But this question is unanswerable, because its premise did not yet exist at the time it was compiled. By analogy, John Barton made a similar comment about questions scholars used to ask about what was and was not "canonical" in Second Temple times. Barton writes that when we ask "about the state of the canon in our period we are asking a question which the available literature cannot be made to answer, for the very good reason that no one had yet begun to think in such terms.... Perhaps we can make some good progress towards this goal by concentrating on the questions that are asked in the literature, rather than those that are not."[86] While Barton jettisons "canon" to turn our attention to new questions about the literature, I would like to similarly treat the "book of Psalms." But can we find ways to imagine psalms traditions in early Judaism—and by analogy, some of the other fragmented and unstable texts in our corpus—other than as a book?

The question of how to describe multiform, uncontained writings has been asked in other text-critical fields that grapple with sources that won't stand still.[87] When we no longer have an ideal original or copy-text that defines the shape and identity of a work, it has sometimes seemed most responsible merely to catalog and describe each discrete version or material artifact on its own, each as an individual piece of "evidence of a precise set of significances at successive points in history."[88]

But D. F. McKenzie critiques such an approach for its "curious conservative dullness." It does not account, he writes, for a concept or theory of text behind its specific instantiations. That is, it only describes what a text is, but does not consider what it might have *seemed like* to its writers, collectors, or readers. It also provides no language for us as modern readers to make sense of the scraps and variants before us. McKenzie, against the impulse of giving up on any sense of an ideal text behind its diverse instantiations, encourages scholars to theorize what notion of a "work" might emerge even if we recognize that Milton's vial has been broken, or, in fact, never existed at all. In the midst of its messy representations, a work, McKenzie writes, "may be the form traditionally imputed to an archetype; it may be a form seen as immanent in each of the versions but not fully realized in any one of them; or it may be conceived of as always potential, like that of a play, where the text is open and generates new meanings according to new needs in a perpetual deferral of closure."[89] How might we think about this for the sacred texts of Qumran and early Judaism more generally?

To be clear, I don't think it is helpful to consider the book of Psalms as a traditional archetype or immanent form never fully realized in the various scrolls listed in table 1. On the contrary, as I have argued, it is quite clear that many of those manuscripts cannot be considered versions of the same work, but instead represent different texts that might more appropriately be grouped with other genres of literature. Moreover, as I also demonstrated, the "book of Psalms" as a discursive concept is not attested until quite late in our literary record. That being said, I do not think we are doomed to the conservative dullness of my chart of individual fragments.

Instead, McKenzie's suggestions for making some conceptual sense of indeterminate and multiform texts can be helpful when taken in a way he did not quite intend. Rather than what "work" stands behind or is immanent in the mul-tiform manuscripts, I want to think about what ancient theory or concept of writing might be behind or immanent in them, and thus, how an ancient writer or reader might imagine them. What kind of language or metaphors might help us imagine morphologies of sacred writing beyond books and Bibles, and how might that help us reframe the texts that have survived?

Digital Metaphors

New metaphors suggest themselves easily: many of us now access the majority of our sources on screens, not in codices. Digital text has given us a powerful ex-ample of how we might conceptualize a nonbook written culture. Since the 1990s, textual scholars have been rethinking concepts of textuality in light of the new material and social conditions that govern the way electronic texts are pro-duced, manipulated and consumed, and how they change our very under-standing of the nature of written communication. Roger Chartier comments that "palimpsestic and polyphonic" digital texts "challenge the very possibility of recognizing...a fundamental identity" for a text.[90] Chartier points out that the threefold link between a material object, a fixed text, and an author, contained in the concept of a book, is deconstructed in electronic text. He writes:

> The electronic representation of texts completely changes the text's status; for the materiality of the book, it substitutes the immateriality of texts without a unique location; against the relations of contiguity es-tablished in the print objects, it opposes the free composition of infi-nitely manipulable fragments; in place of the immediate apprehension of the whole work, made visible by the object that embodies it, it intro-duces a lengthy navigation in textual archipelagos that have neither shores nor borders.[91]

Chartier's characterization of the nature of electronic texts has been chal-lenged—electronic texts certainly do have limits and constraints, although they are not the same ones as those of print media.[92] But what interests me here are the metaphors, the ways of speaking about texts that do not fit neatly into our idea of "books." Instead of the "immediate apprehension of the whole work" in a single physical object—like Milton's vial—electronic texts are "textual archipel-agos that have neither shores nor borders." The same might be said of the over-lapping, multiform collections of psalms found among the Scrolls, collections that cannot be subsumed under the title of a single book and have no set begin-ning or ending, but exist in varying, overlapping scopes, are rearranged, and con-tinue to be expanded.

Digital text, then, offers examples for how we might think about written materials that are not bound (literally and metaphorically) in "books"—that do not have a fixed or bounded identity. In her programmatic theoretical work on electronic text, N. Katherine Hayles suggests a reinvention of the idea of a written "work," which would be understood in terms of texts "spread out along a spectrum of similarity and difference along which clusters would emerge."[93] From this follows her notion of "Work as Assemblage, a cluster of related texts that quote, comment upon, amplify and remediate one another."[94]

Both Hayles's notion of clusters and assemblages and Chartier's borderless, shoreless archipelagos are helpful images for thinking about evidence for the Psalms at Qumran and in early Judaism. I am not arguing that there is a fixed ontological similarity between digital literature and collections found in scrolls, besides the obvious fact that neither format conforms to the rigid conception of a "book" that has dominated the way we think about texts. But neither is there a fixed ontological similarity between *books*, as they intuitively signify to us, and many of the textual traditions of early Judaism. Both, as I explained in the introduction, are metaphors that make different aspects of textual culture thinkable; new metaphors can help illuminate aspects of texts that old ones had obscured.

For a premodern textual culture, alternative conceptual language borrowed from another "nonbook" textuality can give us new heuristic models. To think of and to experience texts as "archives," "databases,"[95] or "assemblages" (Hayles), rather than "books," opens new ways of imagining overlapping and unbounded collections like the Psalms in the context of the ancient communities who compiled and preserved them.

Perhaps we may also consider the concept of text as *project,* which brings human agency and a sense of ongoing development and use back into the production of texts. The presence of textual variants and diverse configurations of psalms is no longer a problem to be solved—no longer to be studied as deviations from a preexistent "book" to which we compare them. Instead, they are part of the very shape of early Jewish literary expectations before that "book" emerged as such.[96]

New textual metaphors will, of course, break down as well; like "book," they will obscure some aspects of the textual imagination while highlighting others. However, looking at ancient writing through the lens of another textual culture, where the relationship between material objects, authors, and texts is quite different from that in the "book," can help us imagine just how differently textual culture could have been conceptualized.

Heavenly Archives and Parchment Fragments

In chapter 3, I discuss this question of textual metaphors in light of the Ben Sira tradition: I show how its composition and reception might be reimagined in terms of a "project," and how Ben Sira's very own metaphors for written tradition, which include channels and rivers, harvest gleaning, and light, enable us to understand Ben Sira's complex textual history and ambiguous identity. We also have some clues for the way early Jews imagined psalms traditions. The language of archive or database may indeed be helpful, as it allows us to see processes of expansion, rearrangement, variance, and incompleteness not as problems requiring explanation, but as basic aspects of the way textual collections were formed. "David's Compositions," the rich passage in 11QPsalms[a] I alluded to above and return to again in chapter 2, gives us one example of such a psalmic imagination:

ויהי דויד בן ישי חכם ואור כאור השמש וסופר ^{2}

ונבון ותמים בכול דרכיו לפני אל ואנשים ויתן ^{3}

לו יהוה רוח נבונה ואורה ויכתוב תהלים ^{4}

שלושת אלפים ושש מאות ושיר לשורר לפני המזבח על עולת ^{5}

התמיד לכול יום ויום לכול ימי השנה ארבעה וששים ושלוש ^{6}

מאות ולקורבן השבתות שנים וחמשים שיר ולקורבן ראשי ^{7}

החודשים ולכול ימי המועדות ולים הכפורים שלושים שיר ^{8}

ויהי כול השיר אשר דבר ששה וא(ר)בעים וארבע מאות ושיר ^{9}

לנגן על הפגועים ארבעה ויהי הכול ארבעת אלפים וחמשים ^{10}

כול אלה דבר בנבואה אשר נתן לו מלפני העליון ^{11}

^{2} And David, son of Jesse, was wise, and luminous like the light of the sun, and a scribe,

^{3} and discerning, and perfect in all his paths before God and men. And ^{4} YHWH gave him a discerning and enlightened spirit. And he wrote psalms:

^{5} three thousand six hundred; and songs to be sung before the altar over the perpetual

^{6} offering of every day, for all the days of the year: three hundred

^{7} and sixty-four; and for the Sabbath offerings: fifty-two songs; and for the offerings of the first days of

^{8} the months, and for all the days of the festivals, and for the Day of Atonement: thirty songs.

^{9} And all the songs which he spoke were four hundred and forty-six. And songs

^{10} to perform over the possessed: four. The total was four thousand and fifty.

^{11} All these he spoke through prophecy which had been given to him from before the Most High.[97]

In this text, there is no notion of anything we might recognize as a *book*; instead, there is a staggering number of imagined compositions—4,050, a typological number that trumps the 4,005 sayings of Solomon in 1 Kings 5, seeking, as James Kugel notes, "to overwhelm us with numbers."[98] While the composition does indicate that psalms were considered prophetic speech, it does not mention "the book of Psalms," or even "the Psalms"—only "psalms," of various types and in great number. This reference is indefinite both grammatically and conceptually. As I discuss further in chapter 2, the 4,050 psalms refer neither to this scroll nor any other specific collection. Instead, it presents us with an open series, overwhelmingly prolific divine writing and speech with no upper boundary. This imagined Davidic repertoire is a divine archive of revealed songs that exists in no single location, but is reflected only piecemeal in the various collections known and available to ancient scribes. This theory of unbounded revealed text makes it possible for new work to emerge that would continue the tradition of Davidic revelation.

From the Psalms Scroll, let us turn once more to Josephus, and consider more closely his description of David's creativity. In *Ant.* VII.305, we read:

Ἀπηλλαγμένος δ' ἤδη πολέμων ὁ Δαυίδης καὶ κινδύνων καὶ βαθείας ἀπολαύων τὸ λοιπὸν εἰρήνης ᾠδὰς εἰς τὸν θεὸν καὶ ὕμνους συνετάξατο μέτρου ποικίλου· τοὺς μὲν γὰρ τριμέτρους, τοὺς δὲ πενταμέτρους ἐποίησεν.

Being now delivered from wars and dangers and enjoying profound peace for the future, David composed songs and hymns to God in varied meters. Some he made in trimeters, others in pentameters.[99]

Josephus is writing for an audience for whom trimeter and pentameter were recognizable ways of describing poetic compositions. He wants to present David as a prolific composer of songs and hymns in a way that would resonate with his Greek-speaking addressees. But although he presents a broad Davidic repertoire, he is not concerned with a specific collection of compositions, and, given his vague reference to Greek poetic forms, he has no stake in making specific bibliographical claims about particular texts. Rather, he presents liturgical compositions as a diverse genre connected to David.

But what is the relationship between these imaginative constructions of psalms—thousands of psalms received through prophecy, or various hymns and songs in pentameter and trimeter—and the actual psalmic texts that were collected and copied by ancient scribes? The imagined concept behind the multiform manuscripts was not a "book of Psalms" with particular boundaries and contents, but a large, yet indeterminate, number of compositions that are imagined to exist somewhere, but are not fully definable or available.

We might compare this version of ideal text to other imagined, divine, but indeterminate theoretical texts: the heavenly tablets, which figure prominently in the book of *Jubilees*, and other heavenly books that make appearances as motifs in early Jewish literature.[100] Loren Stuckenbruck reflects on the relationship between developing Enochic texts and these imagined heavenly writings in the Second Temple period. How is the expansion of Enoch literatures, extant in manuscripts and in translation, related to these theoretical motifs? Stuckenbruck argues that additional writings are authorized by an appeal to the heavenly tablets that contain preexistent revelation: "Within the context of rapid growth of additional revelations in the patriarch's name, the appeal to heavenly tablets reflected writers' claims that their words were not in fact, 'additional' but rather constitute a provision of divine revelation that had existed all along."[101]

For psalmic and liturgical traditions, we might say something similar of the 4,050 compositions named in 11QPsalms[a]—a celestial cache that is partly, but not fully, accessible in various collections, and may still be expected to yield more of its treasures to worthy tradents. Here we might find it helpful to think of some of McKenzie's suggestions for the theory of text that transcends any specific artifact: not in an ideal "work," but in a sense of immanence or potential, never fully present in a specific version, and "in a perpetual deferral of closure." The diverse scribal products are reflections, but never full embodiments, of the totality of revelation. We have, then, a way to think about texts that are sacred, but not stable or contained.

The Book of Psalms Emerges

By the time of the great fourth and fifth century biblical codices—Alexandrinus, Vaticanus, and Sinaiticus—the Psalms are circulating with the same order and contents, though not the same division of compositions, as the familiar Masoretic book of Psalms, plus the additional Ps 151. In medieval Jewish manuscripts, as William Yarchin has shown, the contents of the Psalter are quite stable, but there is variety in how they are divided into discrete textual units: the expected configuration of 150 compositions is not yet standard.[102] I discuss the conflicted boundaries and enumeration of the canonical Psalter in chapter 5.

The Psalms had probably been translated into Greek sometime in the second or perhaps first century BCE,[103] based on text forms that sometimes agree with what became the Masoretic Psalter, and sometimes diverge from it, showing more affinity with other versions found among the Scrolls.[104] The original Old Greek translation and its Hebrew *Vorlage*, before the many layers of editing that produced the earliest extant manuscripts, are still something of a black box: the earliest undisputed Greek Psalms manuscripts are Christian versions dating to the third century CE, and these preserve from a few verses to four psalms, not anything close to a full Psalter.[105] The oldest extensive manuscript is Papyrus Bodmer XXIV, which most scholars date to the third or fourth century (although a second-century date has also been proposed),[106] where Pss 17–53 and 55–118 are preserved. As for literary references, Greek Jewish authors show no interest in thinking in terms of a set, specific collection—a book—although writers like Philo are certainly quoting specific psalms as prophetic speech. As we saw above, it is Luke and Acts, late in the first century CE, that become the first surviving texts to mention a "book of" Psalms (the parallels to Luke in Matthew and Mark do not say "book"). But even this "book" may have had a somewhat different scope from the canonical Psalter. In Acts 13:33, a quotation from Ps 2 is introduced by the words "in the second psalm," but a minority of manuscripts preserve the reading "in the *first* psalm." Perhaps the author of Acts knew a book of Psalms that did not have the introductory Ps 1, with the reference later corrected to match the canonical text.[107]

The book of Psalms as a specific and essentially uniform collection is, however, emerging. Origen writes that the "Hebrews divide the Book of Psalms into five books," listing the first line of the first Psalm in each section in accordance with the numbering in the Greek Psalter.[108] It is firmly set by late antiquity, and it has a history and precursors. We can find versions of these precursors among the Qumran manuscripts, which, for example, tell us that there was far less textual variety among the compositions that now make up Pss 1–89 than among those found in the latter part of the canonical book.

To be sure, reconstructing the evolution of a normative text is one of the tasks of textual criticism. But it is not the only task of literary history. In the last centuries BCE and the first century CE, there was still considerable variation in how psalms traditions could be collected, arranged, expanded—and imagined. We have little evidence that a specific, contained normative collection—a book—structured the way people conceptualized psalms. Approaching this multiform landscape on its own terms, without privileging the precursors of later orthodoxy, helps create a thicker description of a whole imaginative world and conceptual landscape of which those materials that became biblical were only a part, and where sacred texts did not inhabit a unified location.

Conclusion: Bibliographic Surprises in Early Judaism

The Psalms represent only the clearest example of what becomes visible when we read without biblical and bookish lenses. In this chapter, this case study has illustrated *both* how the results of the last two generations of scholarship have destabilized and decentralized our concept of the biblical text *and* how the icon of the Bible-as-book continues to structure our thinking. What is true of the Psalms is true for much of early Jewish sacred literature in general, which was not stable or unified in a single location.

Traditions related to Jeremiah are a key example. What we now know as the book of Jeremiah existed in a similar form in the Second Temple period, but it was only one part of a cluster of material related to the prophet Jeremiah that was not contained in—or conceived in terms of—a single or stable book. We can see this at play on two different levels. First and most simply, we have the text-critical issue: there was no single book of Jeremiah, but two major forms of the text. Scholars have long been aware that the version of Jeremiah in the Septuagint is quite different from the Masoretic one. The LXX preserves an earlier and shorter version, while the MT is longer, with episodes in a different order. Both of these text types were present side by side at Qumran, where six fragmentary Jeremiah manuscripts have been found.[109]

But the second level of the issue is more complicated and more significant. It is not merely that the book of Jeremiah existed in at least two forms: rather, we can see that the tropes and traditions that circulated in connection with Jeremiah did not necessarily converge around a specific bibliographic unit we would call the "book of Jeremiah" at all, in either of its two major textual forms. Instead, they were broader cultural tropes found in multiple locations, which were connected through cultural knowledge about a common persona and shared themes, rather than common dependence on a scriptural text in one or another version.

In his study of Jeremianic traditions at Qumran, especially the *Apocryphon of Jeremiah C*, Kipp Davis brilliantly illustrates how our understanding of Jeremiah's place in the ancient imagination must be unmoored from the biblical book and, instead, placed in culture more broadly. Davis shows that the *book* of Jeremiah is only a minor player in Qumran literature. Extant in only six fragmentary copies, rarely quoted, and without the kind of *pesher*-style commentary written for Isaiah or Habakkuk, "scriptural Jeremiah appears not to have been significant in the reading and interpretation of authoritative or sacred literature."[110] But while the *book* was not central, the *reputation* of Jeremiah as a prophet, exilic leader, and figure associated with the idea of the "new covenant" was more significant, even foundational to the self-understanding of the Qumran community, and inspired other literary products. The *Apocryphon of Jeremiah C*, for example, is not a "rewriting" of a scriptural Jeremiah, in either of its major forms, although scholars have tended to ask how it is related to "authoritative Scripture." But as Davis shows, "the authoritative employment and function of Jeremianic traditions does not appear grounded in the text of scriptural Jeremiah, [but] it rather may be located within the character or persona of the prophet behind the text."[111] Thus, the book of Jeremiah is not necessarily the fountainhead or anchor for Second Temple Jeremiah traditions. Instead, Davis writes, the character participates in "a reputational model for authority that is not primarily textualized."[112] Given this unmooring of the character from the scriptural book, even calling Jeremiah a "biblical character" already misrepresents his place in the Second Temple imagination.

Davis shows the significance of Jeremiah as a cultural figure at Qumran, but the idea of a reputation for Jeremiah and his prophecy that is not specifically "scriptural" can also be traced outside the Dead Sea Scrolls. The second-century book of Daniel is a surprising example. In chapter 9, we read of Daniel consulting written records: "I, Daniel, perceived in the books (בינתי בספרים) the number of years that, according to the word of the LORD to the prophet Jeremiah, must be fulfilled for the devastation of Jerusalem, namely, seventy years" (Dan 9:2). Daniel fasts and utters a penitential prayer. He then receives a visit from the angel Gabriel, who reveals that the prophecy has a cryptic meaning—not seventy years, but four hundred and ninety. This passage is most commonly read as an unprecedented explicit example of inner-biblical interpretation,[113] in which an earlier text is rescued from meaninglessness and obscurity and made relevant through a new interpretation. But Matthias Henze points out that for the character Daniel, "there is nothing odd about Jeremiah's prophecy, so he does not ask for an interpretation."[114] Henze adds, "The biblical author's reworking of earlier materials is altogether different from Daniel's acting as an inspired exegete (which, it turns out, he does not), and the two should not be confused."[115]

But exactly what earlier materials is the biblical author invoking? Surprisingly, Daniel's reference to Jeremiah's prophecy is not, in fact, a reference to the *book* of Jeremiah. As Seth Sanders notes, first, the written source Daniel refers to is not a single book but a collection or archive—*sfarim* in the plural—and second, "the understanding of the 70-year prophecy in Daniel 9 cannot have been received directly from Jeremiah 25."[116] Instead, "the text shows unmistakable signs of being derived not from the text of Jeremiah itself but from a widespread later Second Temple discourse about his prophecy," an observation that Sanders traces as far back as Theodor Nöldeke in 1868.[117] Indeed, the tradition about seventy years of desolation appears in five other places in Scripture (Jer 29:10, Zech 1:12 and 7:4–7, 2 Chr 36:20–22, Ezra 1:1) and, as Michael Fishbane showed, the wording of the prayer in Dan 9 is closest to Chronicles, not to Jer 25.[118]

While Dan 9 is so often cited as the clearest example of inner-biblical interpretation, it is not interpreting the biblical unit we would most readily assume. Instead, it attests to a popular tradition about destruction that is found in multiple locations. Both Davis and Sanders show that the scriptural book as we have it—in either of its two major forms—was not necessarily the central player in the ancient literary imagination, even if it is in ours. In Davis's model, which applies beyond the literature from Qumran, "reputational," not "scriptural," sources of authority stand behind the creation of new Jeremiah traditions.

We have seen, then, how both manuscript evidence and literary references sometimes belie our bibliographic and biblical assumptions. This is not necessarily true to the same extent, or in the same way, for every text. There are, to be sure, other materials that do exhibit more stability and continuity with the normative Bible; few will dispute, for example, that Deuteronomy, highly attested at Qumran, relatively textually consistent, and widely quoted, existed as a scriptural *book*, in the sense of a largely stable text contained within specific boundaries, in the Second Temple period.

But what about the question of Torah as a whole? Further research is needed on what early Jewish writers meant when they said "torah," because it cannot be unequivocally identified with our Pentateuch. Although Pentateuch, Torah, and books of Moses are often understood as synonymous, this not the case in early Jewish texts.[119] This has been noted particularly for Ezra-Nehemiah.[120] In Ezra, the regulations for the priestly courses from a "book of Moses" (Ezra 6:18) do not have a clear referent in the Pentateuch; in 2 Chr 35:4–5 such regulations are attributed to a document of David and Solomon. Other rulings in Nehemiah that are said to be in accordance with what is written in the torah of Moses are either quite different than what is found in the Pentateuch (e.g. intermarriage with the people of the land, Neh 10:31) or do not appear anywhere in the Pentateuch at all (e.g. the law of the wood offering, Neh 10:34).[121] This disconnect indicates either that Ezra-Nehemiah's Torah of Moses was different from the canonical texts that have survived or that it was a broader concept of legal instruction not identified with or limited to the contents and boundaries of specific writings.[122] Daniel 9:11 and 9:13 refer to the "torah of Moses," but give no specific citation, mentioning only that it contains a fulfilled curse on Israel. "Torah" may be a generic term that does not necessarily connote a specific bibliographic entity that includes the continuous narrative from creation to Moses's death,[123] but could point to different interests than a reference to our Pentateuch.

It is also unclear how early the concept of *five* books emerged as a popular or necessary way of conceptualizing the Torah as a bibliographic unit.[124] Reference to a Mosaic collection of five books is not clearly attested as a concept until the first century CE, in Philo (*Eternity* 19) and Josephus (*Ag. Ap.* I.39). One reference in the fragment 1Q30 ("1QLiturgical Text (?)") to "five books," ספרים חומשים, is without context; the damaged text also mentions the numbers three and four. Physical scrolls with Genesis-Exodus, Exodus-Leviticus, and Leviticus-Numbers exist at Qumran. But Deuteronomy seems not to have been copied together with them, with the possible exception of 4QRP, a text that, according to its editors, may have contained the entire Pentateuch, but presents it in a significantly different textual form from the Masoretic Torah.[125]

The *Letter of Aristeas*, a second-century BCE work, is an interesting case for thinking about how Hellenistic Jews imagined Torah without presupposing a Pentateuch. The text narrates the legend of King Ptolemy's commissioned translation of the "books of the law of the Jews" into Greek for the Alexandrian library.[126] The text lauds the wisdom of the law, and shows a particular interest in its materiality: the parchments on which it is written are prepared so beautifully that their joins are invisible, and the law is inscribed in gold. The king asks the scholars he has summoned to take the rolls out of their coverings and bows down to the books (176–77). After the translation is made, a curse is pronounced on those who would change or add anything to the law so that the book would be preserved unchanged for posterity (311).

But the text is surprisingly vague about exactly what texts are being translated, and what precisely the books of the law contain. And nowhere—despite the author's interest in the materiality and accuracy of the texts—does *Aristeas* mention that the books were five in number. Of course, this argument from silence cannot prove that it was not in fact the five books of the Pentateuch that were translated into Greek sometime in the third century BCE. But what *Aristeas*'s silence does show is that, even as the writer has spilled ink on describing the material appearance, quality, and effect of the rolls on the king, it is not obvious or necessary to identify the "books of the law of the Jews" specifically with a *Penta*teuch. In any case, *Aristeas* is interested not primarily in giving specific bibliographic information, but in telling a poetic tale in which ideas about texts are perhaps more interesting than the particulars of the texts themselves.

Despite this lack of clarity in the sources—and the positive evidence that "torah" is a broader genre, and inhabits different forms and locations—the Pentateuch has, like the "book of Psalms," remained a powerful bibliographic lens. This "tyranny of canonical assumptions," in Kraft's words, is present even among those scholars who otherwise strongly critique traditional approaches to the study of the Bible.[127] The default assumption is still that when ancient writers referred to texts, they must have had something like our Bible in mind. But sometimes they meant other traditions, extant or imagined, and sometimes their references were not bibliographically specific. The absolute centrality of the biblical is a theological, not a historical, axiom: a concern with the biblical in the texts that we study must be shown with evidence, not assumed by default. While the history of the field is a history of people seeking the origins, development, and meaning of these iconic texts, the subjects of our study were not necessarily preoccupied with such things; they were living in a culture whose intellectual, religious, and literary creativity cannot be assimilated into one dominant icon.

Milton's book as an essence embalmed in a vial has served as a metaphor for a hypostasized sacred text, unreactive and enclosed. I noted that it has been difficult to imagine sacred text as other than stable and contained in a Bible, and that this has held us back from conceptualizing the religious literature of early Judaism on its own terms, before text and canon had been set, and before scriptural texts could be found in one unique and enclosed site. But perhaps the sacredness of these texts in the literary imagination is dependent, in part, on their indeterminacy, their very lack of containment. Never fully available, they cannot quite be grasped, and don't inhabit a single location where they can be apprehended—like David's overwhelming treasury of 4,050 prophetic psalms, only some of which any scribe has ever seen.

From this perspective, the vial begins to look very small. And while Milton meant his image of an "imbalm'd" essence in the sense of preservation for posterity—to a "life beyond life"—a body that is embalmed is, of course, already dead, prepared for final viewing and burial. It is possible to turn his powerful bookish metaphor on its head, imagining how texts may be affectively imbued with *more* mystery and power when they are still alive, and when we do not think we can fully contain them. I have begun to show that the ancient writers did not think they had all their revealed writing in their grasp, and in the rest of this book, I will explore other sites of this literary humility and wonder. As our record of the past is fragmented, so, indeed, was their present: the horizons of their literary imagination extend far beyond the texts that they actually possessed and controlled. To acknowledge this fragmentation is to begin the work of textual history beyond textual criticism.

with Pss 127 and 129; 1Q16 preserves Ps 68 only. The psalms the scribes chose must have been considered authoritative, prophetic texts of contemporary relevance. But only seven psalms appear in these documents, scattered over three manuscripts in two different caves. The *pesharim* give us no indication about the way the psalms were conceived *as a collection*. Indeed, the nature of these psalms *pesharim* is rather different from, for instance, Pesher Habakkuk (1QpHab), which shows a consciousness of the text of Habakkuk as a unity, commenting on it in order. But it is virtually impossible that these fragments had originally contained commentary on the entire book of Psalms, since even writing out the book of Psalms alone on a single scroll would have produced an extremely long document. Even if the *pesharim* had originally contained commentaries on many more psalms than are now preserved, the most extensive manuscript, 4Q171, indicates that they were not collected in an order familiar from any known psalms collection: it presents commentary on Ps 37, followed immediately by Ps 45.

What, then, did these *pesharim* originally contain? There is no textual overlap between the three manuscripts, so it is impossible to know whether they were originally copies of one larger work. If we note the existence of a smaller collection of psalms and the use of individual psalms as modular unities, as I discussed above, it seems most likely they were separate compositions on different groups of psalms, or perhaps psalms specially selected for their relevance to community concerns.[69] Even if the *pesharim* do reflect parts of one longer work, this document would be a *pesher* on a selection of psalms, rather than on anything like the book of Psalms, the way 1QpHab is a *pesher* on the book of Habakkuk.

Psalms in 2 Maccabees and 4QMMT?

Finally, we must consider two other sources where scholars have found the "book of Psalms": The letter to the Jews of Egypt at the beginning of 2 Maccabees, and 4QMMT, the "Halakhic Letter" from Qumran. Both have been ubiquitous in discussions about the emergence of the biblical canon in general, and the status and popularity of the book of Psalms specifically. Neither of these texts mentions the "book of Psalms" or "psalms" at all. But they both refer their audiences to textual authorities, and in this context, mention the name "David." This reference has almost universally been taken to mean the book of Psalms, and based on this identification, scholars have drawn conclusions about the status and popularity of the Psalter in early Judaism.

But how do we know that "David" refers to the book of Psalms? This identification seems obvious enough—David is the traditional author of the Psalter, so what else could such a reference mean? But it was not quite so simple in the Hellenistic period. As I show more fully in the next chapter, "David" has a far more complex resonance, and is responsible for various discourses—biblical

The Sweetest Voice

The Poetics of Attribution

[W]hen ten righteous men sought to say the Book of Psalms, the Holy
One, blessed be He, said to them, All of you are pleasing, pious, and
praiseworthy to say a hymn before me. But David will say it on behalf
of all of you. Why? Because his voice is sweet.

—Song of Songs Rabbah 4:4

Introduction: What Did Ancient Attribution Claim?
Aesthetics and Authorship

In *The Spirit of Hebrew Poetry* (1782), J. G. Herder presents a theory of Davidic
attribution of the Psalms:

> Not all [of the Psalms] are his or of his age. Only an individual song of
> Moses, however, is from more ancient times, and later writers obviously
> followed him as their model.... The superscription ascribing them to
> David, where it stands without further limitation, seems to be as indef-
> inite in its import, as the ascription to Solomon of whatever proverbs
> and delicious songs belong in any sense to his age, or correspond with
> his character.... [A]mong the Hebrews a beautiful song is synonymous
> with a song of David.[1]

In this brief comment, Herder makes two distinct moves. First, he makes a historical claim about who wrote the Psalms; writing in the eighteenth century,
Herder essentially accepts traditional Davidic authorship. But he also theorizes
something else: what it meant to attribute texts "among the Hebrews." What emerges
is that the modern interest in establishing historical authorship—an interest that
has been central to the kind of historical-critical biblical studies that fully
emerged in the generation after Herder—was not shared by the ancients. Their
conception of what was "Davidic" was not necessarily one of positivistic attribution, but more "indefinite in its import": its resonance could be historiographic

(psalms that belong to David's age), ethical (songs that correspond with his character), and aesthetic (songs that are beautiful).

Herder's theory of the "indefinite" significance of Davidic headings seems oddly unsettling from the standpoint of modern scholarship. This is not merely because the desire to pin down historical authorship and dating of texts remains a key concern of biblical studies; after all, the view that the historical king David wrote the Psalms persists only in conservative apologetics. For those who have long viewed Davidic authorship as pious tradition, not history, there is a different question: didn't at least the *ancients* believe that David really wrote the Psalms?

The idea that ancient people had an uncritical view of biblical authorship already seemed intuitive in the mid-nineteenth century. According to a popular encyclopedia of the Bible, for instance, "[m]any of the ancients, both Jews and Christians, maintained that all the Psalms were written by David, which is one of the most striking proofs of their uncritical judgment."[2] But Herder's remarks suggest that there is something more complicated here: the story is not that once upon a time, people believed the psalms were Davidic, and now, being equipped with the tools of historical-critical scholarship, we know better. Instead, the ancient and modern responses to "are the Psalms Davidic?" are answers to two different questions from two different worlds of literary concepts.[3]

Herder's remarks about the meaning of attribution are also surprising for another reason. In speculating about the meaning of Davidic headings, he offers historiographic, ethical, and aesthetic explanations. But one factor is glaring in its absence: authority. The idea that linking texts with authorial figures is a legitimizing strategy is a powerful one, and has been a dominant way to understand practices of attribution in antiquity. New texts are attributed to great figures— such as Moses, Enoch, Ezra, or David—in order to imbue new traditions with an authority they would not have if they were circulated anonymously or in the name of their true author. For modern scholars, texts need an authoritative source—a reputable author—to be taken seriously; and so the idea that to attribute a text to a figure is intended to give that text legitimacy seems obvious. But was this always the case for ancient writers? What if we took seriously Herder's suggestive passage connecting attribution and aesthetics, and asked if there were other reasons besides authorization that motivated the link between old figures and new traditions?

In chapter 1, I argued that in early Judaism, psalms were not definable by either biblical or bibliographic boundaries, but were imagined as an open archive partially instantiated in texts of various scopes and genres. Without a book of Psalms as such, it follows that we must also rethink its traditional author, David. If he was not the author of a biblical book, how *was* the link between David and psalms understood? In this chapter, I use the figure of David and his relationship with psalms as a case study for reconsidering ancient practices of attribution.

I will suggest two major ideas about how texts and figures were sometimes linked in the Jewish literary imagination. First, attribution can be about other motivations besides conferring authority to a text by linking it to a figure; sometimes, it can be about developing and celebrating a character by staging him in another text. Second, tracing the origins of texts and their historical authorship is a modern scholarly preoccupation, but was not always so important for ancient writers. That is, linking texts to figures was not always about claiming "who really wrote" them. As Annette Reed writes, sometimes the "pseudonymous writer is not so much creator or author as tradent and guarantor," and the appeal to an ancient figure is based on the particular elements of a character's reputation and biography—such as Moses's revelation on Sinai or Enoch's access to antediluvian revelation and cosmic knowledge.[4] The idea that David was considered a "biblical author" in early Judaism is usually taken as an established fact, but there is little in the texts themselves to suggest that early Jews believed, in a consistent or literal way, that David wrote the psalms, or that they were particularly concerned with their authorial origins. Rather, I suspect Herder was right about the range of significance that the "Davidic" had in antiquity, and about the suggestion that attribution is an aesthetic and poetic act.

I first consider the Psalms superscriptions, but then move on to other aspects of how early Jews connected David with psalms, with singing, and with written text. What emerges is that David is not an author—that is, he does not fulfill a bibliographic function—but a developing character associated with psalmody and liturgical tradition. And practices of linking texts to David, which increase through the Second Temple period, cannot be fully explained as strategies of authority conferring, of assigning authors to new texts in an effort to legitimize them. Rather, a fruitful way to explain these practices is to think of them also as effusions of historical, ethical, and aesthetic interest in a compelling character—as biography, not bibliography.

Characters in Search of Stories: Authority, Pseudonymity, and Poetics

One feature of early Jewish literary practices is the pseudonymous attribution of writings to legendary figures of ancient times, rather than to their real authors. This is true not only for the corpus of nonbiblical texts called the Pseudepigrapha, such as the books of *Enoch*, *Jubilees*, or *4 Ezra*, but also for biblical texts, many of which are also pseudonymously attributed: that Moses did not write the Pentateuch, David did not write the Psalms, and Solomon did not write the Song of Songs is no longer in dispute among critical scholars.[5] Among the texts that are linked with ancient figures, some, like the Psalms, originate anonymously, and come to be attributed to ancient figures secondarily over time; while others, like 4 Ezra, are composed from their inception in the voices of old characters. Such texts, writes Hindy Najman, have "deliberately effaced [their] own origin,"[6] and the search to recover their true date and circumstances of composition has taken up most of our scholarly energy. But in recent years the phenomenon of pseudepigraphy itself has become an object of study in its own right. Why might texts, old and new, be linked to legendary figures?

An intuitive way to explain why a text might be connected to an ancient figure is because texts need reputable and identifiable authors in order to be received as legitimate. This concern with attribution as legitimation does seem to be at play, for example, for Josephus, who says the authority of the Jewish sacred books rests on the unbroken succession of prophets who wrote them down:

> [38] [A]mong us there are not thousands of books in disagreement and conflict with each other, but only twenty-two books, containing the record of all time, which are rightly trusted. [39] Five of these are the books of Moses, which contain both the laws and the tradition from the birth of humanity up to his death; this is a period of a little less than 3,000 years. [40] From the death of Moses until Artaxerxes, king of the Persians after Xerxes, the prophets after Moses wrote the history of what took place in their own times in thirteen books; the remaining four books contain hymns to God and instructions for people on life. [41] From Artaxerxes up to our own time every event has been recorded, but this is not judged worthy of the same trust, since the exact line of succession of the prophets did not continue. [42] It is clear in practice how we approach our own writings. Although such a long time has now passed, no one has dared to add, to take away, or to alter anything. (Ag. Ap. 1.38–42)[7]

If a text is to be received as authoritative—as "scriptural"—it must be traced back to an authoritative figure, through the succession of prophets.

This seems consistent with the idea that in the Hellenistic period, there was a "horror vacui" of unattributed texts, which spurred a rush toward authorial legitimation, a drive to fill in these bibliographic gaps.[8] Some scholars take this further, assuming that attribution to an ancient figure could only have one goal: to have newly composed books recognized as Scripture. Jonathan Campbell writes, for example, that the continuing emergence of texts in the name of Moses or the Prophets proves that the scriptural corpus could still admit new texts—because "unless links to the past figures conferred scriptural status, at least potentially, they would have been pointless."[9]

But are authorship and legitimacy so closely linked for all texts? In *Against Apion*, Josephus was speaking about the writing of *history*, which must be traced back through prophetic authors back to Moses. But when he mentions the "remaining four books" (whichever they might be) that "contain hymns to God and instructions for people on life," he does not concern himself with identifying *their* authors. For some types of books in Josephus's conception of a scriptural corpus, attribution to a known figure is not a central concern.[10]

Indeed, given the variety of genres and characters that participate in pseudonymous attribution, we should not expect to theorize this phenomenon in any one way. The idea that attribution is only meaningful insofar as it confers scriptural status overlooks a host of other motivations for writing in someone else's name. Such practices continue today, for reasons that have nothing to do with "getting a book into the Bible," but might instead reflect a literary or spiritual interest in an ancient character. In fact, when we see pseudepigraphy exclusively as authorization, we create a picture of a literary world in which textual choices are highly instrumental, and always primarily political and polemical—perhaps paranoid. This is consistent with a popular way of understanding Second Temple Judaism in general, as a world of warring factions who constantly assert their own legitimacy against competing claims. But early Jewish writers were concerned about more than legitimizing themselves and their creations, and different kinds of discourses used pseudonymous attribution for different reasons.

One example of a multilayered approach to practices of attribution that considers *both* authority conferring and other literary and religious motivations is Hindy Najman's conception of discourse tied to a founder, an idea she charts especially through the figures of Moses and Ezra.[11] To be sure, Najman's most influential contribution is to demonstrate how writers inscribe their creations into older discourses, claiming authority for themselves as genuine continuations of Mosaic or Ezrean traditions.[12] The importance of authorizing *legal* traditions by linking them with their great founder, Moses, now seems evident.

But this is not equally applicable to every pseudepigraphic tradition—and Najman's model, especially as developed in her work on traditions connected to Ezra, has another dimension. Besides claiming authority, linking a text to a figure also extends and enriches narratives about him, transforming the character to make him speak to a new audience. Writing in the name of an ancient hero can also be a kind of spiritual exercise of self-effacement, in which the figure that the author emulates becomes an exemplar and literary guide for both him and his audience—as, for example, *4 Ezra* constructs Ezra as a role model for surviving trauma and building community.[13] In other words, even beyond questions of scriptural authorization, linking a figure with a literary creation is far from pointless.

Recently, Kipp Davis has argued a similar position for Jeremiah materials at Qumran, turning our attention away from a narrow focus on the construction of textual authority to a broader interrogation of what made a figure inspiring enough that scribes composed new texts about him. Davis writes that Qumran texts that are related to the book of Jeremiah—such as his focus, the *Apocryphon of Jeremiah C*—"rarely escape textualized, exegetical treatments"[14] that discuss them in relationship to the scriptural text. Davis begins not with the idea of a previous scriptural text's authority, or with the need to give a new text authoritative status, but instead with the compelling character who serves as a driving force behind new writing. New traditions linked with Jeremiah "served as models for conduct through popular perceptions of their 'founder'—the meaning of Jeremiah's words became secondary to his presentation as the prototypical prophet of exile, and his articulation of the new covenant."[15] Jeremiah's reputation as a prophet went along with his role as an "emblem for community leadership and for propaganda used to distinguish covenant insiders from outsiders."[16] Davis's work shows how looking beyond a narrow focus on textual authorization can help open up a new window into what ignited ancient literary creativity.

"For the Sake of Shrewd Penelope": Characters in Search of Stories

Drawing on theoretical and comparative work from outside the study of early Judaism can also help us imagine pseudepigraphic practices and the creation of new texts linked with old figures. Gérard Genette writes that using a pseudonym "suggests a delight in invention, in borrowing, in verbal transformation, in onomastic fetishism. Clearly, using a pseudonym is already a poetic activity, and the pseudonym is already somewhat like a work. If you can change your name, you can write."[17] What we miss when we read only through the lens of instrumental authority strategies is this positive sense of "delight in invention." Genette speaks of creating a pseudonym, rather than writing as an existing character or linking new texts with old heroes. But in the case of early Jewish pseudepigraphy, we might transpose his idea of "onomastic fetishism" into something broader: an interest not in a name or a previously authoritative text but in a beloved character and his story—in the struggle of Ezra, what Enoch saw in heaven, Jeremiah's prophecy in exile, or the sweetness of David's voice. Rather than beginning with a text and assuming it needed to have its authority gap filled through a link to a figure, might we also think from the opposite end—to imagine that it is the development of the figure, the desire to expand traditions about a character, that generates his links to new texts?

In fact, such a sense of character-driven literary creativity is attested elsewhere in the ancient world, in some theories about Homer from the Hellenistic period, where the character becomes the affective center of the poetic creation. Poetry, notes Mark Payne, is generated from infatuation with one of the characters, who is prior to, and drives the creation of, the narrative. Hermesianax (early third century BCE) lays out such a theory in his *Leontion*, where he writes about the love of Homer for Penelope:

> The Bard himself, whom the justice of Zeus maintains to be the sweet-est spirit of all the race of singers, divine Homer, worked up slender Ithaca in his songs for the sake of shrewd Penelope, on whose account he dwelt on that little island, suffering greatly, leaving his own wide homeland far behind. And he celebrated the family of Icarius, and the people of Amyclas, and Sparta, drawing on his own experiences.[18]

Payne writes that for Hermesianax, "the poet's feelings for his own character are what led him to create and inhabit the poetic world she anchors."[19] This theory, where the longing for a character is a driving force of creativity, extends Aristotle's idea of poetic invention as maternity, wherein poets bring their creations to life and love them as their own children.[20] Hannah Arendt called this *natality*, "being unto life," and opposed it to the "being unto death" of Plato, for whom writing is borne out of a desire to escape mortality.[21] Opposed in modern times to Aristotle's maternal theory and its heir, Hermesianax's poet-as-lover, is Harold Bloom. Bloom, like Plato, sees the poet as someone more conscious of mortality than other people. But Bloom's best known legacy is that of poetic invention as an anxiety of influence, a grappling with an already canonized predecessor in a kind of Oedipal rivalry.[22]

The theories of poetic motivation illustrated by Plato and Bloom begin from an affective core that is negative—characterized by fear and anxiety, about death, loss, obscurity, and legitimacy, anxieties that the labor of writing is supposed to quell. On the other hand, the Aristotelian theory begins not with lack and fear but with excess and love. It is the overflow of affect for a character that causes literature. Hermesianax demonstrates this for the *Odyssey*, written "for the sake of shrewd Penelope." A different version of this trajectory is dramatized in Luigi Pirandello's 1921 play *Six Characters in Search of an Author*, where a group of characters suddenly appear in a theater, clamoring to be staged. Adrift, they need a literary home, "a fecundating matrix, a fantasy which could raise and nourish them: make them live for ever!"[23] Pirandello reflects on the writing of the play as a way to deal with characters he had imagined, who would not leave him alone until he "let them into the world of art by making of their persons...a novel, a play, at the very least a short story."[24] Pirandello, unlike Hermesianax's Homer, had no great love for the characters who pestered him for a stage; but here, too, it is a drive to give characters a "matrix" that drives literary creation.

How does this relate to the central issue of this chapter—the idea of attribut-ing texts to authors in early Judaism? Is there not a vast difference between writing narratives about characters—like the *Odyssey*'s Penelope—and linking texts to figures—as the Psalms are attributed to David? Perhaps the difference is not so great. In the early Jewish literary imagination, I argue, figures like David often function less as authors than they do as characters. Many instances of what we usually call "authorial attribution" are far less clearly meant functionally, to assert authorship—to confer authority on a text by giving it a provenance—and more often are borne out of the compulsion and desire to continue telling stories about a favorite character.[25] Acts of linking a text to a figure are poetic moves, and like Pirandello's theater, they provide characters with a literary matrix where they can live.

In the case of early Jewish Davidic traditions, I see less of a sense of direct authorial attribution *to* David, or pseudonymous writing *as* David, than of expanding traditions *about* David that claim more textual territory as they grow. These traditions tell a story of literary production and pseudonymous attribution that are not motivated only by the anxiety of legitimation of specific texts or filling bibliographic gaps, but where writing is effusion, invention, excess.

The Psalm Superscriptions and Davidic Voice

To explore how an aesthetic and ethical interest in a character can drive practices of attribution, I turn to my major example: the Psalms superscriptions. Studying their creation and reception allows us to trace how the link between the Psalms and David was conceptualized, and how it developed over time. Did ancient people really believe that David wrote the Psalms? How does the development of the superscriptions contribute to our understanding of authorship and pseudepigraphy in early Judaism?

The headings of the psalms are broadly considered later additions, separate from the composition of the psalms themselves, and added at different times over the course of the psalms' transmission and translation. For some time after this consensus developed, scholars paid little attention to the superscriptions, since they could provide no information about the original setting or authorship of the Psalms.[26] But with new interest in the last two generations of scholarship on not only the historical origins of biblical texts but also their transmission and interpretation, the headings have received a great deal more attention, and have been studied for what they might be able to tell us about the transmission of the Psalter and the figure of David.[27]

Of the 150 psalms in the Masoretic Psalter, 73 have Davidic headings, *ledavid*. Other psalms are linked through the *lamed* prefix with different figures: 12 with Asaph, 11 with the sons of Korah, and 1 each with Heman, Ethan the Ezrahite, Solomon, and Moses. Psalms 39 and 62 have a double ascription, to David and Jeduthun. What is the meaning of this *lamed* phrase? Can we discern what such headings meant when they were first appended to the psalms, and how they were understood over time?

While the common translation of *ledavid* is "Of David," suggesting that the superscription is meant to assign authorship, this is hardly a natural reading of the phrase. Indeed, as James Kugel writes, it is probably "the least likely hypothesis."[28] The *lamed* prefix can express multiple kinds of association—"to," "for," "dedicated to," "concerning"—and the name "David" also has a range of possible meanings besides signifying the historical individual. Sigmund Mowinckel, who thinks many of the headings have something to do with their cultic setting, argues that the *ledavid* psalms, particularly the Psalms of Ascent, were related to the liturgical functions of the Davidic king.[29]

Other headings seem to use the *lamed* prefix to mean a composition *concerning* David, in the sense of prayers *on behalf of* the Davidic king, such as Psalms 20, 21, and 61.[30] Thus, the *lamed* indicates something about the subject or purpose of the text. A striking example is Psalm 72, which has a Solomonic heading. The psalm is a prayer *for* the king, that he may judge righteously, that his kingdom span "from sea to sea, and from the river to the ends of the earth," that the "kings of Tarshish and of the isles render him tribute [and] the kings of Sheba and Seba bring gifts" (72:2, 9, 10). Here, the contents of the psalm are thematically related to traditions about Solomon's wise judgment, the expansion of his kingdom, his riches, and his relationships with other monarchs—it is a prayer *for* a Solomonic king.[31]

Other interpretations of the psalm headings have less to do with their performed setting or purpose, and more to do with the transmission of the psalms as texts. One popular view is that the headings indicate smaller collections of psalms associated with particular liturgical "guilds," as Nahum Sarna argues.[32] The "Davidic" and "Korahite" and "Asaphite" headings, then, indicate that these psalms belonged to collections associated with these figures, and do not stake a claim for the authorship of the compositions themselves.[33]

How were these headings understood in the ancient world? The clearest evidence for their early reception comes from the way they are handled in the Septuagint. All the Masoretic superscriptions to David and other figures also appear in the LXX, but thirteen additional psalms that have no attribution in the MT have become Davidic in the Greek. While it is difficult to know for certain which of these superscriptions, if any, were based on a Hebrew *Vorlage* other than the MT and which originated in Greek,[34] it is safe to say that there was an expansion of Davidic headings in the Greek tradition. Based on the strategies of the Greek translators, the way the recensions dealt with the titles, and the proliferation of new, additional headings within the Greek tradition, we can see that the idea of "Davidic authorship" or authorization of the Psalms is not the operative concept in the LXX. Instead, we can trace the continuation of expansive characterization and historiographical processes at work in the MT.

The first crucial observation is that initially, the Greek translator was consistent in rendering לדוד with the dative, as τῷ Δαυιδ.[35] Albert Pietersma writes: "It is quite clear that for the OG translator Hebrew לדוד did not mean Davidic authorship—the articular genitive for a Hebrew ל-phrase is well within his usage. It is equally clear that subsequent Greek tradition was fully aware of the fact that the τῷ δαυιδ of the Greek Psalter did not denote Davidic authorship."[36] Pietersma notes that "subsequent Greek tradition"—that is, the recensions—sometimes replaced τῷ with the genitive τοῦ, "in an apparent effort to clarify Davidic authorship" per se, since these redactors did not read τῷ Δαυιδ itself as an authorial note.

In keeping with the translational strategies of the New English Translation of the Septuagint,[37] Pietersma translates the original dative τῷ Δαυιδ literally as "pertaining to David." This is more than a slavishly literal English translation of a slavishly literal Greek one. Pietersma explains his choice, saying that τῷ Δαυιδ is among the "expressions of general reference" that "indicate without much specificity (partly due to lack of context) that x has something to do with y." The "reasonably neutral phrase 'Pertaining to Dauid' [sic] (et al.) . . . allows for a range of perceived connections with the persons in question."[38] The translation, then, is hardly elegant or clear, but this in itself reflects the vagueness and multivalence of the heading in Greek—which, indeed, reflects the multiple possibilities of meaning of the Hebrew ledavid.

A few Greek superscriptions illustrate the vagueness of a Davidic association by combining David with other figures and other times. Psalm 137 (LXX 136), the famous lament for Jerusalem sung by the rivers of Babylon, has no heading in the MT and Qumran, but Septuagint manuscripts associate it with either David or Jeremiah—or sometimes with both at the same time: "Pertaining to David, (through) Jeremiah," which is followed by the Latin Vulgate.[39] Indeed, 4 Baruch 7:33–36 quotes parts of Ps 137 as sung by Jeremiah, and it appears that both figures could be imagined to voice the psalm and be associated with it for different reasons.

Another example is Ps 65 (LXX 64), where the superscription is "To the end. A psalm for David. A song. Of Jeremiah and Ezekiel from the account of the sojourning community, when they were about to go out." This heading gives a chain of associations and a performance context for the psalm, but does not seem preoccupied with its textual origins. Similarly, Ps 96 (LXX 95) has the heading "When the house was built after the captivity; a song of David." The psalm itself appears in part in 1 Chr 16:23–33 when David brings the ark to Jerusalem, but here it is also placed at the rebuilding of the temple. It is not so much a focus on fixing an origin as a concern with use and aptness that seems to motivate the creation of the headings.

Thus, some of the ledavid headings can be read as indicating a liturgical setting, a prayer for the king, and belonging to a royal collection, or some other kind of Davidic association, and neither the Hebrew originals nor the early Greek reception understands them as authorial notes. But some of the Davidic headings are expanded beyond *ledavid* to connect the psalm with an episode in David's life, and two say outright that David sang or recited the psalm. Thus, in the process of transmission, events in David's biography furnish new narrative settings for these anonymous and timeless compositions, and they come to be put in David's mouth. How do we explain this phenomenon, and what does it tell us about concepts of authorship and the development of David's character?

Expanded Headings and David's Biography

A dominant pattern emerges in the expanded headings: they present a suffering, penitent David, not a triumphant king. Most are attached to psalms of lament and refer to moments of crisis in David's biography. The first expanded heading is in Ps 3, "A psalm of David when he fled from his son Absalom." Psalm 7 is titled "*Shiggaion*[40] of David, which he sang to the Lord, concerning Cush, a Benjaminite," which refers to the Cushite who informed David Absalom had died (2 Sam 18:21–32).

The next expanded heading occurs in Ps 18, which is not a lamentation but a thanksgiving for being saved from distress, introduced thus: "For the leader, regarding the servant of the lord, regarding David, who spoke the words of this song to the Lord when the Lord delivered him from the hand of all his enemies, and from the hand of Saul." The heading to the acrostic wisdom Ps 34, "When he feigned madness before Abimelech, so that he drove him out, and he went away," is also a reference to David's flight from Saul (cf. 1 Sam 21:11–16).

Psalm 51, a song of penitence, is introduced with "When the prophet Nathan came to him, after he had gone in to Bathsheba." The next cluster of psalms with expanded headings—52, 54, 56, 57, and 59—are all laments. Each of the headings invokes a time before David had become king, and was hiding from Saul's pursuit.

The heading of Ps 60 moves us into the period of David's monarchy, invoking the battles he fought as king: "To the leader: according to the Lily of the Covenant. A *Miktam* of David; for instruction; when he struggled with Aram-naharaim and with Aram-zobah, and when Joab on his return killed twelve thousand Edomites in the Valley of Salt." The heading appears to invoke 2 Sam 8, where David is unequivocally powerful and victorious. But it has been attached to a composition about a terrible defeat—a psalm of lament about divine rejection. Next, Ps 63 is introduced with "For David, when he was in the wilderness of Judah," which could refer to several different episodes, such as David's escape from Absalom in 2 Sam 15–17, where the wilderness is mentioned at 15:23, 28, and 16:2.[41] Finally, Ps 142, a psalm of lament and despair has the heading "To David, when he was in the cave," another likely reference to David's hiding from Saul (1 Sam 22).[42]

In the expanded headings, then, we have a distinct concentration of interest in moments of lament, fear, and contrition. Most headings refer not to episodes during David's kingship but to his hardships in the struggle with Saul beforehand.

Of those episodes that do come from his monarchy, several refer to Absalom's revolt and death and one to David's sin with Bathsheba. One refers to David's victorious wars, but is connected to a psalm about defeat. Only Ps 18 is a psalm of thanksgiving, but it is also connected to David's escape from Saul and his enemies. "In these psalms David does not come in view as a king," Rolf Rentdorff notes, but an exemplar that "the individual reader as well as the praying congregation can identify with in times of need and distress."[43]

The expanded psalm headings, then, place the psalms at particular moments in David's life, particularly moments of hardship, and present him as their performer. He thus becomes an example of prayer and worship. But we have no evidence that the composers of the headings were interested in presenting David as the originator of the texts themselves, rather than as a performer of traditional material whose originary authorship was not of particular concern.

To be sure, when a heading contextualizes a psalm in an episode of David's life, it is dramatized in his voice, although only two Masoretic headings have a verb that presents David as singing or reciting the psalm in question:

> Psalm 7: *Shiggaion* of David, **which he sang to the Lord**, concerning Cush, a Benjaminite.

> Psalm 18: For the leader, regarding the servant of the lord, regarding David, who **spoke the words of this song** to the Lord when the Lord delivered him from the hand of all his enemies, and from the hand of Saul.

But even as David is performing the psalm, there is no indication whether the headings mean to claim he *composed* the words. The words themselves remain timeless, generic, and unrelated to David as an individual or to his specific time.[44] Nothing in any of the psalms with expanded Davidic headings suggests the texts themselves were composed or redacted specifically to reflect episodes in David's biography; sometimes, as with Ps 60, they barely seem applicable.

In fact, two texts that make the clearest claims to be David's own autobiographical compositions are not part of the canonical Psalter: the lament for Saul and Jonathan in 2 Sam 1:17–27, and Ps 151. The lament for Saul and Jonathan in 2 Sam 1:17–27 begins:

> [17] David intoned this lamentation over Saul and his son Jonathan.
> [18] (He ordered that The Song of the Bow[a] be taught to the people of Judah; it is written in the Book of Jashar.) He said...

Unlike the canonical psalms, this text contains specific references to people and events from David's first-person perspective, especially the account of his friendship with Jonathan at the end of the composition.[45] While the precise meaning of the introductory phrase is unclear—as are many words in the psalm headings, which may refer to technical musical notations whose meanings are now lost—it is usually interpreted as a reference to traditional material, perhaps a song called "the bow," which is written in the lost "Book of Jashar" or the "book of the upright" (ספר הישר).

Psalm 151 is not part of the Masoretic psalter, but is found in a first-century CE Hebrew version at Qumran in 11QPsalmsª. It is appended to fourth-century Septuagint Psalters with a heading that says it is "outside the number," that is, outside the established number of canonical psalms, underscoring its marginal status in the canon.[46] The text, cited here in its Hebrew version from Qumran, is explicitly presented as David's speech about himself:

> [3] A Halleluia of David, son of Jesse. I was smaller than my brothers and the youngest of my father's sons; he made me [4] shepherd of his flock and ruler over his kid goats. My hands made a flute, my fingers a lyre, [5]and I gave glory to YHWH....[8]...He sent his prophet to anoint me, Samuel [9] to make me great....[11]...[God] anointed me with holy oil, and made me leader of his people and ruler over the sons of [12] his covenant. (11QPsalmsª col. 28)[47]

The first-person references to specific events in David's life contrast with the far more generic, broadly applicable psalms with which his name is linked. Unlike in the canonical psalms, then, this text explicitly presents itself not as something performed by or otherwise associated with David, but specifically as a Davidic autobiographical composition. Interestingly, then, the marginal Ps 151 is the only psalm that *is* a clear Davidic pseudepigraphon.

The superscriptions' connection of psalms to moments from David's life, then, seems to have little to do with finding an author for anonymous texts. Making psalms "Davidic" is not precisely attribution, as little evidence exists for a claim that David personally *composed* the psalms, but dramatization and historicization. But this process of dramatizing and historicizing psalms is motivated not by the texts of the psalms themselves, but by an interest in the *character* who comes to animate the texts. It is the desire to reflect and elaborate on particularly compelling aspects of David's character—David the sufferer, the penitent, the pursued—that is behind the creation of the expanded headings. Put simply, dramatizing the psalms in his voice gives this David more things to say.

Psalm Headings and Midrash

This character-driven understanding departs from the standard way the expanded headings have been understood in the last generation of scholarship: as "inner-biblical exegesis." Brevard Childs argued that the headings are a type of midrash—"the result of an exegetical activity which derived its material form from the text itself."[48] In this model, similarities in wording, themes, and images between particular psalms and the narratives in 1 and 2 Samuel motivate an "exegesis" of the psalm, which becomes interpreted as the words of David in specific situations. Elieser Slomovic compares this to what he calls "connective midrash," rabbinic practices of linking particular psalms with certain events or personalities.[49] This, he writes, shows the roots of rabbinic interpretation are to be found already in the biblical text itself.

The search for midrashic exegesis already within the Bible has been a productive scholarly enterprise, especially since Michael Fishbane's *Biblical Interpretation in Ancient Israel* (1985). Fishbane's magisterial book demonstrated how the layered texts of the Hebrew Bible already show that their tradents interpretively supplemented and reshaped them in the process of transmission.[50] But this approach has become a victim of its own success. Too often, the idea of "interpretation" is used as a catch-all category for many kinds of literary references to older traditions—allusion, reuse of imagery, expanded narratives, even simply the appearance of a common character—that do not necessarily have exegetical aims.[51] And as Steven Fraade has shown, those Second Temple texts that *do* have interpretive features and goals are quite different from later midrashic methods.[52]

Such is the situation with the psalm headings. The idea that they are a kind of inner-biblical exegesis and a precursor to midrash seems to have become something of a scholarly consensus.[53] And yet the headings have little in common with midrash in form, motivation, or effect. To be sure, there is a minimal similarity between rabbinic midrash and psalm titles: some themes and images in the psalms encourage the connection with other traditions, like narratives about David, just as midrash connects texts to one another through shared wording. But there are also key differences in how the psalm titles interact with the text of the psalms themselves.

One major difference is that midrash reveals its exegetical process,[54] interacting deeply with the text verse by verse or word by word. Psalm headings are different: they simply appear appended to the text of the psalm, and interact with it neither directly nor deeply. What counts as "midrash" in the examples offered by Childs and Slomovic is repetition of basic themes and basic verbal similarities between a psalm and a narrative in Samuel to which it is linked—as basic as the verb "I have sinned"[55] in Ps 51 and 2 Sam 12; and as generic as shared references to fear, danger, trust, and deliverance. While networks of verbal similarity may testify to a literary relationship of allusion, to call this relationship "midrashic" is a stretch. The kind of play with the possibilities of language and the generative potential of verbal roots that is characteristic of midrash is absent from the psalm headings. The connections made between the psalms and events in the life of

David are not led by the poetic possibilities arising from the text, but by similarities of theme and event.

The other difference is that unlike midrash, the historical psalm headings in the MT are primarily interested in the life of David, and then only in a limited repertoire of his experiences—with a special focus on his distress and suffering. It is that interest that drives the creation of headings, not the possibilities in the psalm text themselves. There is nothing of the midrashic freedom to read other personages and events out of the text's *form*—even when a heading already gives a different association and the basic meaning of the psalm is clear. For example, the actual midrash to Ps 24, which has a *ledavid* heading and is plainly about the temple mount, connects it to Abraham ascending Mt. Moriah, and continues following lexical echoes to tightly entwine parts of Ps 24 and Gen 19.

Perhaps most strikingly, interpretation of psalms from actual rabbinic midrash seems to have the opposite effect from the psalms superscriptions. Biographical headings to the psalms contextualize originally timeless, generally applicable, anonymous texts by connecting them with a specific episode in the experience of a particular character. Conversely, midrash *undoes* this historicization: it takes the psalms apart into components, and follows a lexical breadcrumb trail to a huge range of other scriptural events, personae, questions, and problems that now make up their expanded web of significance.

To see this in action, let us look at the difference between the heading of Ps 18 and its treatment in *Midrash Tehillim*.[56] The heading reads: "For the leader. A Psalm of David the servant of the Lord, who spoke unto the Lord the words of this song in the day that the Lord delivered him from the hand of all his enemies, and from the hand of Saul. He said...." Thus, this psalm, which expresses praise and thanksgiving for being delivered from one's enemies, is dramatized as David's thanksgiving for being saved from his enemies' wrath.[57]

The midrash on the psalm itself does connect the wording to narratives in Samuel for a few verses. But it is less interested in historicizing the text than it is in unpacking the lexical possibilities of the language, and using words as springboards into other parts of Scripture with seemingly unrelated problems and narratives. For example, for Ps 18:5, "the cords of death encompassed me (*afafuni*)," we get five possible meanings of the verb. The fifth plays on the similarity between *afafuni* and *afafon*, a thick weave of a textile: the image is used to illustrate the "thickness" of the distress that entangled Israel at the hands of Babylon, Media and Persia, Greece, and Edom (symbolically meaning Rome). From the verse "the earth shook and trembled," the midrash draws out a number of questions of theodicy, explaining the divine causes behind natural disasters; in an alternative comment, the verse is connected to Moses's sojourn on Sinai when Israel made the golden calf "and five angels of punishment confronted him"— Moses turned away the angel of anger from Israel even though, as it is written in the book of Psalms, "The earth shook and trembled, the foundations were shaken, because He was wroth."

The rest of the psalm's verses are connected by shared lexical elements to miracles shown to Pharaoh, to God's heavenly chariot, to the Red Sea victory, and to all the battles of Israel where its enemies would be "discomfited" (Ps 18:14, "discomfited them," suggests references to discomfiting enemies in Ex 23:27, Deut 7:23, Isa 10:10, Judg 4:15, 1 Sam 7:10). Other themes and characters that appear, pulled in to populate the midrash on Ps 18 through lexical echoes with other texts, include Gog and Magog, Moses's punishment, Amalek, Leviathan and Behemoth at the eschatological feast, and Abraham and the Messiah sitting on either side of God.

From this dizzying array of associations, it seems that where a superscription intends to historicize and personalize a psalm—place a previously timeless, general song into a specific narrative context in one character's life—the midrash on psalms does just the opposite. It takes the psalm apart into its components, which it then connects with other narratives in the Bible, and dehistoricizes them once again. Indeed, the midrash *on* the heading to Ps 18 is a striking example. The heading says that David "spoke unto the Lord the words of this song in the day that the Lord delivered him." But in the midrash, the second interpretation parses the phrase at "this song," omitting the "day that the Lord delivered him," and looks for other instances of the phrase "this song" in Scripture. "This song" can only be sung after a miracle has been done for the singer, and so the Israelites sing "this song" at the Red Sea, and Deborah and Barak sang "this song" after their victory. Here, in a move *exactly the opposite* of the initial superscription itself, the midrash *de*historicizes the psalm, isolating the phrase "this song" and making it apply, once again, to a variety of historical moments viewed synoptically.

This dehistoricization resonates with the midrash's own statement that the Psalms have a timeless significance: "All that David said in his Book of Psalms applies to himself, to all Israel, and to all the ages" (see this at 4.1, 18.1, and 24.3). We can see a trajectory in the connection of the Psalms with David from the earliest history of the superscriptions through rabbinic midrash: from anonymous and timeless texts that could be reused for a variety of occasions, through texts historicized and dramatized by their link with events in King David's life, and then— as David becomes no longer only an ancient king but a prophetic voice, messianic ideal, and exemplary angelic singer of unbounded horizons—back again to dehistoricized, omnisignificant songs that can belong to almost anyone, and apply to almost any part of Israel's past or future.

As we can see, *Midrash Tehillim* connects psalmic texts to a full range of biblical figures and events, usually based on a verbal link that initiates a chain of others, sometimes in a virtuosic show of lexical memory. But this is not what the psalm titles are doing. They are interested in filling in details in the life of David and enriching his character, and it is in this interest that they must have their starting point. The composers of the psalm headings were not "interpreting" the psalms, but animating and dramatizing them in the voice of a beloved character. An interest in David—especially David the penitent and David the sufferer—leads to an effort to place more texts in his mouth. In this tradition of hagiographic expansion, the royal hero colonizes more textual territories.

Davidic Voice and the Reception of the Psalm Headings

As we have seen, the heading *ledavid* is meant in a multivalently associative way, and the biographical expansions give David's character dimension and make him the face and voice of some psalms. This tradition expands over time and eventually develops into an ascription of authorship, but it does so in fits and starts, and never completely. The reception of the Psalms as Davidic speech is not consistent in the early sources. In the Qumran commentaries on psalms—the *pesharim* (4Q171, 4Q172, and 1Q16)—there is no mention of David, although this may be a factor of the very fragmentary state of the manuscripts. The one Qumran text that cites a psalm as spoken by David is 11QMelch, a first-century BCE composition:

> ... of Melchizedek, and of [his] arm[ies, the nat]ion of the holy ones of God, of the rule of judgment, as is written [10] about him in the songs of David, who said: Ps 82:1 « Elohim will [st]and in the assem[bly of God,] in the midst of the gods he judges» . And about him he sai[d: Ps 7:8–9 « And] above [it,] [11] to the heights, return: God will judge the peoples» . As for what he sa[id: Ps 82:2 « How long will you] judge unjustly and show partia[lity] to the wicked? [Se]lah.» [58]

Here, Ps 82—a psalm of Asaph in the MT—is presented as spoken by David, and is followed by Ps 7, which does have a Davidic heading. The "songs of David" are heard in David's voice, but in a way that is not always consistent with the superscriptions in the MT or any other version.

In the New Testament, passages from the Psalms are presented as David's prophetic speech, usually as fulfilled through Jesus. David speaks "in the Spirit" ἐν πνεύματι (Matt 22:43) or "by the Holy Spirit" ἐν τῷ πνεύματι τῷ ἁγίῳ (Mk 12:36). The Holy Spirit speaks through "the mouth of David" στόματος Δαυὶδ (Acts 4:25). Acts 1:16 states:

> ἄνδρες ἀδελφοί, ἔδει πληρωθῆναι τὴν γραφὴν ἣν προεῖπεν τὸ πνεῦμα τὸ ἅγιον διὰ στόματος Δαυὶδ περὶ Ἰούδα τοῦ γενομένου ὁδηγοῦ τοῖς συλλαβοῦσιν Ἰησοῦν

> Friends, the scripture had to be fulfilled, which the Holy Spirit through the mouth of David foretold concerning Judas, who became a guide for those who arrested Jesus.

The Holy Spirit animates David, who voices the psalms.[59]

But the work of Philo shows clearly that in the first century, hearing psalms as Davidic speech was not a universal tradition. When Philo cites the actual text of specific psalms, he never mentions David, but refers to the psalmist in different ways, even when the LXX contains a Davidic superscription. In fact, sometimes it is Moses, not David, who acts as the exemplary figure for psalms traditions. Philo introduces the speaker of Ps 30—which has a Davidic heading—as "one of the pupils of Moses, praying in songs" (*Conf.* 39). In *On Noah's Work as a Planter* 39, which cites Ps 37, another Davidic psalm, the psalmist is a "follower of and fellow rejoicer with Moses, and not one of the least valued of that body." Philo's introduction to Ps 93—also Davidic—tells us it comes from the "divine man… speaking thus in his psalms" (*Plant.* 29). In *Agriculture* 50, the "guarantor" (ἐγγυητὴς) of the Davidic Ps 22 is "not any ordinary person, but a prophet, whom it is good to believe, he namely who wrote the hymns"[60] (οὐχ ὁ τυχὼν ἀλλὰ προφήτης ἐστίν, ᾧ καλὸν πιστεύειν, ὁ τὰς ὑμνῳδίας ἀναγράψας).[61]

Philo *is* aware that there is a tradition of Davidic psalm writing: in *On the Confusion of Tongues*, he writes of the kings of Israel as "the sons of David[,] who wrote hymns to God; though, during his lifetime, even their great grandfathers had not yet been born (*Conf.* 149)." The reference to hymns is in the context of a statement about virtue and spiritual ancestry. Here, psalm writing is part of David's biography; but Philo felt no compulsion to cite Davidic authorship or authority for the actual psalms, instead connecting them to Mosaic inspiration or prophetic revelation in more general terms.[62] Citing a specific authorial figure was not his concern.

In the first century, then, we still see a range of possibilities for how to "hear" the psalms and understand their connection with David. But when we turn to the second-century CE Septuagint recensions, we see a push toward understanding the Davidic headings as markers of authorship, rather than looser association with a figure. In the recensions, the original dative τῷ Δαυιδ, "pertaining to David," is replaced with the genitive τοῦ Δαυιδ, "of David." This change was made, as Pietersma argues, because neither the Greek translator nor subsequent Greek recensions understood the dative τῷ Δαυιδ as an authorial note. The change to the genitive τοῦ Δαυιδ was a way to assert Davidic authorship or origins in a more direct way not furnished by the original dative.[63]

But the ambiguity of the superscriptions, and the variety of ways psalms are linked with David, persists well into late antiquity. In the fourth-century Tura Psalms commentary—attributed to Didymus the Blind—the commentary on the heading of Ps 24 identifies two kinds of Davidic association, distinguishing between the meanings of τῷ and τοῦ. "Of David," for this writer, is used when David himself composed or played the psalm; and "to David" is used when the psalm refers to him.[64] The Psalms are "Davidic," but in at least two different ways. The multivalence and vagueness of the superscriptions has not fully congealed into a notion of authorship of a scriptural book.

"Every Beautiful Song Is a Song of David"

The first explicit discussions about David's authorship of the book of Psalms qua book appear in rabbinic texts. One statement attributed to R. Meir has it that "[a]ll the praises which are stated in the Book of Psalms, David uttered all of them" (BT Pesahim 117a). And yet this universal Davidicization is not the norm: the rabbis do not see Davidic authorship as monolithic. The best-known Talmudic passage about scriptural authorship recognized multiple "authors" of the Psalms:

> Who wrote the Scriptures?—Moses wrote his own book and the portion of Balaam and Job. Joshua wrote the book which bears his name and [the last] eight verses of the Pentateuch. Samuel wrote the book which bears his name and the Book of Judges and Ruth. David wrote the Book of Psalms, including in it the work of the elders, namely, Adam, Melchizedek, Abraham, Moses, Heman, Yeduthun, Asaph, Korah. (B. Baba Bathra 14b–15a)[65]

Here, David appears as both composer and compiler[66] of a collection of the work of multiple others.

Indeed, the text of the book of Psalms itself calls for such an understanding: several headings ascribe psalms to other figures. This basic textual fact somehow coexists with the strong association between David and the psalms in general, complicating any possibility for a clear sense of authorial unity.

The Midrash Rabbah to the Songs of Songs takes up this problem in its exegesis of the verse "Your neck is like the tower of David, built for *talpiyot*" (Song 4:4, כמגדל דויד צוארך בנוי לתלפיות). The word תלפיות appears only once in the Hebrew Bible, and its etymology and meaning are uncertain; suggestions have included rows of stones, turrets, or an armory. "What is the meaning of תלפיות?" asks the midrash. "The book spoken by many mouths," it answers, playing with the similarity between the words *talpiyot*, armory, and *piyot*, mouths. But then it states the dilemma clearly: "Although ten people composed the Book of Psalms, it is not called by their names, but ascribed to David king of Israel" (Midrash Song of Songs Rabbah 1:1).

How did rabbinic interpreters deal with this dilemma? The midrash drama-
tizes the impasse of the many-authored, yet Davidic psalter:

> [W]hen ten righteous men sought to say the Book of Psalms, the Holy
> One, blessed be He, said to them, All of you are pleasing, pious, and praise-
> worthy to say a hymn before me. But David will say it on behalf of all of
> you. Why? Because his voice is sweet. (Song of Songs Rabbah 4:4)

The midrash connects this to the verse in 2 Sam 23, the "Last words of David,"
which calls David the נעים זמירות ישראל ("the sweet one of the songs of
Israel"), who utters an oracle and has the spirit of God speak through him.
David is the one, the midrash tells us next, who "sweetens the songs of Israel"
(מי מנעים זמירותיהם של ישראל). The rabbis are not concerned with textual origins,
discussing instead how David recited and "sweetened" Israel's songs. Davidic ascription is not one of literal, historical authorship—but might, instead, be closer
to Herder's old view of Davidic ascription as an *aesthetic* claim. David recites the
book of Psalms because David has the sweetest voice. This is one version of
Herder's claim that "every beautiful song is a song of David."

But there is another, even more striking example in Song of Songs Rabbah
that shows that rabbinic interpreters saw Davidic ascription as porous and unstable, and not as a matter of literal religious dogma. Near the beginning of the
midrash, we have a meditation on the title "Song of Songs" itself, with suggestions of how many and which "songs" should be read into the plural form:

> "A Song of Ascents of Solomon" is one, and "a Psalm, a song at the ded-
> ication of the house of David" (Ps. 30) is another. You would think that
> David composed it. But you ascribe (תולה) it to David, as it is said, "Like
> the tower of David is your neck." So here, Solomon said it but ascribed
> (תלה) it to David.

The midrash claims that the ascription to David of Ps 30—a song for the dedica-
tion of the temple, with a *ledavid* heading—does not mean he really composed it.
Instead, the composition is merely ascribed to David, literally "hung" upon him.[67]

Remarkably, this midrashic text is acknowledging a kind of pseudepigraphic
attribution in biblical texts, and presenting its own theory of such a practice.
Ascribing a psalm to David is not forgery, nor, in this case, is it primarily authority conferring. Instead, this practice of attribution is compared to figurative,
poetic language, a simile—"like the tower of David is your neck." To ascribe a
text to David is not a statement of belief in literal authorship or a claim about
textual origins, but an honorific and poetic act. David has the sweetest voice, and
every beautiful song is a song of David.

Sinful King to Angelic Bard: The Making of the Sweet Singer of Israel

How does David become this aesthetic figurehead for the psalms? How does having the "sweetest voice" become such a strong aspect of his character—to the extent that he comes to occupy more and more textual territory, finally claiming, in his own name, a book "spoken by many mouths"?

The creation and reception of the psalm superscriptions is not the only site for tracking the development of David as psalmist. In the rest of this chapter, I read other Persian, Hellenistic, and Roman period texts that connect David to singing, liturgy, and writing to show from another perspective how the link between David and psalms developed and was conceptualized. Here again, the dominant lens for reading these sources has been in terms of what they can tell us about notions of scriptural authorship. But we do not find functional claims about authorial attribution in these texts; instead, we see moments in the dynamic development of a character and his deeds. Inspired singing, establishing liturgy, and transmitting writing become part of David's biography. They are only rarely connected to bibliographic claims about particular, existing texts, but testify to a broader literary imagination of which the biblical is only a part.

"David's Compositions": Paratext or Literature?

I return to a key text I already discussed in chapter 1, where I showed that rather than envisioning a book of Psalms, early Jewish writers imagined psalms as an open genre, a heavenly corpus of texts only partly reflected in available collections. "David's Compositions," which appears near the end of the first-century CE Qumran Psalms Scroll, presents us not only with a vivid illustration of such a vast imagined collection but also with a highly developed picture of David as a character who is connected with psalms and songs:

> [2] And David, son of Jesse, was wise, and luminous like the light of the sun, and a scribe
>
> [3] and discerning, and perfect in all his paths before God and men. And
>
> [4] YHWH gave him a discerning and enlightened spirit. And he wrote psalms (ויכתוב תהלים):
>
> [5] three thousand six hundred; and songs to be sung before the altar over the perpetual
>
> [6] offering of every day, for all the days of the year: three hundred
>
> [7] and sixty-four; and for the Sabbath offerings: fifty-two songs; and for the offerings of the first days of

[8] the months, and for all the days of the festivals, and for the Day of Atonement: thirty songs.

[9] And all the songs which he spoke were four hundred and forty-six. And songs

[10] to perform over the possessed: four. The total was four thousand and fifty.

[11] All these he spoke through prophecy which had been given to him from before the Most High.[68]

In this vivid composition, David is a scribe, sage, and perfect man who is enlightened with divine spirit and prophetically speaks vast numbers of psalms. The text draws on and develops a range of older traditions about David's personality, and foreshadows later traditions in which David becomes a heavenly figure singing the cosmic liturgy. Clearly, too, it is a key source in the development of ideas about Davidic authorship. But before we turn to its literary texture and ask what it can tell us about ideas of attribution, it is important to ask exactly what *kind* of text it is, and its function in the context of the 11QPsalms[a] collection. What is this composition, and what is it doing here, in this collection of psalms and poems that looks so different from the biblical Psalter?

This question is important: our assumptions about a text's genre and purpose determine the kind of information we expect it to reveal, and deeply color how we read it. One major assumption about genre has dominated the reception of "David's Compositions": scholars read this text not as a literary composition but as a functional notation that attributes the collection to David. It is not really part of the collection, but presents information *about* it; in other words, it is not a text but a paratext. For modern writings, "paratexts" are functional elements like the title, preface, table of contents, or copyright page, usually provided by an editor, publisher, or printer to present bibliographic information.[69] Genette, the primary theorist of such features, calls paratext a threshold or a frame—something that marks off a text's boundaries, mediates between the text and its readers, and governs the way it is received. "The paratext in all its forms," writes Genette, "is a discourse that is fundamentally heteronomous, auxiliary, and dedicated to the service of something other than itself that constitutes its raison d'être. This something is the text."[70]

This reflects the common instrumental understanding of what "David's Compositions" is doing in 11QPsalms[a]. It has been called a prose insert, an authorial note, a catalog, an epilogue, a scribal notation, or a colophon.[71] The dominant view is that, like a colophon, it is not part of the collection itself but refers back to it, governing how the Psalms Scroll should be received by offering bibliographical information. Specifically, it ostensibly stakes a claim for the Davidic authorship of the book of Psalms, as represented by *this* specific Qumran collection, by attributing it to David.[72] Thus, according to most scholarship, the text gives the Qumran Psalms Scroll scriptural and prophetic authority, and thus frames how we should understand this unusual collection.

But is this text really a functional, auxiliary frame, and does it do the instrumental work of a colophon? The text does have some traits in common with typical scribal colophons: it enumerates a set of compositions and makes a statement about their origins. But both the physical layout and the contents of the text suggest that reading it as a functional and referential notation does not do it justice. Physically, it is not a threshold or frame: the text is not set apart from the collection, but part of it. Although it is called a "colophon" or an "epilogue" and placed at the end of the published critical edition, it does not come at the end of the scroll itself—but it is followed by several other compositions: Pss 140, 134, and 151A and B (see figure 2.1). And while the critical edition prints the other compositions stichometrically—in verse—and sets "David's Compositions" alone in prose, this does not reflect the physical manuscript (see figure 2.2). There *all* the compositions are in prose format, except the acrostic Ps 119.[73] Publishing decisions, then, have made "David's Compositions" *seem* more distinct from the other compositions on the scroll than it really is. In its placement

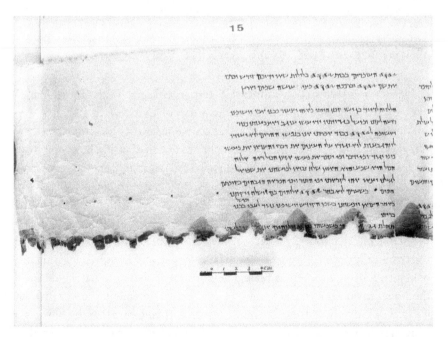

Figure 2.1 The ending of 11QPsalms[a], the most extensive Psalms Scroll from Qumran. This final column (28) contains the end of Ps 134 and a Hebrew version of the two compositions that became the Greek Ps 151. It is followed by uninscribed parchment. The preceding two columns are shown in figure 2.2. Courtesy Israel Antiquities Authority. B-285204, 11Q5–974 Qumran, PAM M43.792

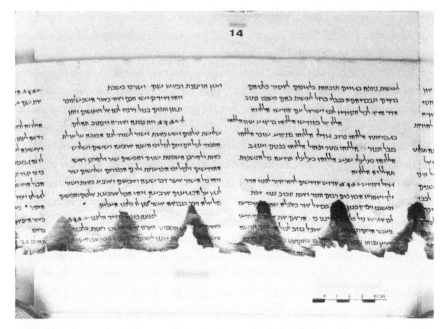

Figure 2.2 These two columns (26 and 27) of 11QPsalmsᵃ contain the end of Ps 149, Ps 150, the Hymn to the Creator (not found in the biblical book of Psalms), David's Last Words (=2 Sam 23:1–7), and "David's Compositions," followed by Ps 140. The next and final column of the scroll is shown in figure 2.1. Courtesy Israel Antiquities Authority. B-285202, 11Q5–974 Qumran, PAM M43.791

and layout, this text is not paratextual, heterogeneous, or clearly "functional": it does not stand outside the collection, but is part of it.

Moving from what the text looks like to what it says, we can still see that the category of a functional paratext or colophon is not an easy fit. The composition makes no claim to refer to the collection in which it is found, and does not make a direct claim for David's authorship of this scroll or any text in particular. We do not read that David wrote *these* psalms—simply psalms, without a definite article. The 4,050 psalms and songs are obviously not referring to the contents of this scroll, but symbolically reflect the idea of a proliferation of inspired writing, the cosmically ordered liturgy of the solar calendar, and David's staggering productivity. Indeed, nowhere is there a demonstrative locution that would invite the reader to take the text as a reflexive, paratextual statement, the way that, say, we read in Proverbs ("These are other proverbs of Solomon that the officials of King Hezekiah of Judah copied," 25:1) or Jeremiah ("Thus far are the words of Jeremiah," 51:64). That genre of paratext, clearly a heteronomous note in the service of the text proper, was available to Second Temple scribes, but "David's Compositions" looks nothing like it. The scribe could have written a colophon, but did not.

Instead, he wrote a composition of praise about David, motivated more by an excess of literary invention than by a need to fill in a bibliographic gap or to legitimize a new collection. In other words, its genre is closer to biography than to bibliography. Why, if it does not clearly perform this role, has this text been interpreted as an instrumental paratext? Such a move reflects a scholarly wish for clarity in how to describe and categorize unfamiliar writings. This is something that actual paratexts, like the scribal colophons in medieval manuscripts, help us do, by providing key information about date, authorship, and provenance.

The purpose of paratexts, after all, is to mediate between text and reader, to help situate a text—otherwise nakedly strange—within familiar discourses. Reading "David's Compositions" this way solves this problem twice over—it helps us frame an unfamiliar psalms collection in a tradition of Davidic authorship, and it keeps the passage busy with functional work so its own strangeness can be safely overlooked. But this is wishful thinking. Scholars who work with fragmentary texts often wish that more "framing" material had been preserved, such as a first column that may once have preserved a title or preface that would clarify the purpose and provenance of a text. And we wish that ancient scribes had been more paratextually forthcoming, that they would more clearly present to us the frameless fragments we encounter. In the absence of "notes to the reader," it is tempting to see "David's Compositions"—with its numbering and listing and reference to writing—as close enough.

But this categorization is based on modern anxieties about bibliographic clarity, not the motivations of the ancient writers. For them, clarity about the authorship of a collection was not necessarily a primary literary value. Many psalms remain anonymous, and the link with particular figures is not, as we saw above, primarily concerned with authorial origins. What happens when we understand "David's Compositions" as a functional paratext, a sort of "byline" attributing the whole scroll, is that we force this psalm collection into a rigid model of a book unified by ascription to an authorial figure. Scholars have imagined that in some positivistic way, the scribes who put the collection together must have thought a psalm ascribed to Solomon, or the hymn to Wisdom we also know from Sir 51, was *actually* authored by David, and so included them in this Davidic collection.[74] But as we saw above, the ancient compilers were not working according to a model of a Miltonian vial, a container for the essence of a single creator's "living intellect." Not even the rabbis believed that David was the author of the book of Psalms in any monolithic way, and no psalter has ever been fully Davidic. A single authorial originator who "really wrote" the text is not the unifying principle of this collection.

"David's Compositions," then, cannot tell us how to read the Psalms Scroll and where to place it in familiar bibliographic categories. But it does offer a rich literary picture of a beloved character in early Judaism. The statement that David "wrote psalms," coupled with these symbolic numbers and diverse genres of his songs, tells us something about David and his impressive characteristics and accomplishments. Psalm writing is one of his praiseworthy deeds—along with praying, having his sins forgiven, and ruling Israel. The number of songs David wrote—4,050—is an allusion to Solomon's 4,005 sayings in 1 Kgs 5. The full passage celebrates Solomon's wisdom:

> God gave Solomon very great wisdom, discernment, and breadth of understanding as vast as the sand on the seashore, so that Solomon's wisdom surpassed the wisdom of all the people of the east, and all the wisdom of Egypt. He was wiser than anyone else, wiser than Ethan the Ezrahite, and Heman, Calcol, and Darda, children of Mahol; his fame spread throughout all the surrounding nations. He composed three thousand proverbs, and his songs numbered a thousand and five. He would speak of trees, from the cedar that is in the Lebanon to the hyssop that grows in the wall; he would speak of animals, and birds, and reptiles, and fish. People came from all the nations to hear the wisdom of Solomon; they came from all the kings of the earth who had heard of his wisdom. (1 Kgs 5:9–14).

This text has several common features with "David's Compositions": besides the echo between the numbers 4,005 and 4,050, both exalt their hero for great wisdom and discernment, both list the categories of discourse he composed, and both emphasize that his knowledge was given by God. Both are in prose, but describe their figures in rich poetic imagery. Nobody, however, interprets 1 Kgs 5 as a functionally oriented editorial note or claim to authorship of a specific collection. Clearly, it is a literary account of Solomon's exemplary, God-given, prolific wisdom. In the same way, "David's Compositions" is a literary celebration of David as a divinely favored, prolific psalmist, liturgical originator, and enlightened sage. We might compare this, once again, to Josephus's statement that David composed "hymns and songs to God in pentameter and trimeter" in the midst of his biography of David. Neither of these texts is interested in making a specific claim about biblical authorship, a concern more of interest to biblical scholars than to ancient writers. Instead, these texts present a portrait of an exemplary figure whose prolific psalm writing is one part of his biography and personality.[75]

The picture of David here goes beyond psalm writing, and develops a number of Second Temple traditions. In the first line of the composition, David is characterized as an enlightened scribe and sage, luminous like the sun, who receives psalms through prophecy. This portrait has strong links with the previous composition on the scroll, "David's Last Words" (2 Sam 23), where David seems to be cast as a prophetic figure, although the term is never used: he utters an oracle

(נאם) and says the spirit of the Lord has spoken through him (רוח יהוה דבר בי) (vv. 1–2).[76] "David's Compositions" makes David's prophetic status more explicit, but still in circuitous language—he is not a prophet (נביא), but he speaks psalms "through prophecy" (בנבואה). As we have seen, other first-century traditions will be more direct about David's prophetic status, including the New Testament (Acts 2:29–30) and Josephus (*Ant* 8.109–11).

Besides using language suggestive of prophecy, "David's Last Words" also says that God's chosen ruler is "like the light of the morning at sunrise" (כאור בוקר יזרח שמש, 2 Sam 23:4), which recalls the description of David's sunlike luminosity in "David's Compositions." In one sense, then, this new text echoes and extends the imagery of "David's Last Words"; indeed, William Brownlee called "David's Compositions" a "midrash" on the 2 Samuel text.[77] But it is more than an interpretive expansion of a biblical passage: David's radiance, together with his characterization as scribe, sage, and calendrical revealer, takes on new resonance against the background of a broader range of nonbiblical traditions about illuminated, quasi-angelic scribal figures. In particular, the description evokes figures like Enoch, who, in the Enochic corpus and the book of *Jubilees*, is similarly described as an inspired scribe and wise man who receives and reveals the correct calendar.[78] Enoch also becomes an angel-like figure with a shining face, participating in a tradition in which both angelic beings and transfigured humans—like Moses and Jesus—are characterized by such luminosity.[79] David's sunlike radiance in "David's Compositions" can, then, also be understood as one version of this motif of light as a sign of divine favor, transfiguration, and prophetic inspiration.

Another striking aspect of 11QPsalms[a] is its characterization of David as "perfect in all his paths before God and men." This characterization is the culmination of a history of idealizing David that we can already see clearly in the Chronicler's whitewashed rewriting of the Samuel narratives. Other Qumran texts also present David as a paragon of virtue, although the language of perfection is unique to "David's Compositions."[80] In the *Damascus Document*'s discussion of the law against a ruler having multiple wives (Deut 17:17), the writer is quick to exonerate David:

> However, David had not read the sealed book of the law (לא קרא בספר התורה החתום) which [3] was in the ark, for it had not been opened in Israel since the day of the death of Eleazar [4] and of Jehoshua, and Joshua and the elders who worshipped Ashtaroth. One had hidden [5] the public (copy) until Zadok's entry into office. And David's deeds were praised, except for Uriah's blood, and God forgave him those. (CD 5:1–6)[81]

Here, David's ignorance of the law exonerates him from the sin of polygamy, and the one sin that remains on his record is forgiven. Interestingly, the reference is essentially an aside without any set-up, which might suggest that the writer assumed his readers would already be familiar with the larger conversation.[82] Another Qumran text also explicitly mentions David's sins while presenting him as a model:

> [1] [forgiv]en (their) sins. Remember David, who was a man of the pious ones (איש חסדים), [and] he, too, [2] [was] freed from the many afflictions and was forgiven. (4QMMTe frag. 14 ii 1–2)[83]

David's ethical exemplarity is based on his reputation as the paradigmatic repentant sinner.

"David's Compositions," then, offers a rich portrait of David that overlaps with and extends a number of biblical and nonbiblical traditions. It presents David as a prophetic figure, a scribe and sage similar to the enlightened sage Enoch, and a revealer of song and calendrical knowledge. It also establishes David as a moral ideal and perhaps a transfigured human being. But it never makes a claim that David is the author of this collection, or any particular text: it is not interested in making a functional authorial claim, but in transmitting an imaginative and inspiring picture of a character.

What Texts Are Davidic? Second Temple Perspectives on David the Writer

To be sure, the association of David with psalm writing is clear in "David's Compositions," but it is part of a much broader picture in which David is responsible for founding other kinds of traditions[84]—including written texts—besides the biblical psalms. It is common to assume that a belief in the Davidic authorship of the book of Psalms already existed when the Psalms Scroll was composed, and thus that "David's Compositions" also stakes such a claim, merely confirming and developing an existing tradition. But there is surprisingly little evidence for this claim as such. Davidic creativity and the discourses connected with him are far more complicated than a simple association with the Psalms might suggest. Texts from Qumran and early Judaism more generally show a tradition of Davidic discourses linked with liturgy and revelation, but not identifiable with scriptural psalms. David in the Second Temple period is many things: a musician, wise man, exemplar, transmitter of written revelation, forgiven sinner, liturgical founder, exorcist, and, indeed, psalmist—a character who sings (and, in a few first-century CE texts, even writes) psalms—roles related to, but not identical to, his later role as "the Psalmist."

In Samuel, Chronicles, and Ben Sira, David sings, plays music, prays, receives revelation, transmits liturgical instructions, and serves as the ideal man and forgiven sinner. The earliest articulations of David as an inspired musician appear in Samuel, where David plays music to rid Saul of an evil spirit (1 Sam 16:13–23). This efficacious, exorcistic musicianship is developed in later traditions: Pseudo-Philo's *Bib. Ant.* 60:2–3, for example, gives the text of the song David would have sung to exorcise the demon:

> Darkness and silence were before the world was made,
>
> And silence spoke a word and the darkness became light.
>
> Then your name was pronounced in the drawing together of what had been spread out,
>
> The upper of which was called heaven and the lower was called earth…
>
> As long as David sang, the spirit spared Saul.[85]

The words placed in David's mouth are not at all reminiscent of biblical psalms. But Davidic songs against demons appear also in the exorcistic collection 11Q11 (see chapter 1), and "David's Compositions" also mentions "four songs for the stricken" among his repertoire.

The tradition continues into late antiquity: a version of "the words of David, the singing songs that he would recite over King Saul," appears in a trilingual (Hebrew, Greek, and Aramaic) silver amulet from Tell el-Amarna from around the fifth century, which was likely copied from a written magical text.[86] A Babylonian incantation bowl, inscribed in Hebrew and Aramaic, preserves another version of this exorcistic song followed by adjurations against demons.[87] The importance of David as exorcist persists in the popular piety of late antique Jews.

"David's Compositions" tells us David is a scribe and wrote psalms, but other sources connect him with different written texts. The earliest connection between David and writing seems to be in 2 Sam 1, discussed in the second section of the chapter: David's lament for Saul and Jonathan, which is "written in the Book of Jashar" or "book of the upright" (ספר הישר). In Chronicles, however, David is linked with writing of another kind: he receives the written blueprint, *tabnit*, for the temple and instructions for its functioning, which he hands down for Solomon to follow (1 Chr 28:11–19). He says:

הכל בכתב מיד יהוה עלי השכיל כל מלאכות התבנית

> All this that the LORD made me understand by His hand on me, I give you in writing—the plan of all the works. (1 Chr 28:19)[88]

The Chronicler's idealized David is the recipient of written revelation—the temple plan and instructions "by the spirit" (1 Chr 28:12) and from the hand of

God, language that opens the way for the more explicit connection between David and prophecy in 11QPsalms[a]. This tradition of David's architectural blueprint evidently inspired a later tradition in the *Lives of the Prophets,* dated between the first and fourth centuries CE,[89] which credits David with the design of priestly and prophetic tombs: "[Isaiah's] tomb is near the tomb of the kings, west of the tomb of the priests in the southern part of the city. For Solomon made the tombs, in accordance with David's design" (1:7).[90] David, who gives Solomon the plan for the temple, has become the architect of other sacred structures as well.

The Chronicler's David also delineates the cultic roles of the priests and Levites and commissions the praise of God with musical instruments and song. This is effected both through David's own example of leading psalm singing and through written instructions handed down to future kings.[91] The Temple cult becomes a legacy that is both Mosaic and Davidic—while Mosaic law governs sacrifice,[92] Davidic prescriptions, also in writing, are consulted by later rulers as authoritative instructions for liturgical practice (2 Chr 35:4).[93] This writing is not the Psalms or the words of liturgy at all, but divinely received guidelines for the organization of worship services and cultic architecture.

David's exemplarity and liturgical legacy are also strong in Ben Sira's "Praise of the Ancestors" (47:8–11):

> In all his deeds he praised God Most High with words of glory,
>
> With all his heart he loved his maker, and praised him constantly all day.
>
> He established music before the altar, and the melody of instruments,
>
> He added beauty to the feasts, and set the festivals in order for each year
>
> (ויתקן מועדים שנה בשנה),
>
> So that when his holy name was praised, justice would ring out before daybreak.
>
> And the Lord forgave him his sins, and exalted his might forever.

Here, as in Chronicles, David both serves as an example in his personal acts of praise and hands down a liturgical legacy. This legacy is aesthetic and calendrical: he established temple music, "added beauty to the feasts," and "set the festivals in order for each year." This focus is also present in 11QPsalms[a]'s cosmically ordered songs (where they are listed according to the solar calendar, endorsed by Qumran texts and the book of *Jubilees*). Finally, Ben Sira asserts that "the Lord forgave him his sins," celebrating another aspect of David's exemplary character. Curiously, some scholars have nevertheless read a claim for authorship of psalms here,[94] even though no reference to either psalms or writing appears: Ben Sira says only that David praised God, established temple music, beautified and arranged the festivals, and was forgiven—claims that are biographical, not bibliographical.

In the *Ascension of Isaiah*, a Christian compilation likely completed in the late second century CE but containing older materials,[95] David is also credited with revealed writing. In this section, which Michael Knibb dates to the first century CE,[96] Isaiah prophesies about the Beloved's descent into Sheol:

> [20] And the rest of the vision about the LORD, behold it is written in parables in the words of mine that are written in the book which I prophesied openly. [21] ... And all these things, behold they are written in the Psalms, in the parables of David the son of Jesse, and in the Proverbs of Solomon his son, and in the words of Korah and of Ethan the Israelite and in the words of Asaph and in the rest of the psalms which the angel of the spirit has inspired, [22] (namely) in those which have no name written. (4:20–22)[97]

Here, David utters prophetic "parables," a word the Isaianic narrator also uses for his own written prophecies. References to psalms are among a broader variety of writings, including the Proverbs of Solomon, and are attached to other figures, named and anonymous. David and the Psalms are not directly identified as a textual unit—"David" is not an umbrella term for psalms materials. Neither are psalms imagined as a coherent collection or "book" that can be simply cited by title; rather, the text paints a picture of a large, multivocal collection of compositions inspired by "the angel of the Spirit."

We see, then, an expanding tradition in the Persian, Hellenistic, and Roman periods of linking David with song, liturgy, and writing of different kinds. David's cultural production and authority is frequently related to discourses other than biblical psalms, and his portfolio continues to expand as he develops as an exorcist, an architect, and a liturgical impresario. The earliest Jewish texts that claim David *wrote psalms* come from the first century CE: "David's Compositions," which says he wrote 4,050 psalms; Josephus, who says he wrote hymns to God in various meters and made musical instruments, then moves on to the rest of his biography; and Philo, who says that those who live blameless lives are known as "sons of David who wrote hymns to God," but never mentions David when he cites psalms themselves. In each of these examples, the writing of psalms contributes to the story of David's biography and exemplary deeds.

Finally, in the Greek philosophical text 4 Maccabees, also likely datable to the first century CE, the father of seven martyrs teaches his sons "the law and the prophets," listing passages that are loosely related to overcoming adversity. As part of this pedagogical repertoire, he sings to them "songs of the *hymnographer* David, who said, 'Many are the afflictions of the righteous'" (τὸν ὑμνογράφον ἐμελῴδει ἡμῖν Δαυεὶδ τὸν λέγοντα Πολλαὶ αἱ θλίψεις τῶν δικαίων, 18:15). The citation is from Ps 34, whose superscription places it in David's mouth "when he feigned madness before Abimelech." These are the earliest references to David as a *writer* of psalms, all from the first century, and all in the context of setting him up as an exemplary figure.

One final group of texts has often been connected to ancient Davidic authorship, but is more clearly an example of modern scholarly discourse around it: the Genizah Psalms, four songs of praise and thanksgiving for four successive days, spoken in a voice that claims visionary inspiration. Tentatively dated by most to the late Second Temple period, the texts were published by David Flusser and Shmuel Safrai in 1982 and called "the apocryphal 'Songs of David.'"[98] Subsequent scholarship has also presented the texts as a "Davidic pseudepigraphon," emphasizing the idea that the first-person voice is meant to be David's.[99] But what are the grounds for seeing the Genizah Psalms as Davidic?

A fresh reading of the text shows that it is modern scholars, not the ancient poet, who have attributed it to David. The headings to the texts never mention David. In the entire collection, his name is mentioned once—in the third person: he is praised as an eternal king who has defeated all his enemies, who sings praises every day, and whose greatness is like the angels (1:15). David is invoked as an important figure, but there is little ground for arguing for a consistent Davidic voice in a collection that invokes various personae and traditions—not only David's greatness but also Solomonic wisdom, Isaiah's suffering servant, and perhaps personified Israel—into a shifting poetic "I." Meir Bar-Ilan writes that "the author considered King David to be his hero," but "David's authorship was attributed to the text without textual evidence."[100] In other words, scholars have mistaken a character for an author—biography for bibliography.

Why this drive to attribute a text that, read on its own, is an anonymous collection of ancient poetry? Although the attribution of texts to ancient figures is a common and important literary move in early Judaism, not all new literature needed to be attributed to an ancient author. Perhaps, besides our own modern *horror vacui* of authorless texts, the desire to attribute this text to David is partly based on the need to place it in a familiar category—in this case, the Pseudepigrapha.

The case of the Genizah Psalms illustrates the problematic nature of this category, and the confusion between Pseudepigrapha (a catch-all name for a corpus of noncanonical texts, many of which are attributed to ancient figures) and pseudepigraphy (the literary practice of false attribution, present in both biblical and nonbiblical texts). In the *Old Testament Pseudepigrapha: More Non-Canonical Scriptures*,[101] the Genizah Psalms are published as "Songs of David," and the analysis begins with the claim that the "I" is to be understood as David's voice—and therefore, "the songs can be called a Jewish pseudepigraphic writing," apparently justifying its place in the collection. Here, it seems that these texts must be attributed to an ancient figure in order to qualify as Pseudepigrapha. But it is modern scholars who have done the work of attribution; titling these texts "Songs of David" or "Apocryphal Psalms of David" makes a bibliographic move that the ancient poet himself did not make.

David's Celestial Afterlife

In the history of Jewish and Christian traditions, David is a character without an upper limit. Rising above his identity as a statesman and a king, then a perfect man and wise scribe, David becomes an angelic being, and finally reaches heaven. An angel-like luminosity is part of his persona in "David's Compositions," and in the *Apocalypse of Zephaniah*, David dwells in heaven along with Enoch and Elijah—the two deathless, ascended figures of early Jewish tradition[102]—and speaks with the angels in their own language. The Genizah Psalms praise David's great power, saying that God sanctified him

> Because he established your praise to the ends of the earth.
> You named him Everlasting Pillar,
> And Repairer of the Breach and Rebuilder of Ruins....
> By his mouth you have sanctified the Great Name,
> And every day he recounts the songs of your might.
> You have made his greatness the greatness of all the angels,
> And you have made him king of all the peoples for ever.
> (1:16–17, 22–23)[103]

David's greatness is like the angels', and he is an "everlasting pillar" (עמוד עולם)— or perhaps, the "pillar of the world," a cosmic figure who sings praises every day.

David's heavenly throne—sometimes a throne of fire—is a motif in several rabbinic traditions. In one apocalyptic vision of Rabbi Ishmael that appears in some manuscripts of *Heikhalot Rabbati*, David wears a crown with the sun, moon, and twelve constellations, luminous with heavenly light. The visionary wants to witness David's glory, and first sees seven bolts of lightning, ofanim, seraphim, the hayot (living creatures), treasuries of hail and snow, clouds of glory, the stars and constellations, the ministering angels, and the seraphim, all singing Ps 19 as they come to greet David. David's crown is so brilliant that its radiance extends to the ends of the earth, and he comes to sit on an enormous fiery throne. He sings hymns and praises "like no ear had ever heard," and the angelic beings and heavenly bodies respond.[104] In the midrash *Gan Eden ve-Ge-hinnom*, David's throne is opposite God's at the great Judgment Day banquet.[105] As God passes the wine cup to be blessed, Abraham, Jacob, Moses, and Joshua each refuse to say the blessing, saying they are unworthy. Finally, God passes the cup to the sweet singer, who pronounces the blessing. Then, as God reads the Torah, David recites a psalm, the righteous and the wicked both answer "Amen," and God sends angels to bring sinners from hell to paradise.

In these two rabbinic traditions, a luminous, incomparable David has the special task of leading cosmic liturgy. While these texts have not been securely dated, we find a remarkably similar set of features in a Christian apocalypse from the fourth century, showing that this tradition had broader influence and older roots. The *Apocalypse of Paul*[106] recounts Paul's guided tour of heaven, where a powerful being whose face shines like the sun plays his harp and sings praises by a high altar. His mighty voice fills the entire seventh heaven, and the foundations of the celestial city shake when all the righteous repeat his "Alleluia." Like the visionary in the *Heikhalot* text, the Paul character asks about the identity of this luminous cosmic figure. This is David, replies the angelic guide, who sings eternal praises before the throne of God. The visionary asks, "How did David alone above all the other saints lead the psalm-singing?" The angel responds that "as it is done in the heavens so also below," and no sacrifice—here, the Christian Eucharist—can be performed without David's singing "Alleluia" in the language of God and the angels, for all the righteous to repeat (*Apoc. Paul* 29–30).

While there is no reason to suspect textual dependence, the question "Paul" asks—why is it David who sings these psalms?—is evocative of another rabbinic text we have already seen: the question in Song of Songs Rabbah. Why, among all the other worthy men, is David the one to whom the Psalms are ascribed? In the midrash, the Holy One explains that David sings on their behalf because his voice is sweet. The angel in the Christian apocalypse has a less clear answer about David's uniqueness, but points to his heavenly power and exemplarity: "as above, so below."

This returns us to the question of our chapter—what did ancient people mean when they called the psalms Davidic? Ancient attribution is not precritical religious dogma about literal authorship, but a poetic and honorific association of a body of texts with a character who becomes more and more powerfully linked with efficacious prayer, beautiful song, and divine favor. The growth of the figure to celestial proportions transforms him over time from a psalmist to the Psalmist.

Conclusion: The Life of the Writer

In his essay "Eternal Writing and Immortal Writers: On the Non-Death of the Scribe in Early Judaism," Samuel Thomas asks why so many legendary scribal figures, in the course of the transmission of traditions about them, seem to evade death and enjoy heavenly afterlives. Thomas notes this trope in Second Temple traditions related to Enoch, Moses, Ezra, Baruch, and some of the scribal figures in the Dead Sea Scrolls, highlighting the "complex association between right-eous scribal figures, the appeal to heavenly or eternal forms of writing or speech, and some version of immortality."[107] He adds, "Being a scribe makes one im-mortal at least insofar as death may be overcome in the transmission, elabora-tion, and new life of sacred tradition, which itself is understood to come from an eternal and often esoteric source."[108] I have shown that David, too, gradually comes to be a patron of the written psalms traditions copied by scribes on earth, but he is also responsible for celestial song that is still occurring in heaven—just as some of Enoch's knowledge is available in scribal products, but his writing will continue unbroken in Eden until Judgment Day.[109] The writing activity of these characters is not isomorphic with the available books ascribed to their names: that is, writing heroes are never replaced or subsumed by their books.

Rather than being authors who serve to vouchsafe new scriptures and doc-trines, filling in bibliographical gaps, such figures take on new lives and colonize new texts about heavenly knowledge, prayer, and prophecy. Writing becomes one part of a broader network of activities and features that make up the leg-endary character's exemplary reputation and biography. If, following Roland Barthes, we can talk about the "death of the author"[110] in early Jewish textual production, we also have something positive with which to replace it: the effu-sive, overflowing "life of the writer."

The first two chapters of this book have shown how our major bibliographic categories—books and authors—have constrained a dynamic literary culture where revelation can be found in multiple and shifting fragments, and writing figures are the main characters in narratives about an effusion of revelation that cannot be contained in any human scribal collection. My major case study has been the Psalms, to which we will return in the final chapter. But for now, I will turn to a different textual tradition: the book of Ben Sira. We shall see how this text—commonly considered the first book with a named author in Jewish lit-erary history—can help us draw a fuller and sometimes surprising picture of how early Jewish writers imagined their own work.

Like a Canal from a River

Scribal Products and Projects

> The first man did not know wisdom fully,
> Nor will the last one fathom her.
> For her thoughts are more abundant than the sea,
> And her counsel deeper than the great abyss.
> As for me, I was like a canal from a river,
> Like a water channel into a garden.
> I said, "I will water my garden and drench my flower-beds."
> And lo, my canal became a river, and my river a sea.
>
> —Ben Sira 24:28–31

Introduction: The Poetic "I": Historical or Legendary?

An acrostic hymn to Wisdom—sensuously evocative—appears near the end of the Qumran Psalms Scroll. In the first person, the poet describes his desire for Wisdom since his youth, and his tireless, passionate seeking of her beauty:

¹¹ אני נער בטרם תעיתי ובקשתיה באה לי בתרה ועד

¹² סופה אדורשנה גם גרע נץ בבשול ענבים ישמחו לב

¹³ דרכה רגלי במישור כי מנעורי ידעתיה הטיתי כמעט

¹⁴ אוזני והרבה מצאתי לקח ועלה היתה לי למלמדי אתן

¹⁵ הודי זמותי ואשחקה קנאתי בטוב ולוא אשוב חריתי

¹⁶ נפשי בה ופני לוא השיבותי טרתי נפשי בה וברומיה לוא

¹⁷ אשלה ידי פת[   ]מערמיה אתבונן כפי הברותי אל

¹¹ I was a young man before I had strayed when I looked for her. She came to me in her beauty when

¹² I finally sought her out. Even as a blossom drops in the ripening of grapes, making the heart glad,

¹³ my foot trod in uprightness; for from my youth I have known her. I slightly inclined

¹⁴ my ear and great was the teaching I found. And she became a nurse for me; to my teacher I give

¹⁵ my praise. I purposed to make sport; I was zealous for pleasure, without pause. I kindled

¹⁶ my soul for her and I did not turn my face away. I bestirred my soul for her, and on her heights I did not

¹⁷ waver. I opened my hand(s) […] and perceive her unseen parts. I cleansed my hands … ¹

Since the bottom of the Psalms Scroll is damaged, much of the end of the composition is cut off just as the erotic imagery moves toward its climax. But the poem is better known from another place: in a slightly different form, it also appears in the last chapter of the book of Ben Sira.² There, it continues with a call to "draw near to me, you who are uneducated, and lodge in the house of instruction" (Sir 51:23) and the promise, "Hear but a little of my instruction, and through me you will acquire silver and gold" (Sir 51:28).

How do we make sense of the presence of the same composition in two such different texts? The Psalms Scroll and Ben Sira seem to inhabit two distinct literary worlds. Generically, the Psalms Scroll collects liturgical hymns, and Ben Sira is a wisdom book, with conservative, practical advice for young men. One is strongly linked with the legendary and visionary king David, and its contents developed over centuries; the other is firmly datable to the early second century BCE, and, uniquely among early Jewish texts, its "author" is not a pseudepigraphic ancient hero, but tells us his own name—Joshua ben Eleazar ben Sira, presumably a teacher in Jerusalem. So who is the "I" in this composition? And what does this hymn, shared between these two disparate textual traditions, tell us about literary processes and concepts in early Judaism? If a widespread liturgical Davidic "I" is a voice that can be adopted by anyone praying, what does it mean that it's Ben Sira's voice too? If both are personal, whose autobiography is this? Is it somehow meant to be everybody's, with "Ben Sira" almost as much of a generic narrative device as David—and, if so, what does this tell us about the difference or continuity between pseudepigraphic and "genuine" authorship in early Judaism?

In separate studies, scholars have attempted to connect this text to both "authors"—asking literary questions about how it is connected to the pseudepigraphic "author" David, and biographical questions about what it tells us about the "real" author, Ben Sira. Peter Flint sees it as part of a "Davidic cluster" of compositions in the collection, and Bodil Ejrnæs considers it as part of a pair with another text in the Psalms Scroll, the *Apostrophe to Zion*. Seen in this context, the speaker of these two poems is David; their themes are his relationship with two women—personified Wisdom and personified Zion—and they serve to bolster Davidic authority.³

Conversely, in its context in Ben Sira, many scholars argue that the text is authentic, that is, written by Ben Sira himself, about his own personal path to wisdom. For example, the "house of instruction" in Ben Sira 51:23 becomes a reference to an actual school Ben Sira ran, the earliest mention of a school in Jewish literature. But these attempts to tie a text tightly to an authorial figure—whether a pseudepigraphic one like David or a "real" one like Ben Sira—impose foreign ideas about the unity of "authors" and "books" onto literary products that follow a different logic.

In the first two chapters of this book, I showed how the example of the psalms can help us think about an ancient literary imagination that was unbound by these modern concepts of "books" and "authors." The diversity of psalms collections and the cultural discourse about psalms shows that other metaphors—such as databases, projects, and even archives, heavenly and earthly—are helpful for imagining an ancient bibliographical poetics that does not assume that revealed writing is entirely graspable or entirely known, but exists beyond the horizons of available text.

These broader horizons of writing that do not coincide with "books" also affect the way we imagine authorial figures. When there is no "book of Psalms" as a concrete entity, but the writing of songs and liturgical instructions is a powerful trope, David is not an author of a specific textual unit, but a character who writes. Anonymous texts are not necessarily "texts in search of an author," whose vacuum of authority is filled by an authorial name. Instead, fertile characters like David search for more and more textual homes, such as psalms superscriptions, in which to settle and generate new lore. That is, the developing figure colonizes more and more texts, and his own personality grows as he stakes out new textual territory.

At first glance, the second-century BCE book of Ben Sira is part of a different story. While David is a pseudepigraphic hero, Ben Sira has put his own name on his work, and is typically known as the first named author in Jewish literary history. In this way, the author Ben Sira and the book that bears his name might seem to fit rather neatly into our own bibliographic imagination—into our own practices of identifying and organizing texts.

And yet, while this text is always singled out in discussions of early Jewish textuality as the first "authored book," Ben Sira is neither an author nor a book. The idea of a "book" in anything close to the Miltonian sense, as an iconic contained text, is not to be found. It does not describe how the scribe understands his own work, or how he thinks about the sacred traditions he has inherited. In fact, it is likely that Ben Sira never used the word *sefer*. The word βίβλος appears several times in the Greek translator's prologue to the text, and in the body of the Greek text it can be found twice: the first, referring to the "book of the covenant of the Most High, a law that Moses commanded us" (24:23), is in a chapter that has not survived in any Hebrew manuscripts. The second instance, the famous line in Greek that says Jesus son of Eleazar son of Sirach has written "instruction of understanding and knowledge... in this book" (50:27), is extant in one Hebrew manuscript—but there, the Hebrew mentions only ben Sira's instruction and wisdom, and the word *sefer* does not appear.

While we cannot reconstruct the Hebrew behind the Greek translation with absolute confidence, what we do see is that the concept of a book is barely, if at all, present in the Hebrew Ben Sira, and certainly not in the sense of textual stability and containment. Ben Sira's traditions—the ones he inherits and the ones he creates—do not stand still, but are imagined in dynamic metaphors of flow, growth, and elusiveness, as water, light, a harvest, and a woman. Torah and wisdom are never fully graspable, and the text of Ben Sira itself, as I will demonstrate, is an ongoing sapiential project that was expanded and reconfigured over time.

Given all this, what about Ben Sira's authorship? Despite the use of his name, Ben Sira is continuous with the anonymous and pseudepigraphic textual culture of early Judaism, and the text associated with him is *not* the originary intellectual product of an individual author—and was not understood to be either original or complete, either by Ben Sira or by his heirs. The celebration of Ben Sira as the first authored book, a watershed in Jewish literary history, has been overstated: it is colored by the Greek translation and prologue to the text, and by modern desires to uncover concrete sociohistorical and biographical evidence in an ancient literary source. Instead, "Ben Sira" is a personality as constructed as a pseudepigraphical hero, and likewise becomes a generative character or figurehead in later traditions that are not necessarily identical to the "book of Ben Sira" as we know it.

While it is often set apart from contemporary anonymous and pseudepigraphic texts, then, Ben Sira surprisingly allows us to flesh out the kind of literary imagination I began to describe in the first two chapters. Two kinds of evidence help us conceptualize how its producers and audiences imagined Ben Sira as a textual tradition: the complex textual history of Ben Sira and the imagery the writers themselves use to describe their own textual activities.

The text's own images for tradition—harvest gleaning and flowing rivers—illuminate its dynamic compositional history, which underwent several editions, likely during Ben Sira's lifetime and certainly in the centuries that followed. These ways of imagining textual tradition also help us understand its reception history in rabbinic literature. There "Ben Sira" signifies neither an author nor a book but an exemplary *character* known for wisdom teaching, or a looser, generic *tradition* of pedagogical lore—some of which is found in our "book of Ben Sira," and some of which is not.

In this chapter, I first discuss how the truism of Ben Sira as the "first Jewish author" must be challenged, and use the text's own literary imagery to reimagine what this text meant to its producers. Second, I trace the development of Ben

Sira as a text, and show how the difficulties of preparing a modern edition of the text highlight the problems of "book" metaphors applied to a tradition that was imagined as neither original nor complete. Finally, I discuss the reception of Ben Sira—as both text and figure—over time. What do both the manuscript and the literary evidence tell us about what ancient people meant when they said "Ben Sira"?

The First Jewish Author? Ben Sira and the Authorial Name

The book of Ben Sira, written in the first quarter of the second century BCE, was known primarily in the Greek translation by the author's grandson until the discovery of the Hebrew Cairo Genizah manuscripts (MSS A–F)[4] and the fragments from Qumran (2Q18)[5] and Masada.[6] The text exists in two major textual forms: the short text, Greek I, translated from Hebrew I; and the revised long text or Greek II, translated from Hebrew II, found in the Genizah manuscripts as well as the Syriac and Old Latin translations.[7]

The main issues in scholarship on Ben Sira, particularly its Hebrew manuscript tradition, have several parallels to those of Dead Sea psalm collections. Both traditions testify to a complex transmission history, including expansions and rearrangements, whose authority, originality, or canonicity has been variously assessed, although this debate has been far less intense for Ben Sira, likely because it is not canonical for most communities.[8] Also, the compositional history of both traditions has, to varying extents, been connected to sectarian activity. Although the Dead Sea Scrolls have yielded only a very fragmentary portion of Ben Sira chapter 6, the affinities between Ben Sira and some Qumran texts have long been recognized by scholars, with some going so far as to suggest that the expanded text (HII//GII) was largely an "Essene" creation, and ended up in the Cairo Geniza through the same channels as the *Damascus Document* and the Aramaic Levi materials.[9] The scholarly publication of these texts, as well, presents parallel problems, as determining how to produce a scholarly edition has historically involved concepts of authoritative or original texts that do not apply in the texts' own contexts.

As I showed for psalms traditions, these concrete matters of manuscripts and textual shaping should be considered together with the literary evidence that tells us how the ancient writers themselves imagined their work. Ben Sira gives us some important clues: the first-person speaker is self-conscious about his role in transmitting tradition to future generations. The text also includes an extended composition in praise of the scribe (chapter 39), who seeks out and passes on wisdom. Like the Qumran Psalms Scroll's description of David, scribe and sage whom God endowed with an understanding and enlightened spirit (col. 27 ll. 3–4), Ben Sira's scribe will be "filled with the spirit of understanding" if the Most High so desires (39:6). The scribe is a man of prayer and a forgiven sinner.[10] Ben Sira's famous claim that he will "pour out wisdom like prophecy" (24:33) has also been linked to the statement in the Psalms Scroll that David, too, spoke his psalms "through prophecy which had been given to him by the Most High" (11QPs^a col. 27).[11]

In both the Psalms Scroll and Ben Sira, the scribe is a sage, a writer of texts, and an ethical exemplar who enjoys prophet-like inspiration and God-given enlightenment. But there is a key difference between the scribal figures in Ben Sira and the Psalms Scroll: Ben Sira's self-identification in 50:27.[12] The work's self-attribution is unparalleled among the corpus of writings from this period, which are otherwise anonymous or pseudepigraphic. What are we to make of this new development? What kind of change in literary values does it represent?

It is common to think of Ben Sira as the first individual "author" in Judaism, an idea that is tied closely to the assumption that the text presents us with his individual personality. Martin Hengel writes that "Ben Sira was the first to venture to emerge clearly as a personality (50:27). Here is the beginning of a new development, for the stressing of the personality of the individual teacher derived from Greek custom."[13] But I argue that Ben Sira does not represent such a dramatic shift in literary history, and that his persona and his relationship to his text is closer to that of a pseudepigraphic hero than that of a modern author. Indeed, the way the work developed as a text, and the way its producers and audience imagined it, is not utterly different from other works of this era. By this, I mean to say that the book of Ben Sira is fluid and open to expansion and rearrangement, despite the attribution of the text to an identifiable author, and was neither intended nor received as an originary or finished intellectual product. This comes through in three ways that challenge any fixed interpretation of Ben Sira as the "author" of a "book": Ben Sira's own understanding of his role in the production of his "book," the compositional history of Ben Sira, and the ways in which Ben Sira was understood as a figure and a text in Jewish interpretation.

How does Ben Sira conceive of his own role in the production of his text? Let us begin with the Greek and Hebrew versions of the key text where his name appears. Ben Sira identifies himself in 50:27, and urges his readers or listeners to take his words to heart. The Greek translation has most strongly shaped our reception of Ben Sira:

27 παιδείαν συνέσεως καὶ ἐπιστήμης ἐχάραξεν ἐν τῷ βιβλίῳ τούτῳ ἰησοῦς υἱὸς σιραχ ελεαζαρ ὁ ιεροσολυμίτης ὃς ἀνώμβρησεν σοφίαν ἀπὸ καρδίας αὐτοῦ

28 μακάριος ὃς ἐν τούτοις ἀναστραφήσεται καὶ θεὶς αὐτὰ ἐπὶ καρδίαν αὐτοῦ σοφισθήσεται

²⁹ ἐὰν γὰρ αὐτὰ ποιήσῃ πρὸς πάντα ἰσχύσει ὅτι φῶς κυρίου τὸ ἴχνος αὐτοῦ

²⁷ Jesus son of Eleazar son of Sirach of Jerusalem, whose heart poured forth wisdom, has written instruction in understanding and knowledge in this book;

²⁸ Happy is the one who concerns himself with these things, and he who lays them to heart will become wise.

²⁹ For if he does them, he will be equal to anything, for the light of the Lord is his path.[14]

The Hebrew manuscripts of Ben Sira are fragmentary, but in the one instance where this passage is preserved (MS B), it reads rather differently:

²⁷ מוסר שכל ומושל אופנים לשמעון בן ישוע בן אלעזר בן סירא

אשר ניבע בפתור לבו   ואשר הביע בתבונות

²⁸ אשרי איש באלה יהגה   ונותן על לבו יחכם

כי יראת ייי חיים

²⁷ Instruction in enlightenment and appropriate sayings of Simon[15] ben Yeshua ben Eleazar ben Sira,

Whose heart overflowed with understanding, and who poured forth wisdom.

²⁸ Happy is the man who meditates on them, and he who lays them to heart will become wise. For the fear of the Lord is life.[16]

The Greek version of 50:28 has evidently been reworked, and Greek 50:29, which O. Mulder calls "an expanded version of the epilogue,"[17] appears to be a Greek interpolation not extant in Hebrew. The differences between the one Hebrew witness of chapter 50 and the Greek translation are notable with regard to Ben Sira's authorial persona. In the Greek, we read ἐχάραξεν ἐν τῷ βιβλίῳ τούτῳ, "he 'engraved' [wrote] in this book." Conversely, no reference to writing or books appears in the Hebrew. Rather, the Hebrew states simply that these are the wisdom and sayings associated with Ben Sira, the *lamed* prefix recalling the *ledavid* psalm headings. At the end of the manuscript, MS B adds a colophon once again linking the text with Ben Sira, but without making a reference to writing or a book, only his "words" and "wisdom":

עד הנה דברי שמעון בן ישוע שנקרא בן סירא

חכמת שמעון בן ישוע בן אלעזר בן סירא

יהי שם ייי מבורך מעתה ועד עולם

These have been ["up to here"] the words of Simon ben Yeshua who is called Ben Sira.

The wisdom of Simon ben Yeshua ben Eleazar ben Sira.

Blessed be the name of the Lord from now until eternity.[18]

MS B most likely dates from the twelfth century, and it is a matter of debate to what extent it reflects an older or more "original" version of the text than the Greek translation. However, the copyist of MS B seemed to have at his disposal an older text, as many of the marginal notes there reflect readings close to the Masada scroll.[19] If the older, second-century BCE Hebrew text is closer to our one Hebrew witness in MS B than to the Greek translation, we must ask whether the construction of Ben Sira's self-presentation as an author of a book is a function of reading the Greek version of this work.

Textual Fluidity and Metaphors of Overflow

If he is not the author of a book, how does Ben Sira conceptualize his own activity, and what does this mean to our understanding of the textual landscape he inhabits? Ben Sira does not understand his work as a "book" in the sense of an original and final written composition, but as the malleable and necessarily incomplete continuation of a long tradition of revealed wisdom. One key source for how Ben Sira understands the transmission of tradition is in chapter 24, which has not survived in any Hebrew manuscripts. It is here that we encounter a speech by divine Wisdom. This chapter takes up and extends tropes we can find in the book of Proverbs, which also gives personified feminine Wisdom her own voice. In Ben Sira 24, Wisdom says that God had her encamp in Israel, where she took root. She compares herself to a variety of plants that give fruit, emit fragrance, spread their branches, and shoot vines. She invites the listener to eat of her produce: "Those who eat me will hunger for more, and those who drink me will thirst for more" (24:21).

Then comes Ben Sira's famous identification of Wisdom with Torah: "All these things are the book of the covenant of the Most High God, a law that Moses commanded us, an inheritance for the gatherings of Jacob" (ταῦτα πάντα βίβλος διαθήκης θεοῦ ὑψίστου νόμον ὃν ἐνετείλατο ἡμῖν μωυσῆς κληρονομίαν συναγωγαῖς ιακωβ, 24:23). If the Greek βίβλος translates a Hebrew *Vorlage* that had the word *sefer*, this would be the one place where Ben Sira mentions the word "book," in the context of the personified Lady Wisdom as the law of Moses. But even if so, this is still not an authored "book" in the Miltonian meaning. There is no sense that any "book" contains—binds—this personified Wisdom and Law.

As Claudia Camp has written, we may trace precursors for the emergence of authoritative texts and canons in Ben Sira.[20] We may see precursors for the iconicity of the Bible as a book, in some of the cosmic imagery associated with divine Wisdom. But in the imaginative world of the text, not from the perspective of later Bibles, Wisdom-Torah's iconicity is not tied to its bookishness. The copious metaphors that represent the inherited tradition of Israel all grow, flow, and move; none stand still, and none can fully be possessed. For one thing, the personified Woman Wisdom continues to speak; and as she morphs into a tree of many varieties, she promises endless produce but continuing hunger.

Then, the metaphor shifts once again: the tradition is now pictured as water—powerful rivers whose currents cannot be contained.[21] The writer can imagine the tradition he inherits as something without beginning or end, continuously overflowing, and it is here that he can inscribe himself as one of its channels:

[25] It overflows, like the Pishon, with wisdom, and like the Tigris at the time of the first fruits.

[26] It runs over, like the Euphrates, with understanding, and like the Jordan at harvest time.

[27] It pours forth instruction like the Nile, like the Gihon at the time of vintage.

[28] The first man did not know wisdom fully, nor will the last one fathom her.

[29] For her thoughts are more abundant than the sea, and her counsel deeper than the great abyss.

[30] As for me, I was like a canal from a river, like a water channel into a garden.

[31] I said, "I will water my garden and drench my flower-beds." And lo, my canal became a river, and my river a sea.

[32] I will again make instruction shine forth like the dawn, and I will make it clear from far away.

[33] I will again pour out teaching like prophecy, and leave it to all future generations.

[34] Observe that I have not labored for myself alone, but for all who seek wisdom.[22]

This sacred tradition cannot be contained even within the banks of great rivers—the very opposite of the Miltonian book as a vial of preserved essence. As with the 4,050 songs of David, Wisdom-Torah has sacred power *because* it is not stable or contained.

With the beginning of the first-person speech in v. 30, Ben Sira describes himself as tapping into this vast, overflowing body of holy wisdom, which he carries forward like a current. Benjamin Wright explains how, "using water as the basic metaphor, Ben Sira argues for continuity between his teaching and Wisdom. As his small canal becomes a river, then becomes a sea, the metaphor finally links 'the sea' of heavenly Wisdom described in verse 29 directly with wisdom/teaching of the sage, who serves as a channel for Wisdom."[23] Ben Sira's work carries forward part of a larger, overflowing tradition—and it becomes a growing tradition itself. In v. 28, he writes that "[t]he first man did not know wisdom fully, nor will the last one fathom her," presenting the collection and transmission of wisdom as a multigenerational process that is never complete.

Another metaphor expresses a similar sentiment: the gleaner in chapter 33:16–18, which we do have partially preserved in the Hebrew MS E.

> ¹⁶ I also have been vigilant as the last person, and like a gleaner after the grape harvesters.
> ¹⁷ By God's blessing I also have advanced, and like a grape harvester I have filled my wine vat.
> ¹⁸ See that not only for myself have I toiled, but for all those seeking instruction.

The last verse of this passage echoes 24:34. Not only this, but the passage also takes up the idea of the intergenerational chain of transmission of traditions that was expressed in the previous text's comment about the "first" and the "last" being unable to fathom the whole of wisdom. Here, Ben Sira sets himself up as the "last person," the most recent link in the chain of transmission—"a gleaner after grape harvesters," that is, his sagely or prophetic predecessors. As Jeremy Corley and Wright both observe, the reference to being "vigilant" echoes the call of Jeremiah (in Jer 1:11–12), and the imagery of the vintage harvester echoes Isa 5:1–7, the vineyard planted on Zion. Ben Sira's ingathering of wisdom after it has already been "picked over" by his predecessors still produces a full wine press, which becomes the teaching he transmits to his students and successors.[24]

In fact, we encounter hints of such images elsewhere in Ben Sira, outside these passages. Chapter 39 also describes the scribe and sage as a channel and a gatherer:

> ¹ [The scribe] seeks out the wisdom of all the ancients, and is concerned with prophecies;
> ² he preserves the sayings of the famous, and enters into the subtleties of parables;
> ……………………………………… .
> ⁵ He sets his heart on rising early to petition the Most High.
> He opens his mouth in prayer and asks forgiveness for his sins.
> ⁶ If God Most High is willing, he will be filled with the spirit of understanding; he will pour forth words of wisdom and give thanks to the Lord in prayer.
> ⁷ He [God] will direct his counsel and knowledge, as he meditates on his mysteries.
> ⁸ He will pour forth wise teaching, and will glory in the Law of the Lord.

Ben Sira's text shows the scribe as a channel for preserving and transmitting sacred traditions who seeks, preserves, and pours forth the wisdom of the ancients, all with the help of divine inspiration, recalling 24:33 where Ben Sira says he will "pour out teaching like prophecy." But what exactly does it mean to "preserve the sayings of the famous" and "pour forth words of wisdom"?

As James Kugel has argued, the activity of the sage was collecting units of wisdom—which were already "out there," not created by the sage himself, and knowable only gradually and in part—and handing them down to posterity.[25] Wisdom is an anthological enterprise. It is concerned with the *quantity* of things known; hence, for example, the import of the staggering number of sayings that Solomon knew in 1 Kgs 5:12. We might connect this to the repeated references to the Law or Wisdom as *overflowing,* and to Ben Sira's full wine vat after his grape harvest—and, by extension, to the overwhelming thousands of songs sung and written by David, the scribe and sage in 11QPsalms[a]. The scribe-sage is an anthologist, indeed, like Ben Sira himself, who has gleaned and transmitted the revelations of his age.

How do the images of the river and sea, the light, the gleaner, and the scribe as the gatherer and transmitter of traditions shed light on the production of texts? There is an element common to all these descriptions, and that is the sense of a continuity or *movement* that traces itself back to the past and flows out toward the future. Perhaps we might use such metaphors to conceptualize the writings of this period as traditions without delineated origins or end points. This imagery has a key advantage over "book" language, which requires us to posit, in Chartier's words, a fundamental identity for a work—either its "original" or its "completed" form, following the requirements of modern editing, where "establishing the text" means returning to one of those forms. In contrast, from the way in which Ben Sira describes his own task and the work of the scribe in general, we can see that he did not consider his work to be either original or complete.

Somebody's Grandfather: Ben Sira the Individual in Hebrew and in Greek

Indeed, Ben Sira did not consider his work to be a "book" (with a definite identity and shape) at all, and his own understanding of his activity does not allow us to set him up as a unique, first individual "authorial" figure in the history of Jewish texts. This is in contrast to the claims of earlier Ben Sira scholarship, such as Hengel's assertion that Ben Sira is the first to "emerge clearly as a personality," following Greek custom that emphasizes the personality of the individual teacher.[26] But we must consider to what extent Ben Sira's Hebrew text allows us to make such strong claims about his individual personality. As I began to suggest above, perhaps our familiarity with the Greek text of Ben Sira colors our understanding of Ben Sira's own self-presentation. The Greek version includes not only the mention that Ben Sira of Jerusalem wrote a book (50:27) but also the prologue of the translator, who identifies Ben Sira as his grandfather, and who presents his work as a "book" to be translated and published:[27]

> Iesous, my grandfather, since he had given himself increasingly both to the reading of the Law and the Prophets and the other ancestral books[28] and since he had acquired considerable proficiency in them, he too was led to compose something pertaining to education and wisdom.... [W]hen I had discovered an exemplar of no little education, I myself too made it a most compulsory task to bring some speed and industry to the translating of this tome...with the aim of bringing the book to completion and to publish it also for those living abroad.[29]

I will return to the difficulty with thinking of Ben Sira as a "book" later in this chapter. For now, I wish to stress that this Greek prologue, in which Ben Sira is a concrete person, has inflected the way we read Ben Sira's Hebrew text. In our reception of the prologue, Ben Sira is more than just a personality: he is somebody's grandfather.

This encourages us to read all the first-person passages throughout the text in terms of an individual authorial figure—a biological person, a concrete human being. But in his study of the "autobiographical" texts in Ben Sira, Benjamin Wright points out:

> While it is tempting to see the "real" or autobiographical Ben Sira as the primary subject of these passages, and most scholars read the book this way, we cannot assume that this is the case. Besides whatever personal experience might be reflected here, these sections offer a deliberate *self-presentation*. That is, through his authorial "voice" we hear how Ben Sira wants his reader to perceive the "I" who speaks here, and...the "I" passages serve a specific function in the book. Consequently, we should exercise caution when claiming that we can gain any significant insight into Ben Sira's personality, since upon reflection we find the "I" of Ben Sira to be just as constructed as the "I" of Moses in *Jubilees* or the "I" of Ezra in *4 Ezra*.[30]

To this, we might add that the parallels between David and Ben Sira as constructed textual figures are many. Neither figure is connected with a "book" but with a continuous *tradition* that is handed on in writing. Neither is directly called a prophet, but each is credited with prophet-like inspiration to either "speak psalms" (11QPsalms[a]) or "pour forth teaching" (Sir 24).

Both figures also serve as exemplars. For Wright, Ben Sira's "I" passages construct an authoritative voice to be obeyed, and an ideal sage to be emulated. His mode of self-presentation is not primarily as the author of a book, but as a link in the chain of the inspired transmission of revealed wisdom. And while we do have Ben Sira's own name in one verse of the book, we should, as Wright warns, not be so quick to assume that all the first-person passages reflect his own individual "personality." After all, the book of Proverbs uses the first person abundantly as a feature of its pedagogical rhetoric, along with a variety of sapiential texts from the Second Temple period, and Ben Sira stands in continuity with this tradition. This is clear, for instance, from his references to his listeners or students as his children.[31] This does not mean that the first person speech reflects no subjective experience; but we must reckon with the fact that the "I" voice is first and foremost that of a narrator who takes on the persona of an idealized sage and teacher, not someone who is communicating raw autobiography.

Another example of such a rhetorical strategy is the so-called Teacher Hymns in cols. 10–17 of the *Hodayot* or *Thanksgiving Hymns* from Qumran. These first-person compositions have been read by some Qumran scholars[32] as the *ipsissima verba* of the Teacher of Righteousness, an enigmatic figure who appears as a founder and leader of the sectarian community in some Qumran texts. The hymns, then, were imagined to be the creative autobiographical work of this putative individual, and were mined for information about this mysterious figure's life. For example, Michael Wise has extracted from these hymns not only data about the Teacher's life, persecution, and exile but also insights into his spiritual life—and even his name.[33]

But over time, as Max Grossman has shown, scholars began to question the idea that the Teacher of Righteousness is the "author" of these texts—that this figure is a historically locatable individual who can be imagined as an individual creator of the textual products of the Qumran community.[34] With regard to the poetic *Thanksgiving Hymns*, it is doubtful that they can be used to reconstruct the historical and interior life of a specific individual. An excellent critique of the tendency to read the *Hodayot* as autobiography comes from Angela Harkins,[35] who argues that such a reading is rooted in Romantic ideas of individual authorship that are foreign to Jewish antiquity. The search for the individual, historical Teacher of Righteousness, Harkins writes, privileges "Romantic notions of individuality and interiority,"[36] and sees literary texts as the expression of an individual creative genius. Part of this conception is already in place prior to the Romantic period: for Milton, as we saw in chapter 1, a book is a container for "the purest efficacie and extraction of [a] living intellect...the pretious life-blood of a master spirit."

But no specific historical figure can be reconstructed from poetic hymns: they use familiar images and literary tropes, including first-person references to suffering and persecution that are not to be understood as biographical accounts of specific historical experiences. The "I" of the hymns can, instead, be understood in other ways that do not privilege either historical reconstruction or anachronistic concepts of individual genius. The first-person voice is perhaps representative of the "office" of an inspired community leader and the ideal, exemplary teacher, rather than reflective of a specific historical personality.[37] Or, as Harkins suggests, it is a "rhetorical persona" to be actualized by the reader in ritual performance: the reader embodies the "I," and the text becomes an "affective script for the reader to reenact."[38]

In Ben Sira, I suggest, the situation is not so different. Surprisingly, it is not much easier to pin down a historical individual and his interior states for Ben Sira than it is for the putative Teacher of Righteousness. Elias Bickerman writes that "there are no self-revelations in Ben Sira,"[39] and indeed, were it not for the single mention of Ben Sira's name in the Hebrew 50:27, little would remain to help us identify a distinct, historical personality in the text—the first-person voice notwithstanding.

Some scholars, however, have attempted to mine the first-person passages for concrete autobiographical information about Ben Sira as an individual, just as many have done for the Teacher of Righteousness. One such attempt is an article by Paul McKechnie,[40] who argues that the first-person passages that mention persecution faced by the narrator (12:10–12, 25:7, 27:21–24, and 51:1–7) refer to real, specific events in Ben Sira's life. The mention of a false accusation before the king (51:6) is key to his argument. According to McKechnie's reconstruction, Ben Sira left Jerusalem at around 200 BCE, was a courtier in Alexandria until accusations against him were brought before Ptolemy IV, V, or VI, faced trial, was exonerated, retired from royal service, opened a school, and wrote his book—all in Alexandria.

This elaborate life story and revisionist argument about Ben Sira's geographical provenance reflects a scholarly ambition to reconstruct specific, concrete, historical facts from sources that cannot yield this kind of information. In particular, McKechnie's reconstruction has two flaws. First, it is more likely that these passages about the persecution of a righteous man by his foes are literary creations that echo themes in psalms of lament, not autobiographical reports. Second, much is made of the mention of lying accusations before the king, which are interpreted to mean that Ben Sira was in the court of a Ptolemaic ruler and experienced persecution there. Since other political and historical clues to Ben Sira's context are missing, the mention of a king is taken seriously as the one feature that may help us place Ben Sira precisely in space and time. This does not make for a strong case, since accusations and persecutions against a sage before the king are a conventional part of sapiential narratives, such as the stories of Daniel and Ahiqar (we might also cite those parts of Proverbs that warn about

the wrath and judgment of kings, e.g. 16:10, 13, 19:12, 20:2, 24:21–22, or instruct how to conduct oneself in their presence, e.g. 23:6–8).

But even more than this, the picture of Ben Sira as a historical, individual
personality may be inflected by our reading of the Greek translation rather than
the Hebrew. In 51:5–6, the speaker thanks God for protecting him

ἐκ βάθους κοιλίας ᾅδου καὶ ἀπὸ γλώσσης ἀκαθάρτου καὶ λόγου ψευδοῦς
βασιλεῖ διαβολὴ γλώσσης ἀδίκου ἤγγισεν ἕως θανάτου ἡ ψυχή μου καὶ ἡ
ζωή μου ἦν σύνεγγυς ᾅδου κάτω

from the deep belly of Hades, from an unclean tongue and lying words—
the slander of an unrighteous tongue to the king. My soul drew near to
death, and my life was on the brink of Hades below.

The extant Hebrew (found in MS B only) for 51:5–6, however, reads:

‫... וחצי לשון מרמה ותגע למות נפשי וחיתי לשאול תחתיות‬
... and the arrows of a deceitful tongue. My soul drew near to death,
and my life to the depths of Sheol.

Although there is no way to be certain which version best reflects Ben Sira's own
text, if we assume the reliability of the Hebrew MS B here, we find no mention of
a king—no reference to a ruler whom we can then try to identify in order to situate Ben Sira's first-person passages in a specific geographical location and historical moment.[41] Like references to persecution by one's enemies in the Psalms[42]
and warnings about lies and deception in Proverbs, these are generic and conventional literary accounts, not references to concrete historical events, and
cannot be used to historicize Ben Sira as an individual.

Poetry and the Myth of Ben Sira's School

While McKechnie's reconstruction and relocation of Ben Sira in Alexandria is
rather extreme among the would-be biographers of the sage, many scholars have
taken the wisdom poem in 51:13–30 as an autobiographical account of the author's search for wisdom. They have had a particular stake in 51:23:

MS B: ‫פנו אלי סכלים ולינו בבית מדרשי‬

Turn to me, simple ones, and lodge in my house of study (*beit midrash*).

Greek: ἐγγίσατε πρός με ἀπαίδευτοι καὶ αὐλίσθητε ἐν οἴκῳ παιδείας

Draw near to me, you who are uneducated, and lodge in the house of instruction.

This verse has not survived in the Psalms Scroll, and scholars have questioned the reliability of the Hebrew MS B for this verse. It has garnered a great deal of attention because it is considered to be the earliest clear reference to a school in a Jewish text.[43] It is also taken specifically as evidence that Ben Sira opened his own wisdom school in Jerusalem. Thus, this verse is pressed into service as concrete textual evidence for both the social history of Jewish education and author's biography, and so, much seems to be at stake in the "authenticity" of the poem as a composition of Ben Sira himself.

We have already seen the difficulty of pinning down this poem's origins and speaker at the beginning of this chapter. The poem is considered to be authentic by many scholars, despite the arguments of Sanders and García Martínez that its presence in 11QPsalms[a] indicates its independence, and despite the existence of a previous "colophon" at 50:27–29 that might suggest that the poem is a later addition.[44] Maurice Gilbert considers this acrostic to be a conclusion to the book, similar to the acrostic in Prov 31.[45] Jeremy Corley also considers this poem a conclusion to the book that already formed part of the first of five "editions" of the text as it was developed by Ben Sira himself.[46]

But the arguments for authenticity seem to be motivated mainly by scholars' desire to derive some concrete historical and biographical facts from the scant sources we possess. As Jacqueline Vayntrub argues for the book of Proverbs, when scholars attempt to trace the social history of ancient Israelite and early Jewish education, they sometimes overlook the literary self-presentation of the ancient sources.[47] But poetry is not a transparent window into social practice. This is also true of the role of Ben Sira's reference to a *beit midrash* in the history of scholarship. Even if someone named Ben Sira did compose this text, which is impossible to determine, it is an acrostic poem, full of metaphors and images about the elusive Lady Wisdom that recall her personification in Proverbs. Indeed, the invitation to enter the "house of instruction" may echo a text like Prov. 9:1:

חכמות בנתה ביתה חצבה עמודיה שבעה

Wisdom has built her house, she has hewn her seven pillars.

In this chapter, personified Wisdom calls throughout the town and invites the "simple" (פתי) and the "lacking understanding" (חסר־לב) to enter her house; specifically, she says that the simple should *turn* there, יָסֻר, so that they may receive instruction. This is semantically, though not lexically, parallel to Ben Sira's command to the unschooled to *turn* to him, פנו אלי, in the Hebrew MS B[48] (or is it

Wisdom herself who is calling in this verse of Ben Sira just as she is in Prov 9, which, given the frequency of shifting subjects in Hebrew poetry, would not be wholly surprising?).[49] The Greek, on the other hand, uses ἐγγίσατε, "draw near." The references to thirst and lack in Sir 51:24 may also allude to the metaphorical banquet of wine and meat that Wisdom has waiting (Prov 9:2, 5).

In the context of this composition, the invitation to the simple to enter a "house of instruction" may well be a metaphor, infused through and through with the flavor of Proverbs. It is a poetic account of a search for wisdom that is literary and idealized, rather than specifically personal, despite its first-person form. This does not mean that Ben Sira was not in the business of educating students—a pedagogical context is the most likely origin for his text. But to read Ben Sira in the context of education is plausible because the rhetoric and contents of the work as a whole suggest it, not because of the reference to a *beit midrash* in the acrostic poem in chapter 51. That reference cannot be used to make a historical argument about any actual school in Jerusalem (or Alexandria).

The sense of Ben Sira's individuality as a person with a discoverable biography seems to be a function of modern scholars' desire to reconstruct the concrete and historical.[50] It is encouraged by some features of the Greek text, particularly the translator's presentation of his grandfather's biography and characteristics. But all we know about Ben Sira, besides his name and his putative grandson's later report, is an idealized self-presentation as a sage.

To further challenge the idea of Ben Sira's uniqueness as a figure, I would suggest that another individual teacher had to some extent already "emerged as a personality" in Hebrew literature—Qohelet. Of course, this teacher is not named and not identifiable, and shrouded in a pseudepigraphic or legendary narrative framework. He is introduced as "Qohelet, son of David, king in Jerusalem," a persona that alludes to Solomonic wisdom and wealth, without naming Solomon directly.[51] But his personality and activity are described in fairly concrete detail by the book's epilogist:

ויתר שהיה קהלת חכם עוד למד־דעת את־העם ואזן וחקר תקן משלים הרבה:
בקש קהלת למצא דברי־חפץ וכתוב ישר דברי אמת:

> Besides being wise, Qohelet also taught the people knowledge, and weighed and studied and arranged many proverbs. Qohelet sought to find pleasing words, and he wrote words of truth plainly. (12:9–10)

Qohelet, although he takes on Solomonic garb in the introduction to the book (while never being explicitly called Solomon), is presented as an individual teacher in concrete, realistic terms here—indeed not so differently from the translator's description of his grandfather Joshua Ben Sira as a learned writer and teacher, and certainly *more* concretely and realistically than the very dubious reference to Ben Sira's Jerusalem school in 51:23. In addition, the personality and activities of Qohelet, expressed in the first-person accounts of his search for wisdom earlier in the book, seem quite sharply drawn—no less sharply than the idealized personality of Ben Sira in his own first-person passages.

The key difference, of course, is that Ben Sira includes his name, and his historical individuality is emphasized by a personal report from the translator, who claims to be his grandson. Conversely, Qohelet remains anonymous and, in the book's narrative frame, allusively pseudonymous.[52] But if we bracket Ben Sira's name in 50:27, we can read his book not much differently than Qohelet, the book of Proverbs, or the "Teacher Hymns," which, too, feature the first-person voice of wisdom teachers. The implications of Ben Sira's name for the conceptual development of individual authorship in Jewish texts, then, have been overstated.

Ben Sira's self-identification, first, is not personal and specific, but, with the exception of his individual name, draws on conventional and stylized language to place him in a chain of inspired, ideal teachers and pious men. Second, putting his name on the work does not imply a sense of authorial property; it is not the equivalent of Ben Sira's "copyright." That is, the fact that he mentions his own name does not necessarily mean that he considers his text to be his own coherent, fixed intellectual creation, extends his authority over it, and identifies it as both *originating and coterminous* with his own textual activity. Rather, Ben Sira presents himself by name as the recipient and heir of some revealed wisdom and received instruction. He considers himself to stand in continuity with earlier inspired figures and sages and he understands his work as collection and transmission. He presents his persona as an ideal scribe, a gleaner following his predecessors, and a channel for the great sea of revealed wisdom. But channels and streams, by definition, do not suddenly solidify but continue to flow. They remain open to further expansion and supplementation by those who consider themselves to be in continuity with his legacy, like gleaners after the next grape harvest.

What Is "The Book of Ben Sira"? Open Books and Authentic Text

This discursive evidence, including Ben Sira's images and metaphors, can give us a glimpse into how early Jewish writers conceptualized their own textual production, and how the imagined morphology of writing differed from our own. While it is not a systematic "native theory" of texts, it does give us a glimpse into what the world of literary production seemed like to early Jewish writers.[53]

The text's own figurative language can help illuminate its formal, compositional development—that is, the text's literary choices shed light on, and perhaps open the way for, its own complex transmission history. The diversity among the Hebrew manuscripts indicates that the transmission process of the text is in line with the understanding that Ben Sira's work is, like the 11QPsalms^a collection, *neither original nor complete*, but a moment in a long process of inheriting, preserving, arranging, and teaching the tradition. Indeed, the text flows like channels from a river, from generation to generation and language to language. As mentioned already, there are two major recensions, a shorter and an expanded version; each Hebrew manuscript differs from the others in minor or major ways in contents and arrangement, from differently ordered verses through an "additional" hymn (MS B, at 51:12) to an excerpted and completely rearranged text (MS C).

In chapter 1, I argued that the "*book* of Psalms" is not a productive concept through which to consider psalms traditions. This is also the case for the Ben Sira materials. The incongruence of using "book" models to conceptualize Ben Sira traditions is most clearly evident in the practical task of publication of these manuscripts. Pancratius C. Beentjes was faced with this problem when preparing his 1997 edition of all the Hebrew manuscripts of Ben Sira. How to present the texts in a way that would be usable for the modern reader, possible to render in a printed book, and true to the diversity of the manuscripts themselves?

Both MSS A and B contain verses that appear out of order compared to the Greek text: for example, in A, 27:5–6 appears between 6:22 and 6:23. "How should one process such 'erratic verses'?," Beentjes asks. "By lifting them out of their original context, the editor is *creating a new text* that has never existed."[54] Particularly problematic is MS C, the oldest medieval manuscript, which contains a selection of material in a radically different arrangement and has been called an "anthology," "abstract," or "compendium" from Ben Sira. Solomon Schechter wrote that "the codex from which these leaves come never represented a complete Ms. of Ben Sira, but merely formed an abridged collection of extracts from the Book, prepared by the scribe for some special purpose of his own."[55] Beentjes has argued that the compiler of MS C creatively rearranged passages from Ben Sira according to his own hermeneutical principles to form a "gnomic anthology."[56] He arranged material from Ben Sira thematically, according to at least three subjects—shame, the wise man, and the wife.[57] For Beentjes, if the first leaf, which begins with Sir 3:14, was the first page of the anthology, this would suggest that the text was to be used in a school context. Beentjes comments on his methodological difficulties he faced when deciding how to present this text:

> To the editor who wants to 'synopticize' this manuscript with the parallel texts of MSS A, B and D, the 'chaotic' sequence of the verses of MS C (e.g. Sir 3,14–18.21–22; 41,16; 4,21; 20,22–23; 4,22–23) poses a serious problem. To present MS C synoptically, one has to rearrange the anthological verses into an assumed 'original' order, but then all characteristics of the anthological MS C disappear at once.[58]

The problem is a practical one, but it reveals deeper conceptual questions about the definition of a book that Beentjes does not engage, although his use of quotation marks around the word "original" suggests some discomfort with this term.

This discomfort is not thematized, but it seems to me that the problem of using such language lies in the impossibility, to return once again to the words of Roger Chartier, of positing "a fundamental identity" for the text. These are questions of editorial theory and practice now posed by Benjamin Wright, who draws out both the theoretical difficulty of pinning down a "definitive text" or the "real Ben Sira" and its practical implications for deciding how to choose and present a base text for a commentary.[59] What is the "original" or "final" Ben Sira, the authoritative version of this book, which is to serve as the standard to which all other versions are compared? "Where and how do we locate a definitive text of the book of Ben Sira?," Wright asks. "Can (not will) the real Ben Sira stand up?"[60]

Perhaps not, because the text has not stood still. Scholars must make practical decisions in presenting an approximation of the text of Ben Sira at some moment in its transmission history. But it is important to recognize, as Wright does, that our categories don't quite fit. Different "editions" of Ben Sira may have existed already during his or his students' time. And the idea of a definitive text does not match Ben Sira's own understanding of his text as an overflow or ingathering of older traditions, and a compendium of wisdom that is necessarily unfinished: "The first man did not know wisdom fully, nor will the last one fathom her" (24:28). With such attitudes toward the gathering, production, and transmission of wisdom, it becomes clear that the criterion of either *Urtext* (i.e., determining the "original" form of a text before its later additions and corruptions) or the related criterion of "final authorial intent"[61] (determining the ideal form the author intended his work to have) that have long informed editorial decisions about the authoritative form of books does not apply in this context: there is no understanding of individual books and authors as clearly delineated, separate entities, but as moments in a multigenerational process.

Here, I would like to draw on Peter Schäfer's work on the diversity of the Heikhalot manuscript tradition, which evolved continuously long after the composition of its constituent parts. The rearrangements, omissions, and additions to this literature over time prevent us from talking about, or publishing, a stable literary text that can be called the Heikhalot. Schäfer develops the language of "microforms and macroforms,"

> instead of the terms writing or work, to accommodate the fluctuating character of the texts of the Hekhalot literature. The term *macroform* concretely denotes both the fictional or imaginary single text ... as well as the often different manifestations of this text in the various manuscripts. The border between micro- and macroforms is thereby fluent: certain definable textual units can be both part of a superimposed

entirety (and thus a "microform") as well as an independently transmitted redactional unit (thus a "macroform").[62]

The manuscript history and compositional diversity of Heikhalot literature is far
more complex than that of Ben Sira, but Schäfer's departure from the language
of "book" or "work" is a helpful approach for rethinking the goals of the editorial
process for ancient texts in general. Ra'anan Boustan, explaining and drawing
upon Schäfer's work, writes that "an editor must be prepared to forgo the creation of a misleading 'finished product.'"[63]

Ben Sira and the "Open Book"

For Ben Sira, the idea of a "finished product" is misleading not only because of
the evidence of compositional fluidity and expansive recensional work[64] but
also because of how Ben Sira understands the "incomplete" nature of wisdom
(as a tradition in constant movement and striving toward greater insight and dis-
closure) and the continuity between the work of successive generations of sages.
In other words, it is not merely a question of the practical, text-critical impossibility
of determining an authentic or original Ben Sira, due to its messy compositional,
translational, and scribal history. Rather, it is a question of a deeper *conceptual*
incongruence, in that the modern scholarly impulse to produce an authoritative
editio princeps, a definitive edition, does not reflect the way texts were produced
and imagined in antiquity—as projects, not as products.

This point is related to Brennan Breed's important critique of the distinction
between "text" and "reception" in biblical studies, and of the continued privileging of an original text. Instead of looking for stable textual products or privileging particular moments of historical context, Breed sees the creation, transmission, and interpretation of writing always in terms of a process: texts are
"nomads," with "no origin and no endpoint."[65]

Texts, then, can be unstable not only because of the vagaries of scribal revision and copying but also because of deeper ideologies about what texts are supposed to look like. Such ideologies of process appear not only in the world of
scrolls but also in codex-based literary cultures: the material forms of front and
back covers do not always go hand in hand with conceptual morphologies of
closure and completion. In their work on medieval Hebrew manuscript books,
Malachi Beit-Arié and Israel Ta-Shma have identified a phenomenon they have
called the "open book"—texts that continued to undergo revision, not only by
later readers but also by their first authors, even after they were in circulation.
Ta-Shma writes that the medieval manuscripts are a window into some surprising ways that authors understood their own textual creations:

[Q]uite often books were not meant by their authors to serve as final statements, but rather as presentations of an interim state of knowledge or opinion, somewhat like our computerized databases, which are constantly updated and which give the user a summary of the data known at the time of the latest updating. In a similar way, the medieval book was sometimes conceived of as no more than a solid basis for possible future alterations by the author himself. There were many reasons— some philosophical and psychological, others purely technical—for this profound phenomenon, which can give rise to serious problems as to finality, authorship and authority of a given text of a work.[66]

One of the major principles of modern scholarly editing, the idea of "final authorial intent," becomes meaningless: some authors' "intent" was precisely *not* final. In addition to books that were conceptualized as "open" by their authors, there were also books that were "opened" by later readers who adapted the texts for their own needs.[67] This model of an open project seems to hold for Ben Sira: as Judith Newman writes, "[t]he question of who has the last word is something of a trick question because the book seems to have invited others to add to the collection upon attaining their own wisdom."[68]

If Ben Sira is an "open book," was it born open or opened up by its readers? It seems, based on both Ben Sira's own imagery and the manuscript history of the text, that it may be both. There are no criteria to determine what stage of Ben Sira to treat as the "fictional or imaginary single text," since anthologizing is the mode of both composition *and* transmission of these materials. Jeremy Corley argues that the text existed in several "editions" already during the author's lifetime:

> It is likely that the first edition of the book consisted of 1:1–23:27 and 51:13–30. Thereafter, three new editions cumulatively added supplements, each one beginning with a wisdom poem (24:1–29; 32:14–33:15; 38:24–39:11) and an autobiographical note (24:30–34; 33:16–18; 39:12). Since the Praise of the Ancestors (44:1–50:24) is a self-contained unit of its own, it forms the last supplement for the book's final edition (the fifth).[69]

For Corley, the work has a thoughtful arrangement, and the acrostic Hymn to Wisdom in chapter 51 was the original ending of the composition. Nevertheless, it appears that the text has "ended" more than once: the "colophon" in 50:27–29 that includes Ben Sira's name still allows for more material to run over like the Euphrates, bringing to mind the "ending" of David's psalms at Ps 72 and the layered endings of the 11QPsalms[a] collection.

While Corley's thesis is attractive in its delineation of the different genres within Ben Sira and comparisons to the structure of Proverbs, not everyone shares his view that the structure of Ben Sira is so carefully thought out. Lutz Schrader has argued that the structure of Ben Sira is too haphazard, with too many repetitions and disconnected segments, to be the work of the sage, and must have been compiled from his notes by one of his students after his death.[70] But once again, such a view betrays a modern sense of individual creativity and textual coherence, not taking into account the collective anthological nature of sapiential traditions. Whether we assume that the arrangement of the book comes from Ben Sira or from his students, the text likely underwent several re-dactional stages and was motivated by the impulses to both preserve and renew.[71]

If we allow that some of the redactional and compilational work was done by Ben Sira's students, using the teacher's demise as a cutoff point for the "authentic" form of his text seems arbitrary, informed by modern assumptions of individual intellectual property.[72] After all, in the pedagogical rhetoric of wisdom literature, the teacher-student relationship is not only personal but textual as well. As Carol Newsom explains in her work on Proverbs, the strategy of direct address, "I" and "you," "recruits" readers as students and sons, who "are called upon to take up the subject position of son in relation to an authoritative father. Through its imi-tation of a familiar scene of interpellation the text continually reinterpellates its readers."[73] Wright considers such "interpellation" in the context of Ben Sira as well, whose teaching function continues through his text as his addresses to his "children" are read.[74] If the creator of a textual tradition like the Wisdom of Ben Sira did not consider his work to be bounded and self-contained, as I have shown above, then the expansion and morphing of his text by later generations of his students (including, I would suggest, his translator) is *continuous* with his own process of expanding and compiling his writings.

All this complicates the very question of authenticity, of determining what the "Book of Ben Sira" *is*; this has traditionally been assumed to be what the in-dividual Joshua ben Eleazar ben Sira actually wrote. This question is, I think, comparable to the myriad scholarly discussions of what was or was not believed to be "Davidic" in ancient communities, which is understood to have bearing on the status of such collections as 11QPsalms[a].

I am comparing a "historical" author as studied by modern scholars to a pseudepigraphic hero as viewed by ancient people. But scholarship on both what is authentically Psalmic and what is authentically Ben Sira rests on the same assumption: that ancient texts functioned along similar concepts of au-thenticity and authorship as modern ones. It seems to me that the question of whether ancient audiences believed that David "really wrote" a certain composi-tion was simply not that important to their conception of the authority or status of a psalms collection,[75] just as whether a text or arrangement is "authentically"

Ben Sira seems foreign to the textual context in which he himself wrote. But, as we have seen, the ideologies and realia of this text befuddle modern scholarly attempts to make them fit into our bibliographic categories. The focus on the *ipsissima verba* of Ben Sira (or of David according to putative ancient beliefs) is an anachronistic concern, and blocks other, more interesting questions about the formation of traditions in antiquity.

A case in point is the "additional" psalm after 51:12 in the Hebrew MS B of Ben Sira (Sir 51:12a–o), another example of Ben Sira's compositional diversity:

> Praise the LORD, for he is good, for his mercy endures forever;
>
> Praise the God of glory, for his mercy endures forever;
>
> Praise the Guardian of Israel, for his mercy endures forever;
>
> Praise the creator of all things, for his mercy endures forever;
>
> Praise the redeemer of Israel, for his mercy endures forever;
>
> Praise God who gathers the dispersed of Israel, for his mercy endures forever;
>
> Praise God who builds the city and sanctuary, for his mercy endures forever;
>
> Praise God who makes a horn sprout forth for the house of David, for his mercy endures forever;
>
> Praise God who has chosen the sons of Zadok as priests, for his mercy endures forever;
>
> Praise the Shield of Abraham, for his mercy endures forever;
>
> Praise the Rock of Isaac, for his mercy endures forever;
>
> Praise the Mighty One of Jacob, for his mercy endures forever;
>
> Praise God who has chosen Zion, for his mercy endures forever;
>
> Praise the King, the king of kings, for his mercy endures forever.
>
> He has lifted up the horn of his people! Let this be his praise from all the faithful,
>
> From Israel, the people near to him. Hallelujah!

This hymn has been largely ignored in scholarship because, missing from the Syriac and the Greek and preserved only in MS B from the Geniza, it is generally not considered "authentic," that is, not representing the creativity of Ben Sira himself.

In a recent pair of articles, Françoise Mies describes how the question of authenticity has dominated the little scholarly work that exists on this hymn, to the exclusion of any analysis of the composition.[76] Mies does analyze the hymn in detail, but in essence, her work also focuses on the question of probable authenticity. She argues that the text is very much at home in Ben Sira's own work, pointing out the biblical language, connections with Second Temple literature and Jewish liturgy, and congruence with the rest of Ben Sira. She also makes a case for reading it as a natural part of the "concluding" pieces in chapter 51, a hymn of praise between the first-person thanksgiving prayer, 51:1–12, and the first-person acrostic to Wisdom, 13–30. Mies also observes that the unique attestation of the composition in MS B should not marginalize it, since chapter 51 is not extant in any other Hebrew manuscript. As for its absence from the Greek, Mies points to the mention of the priesthood of the sons of Zadok in line i; at the time Ben Sira's grandson made his translation, the Zadokites were not in charge of the priesthood, and the composition was left out on this account.[77]

This work makes an excellent case for the antiquity of this composition and its relationship with other Second Temple literature. But a text's value should not depend only on its authenticity. Whether Ben Sira or a later sagely heir composed this psalm and placed it in its penultimate position in the text, it is still an important witness to the way liturgical compositions were compiled and combined with other texts, and the way traditions about the divine names and the deeds of God were formed.

The Afterlives of Ben Sira as Text and Character

If we cannot pinpoint a fundamental identity for the text, what, then, did ancient people mean when they said "Ben Sira"? And when we do not have an authorial product, who is "Ben Sira" the figure?

I argued earlier for a looser understanding of the idea of "psalms," and maintained that no concept of the book of Psalms as a coherent collection existed. I also showed how the figure of David is not straightforwardly identified with the psalms, but associated in a looser way with a more amorphous, undefined idea of liturgical tradition. While no exact comparison is possible, rabbinic references to Ben Sira, as a figure and as a text, serve as another interesting example of this less definite way of imagining a textual tradition, and show that ancient references to writings or their "authors" should not be automatically identified with books as we know them.

As many scholars have noted, the overlap between extant versions of Ben Sira and its rabbinic "citations" is not exact.[78] Some sayings attributed to Ben Sira are close to the extant manuscripts, and some are similar but rearranged or otherwise altered; still others do not exist in any known version, but are in fact biblical texts.[79] Conversely, some rabbinic sources quote a verse that is found in Ben Sira, but do not attribute it as such, pointing instead to a different source, such as a rabbi.[80] What accounts for such variability, or, we might say, lack of precision? Michael Segal suggests that the only explanation is that the passages were cited from memory.[81] Other scholars point to the noncanonical status of Ben Sira, arguing that this meant the rabbis could be less accurate and literal in the transmission of this text.[82] However, it appears that the variability of these citations and pseudocitations reflects a far more complex relationship between rabbinic communities and Ben Sira as a character and as a textual tradition. This relationship depends on the kind of access to and knowledge of the text at different times and places, the continuing development and rearrangement of the text in anthological compilations, and the "notoriety" of the figure of Ben Sira[83] as a sage and teacher in rabbinic circles.

In her study of rabbinic knowledge of Ben Sira, Jenny Labendz shows that "at different times and in different places, the Rabbis possessed different materials."[84] Her key argument is that the early Palestinian rabbis cited Ben Sira accurately because they had the text available for study, but, based on their citation formulae, treated Ben Sira as an oral source—that is, cited him as a protorabbi ("Ben Sira said," or "So-and-so said in the name of Ben Sira"), rather than the author of a book ("It is written in the Book of Ben Sira"), in order to distinguish the text from canonical texts.[85] On the other hand, the text did not seem to have been available in Babylonia until after the fourth century;[86] while Ben Sira is cited numerous times in the Babylonian Talmud, the citations are not accurate, and "there is no indication that those who cite Ben Sira in the [Babylonian] Talmud actually had a physical book from which they were quoting."[87] The one exception to this seems to be R. Joseph, whose unique *textual* relationship with Ben Sira is evident in the accuracy of the citations attributed to him in Sanhedrin 100b, which reports a dispute with R. Abaye about the merits of Ben Sira.[88]

Despite its noncanonical status, Ben Sira's wisdom was a popular source for Jewish homiletics and liturgy. Since it was not a canonical text and thus there was no set "official edition," the text was altered, expanded, and excerpted for different circumstances.[89] We know from the existence of MS C that anthologies of this material were created, where the sayings were selected and rearranged.[90] This phenomenon was not unique to Jewish contexts of transmission. The third- to fourth-century Syriac Christian translation is comparable to the uneven, "inaccurate" citations of Ben Sira in the Babylonian Talmud.[91] The Wisdom of Ben Sira was used in Christian homiletics just as it was among Jews, and, since its text had not been "sanctified by tradition,"[92] verses were altered in the course of usage, according to the pedagogical needs of the ancient teachers. These altered passages found their way into later written editions of Ben Sira, exemplifying the way in which texts evolve in the interplay between writing and community use.

This dynamic process is also connected to the reputation of Ben Sira as a wisdom teacher and an expert in the Law, which made him one of the rabbis' own. The figure gained a certain "notoriety" in rabbinic circles,[93] and so—just as David was considered not so much as the author of a book of Psalms but as an exemplary liturgist, linked to a more amorphous tradition of liturgical material—Ben Sira was considered not only as the author of a concrete and particular book but more generally as a representative of a tradition of wise sayings. Because of this character's reputation, new sayings "accumulated around and circulated in his name," some of which made it into "popular anthologies."[94] Other sayings found in Ben Sira circulated without attribution to this figure, as part of a large "amorphous body of sayings" that circulated "atomistically and anonymously."[95] Labendz summarizes this complexity: "The contents of Ben Sira were spread within the rabbinic community. They were preserved and remembered with varying degrees of accuracy, and sometimes they were conflated with other wisdom sources. The title of the work was attached to a variety of wisdom traditions, only some of which were actually in Ben Sira."[96] Thus, in these communities, there is no precise identification between the figure of Ben Sira and the work we possess that bears his name; rather, we discern a more complex overlap and sense of generative potential, showing the inadequacy of "book" language to characterize the production and reception of ancient Jewish texts.

Conclusion: Metaphors and Manuscripts

In this chapter, I have discussed the way in which the author-compiler of Ben Sira understands his own role in the transmission of traditions, the compositional history of the text, and the later reception of his work and his status. Although Ben Sira is commonly accorded unique textual status in Jewish antiquity as an individually authored book, this designation is misleading, for its authorial figure understands himself to stand fully in continuity with a broader, more ancient tradition of seeking out, preserving, and transmitting wisdom, which neither begins nor ends with his own activity, but hearkens back to the past and remains open to the future. Thus, the processes of textual creation and its later transmission are not separate, but continuous. The individual personality and life of Ben Sira are not the boundaries of the textual tradition he transmits. Here again, the idea of a "fundamental identity" for a text, which I have discussed in the context of the Psalms Scroll and metaphors from digital textuality, does not apply. Hence my articulation of Ben Sira's work not as a "book" (which brings to mind an isomorphic identity of object, figure, and text) but as a "project" (which does not combine these three components into a single entity, but configures their relationship as more loosely overlapping).

Reading psalms traditions and Ben Sira alongside each other is also useful when it comes to the reception of Ben Sira in later traditions. The transmission and reception of a noncanonical, but highly regarded and popular textual tradition can, I think, shed light on the way texts were imagined in a precanonical age. Texts are not listed in a catalog or cross-checked systematically; they exist in different forms, without anything like an *editio princeps* that sets the standard for all others; and they have different levels of availability and awareness in various communities. My sense is that this multiform, "unauthorized," and variable nature of Ben Sira's wisdom is comparable to the way that psalms collections existed in the Second Temple period, when we have no evidence to suggest that any official or conscious decisions were being made about their shape and form, when they celebrated the character of the exemplary psalmist, and when they grew and changed over the course of community use.

My other broad methodological point is that the literary study of themes and tropes—images, rhetoric, and voice—cannot be separated from the history of the production and reproduction of the texts in which they are found. D. F. McKenzie writes that no border exists

> between bibliography and textual criticism on the one hand and literary criticism and literary history on the other. . . . In the pursuit of historical meanings, we move from the most minute feature of the material form of the book to questions of authorial, literary, and social context. These all bear in turn on the ways in which texts are then re-read, re-edited, re-designed, re-printed, and re-published. If a history of readings is made possible only by a comparative history of books, it is equally true that a history of books will have no point if it fails to account for the meanings they later come to make.[97]

Indeed, what these texts say about themselves—the literary reflections on their own origins and purposes and the nature of the figures responsible for their creation—can help us understand their textual development and transmission.

In other words, what Ben Sira says about the role of the scribe and wise man as a transmitter of traditions and what imagery he chooses to reflect on the work of writing—all this already points to the possibility of a complex bibliographical history. The imagery of movement and progression—channels and rivers, growing trees, and gleaners after grape harvesters—places Ben Sira's textual activity in a longer history that is both ancient and ongoing. It is as if the text itself was highlighting, or even enabling, its own openness, as a moment in a long process of writing, reading, and collection.

4

Shapes of Scriptures

The Nonbiblical Library of Early Judaism

> [Jacob] gave all his books and the books of his fathers to his son Levi so
> that he could preserve them and renew them for his sons until today.
>
> —Jubilees 45:16

Introduction: "Collecting, if Possible, All the Books in the World"

Just as the text of Ben Sira presents itself as an unfinished project, so the gathering of wisdom is a process that is never complete. After the harvest there is a gleaner (Sir 33:16–19), and the horizons of wisdom perpetually recede, escaping human grasp. But the awareness of incompleteness and openness finds a counterpart in the desire for full possession: totalizing ambitions for the completion of the project after all—the dream of collecting all of human knowledge in one place.

The dream of a universal library, a complete repository of all writing ever produced, is a recurring theme in Western culture. In "Libraries without Walls," Roger Chartier writes—from the perspective of early modern European history—that this desire to grasp and tame the totality of human knowledge "underlay the constitution of great princely, ecclesiastical, and private 'libraries'; it justified a tenacious search for rare books, lost editions, and texts that had disappeared; it commanded architectural projects to construct edifices capable of welcoming the world's memory."[1]

This aspiration for totality, according to some ancient reports, was also the dream behind the famed library of Alexandria. Its aim to collect all the world's knowledge drove its vigorous, sometimes aggressive practices of acquiring manuscripts, new modes of cataloging and organizing texts, and extensive work of copying and translation. For the second-century BCE *Letter of Aristeas*, this value of universality and completeness was also the driving force behind the translation of the Law into Greek, so it could be included in the repository of all human knowledge. *Aristeas* tells us that "[w]hen Demetrius of Phalerum was put in charge of the king's library he was assigned large sums of money with a view to collecting, if possible, all the books in the world; and by arranging purchases and transcriptions he carried the king's design to completion as far as he was able" (9).[2] Demetrius is reported as saying there were over two hundred thousand volumes already collected, and the goal was half a million books.

Nobody knows how many volumes really were collected in the Alexandrian library. What we do know is that the ideal of total possession of all the world's wisdom is a desire that is inexorably deferred. Chartier points to the invention of print, and the ensuing "proliferation of titles and editions," as a breakthrough that "ruined all hope for an exhaustive collection."[3] But the dream of totality was a hopeless one long before print:[4] ideas about the uncontrollable proliferation of writing, and questions about what has already been lost or remains inaccessible, were voiced in the ancient world as well.

The totalizing dream is impossible. But for some, there is a theological solution: the universal library, a "complete set," already exists—and it is the Bible. As Chartier writes, the concept of a "library" holds a variety of meanings in Western culture, including not only an institution or building but also a collection of books, a published series of books of the same nature, a catalog of works, or a collection of texts in a single volume.[5] Some ways of imagining the Bible as the totality of revelation, as the complete repository of the divine word, seem to reflect the powerful human desire for the elusive universal library. According to some rabbinic and kabbalistic tropes, we are already in possession of everything worth knowing: it had all been revealed on Sinai once and for all. Everything was either explicit in Scripture or latent in it, only waiting to be discovered within its letters through diligent study. "Turn it and turn it," the rabbinic composition *Pirkei Avot,* "Sayings of the Fathers," says about the Torah—"for everything is in it" (5:21).[6]

Chartier begins his essay on the universal library with Jorge Luis Borges, who by now is a familiar guide to mythical libraries and imaginary books. In his famous short story "The Library of Babel," Borges imagines an infinite library: a library that, through accidents of permutation, contains all the books that have ever been written or could ever possibly be written in the future—a collection in which everything could be found. Borges articulates the effect such a library has, and how certain anxieties about knowledge and its access motivate this idea:

> When it was announced that the Library contained all books, the first reaction was unbounded joy. All men felt themselves the possessors of an intact and secret treasure. There was no personal problem, no world problem, whose eloquent solution did not exist—somewhere in some hexagon. The universe was justified; the universe suddenly became congruent with the unlimited width and breadth of humankind's hope.[7]

There is an "unbounded joy" at the completion of the library—a sense of relief and resolution when the available information coincides with the possible questions. And yet: these books can never *really* be found or read in Borges's infinite library.

Some theological modes of imagining the Bible as a complete repository of knowledge satisfy the same kind of desires for resolution and totality. They placate anxieties about the limits of knowledge and control over information. Everything worth knowing is accessible—even if encoded—in a single location. "Turn it and turn it": all the answers to every question are already there, to be found "somewhere in some hexagon," somewhere within the biblical corpus.

This view has some support in one thread of rabbinic ideology about the biblical canon—Scripture as a self-contained entity, sufficient unto itself (although this does not represent all rabbinic attitudes toward the Bible).[8] But this idea does not hold for times before the texts that were meaningful for Jewish communities had been bound into a unity, or imagined as a limited corpus existing in a single location from which all knowledge sprang.

Even so, the idea of the Bible as a universal library is so powerful that this sense of biblical totality is still sometimes projected by biblical scholars upon earlier times. For example, Menahem Haran argues that no libraries as such existed in Second Temple times because the corpus of literature was too small for libraries to be necessary. The Jewish "library" was complete at twenty-two scriptural books, and "[i]n these twenty-two books," Haran writes, "the Jews find everything."[9] (In this scheme, the many more books found at Qumran are considered irrelevant, evidence from an outlier sectarian group, although scholars agree that most of the texts were written outside Qumran and represent Jewish traditions far broader than the sect.) Similarly, Michael Fishbane has asserted that, for the Qumran community, the Bible was "the literary expression of Divine Truth; at once the unique resource of past revelations, and the mediating source of all subsequent ones."[10]

But this chapter paints a different picture of the shape of sacred writing before the Bible existed as such. As most scholars now recognize, there was no coherent entity called "the Bible," and so no sense that any corpus constitutes a universal or complete body of knowledge, an "intact and secret treasure" or a complete set. In many Second Temple texts, we see an awareness of a literary world that is ancient, varied, and not fully accessible. In texts like *Enoch*, *Jubilees*, and many traditions about the patriarchs from the Dead Sea Scrolls, for instance, we see the notion of a long history of revealed writing stretching back long before Sinai, and forming part of the stories about Israel's ancient ancestors. We see scribes recognizing the authority and divine origin of texts like the *Enoch* literature, *Jubilees*, and these patriarchal traditions, which present themselves not as derivative of or dependent on material we now call biblical, but indeed, prior to it. And while specific texts that have come down to us, like the Enochic material, are recognizably used in other literature, early Jewish texts also mention many writings that we cannot identify with any extant texts—writings that may have been lost, like the book of Noah, or were always only imagined, like the heavenly Book of Life.[11]

This chapter, then, is about the morphology of the imagined sacred library in early Judaism. If the early Jewish "library"—the inventory of writing that was known or imagined—is not yet shaped like and configured in relation to a Bible, if the Bible was not a totalizing entity from which all knowledge was imagined to flow, how do we describe it? What was Scripture, before Scripture meant the same thing as Tanakh? What did early Jewish writers know or imagine about their own literary world? What texts *were* there—whether available and cited, or known only by hearsay and legend? Where did these writings come from, and how did they travel through time?[12]

The first part of the chapter discusses the "mental architecture" that structures how we imagine the shape, limits, locations, and hierarchies of ancient sacred writing. I discuss a selection of sources that suggest biblical and nonbiblical texts should be considered in a horizontal, not hierarchical, relationship to each other. But powerful scholarly categories like "rewritten Bible" and "biblical interpretation," while illuminating some key aspects of early Jewish writing, make it difficult to reconfigure this intellectual scaffolding.

The way the sources are collected and published for our consumption plays a large part in building these mental structures, and the second part of the chapter shows how the modern publication history of nonbiblical writings has contributed to creating the categories through which we view the ancient literary world. I argue that the selection and framing of our sources in their modern published form, from the first major published collection of nonbiblical early Jewish texts in 1713 through the most recent one in 2013, both enables and constrains the way we can think about what sacred writing was like before biblical hegemony was entrenched. Nonbiblical literature has invariably been collected as a corpus separate from the Bible and defined by its relationship to it, and this has colored the way we imagine the shape of early Judaism's sacred library.

In the third part of the chapter, I focus on one example—the book of *Jubilees*, which has largely been studied as "rewritten Bible" and "biblical interpretation"— for insight into what the scriptural world *seemed like* to its producers, before the idea of the Bible as a complete repository or bounded corpus was an available concept. While *Jubilees* retells a history of Israel that we know from Genesis and Exodus, sacred writing itself plays a key role in its narrative: *Jubilees* gives us its own presentation of a history of books—its own account of the inventory, provenance, and transmission history of sacred texts.

In the previous chapter, I showed that for the Ben Sira collection, the poetic imagery of the text itself reveals something about its own native theory of itself—its origins and boundaries, and the role of the figures who transmit it.[13] Here, I broaden the scope to other texts, paying attention to the clues they have left about how they themselves imagine the morphology of their library: the shape, limits, locations, and hierarchies of sacred writing more generally.

Mental Architecture and the Shape of the Sacred Library in Early Judaism

The major contention of this chapter is that beginning with questions about the Bible's origins and interpretation and assuming its centrality to early Jewish literature obscures the possibility of describing a prebiblical literary imagination, in which textual traditions took fundamentally different shapes. A different starting point can help reveal some aspects of a "native theory" of textual tradition, before Bibles and books were available as concepts that structure and limit writing.

But this is not an easy task: in the very language we use to describe and categorize our sources, and the way they are published for our consumption, the "Bible" is the totalizing concept that gives structure to the literary world as a whole. Even if we are consciously aware such categories are anachronistic, this deeply ingrained mental architecture powerfully affects the way we imagine the world of early Jewish writing.[14] But architecture, by its nature, is constructed, not natural. We need not stay in the same house where we grew up. Can we redesign our structures or visit other palaces?

"Rewritten Bible" and "Biblical Interpretation" as Structuring Concepts

Among the ways we construct the world of early Jewish texts are two major concepts: "rewritten Bible" and "biblical interpretation." The term "rewritten Bible" was coined by Geza Vermes in 1961 as a description of works like *Jubilees*, the *Genesis Apocryphon*, Josephus's *Antiquities*, and the *Biblical Antiquities* by Pseudo-Philo: works that offer a sustained and adapted retelling of biblical narrative.[15] Since Vermes, the designation has been extended by various scholars to describe a plethora of other works, many newly discovered at Qumran, that "rewrite" other kinds of biblical texts, such as the rewritten law in the *Temple Scroll* or reworked prophetic texts like Pseudo-Ezekiel. Since the term "Bible" is recognized as anachronistic by an increasing number of scholars, many now use the less loaded "rewritten scriptures" instead, to acknowledge that the biblical canon was not yet set, but that authoritative scriptures did exist and generated reworking and interpretation.

But a different name does not change the mental blueprint that structures how we imagine groups of texts and the relationships between them. Assumptions about textual hierarchies remain: the sense that the scriptural text remains primary or central and the "rewritten" work is secondary, derivative, and *in the service of* its scriptural source is implicit in the concept.

Yet this is not how such texts present themselves or—as far as we can tell—how they are used and received in Second Temple Judaism. Thus, the designation "rewritten scripture" is apt and illustrative in a limited sense, and only for a specific moment of the text's biography: it is true that the *process of composing* these works included reworking, adapting, and embellishing earlier texts that would later be classified as Scripture. But this observation does not help us understand either the text's self-presentation or the place that such texts, once written, might occupy in the ancient literary imagination.[16] We might, then, talk about rewriting scriptures *as a verb*, but not rewritten scriptures *as a noun* that names a genre.[17]

To use "rewritten scripture" as a generic category that puts texts into groups risks constructing a misleading picture of textual hierarchies. While a text may in some way be "derivative"—or, better, may use and respond to earlier traditions—it typically does not present itself as such; neither do we typically have evidence that it was received this way. We can see this more clearly by comparison with one that *does* claim such a relationship with its textual past: the book of Deuteronomy. Deuteronomy—unlike *Jubilees*, the *Genesis Apocryphon*, and other texts classified as "rewritten Bible"—actually does present itself as a retelling of previously given laws; it was already called *deuteros nomos*, "repeated" or "second law" in Greek, by its ancient readers; and scholars from virtually every school of pentateuchal criticism recognize it as such (although they disagree on whether Deuteronomy intended to supplement and clarify or replace the prior law).[18] But other texts that "rewrote" older traditions did not position themselves in such a hierarchy vis-à-vis their precursors. They claimed a place alongside works that are now in the biblical canon: we can position them beside one another on the same mental bookshelf.

The concept of biblical interpretation is another popular lens through which early Jewish literature is commonly studied. From the critical mass of monographs, collected volumes, and articles that focus on the interpretation of Scripture in specific Qumran texts and the Pseudepigrapha, one would get the impression that the major activity of early Jewish writers was the exegesis of Scripture, the central fountainhead of the literary world, from which all other texts flow and around which all other texts converge. Indeed, sometimes this case is made explicitly. James Charlesworth, for example, writes that "the main reason [the Apocrypha and Pseudepigrapha] were composed was the appearance of biblical exegesis, that is, interpretation of the writings that would come to compose the Tanak." Biblical exegesis is the "crucible of the extracanonical writings"[19]—the purpose of nonbiblical texts is to fill in the gaps or explain the inconsistencies in Scripture, making the nonbiblical both derived from and in the service of the biblical.

But again, this does not reflect the way the writers present their own work. Although many texts, such as the book of *Jubilees* or the *Temple Scroll*, do contain exegetical elements that harmonize inconsistencies or fill in gaps in the earlier texts on which they rely, they do not frame themselves as exegesis—but as new revelation from a divine source. Crucially, in their form and rhetoric, they do not position themselves as secondary works in the service of these earlier scriptures.

Neither do they take a generic form associated with exegetical commentary, which presents a biblical lemma and its interpretation, as in rabbinic midrash. There is one exception: the *pesher* texts from Qumran, which present citations from prophetic texts—lemmata—and then give their commentary, beginning with the word *pishro*—"its interpretation." But as Steven Fraade has convincingly argued, the Qumran *pesharim* should not really be considered the direct precursors of midrashic exegesis.[20] These texts, like Pesher Habakkuk, Pesher Isaiah, and the fragmented *pesharim* on psalms I discussed in chapter 1, give their lemmata actualizing meanings that read them in light of the present situation of the community and its expectations of history's imminent end. In terms of their exegetical content and interests, the *pesharim* are, therefore, unlike rabbinic midrash. Midrash tends to provide multiple, dialogically arranged options for the interpretation of biblical passages, including extensive embellishments, smoothing out of inconsistencies, and filling in of perceived gaps in the text. Explicitly actualizing readings do not dominate midrash the way they do the *pesher* literature.[21] But when it comes to their literary form, the *pesharim* are the closest we get in the Second Temple period to later traditions of Jewish commentary: they foreground the particular scriptural texts explicitly as their sources and starting points, and clearly mark the commentary as both *separate from* and *dependent on* them.

This, however, is not the case for other Second Temple literature. Like rewriting, exegesis is one implicit part of these works' compositional process. But this is not an apt description of the purpose or genre of the works as a whole. Indeed, in many cases, the later, noncanonical work is *of the same genre* as the scriptural text it is supposed to be interpreting. That is, we have texts that draw on narrative, law, or prophecy we now call scriptural to create new narrative, law, or prophecy.

The assumption that the texts we call biblical are necessarily hierarchically superior, primary, or central—and the demotion of other materials to secondary, derivative, or auxiliary status—is based on their privileged place in later, normative Jewish and Christian traditions. But for the Second Temple period, John Reeves suggests that

> the more responsible hermeneutic stance would be to position the cod-
> ified traditions now found within "the Bible" horizontally alongside "its

interpreters" (as opposed to constructing a vertical—and hence hierarchic—genealogical chain) and to view each of these written streams of tradition as formally parallel currents of narrative expression. Making a synoptic or synchronic perspective our default position for exegetical assessment offers a very different vantage point for observing the distribution, thematic dimensions, and ideological affiliations of the common characters, motifs, and story cycles found in most of our texts. It also allows us to pose questions or to consider possibilities that are automatically precluded when we uncritically privilege "the Bible" as the exegetical fountainhead for all of its allied discourse.[22]

I want to dwell here on the way that Reeves articulates his critique. This short passage abounds with spatial metaphors: Reeves calls for seeing the relationship between what we call "biblical" and other texts horizontally, or in parallel, rather than vertically or hierarchically—synoptically or synchronically, rather than as a chain that privileges what is earlier and sees later material as linearly derivative or peripheral to a central source or focus, a "fountainhead." To return to my earlier metaphor, we can shelve these texts side by side on our mental bookshelf.

Reeves's spatial metaphors are more than rhetorical flourishes. Rather, as I have shown in the first three chapters of this book, the way we imagine texts is often structured through material and spatial categories that predetermine how we read them. As I demonstrated in the first chapter, the very category of "book" is a material and spatial category that implicates concepts of borders and unity, as well as order, beginnings, and ends. This category acts like a mental container that arranges the fragments we have into shapes that do not always correspond with their material distribution or their morphologies in the ancient imagination. Alternative metaphors, like projects or archives, suggest new ways to visualize the sources spatially, unbinding them from anachronistic bookish constraints and making it possible to see new ways in which texts might go together.

In the same spirit, James Bowley has compared our most common picture of early Jewish literature to a wheel, and "at the hub are the major canonical texts and all the other texts revolve around it, some closer, some farther away," suggesting that we must instead visualize the texts in a "large web of interaction."[23] For Reeves, too, visualizing "biblical" and "nonbiblical" material horizontally or in parallel, rather than in relationships of derivation and periphery, is a wholesale reconfiguration of the conceptual structures that intuitively shape the way we talk about the relationships and functions of early Jewish texts.

This is what I mean when I suggest that the early Jewish library was *shaped* differently than the categories of "Bible," "rewritten Bible," and "biblical interpretation" imply. We must visit and inhabit new mental structures—not simply adjust terminology, such as "scriptural" rather than "biblical"—if we wish to integrate the emerging scholarly consensus that there was not yet a "Bible" as such into our reading of the sources. It is a matter of reorganizing our mental library, not merely changing the names of its wings.

Rearranging the Early Jewish Library: the View from Qumran

Later in this chapter, I discuss these ideas with special attention to the book of *Jubilees*. But the call to read synchronically or synoptically, rather than hierarchically with the (proto)biblical at the top or in the center of the literary world, is helpful for reconsidering Second Temple literature more broadly.

This work of reimagining the shape of the sacred library in a broader sense is already underway, with the Dead Sea Scrolls at the forefront of the discussion. It is in the Scrolls that we get the most direct evidence for what texts early Jewish scribes had at their disposal and what their own mental libraries may have looked like. In one exemplary study in *Revue de Qumran*, Florentino García Martínez takes on this question directly, presenting a broad selection of Hebrew and Aramaic texts from Qumran that draw on and refer to earlier writings.[24] García Martínez demonstrates that the uses of sources and references to textual authority give us a picture of a literary world where what came to be the "Bible" is neither conceptualized as a corpus nor given unique or preeminent status as *the* "exegetical fountainhead." In the Enochic texts, for example, we do find dependence on texts found in the canonical Bible;[25] but as García Martínez puts it, "it is also equally clear that the Scripture is not the only, or even the most important, source of authority: angelic revelation and the knowledge of the heavenly books are the prime source of authority of the composition."[26] Thus, he has traced textual relationships between the sources in ways that correspond to Reeves's suggestion of a horizontal or parallel view of biblical and nonbiblical traditions.

In turn, Enoch's knowledge, as transmitted in writing, claims supreme status for itself. In the *Astronomical Book* (now *1 Enoch* 72–82, preserved in a different version at Qumran in the manuscripts 4Q208–11), the angel Uriel shows Enoch the laws of the heavenly bodies, and Enoch writes them down (74:2); later, Enoch is shown the heavenly tablets and the book where all the deeds of humanity are recorded (81:1–2). The angels permit Enoch to return to earth for one year so he can write down all that he has seen and teach it to his children. In his final speech to Methuselah, Enoch emphasizes the writtenness of his legacy and adjures his son to preserve and transmit it:

> Now my son Methuselah, I am telling you all these things and am writing (them) down. I have revealed all of them to you and have given you the books about all these things. My son, keep the book written by your father so that you may give (it) to the generations of the world.

Wisdom I have given to you and to your children and to those who will
be your children so that they may give this wisdom which is beyond
their thought to their children for the generations. Those who understand will not sleep and will listen with their ear to learn this wisdom. It
will be more pleasing to them than fine food to those who eat.[27]

Claims to the authority of Enochic writings persist in other parts of the corpus
we now call *1 Enoch*. In a later composition, the Epistle of Enoch (*1 Enoch* 91–
105), Enoch communicates that his books will be given to "the righteous and
pious and wise, and they will believe in them, and in them all the righteous will
rejoice and be glad, to learn from them all the paths of truth" (104:12–13).[28] The
book of *2 Enoch*—which has survived only in Slavonic translation, but likely
dates to the late Second Temple period[29]—relates that Enoch, taking angelic dictation, wrote 360 books (*2 Enoch* 23) filled with knowledge about the heavens,
the earth, and human souls. The pervasive tradition of Enoch as a writer, entrusted with both cosmic knowledge and instructions, is now imagined as a vast
library, more extensive than has ever been collected, like the 4,050 revealed
songs of David.

   While Enoch literature is more prominent, other Aramaic texts also present
us with a richly bibliographic world where the writing and transmission of books
is inextricable from the history of Israel's ancestors.[30] The fragmentary *Testament
of Qahat*, placed in the mouth of Levi's son, relates priestly instructions and admonitions:[31]

> [9] And now to you, Amram, my son, I comma[nd ...] [10] and [to] your [son]s
> and to their sons I command [...] [11] and they have given to Levi, my father,
> and which Levi, my father, has gi[ven] to me [...] [12] all my writings as wit-
> ness that you should take care of them (כול כתבי בשהדו די תזדהרון בהון) [...] [13]
> for you; in them is great worth (זכו רבה), in their being carried on with
> you (באתהילכותהון עמכון). (4Q542 1 ii 9–13)[32]

Ancestral writing is of great value, and is passed down and taken care of through
the generations. It serves as a "witness," an Aramaic term that corresponds to
תעודה, "testimony," in *Jubilees*, which, as we will see, tells a rich story of the revelation and renewal of ancestral writings at every juncture of Israel's history.

The *Genesis Apocryphon*

The *Genesis Apocryphon* provides another example of a work for which canonized Scripture is not always an exegetical fountainhead.[33] This work is frequently
studied under the rubric of biblical interpretation or rewritten Bible. And indeed,

it does offer new Aramaic versions of narratives about Enoch, Noah, and Abraham, presented as first-person speech. But this is not merely an embellished Aramaic representation of a biblical blueprint. The text relies on both biblical and nonbiblical sources for its composition, *and*, in the course of the narrative, explicitly refers to sources of written authority that cannot be identified with the Bible.

Thus, we can ask two interrelated questions: what textual repertoire does this work draw on, and what textual world does it imagine and present to its readers? First, we can consider its sources, the "library" the writer had at his disposal. The latter part of the composition, which covers the last part of the Abraham story, stays very close to the text of Genesis, clearly a direct source for the Aramaic writer. But the earlier parts of the text—especially the material on Enoch and Noah—do not rely on Genesis as their source. Indeed, for the first five columns of the text, Moshe Bernstein has noted that "there is virtually nothing substantial which can be linked to the actual words of the Bible. The outline of the biblical story is followed, more or less, in Part I, but the biblical text itself is of little import, and even the details of the biblical narrative do not play a significant role in the retelling."[34] This material is closely related to *1 Enoch* 106–7, either based on it directly or sharing a common source.

What about the textual authorities that the *Genesis Apocryphon* explicitly claims? Famously, the section where Noah tells the story of his life is prefaced by the words: כתב מלי נוח. The first word of the phrase was likely פרשגן, "copy," making the full introductory formula "a copy of the book (or written record) of the words of Noah." There is a continuing debate about whether the "book of Noah" was a real text now lost or an imagined book, as fictional as the celestial Book of Life or Enoch's heavenly tablets. I discuss this further in my treatment of *Jubilees* later in this chapter, which also attests to a tradition of writings associated with Noah. For now, regardless of whether the book of Noah was real or imaginary, a reference to it in a text like the *Genesis Apocryphon* achieves the same purpose: mentioning such a book gives the tradition an aura of authority and mystery, an association with precious writing from hoary antiquity.

Enochic literature also makes an appearance in the *Apocryphon*—not only as a textual source for its writer but also as a source for the characters, inside the narrated world of the text. The reference to "the book of the words of Enoch" appears in a fragmented account of Abraham and Sarah's sojourn in Egypt. The Egyptians, who have taken Sarah, have apparently heard about Abraham's wisdom, and request that he share it with them: "They asked scribal knowledge (ספרא) and wisdom and truth for themselves, so I read before them the book of the words of Enoch."[35]

Here, the writings of Enoch are the source of Abraham's internationally renowned wisdom, and the content of what he presents to the Egyptians who ask to know it. Inside the imagined world of the *Apocryphon*, the Enoch literature is the textual ambassador between Israel's patriarchs and the world outside. It is the fountainhead of the *Apocryphon*: both as the textual source for its writer, and as the textual source for Abraham's wisdom.

The *Genesis Apocryphon*, then, inscribes its own version of the history of Jewish written culture: a culture that is retrojected all the way into the days of Abraham, who already draws on its heritage and even transmits it to outsiders, and further back to its origins with Noah and Enoch. But besides the pre-book, pre-Sinai, nonbiblical "book history" that is imagined *within* the narrative, the *Genesis Apocryphon* is itself an example of a text that is part of such a literary culture—a library of traditions about Israel's ancestors in which the biblical texts participate, but where they are not always the focus.

To be sure, the *Apocryphon* does perform brilliant feats of rethinking and problem solving with the text of Genesis. One example is its treatment of the episode in Gen 12 where Abraham passes Sarah off as his sister, in fear that the Egyptians would kill him in order to take her away. This unflattering portrayal of Abraham as a liar and coward who grows rich when his own wife is taken away, presumably into Pharaoh's harem, is radically transformed in the *Genesis Apocryphon*. There, Abraham has an allegorical dream—clearly, in the world of the *Apocryphon*, a divine message—about a cedar and a date palm. Men come to cut down the cedar, but the date palm asks that the cedar be spared, because both come from the same root. Upon waking, Abraham tells Sarah about his prophetic dream, and requests that she tell the people they meet on their travels that he is her brother. "I will live under your protection," says Abraham, "and my life will be spared because of you" (19:20).[36] The *Apocryphon* has not only turned Abraham into a visionary: it has also given his strategy a divine source, and granted Sarah some participation and power—here, at least, she is in on the plot.

This vibrant retelling of an older text comes immediately before the account where Abraham reads to the Egyptians from a book of Enoch, referring explicitly to another ancient and authoritative textual tradition. The exegetical elements of the *Apocryphon* are important, but they are only part of the story. It also presents the lives of ancient heroes through the lens of its own interests and distinctive aesthetic, imagining a world already populated with writing in patriarchal times.

The Case of 4QTestimonia

García Martínez points to one Qumran text, 4QTestimonia, as another window into a nonbiblical religious library, showing how, in order to give a fuller picture of what the literary world was like, the concept of Bible as a unity must be unbound.[37] 4QTestimonia is a compilation of four quotations about eschatological figures—a messianic prophet, a king, a priest, and a cursed figure—taken from four different sources, presented without commentary. As a compilation of citations or proof texts, the composition as a whole seems to exhort obedience to divinely authorized leadership. What sources did this compiler have before him, and what might they tell us about the way he imagined his inventory of authoritative literature?

The first passage is often presented as Deut 5:28–29 plus Deut 18:18–19, but it turns out that it is not the book of Deuteronomy that is being quoted here, but an alternative version of Exodus—the proto-Samaritan Exodus 20:21 (reflected in 4QRP and 4QPaleoExod). There, the introductory formula—"And YHWH spoke to Moses saying"—is identical to 4QTestimonia, while no such formula exists in Deuteronomy's version. The text emphasizes the fear of God, promises a prophet like Moses, and warns of punishment for those who do not heed him.

The second passage cites Num 24:15–17, Balaam's oracle about hearing and seeing the vision of God and about "the sceptre and the star," who will crush Israel's enemies. The third contains Deut 33:8–11, Moses's blessing of Levi and the priests, who "observed your word and kept your covenant" and who made God's law "shine," complete with the curse on their opponents. Neither the Numbers nor the Deuteronomy citations are identical to the versions in the canonized Masoretic Text.

Finally, the fourth paragraph cites Joshua's curse on the rebuilder of Jericho with additional curses on an "accursed man, one of Belial" who will rebuild the "fortress of wickedness." This fourth passage has sometimes been represented as a citation of Josh 6:26 followed by an interpretive supplement from the *Apocryphon of Joshua* (4Q379 22 ii), one of several nonbiblical texts related to Joshua that were found at Qumran and Masada.[38] But this is misleading: the *Apocryphon of Joshua* itself contains Josh 6:26 with the same introductory note as 4QTestimonia: "At the moment when Joshua finished praising and giving thanks with his psalms, he said...." The *entire* fourth passage, then, is taken from a text like the *Apocryphon of Joshua*, a "rewritten" Joshua tradition, unknown before the discovery of the Dead Sea Scrolls.

Separating the "biblical quotations" in this text from "interpretive commentary"—and citing the first and fourth passages as coming from the Bible at all—misrepresents the scribe's sources. It sets up an anachronistic boundary between biblical and other texts that did not exist from this text producer's point of view. When the sources are presented without canonical bias, 4QTestimonia emerges as a balanced compilation, containing four quotations from four authoritative sources without any additional embellishment. García Martínez characterizes this scribe's use of sources in the following way:

[T]hese quotations, which are all set at the same level, with the same introductory formulae, were considered as providing proof from authoritative writings of the ideas of the collector. They can thus tell us something about the shape of the authoritative writings at that time. As said, these authoritative sources are:—an expanded and harmonised version of Exodus, attested at Qumran in several scrolls, which later came to be the "Bible" of the Samaritans, and considered by Tov as closely related to the "rewritten Bible compositions";—two slightly modified versions of Numbers and Deuteronomy, two books which later become part of the Tanak;—and a composition completely unknown before, very similar to other compositions found at Qumran that are usually classified as "rewritten Scripture," but which is considered here as authoritative as the other three writings. Thus the authoritative Scriptures of Qumran were clearly not identical with the books of Tanak, but rather included other compositions.[39]

Implicit in García Martínez's assessment is a crucial point about common ways of categorizing early Jewish texts as "rewritten Bible" or "rewritten Scripture." The designation may be correct as a description of the process by which the texts were created, since the producers of a text like the *Apocryphon of Joshua* did, in fact, use the now-biblical Joshua as a source. But insofar as the designation suggests a hierarchical relationship vis-à-vis authoritative scripture, it does not adequately describe how the texts, once composed and circulated, fit into the literary landscape of the Second Temple period or the status they claim for themselves. Examples of "rewritten Bible" take their place as new scriptures alongside older sources.

This seems to be the case for the *Apocryphon of Joshua* in 4QTestimonia, but also for other "reworked" materials, most prominently *Jubilees*, which I discuss more fully below. The 4QTestimonia text shows us a literary repertoire that overlaps in many ways with our Bible—but one that diverges from it as well, showing us that no later boundaries unite or delimit the corpus of sacred texts used in early Judaism.

The case of 4QTestimonia stands as a warning to scholars in another way: even if a quotation looks biblical, we cannot always assume it came from a text that is now in the Bible. Here, what looks like the biblical Joshua—embellished with an interpretive flourish—is in fact a citation from a different text. By accident of preservation, we happen to have access to these other sources that were part of this compiler's sacred library.

But what if the two manuscripts of the *Apocryphon of Joshua* had not been preserved? If those texts had disintegrated over two thousand years, or were lost somewhere on the antiquities market, we would simply assume that the scribe had used the biblical book of Joshua and added an interpretive expansion. To imagine a different source would never have occurred to us at all. But—as Kraft, Stone, and others have long warned—surviving texts are only a fragmentary reflection of much fuller, more complex pasts. How many more writings have perished that were once part of the sacred library—and how many other citations have we misidentified as biblical?

From Forgery to Exegesis: The Nonbiblical Libraries of Modern Publishing

As we have seen, some biblical and nonbiblical texts had a horizontal, not hierarchical, relationship to one another. For those texts, the categories of biblical or nonbiblical do not provide much meaningful information about the place these texts had in the ancient imagination. To say, then, that the texts that would become biblical were the center of Jewish life is to organize and group the sources in a way that their ancient readers did not. To be sure, most of the texts that would become biblical were critically important to Hellenistic Jewish writers. But we can never safely assume that these texts—the Torah, some prophets, and some psalms—were the only center. They shared attention and authority with many texts that did not end up in the later canon. The imagined bookshelf of sacred texts contains biblical and nonbiblical texts side by side, not always in a relationship of hierarchy, derivation, or center and periphery.

Why has it been difficult to imagine early Jewish writings without the Bible as the only touchstone and organizing category? In earlier chapters, I showed how the iconic status of a Bible structures our thinking, superimposing itself on pre-biblical data, and how bibliographic unities—authors and books—have both enabled and constricted the way we imagine the shape of literature. But the other reason why canonical boundaries are so powerful has to do with another kind of "book history": the way that the nonbiblical texts have been collected and published in modern times. From the earliest major publication of "Pseudepigrapha" under that title in the eighteenth century by Johann Fabricius, through the most recent, three-volume set *Outside the Bible* by Louis Feldman, James Kugel, and Lawrence Schiffman, the way the primary sources are collected and presented to us shapes our understanding of their literary world.

A key tenet of book-historical work—still relevant today—is that the material form of texts, the choice to group together certain writings, and the paratextual material that frames them affect the way they are received. While we readily apply this principle to the study of how texts were received in antiquity, it is less common to think about its relevance to how we ourselves receive our ancient sources in their published form. But just as our picture of literature that became biblical is already predetermined by our experience of holding a Bible—specific texts mechanically reproduced and bound in a particular order between two covers—so the way the literature of early Judaism is mediated to us determines how we are likely to imagine its shape, intertextual relationships, and hierarchies. Collection and curation matter: which texts are grouped together and what paratextual materials frame them inform how these never-quite-raw materials are understood. How we imagine the shape of ancient literature depends in part on where they're kept on our *physical* shelves.

Because of the Bible's special cultural status, it is no surprise that the literature of early Judaism has always been, and primarily still is, collected and presented in distinction from and in relation to the biblical canon. Though this is obvious, it is still important to think more precisely about how publication practices have changed, and how they have contributed to the mental architecture through which we imagine early Jewish literature. My analysis here is necessarily selective: while there is no room for a comprehensive history of publication, I will highlight four key moments that influence and illustrate the development of our ideas about the shape of early Jewish literature.

Fabricius, 1713: Fabula, Fraudes, Pseudepigrapha

Our story begins in the eighteenth century. Johann Fabricius, a Lutheran antiquarian in Germany, published the first major collection of noncanonical texts under the title "Pseudepigrapha" in 1713.[40] Fabricius's work was part of the impulse to preserve and organize the great influx of knowledge that both Renaissance scholarship and the invention of the printing press had facilitated. But the publication of noncanonical texts was also religiously charged. Martin Luther had condemned these texts to be burned. Fabricius—as the librarian of a prominent Lutheran theologian—needed to present them in a theologically acceptable way.

But there was more to the problem. The very existence of ancient religious texts that were not biblical brought up difficult questions about the nature and boundaries of Scripture. These nonbiblical texts were about figures known from the Bible and revered in Jewish and Christian traditions. They claimed to transmit divine revelation. How can we be sure they didn't? Why weren't these texts included in the Bible? And who got to decide?

It was Luther's own changes to the biblical canon that had added fuel to such questions: he had redrawn the boundaries of the biblical canon, removing the deuterocanonical books or "Apocrypha"—texts like Judith and Tobit that are found in Catholic and Orthodox Bibles, but not in the Jewish Tanakh—from the biblical canon that is still binding in Protestant churches. This canonical reshuffling challenged the Catholic apostolic succession as the guarantor of Scripture;

now, criteria besides institutional pronouncements would be needed to support the stability and unity of the Bible. So, what is biblical about biblical texts? Besides relying on the pronouncements of churchmen, is there any way to tell biblical and nonbiblical books apart?

Fabricius's collection of the Pseudepigrapha *under that title* attempts to show that, even if they resemble each other in some respects, there is still a way in which biblical and nonbiblical texts are qualitatively different—that canonical divisions are based on a criterion other than church authority. That criterion is the authenticity of their attribution to their authors. The noncanonical texts are inferior because they are pseudepigraphic: Enoch did not really write *1 Enoch*, and Moses was not the author of *Jubilees*, and who could ever believe that Ezra wrote *4 Ezra*? In his introduction, Fabricius writes that he wants to show they are worthless forgeries, and to expose them to the "contempt of everyone." Annette Reed writes that the collection presents the reader with the information needed to "adjudicate their authenticity...to 'unmask' works that might otherwise be mistaken for scriptures with authority and antiquity akin to 'the Bible.'"[41]

Perhaps Fabricius protests too much. He was an antiquarian, not a theologian or apologist: he surely thought these texts were worth preserving and collecting. And his broader interest in forgery must have made ancient pseudepigraphic literature a beguiling object of study. But because the question of canonicity could be theologically volatile, he had to present the writings in a way that would neutralize their danger. Thus, the framing of these texts as worthless forgeries is a defensive move: it buttresses biblical stability and unity in the face of challengers who would question whether there are clear criteria that differentiate canonical texts from others. Fabricius attempted to safeguard the *qualitative* superiority of canonical texts by collecting the Pseudepigrapha as a group under that name, and presenting them as contemptible fraud, worthless trash compared to the authentic Bible.

To be sure, today, no modern critical scholar sees the biblical Deuteronomy, for example, as any more authentically Mosaic than *Jubilees*, so the distinction between "biblical" and "pseudepigraphic" texts is no longer made by criteria of authenticity. As we saw in chapter 2, the distinction between "Bible" and "Pseudepigrapha" as categories of texts is no longer based on the presence or absence of pseudepigraphy as a textual feature. But the categories, though now empty of their qualitative features, have persisted. Fabricius's collection and its title set a publishing precedent, and succeeded to a large degree in building thick walls between the Bible and its outsiders.

R. H. Charles, 1913: "A Vast Advance on the Old Testament"

The next major published collection—the *Apocrypha and Pseudepigrapha of the Old Testament* edited by R. H. Charles in 1913[42]—treated the sources rather differently. With the advent of historical-critical scholarship, no informed person believed anymore that texts like *1 Enoch* and *4 Ezra* were really written by biblical figures. It was no longer necessary to demonstrate they were not "authentic"; the "pseudo" in "Pseudepigrapha" had stuck. But while, for Fabricius, this reduced them to contemptible fakes that were worthless or even dangerous, in Charles's collection, the ethical resonance of the "Pseudepigrapha" label was completely different. For Charles, paradoxically, pseudonymity pointed to their *authenticity*: their real ethical, spiritual power.

How did false attribution become a marker of value and authenticity? The answer lies in supersessionist theology. This is a familiar scheme: according to stereotypical Christian supersessionism, the Judaism of the Second Temple period was spiritually bankrupt, its vitality shackled within a legalistic system. The law had a stranglehold on religious culture, and there was no more room for prophecy. The constraints of legalism quashed claims to new, living revelation.

But, in Charles's account, inspiration had not really died: it was only pushed underground. Second Temple apocalyptic writers inherited the best of the biblical prophets' "moral depth and inwardness,"[43] but in a rigid system of law and institutional control, they could not write in their own names; prophecy, according to the establishment, had come to an end.[44] Charles writes that "[a]ll Jewish apocalypses from 200 onwards were of necessity pseudonymous if they sought to exercise any real influence on the nation; for the Law was everything, belief in inspiration was dead amongst them, and their Canon was closed."[45] True spiritual insights, then, required false attribution. Since authentic inspiration was antiestablishment, it had to go undercover.

But what about the relationship of the Pseudepigrapha to the Bible? If Fabricius had collected these texts to denigrate them and to distinguish them from their canonized counterparts, how does Charles present them vis-à-vis the biblical canon? Like all editors of pseudepigrapha collections until today, Charles assumes canonical priority—that biblical texts are already stable and established when these other works are written. But he does not assume canonical superiority, at least not for the canon of the Old Testament, which, in his theology, was quickly being surpassed. Charles writes, "If the Canonical and Apocryphal Books are compared in reference to the question of inspiration, no unbiased scholar could have any hesitation in declaring that the inspiration of such a book as Wisdom or the Testaments of the XII Patriarchs is incomparably higher than that of Esther."[46]

Again, this is part of a story of religious evolution. Apocryphal texts were superior to biblical Old Testament literature—because they are a sign of spiritual progress that culminates in the New Testament. Christianity inherits their ethical and spiritual richness, their apocalyptic energy, while rabbinic Judaism regresses into a dead tradition. Charles writes that the ethical teaching in noncanonical apocalyptic texts is "a vast advance on that of the O.T., and forms the indispensable link with the N.T. This ethical element is present also in Talmudic literature, but somehow it lacks the fire and inspiration that distinguish it in the Pseudepigrapha."[47] The valuation of pseudepigrapha as worth studying for ethical and spiritual reasons is part of an overtly supersessionist and anti-Jewish message. If Fabricius was presenting the texts as worthless vis-à-vis the canon, Charles was presenting them as a bridge between the testaments, an "intertestamental" library that illustrated the spiritual development from the Old to the New.

The most curious feature of Charles's publication of the *Apocrypha and Pseudepigrapha* is the presence of the rabbinic *Pirqe Avot*, "Sayings of the Ancestors," among his sources. This text is found in no other collection of Pseudepigrapha: it is not pseudepigraphic but anonymous, and having circulated as part of the Mishnah, it is part of the normative canon of rabbinic Judaism. But Charles includes this text to make a point about the ethical evolution of Judaism and Christianity. He explains outright why it is there: "in order that the student might have before him the best that Later Judaism produced in the domain of Ethics."[48] The message is that *Pirqe Avot* was the best that rabbinic Judaism could manage: in terms of spiritual "fire and inspiration," it represented a degeneration from the religious vigor of the "intertestamental" texts that was then most fully developed in the New Testament.

Between Fabricius and Charles, we see a radical change in the way that the noncanonical texts of early Judaism are evaluated—a completely different assessment of their significance and authenticity as religious literature. But both collections show that the practice of publication is an act of creating a library. Both build their library as a separate edifice from the biblical, and use the Bible as the touchstone not only for categorizing but also for evaluating other texts.

Charlesworth, 1983 and 1985: "The Heritage of Both Jews and Christians"

We move now to the 1980s, which saw the publication of two major collections of nonbiblical texts from the Second Temple period. By then, the Dead Sea Scrolls were transforming biblical scholarship, as well as the study of early Judaism and Christianity. A new picture of a textual landscape not yet unified into a Bible was emerging, but slowly. By the time of Charlesworth's *Old Testament Pseudepigrapha* (1983, 1985) and Hedley Sparks's *Apocryphal Old Testament* (1984),[49] the work of integrating the Dead Sea Scrolls into a new picture of early Jewish literature was only beginning.

Sparks self-consciously claims continuity with Charles, and the assumption of canonical priority is unexamined in the publication.[50] In the interest of space, however, here I will focus on Charlesworth's *Old Testament Pseudepigrapha*, which has remained the standard collection for students of the Pseudepigrapha, and which Robert Kraft has called the "bolder and brasher" of the two collections.[51] The publication contains a wealth of reflection on its own methodology and its departures from its precursors, making it a rich source for studying change in how our sources are framed.

In Charlesworth's volumes, we are worlds away from Charles's editorial framing from 1913, at least when it comes to the supersessonist message the texts are collected to present. Charlesworth's publication presents the same materials in a radically different way: rather than demonstrating the superiority of Christianity, they are ecumenical, the shared heritage of both Jews and Christians. Indeed, the very production of the volume itself is the result of collaboration between modern Jewish and Christian scholars, a fact mentioned several times in the introductory material. And it is not only scholars but also nonacademic readers from the two traditions who are the intended audience of the collection, as we can see from the "Foreword for Christians," "Foreword for Jews," and "Foreword for the General Reader" that precede the collection. In his "Foreword for Jews," Samuel Sandmel writes:

> A complete turnaround in the approach to the Pseudepigrapha in the last decades has been most gratifying. These writings have become the object of study for their own sake, part of the wish to illuminate the totality of the Jewish creativity of that bygone age. The recent scholarship has not tried to make the literature fit into a procrustean bed for some parochial purpose. The cooperative study enlisting the gifted minds of Christians of various denominations and Jews of varying backgrounds is surely as moving and exciting a development as any cooperative academic venture could be. How gratifying that cooperative study is reviving this literature. How much such study contributes to understanding the richness of the Jewish legacy, now the heritage of both Jews and Christians.[52]

If Fabricius called the texts contemptible frauds, and Charles presented them to support Christian supersessionism, Charlesworth's volumes celebrate them as a treasure trove of the religious imagination and as a site of ecumenical potential (even as they retain the specifically Christian term "Old Testament").

We can see in this paratextual material a multiplicity of interests and audiences that complicates the way noncanonical texts are published and studied. For what purpose are these texts to be used? Are they collected for scholars of religion, for theologians, or for religious audiences? It seems to be all of the above. In his general introduction, Charlesworth finds it necessary to write that these writings "are not gathered here in order to replace or add to those scriptures considered canonical by Jews or the larger collections claimed to be canonical by various groups of Christians."[53] At the same time, the writer of the "Foreword for Christians," James T. Cleland, suggests that a text like the Prayer of Manasseh should actually be used as Christian prayer, assigning it normative value beyond historical interest.[54]

There is, then, a significant blurring of purposes here: the collection attempts to speak to all of its audiences at once, whether they use the texts for historical understanding or to make religious meaning. But this confusion is also positive. The Charlesworth volumes do not assimilate all the Pseudepigrapha into any single agenda—they are not collected, as in Fabricius, to be denigrated whole-sale as forgery; neither are they displayed as evidence for Christianity's spiritual superiority. Indeed, Sandmel's comment that they "have become the object of study for their own sake, part of the wish to illuminate the totality of the Jewish creativity of that bygone age," does reflect something important about the collection, at least when it comes to its self-presentation.

There is also an acknowledgment that the very category of "Pseudepigrapha," dependent as it is on the boundaries of the biblical canon, is problematic. Charlesworth uses the term as a matter of convention. But he does recognize the risk of anachronism in separating "Bible" and "Pseudepigrapha": "to call the Pseudepigrapha 'non-canonical,' or the biblical books 'canonical,' can be histori-cally inaccurate prior to AD 100. ... It is potentially misleading to use the terms 'non-canonical,' 'canonical,' 'heresy,' and 'orthodoxy' when describing either Early Judaism or Early Christianity."[55]

And yet this caveat does not change the approach. Canonical priority is still assumed, and the Bible continues to set the agenda for the collection as a whole and for its individual contributions, giving the strong impression that early Jewish creativity was organized around a protocanon. Robert Kraft already pointed this out in his 1988 review: the assumption remains that

> "OT" precedes "Pseudepigrapha" and becomes the standard by which to recognize and with which to compare the forms and contents of the latter, e.g., "the Pseudepigrapha illustrate the pervasive influence of the OT books upon Early Judaism" (xxviii), "the traditions in the OT pro-vided the framework and most of the presuppositions for the following testaments" (773). "Early Judaism was a religion bound to and defined by the Book, the Torah. ... The biblical narratives were clarified, en-riched, expanded, and sometimes retold from a different perspective" (2.5, introducing the section called "expansions" of "OT" and legends).[56]

The texts in the collection are satellites circling the Bible, which is their source and model. "This sort of approach," Kraft continues, "tends to preclude the possibility of recognizing in the 'expansions'…materials that may predate, or be independent of, what came to be the 'biblical' tradition."[57]

For Kraft, imagining the literature of the Second Temple period along canonical lines is not only a problem because it is an anachronism, and anachronisms should in principle be avoided. It is also a problem because keeping such mental architecture in place makes it difficult to imagine these texts in any other configurations. Writings may also be grouped according to interests like the periodization of history, which might include, say, Daniel, *Jubilees*, and Josephus; or generic categories like hagiography, which might include a range of biblical and nonbiblical materials. It is time, Kraft writes, to abandon the "obfuscating traditional and/or theological structures"[58] that keep ancient writings in categories that their producers and early readers would not have recognized.

Kugel, 1997; Feldman, Kugel, and Schiffman, 2013: When the Forger Became an Exegete

Finally, we turn to the newest collection of early Jewish literature: *Outside the Bible: Ancient Jewish Writings Related to Scripture*[59]—the largest collection to date, and the most beautifully presented. What kind of library does *Outside the Bible* present to its readers, and how does it fit the story we have told? Before we turn to the collection, I want to point out that it belongs to a tradition of reading early Jewish texts that has been popular since at least the 1990s: we now tend to encounter noncanonical texts as biblical exegesis. I have discussed this framework in the first part of this chapter; here, I place it in the ongoing history of the reception of Second Temple literature and discuss how it has also informed the newest collection.

The paradigm is most vibrantly expressed in the work of James Kugel, especially *The Bible as It Was* and its expanded version *Traditions of the Bible*, and more recently *How to Read the Bible*.[60] Kugel's work is remarkable not only for its brilliant close readings but also because it brings the entire range of available sources into a theory of how Jews read and wrote. For Kugel, the return from the Babylonian Exile brought a new phase in literary production: the rise of interpretation. In the postexilic "Age of Interpretation," scribes, priests, judges, and teachers—a diverse group that Kugel dubs "the Ancient Interpreters"—now read their inherited texts in a distinctive way that was shared across linguistic, sectarian, and eventually religious boundaries. These ancestral texts, identified by Kugel with the Bible, particularly the Torah, were now being read *as Scripture*: they were considered divinely inspired and fundamentally relevant to human life, full of moral instruction and hidden meanings. While on the surface, the ancient scriptures were often literarily inconsistent and lacked obvious "moral lessons," exegetical work could reveal the divine truths they held.

For Kugel, this "interpretative revolution"[61] turned a mass of ambiguous or even contradictory writing into a coherent sacred text, a divine rulebook. It was the work of the Ancient Interpreters of the postexilic period that made "the Bible biblical."[62] And it is primarily in the Apocrypha and Pseudepigrapha that we find evidence for this work: these texts "allow us to reconstruct in some detail how the Bible was read and understood during this crucial period."[63]

But to return to the issue of collection and publication: how are the texts of the Second Temple period curated for consumption? Here, the formal structure of Kugel's popular publications is crucial to his theory. In *The Bible as It Was* and *Traditions of the Bible*, Kugel goes through the Torah in order, beginning each chapter with a summary of a biblical episode. Then, he mines noncanonical literature, from the Second Temple period but also from rabbinic Jewish sources and late antique Christian ones, for short passages that are related to that episode, resolving their ambiguities and contradictions, and embellishing the often laconic biblical accounts. Short excerpts from a range of nonbiblical sources, from *1 Enoch* through Philo to Augustine, are gathered together around the biblical passages they respond to, with editorial commentary.

This is a powerful move. By presenting a biblical lemma at the beginning of each chapter, followed by fragments of commentary from different sources, Kugel has created a collection that, formally, has a great deal in common with rabbinic midrash. This arrangement also replicates the dialogical structure of midrashic literature: the diverse interpretations of rabbis from different generations, arranged to follow the biblical passage and introduced by the editorial phrase *davar aher*, "another interpretation." Here, it is the Ancient Interpreters who are in a cross-generational and cross-linguistic conversation about a shared textual tradition.

This arrangement illuminates much about early Jewish reading. We see how microform interpretive motifs recur in texts of different genres and languages, suggesting a cultural matrix of shared traditions that is only partly reflected in the surviving sources. And in an important corrective to the tendency to see Greek-speaking and Hebrew- and Aramaic-speaking Judaism as intellectually distinct traditions, Kugel shows the deep affinities between them in the way they related to their textual past.[64]

But in the very way this presentation is structured, we encounter a literary world that is already shaped like the medieval and modern Bible. Short excerpts from the noncanonical texts are clustered around the biblical texts and respond to them, filling in their gaps and smoothing out their contradictions. The result is a new picture of the Bible, mostly the Pentateuch, harmonized, embellished, and illuminated. This is a matter of modern shaping, not the way the ancient texts themselves were configured. The texts from which the interpretive excerpts are taken and grouped according to their relationship to biblical passages do not, for the most part, present themselves as exegesis, but as stand-alone compositions with multiple sources and their own genres and concerns.

This model tells us a great deal about how biblical interpretation emerged in an atomistic, nonlinear way. But scholars who want to describe what the literary world was like in the period *before* the Bible was an available structuring category risk being misled by this bibliomorphic presentation. We need to work to dismantle the biblical architecture that has always structured our experience of the sources, because, as Kraft, Reeves, Reed, and others remind us, we can no longer assume biblical centrality and priority as a given for Second Temple authors. This is the work, as John Reeves writes, of "re-embedding 'the Bible' among, as opposed to prior to, its alleged derivatives."[65]

We can now return to the latest published collection of nonbiblical early Jewish sources, *Outside the Bible*. This monumental collection was edited by Kugel, Louis H. Feldman, and Lawrence H. Schiffman, and the scholarly interests and approaches of all three scholars have shaped the final product. Feldman's scholarship has focused on Greek-speaking Judaism, most notably Josephus, including a particular interest in his modes of rewriting and interpreting the biblical text.[66] Schiffman has done extensive work on early Jewish liturgy and law, and an important part of his oeuvre has searched out continuities and discontinuities between Qumran and rabbinic Judaism, especially *halakhah*.[67]

How does this collection fit into the story I have told about shifting ways to frame and value nonbiblical texts—from Fabricius's denigration as forgery, Charles's supersessionism, and Charlesworth's vague ecumenism? *Outside the Bible* advances the conversation in an important way: it has dropped "Pseudepigrapha" not only as a title but also as an organizing category. Besides those writings commonly gathered under this name, the collection also includes named authors Philo and Josephus, as well as parts of the Septuagint. This gives a richer account of the literary world of early Judaism and does not create categories based on the criteria of authorial attribution, which is only one of many ways literature can be grouped.

But one thing stands out in the collection: its explicitly biblical shaping. The collection converges around the Bible, and many texts are presented as biblical exegesis. Its subtitle is *Ancient Jewish Writings Related to Scripture*. And the titles of the collection's subsections present many of these texts specifically as interpretation: "Sustained Biblical Commentaries," "Greek Jewish Interpreters," "Interpretive Texts Centering on Biblical Figures," "Stories Set in Biblical and Early Post-Biblical Times." The morphology and horizons of the collection are coextensive with the Bible. Texts that are not "exegesis" but separate literature that shares characters with the Bible—such as the Enochic texts—are included under the genre of biblical "commentary" or "interpretive texts." This is part of the collection's goal to stress the Jewish context of the texts, and to posit continuity: the

texts' relationship with the Hebrew Bible before them, and rabbinic interpretation after. Structurally, the collection presents them as a kind of bridge between
two canonical corpora, the biblical and the rabbinic.

Using the Bible as an organizing principle is deliberate. It is not a matter of
unquestioned presuppositions, but of conscious choice. The editors reflect on
the principles that governed the framing of the collection:

> Organizing the wide variety of materials presented a particular challenge....
> To sort materials by more or less traditional categories (Apocrypha,
> Pseudepigrapha, Hellenistic writings, Dead Sea Scrolls), we felt, would
> only perpetuate the fragmented perception of these writings as the sin-
> gular products of isolated Second Temple Jewish writers. To classify
> them primarily by literary genre...would risk missing a central feature
> that unites most of these documents—their prevalent stylistic and the-
> matic connection to Hebrew Scripture. Therefore, we have arranged the
> selections in a way that highlights their closeness to the Hebrew Bible,
> starting with actual translations, then moving to various types of bib-
> lical commentary and rewritten biblical narratives, and proceeding
> from these to laws, liturgies, and rules for living drawn from the lan-
> guage and themes of the Hebrew Bible.[68]

What unites these texts, what makes them into a coherent library, is their closeness to—and dependence on—the Bible. Thus, the editorial framing of *Outside
the Bible* assimilates the noncanonical texts *inside* the Bible's contours and authority. The collection puts the sources in an order that reflects this shaping: it
begins with translations, and proceeds outward in diminishing degrees of closeness to the biblical text, presenting a literary world that is shaped like the Bible
and its emanations. The Bible is the collection's governing principle more explicitly than it was for Charles (1913) or Charlesworth (1983, 1985). As critics like
Kraft have pointed out, those publications *assumed* the biblical as their touchstone. *Outside the Bible*, instead, asserts it explicitly.

I have traced a story of publication that began with forgery and ended with
exegesis. That is, for Fabricius in 1713, the writers of the Pseudepigrapha were
frauds: their works might look like biblical texts, but they are in fact worthless
fakes that must be exposed. But in the latest collection, and for much scholarship
on the Second Temple period today, the forger has become an interpreter. The
same writers have become brilliant exegetes of Scripture, and the texts are celebrated as a valuable window into the earliest Jewish Bible reading.

In this way, the writers of early Jewish noncanonical literature have been re-
deemed. But they have also been neutralized. In fact, while the 1713 and the 2013
collections value the noncanonical texts in opposite ways, they have something

crucial in common: both respond to challenges to the stability and unity of the Bible, and effectively bolster biblical boundaries. For Fabricius, such challenges come from Luther's redefinition of the canon and challenges to church authority, and the increased availability of texts thanks to printing; for contemporary scholarship, the challenge has come largely from the publication and study of the Dead Sea Scrolls and the new scriptural world they revealed. The eighteenth-century collection defends biblical boundaries by collecting these texts under the title of forgeries and separating them from the canon; the 2013 volumes do so by integrating them into a history of exegesis and fitting them within canonical horizons, so they can take their place on the shelf as a precursor to midrashic interpretation.

What can we learn from historicizing how we have published and judged the texts? Collecting primary sources is an act of creation and shaping—no less when modern scholars do it than when ancient ones did. The very act of making sources usable *requires* taking them out of context and arranging them in ways that may never have been possible for their writers and earliest readers. Each publication constructs a library, giving it a specific shape and character. These collections are not raw data. Implicitly or explicitly, each presents an argument about the sources it makes available.

We can see that the current paradigm in the field—that the major literary activity of early Judaism revolved around interpreting, embellishing, or rewriting Scripture—is not a raw reading of the sources, but the latest moment in a longer history of reception. Once we realize that such a model both illuminates and constrains our reading of the ancient texts, we can try to tell the story in alternative ways.

Jubilees as Bibliography: A Native History of Written Revelation

In the rest of this chapter, I use the book of *Jubilees* as a case study for how this might be done. Likely written in the early second century BCE, *Jubilees* had been known to Western scholars in Ethiopic translation before approximately fifteen Hebrew manuscripts were found at Qumran. The book is framed as an angelic revelation to Moses of the history of Israel and the teachings that are inscribed on the heavenly tablets, during his forty days on Sinai. The story follows the biblical narrative, from the creation and primordial history through the Exodus, although it also uses *1 Enoch* 6–11 for the account of the fallen angels. James Kugel describes it as "arguably the most important and influential of all the books written by Jews in the closing centuries BCE."[69]

In some ways, *Jubilees* seems like a contrarian choice for "debiblicizing" our picture of Second Temple literature. After all, *Jubilees* is a parade example of both

"rewritten Bible" and "biblical interpretation." Already called "Little Genesis" by
Christian writers of late antiquity,[70] *Jubilees* is one of the very texts that originally
inspired Geza Vermes's definition of "rewritten Bible." The book presents a sustained reworking of biblical narrative, following the text of Genesis and Exodus
closely, often verbatim. Kugel describes it as "a treasure-house of ancient biblical
interpretation, composed by an unknown author who thought deeply about the
Torah and Judaism....Although it retells much of the material in Genesis and
Exodus, its retelling is accompanied by all sorts of new information designed to
answer questions about the biblical narrative."[71] For an audience interested in
the way biblical interpretation developed, *Jubilees* is indeed a treasure house of
embellished and harmonized versions of familiar biblical episodes. Its interaction with Genesis sheds important light on the process by which older traditions
were transformed and brought forward, and shows what this important writer
found compelling and troubling about the biblical text.[72]

But *Jubilees* is a text with its own purposes and integrity, and a narrow focus
on what it shows about exegesis of the Bible obscures the fact that *Jubilees* is both
participating in and presenting a literary world that is not configured in relation
to the Bible. It presents itself as immediate revelation to Moses, not an interpretation of a prior one, and evidence for the reception of *Jubilees* shows us that this
claim was taken seriously.[73] The Qumran *Damascus Document* cites *Jubilees* as an
authoritative source with the same introductory word as its reference to the Law
of Moses, putting these sources "in a strict parallel":[74] "Therefore, one will
impose upon <him>self to return to the law of Moses, for in it all is defined
(מדוקדק). And the exact interpretation of their ages about the blindness of Israel
in all these matters, behold, it is defined (מדוקדק) in 'The book of the divisions
of the periods according to their jubilees and their weeks'" (CD 16:2–4).[75]
Jubilees is presented as a source in a horizontal, not a hierarchically lower or derivative, relationship with Mosaic Torah. And it even generated its own tradition of reworking, found in compositions scholars have called *Pseudo Jubilees*
(4Q225–28).[76] It later enjoyed a prolific career in translation in Christianity, and
as I discuss in the next chapter, it is considered part of the canon of Scripture in
the Ethiopic church.

But even if we did not have evidence for its reception, seeing *Jubilees* through
the lens of exegesis and rewriting illuminates only an aspect of its compositional
process, and takes little account of its own claims. John Collins emphasizes that
"[w]hile much exegetical activity undoubtedly went into the composition of
Jubilees, it is not presented as an exegetical text."[77] While such labels are, as Hindy
Najman writes, adequate for understanding aspects of *Jubilees*, they are "inade-
quate for characterizing the book as a whole."[78]

Using such designations to organize whole texts into groups depends on anachronistic canonical boundaries their earliest readers would not have recognized,

and assumes the most important aspect of these texts is their relationship to, and what they illustrate about, the Bible. As one example of an alternative, Najman suggests considering *Jubilees* within the genre of prophecy: this would focus more on what *Jubilees* claims for itself and how its understanding of revelation and mediation can be compared to other texts, whether they are now in the Bible or not.

A comparison with another example may show more clearly in what ways the category of "rewritten Bible" can apply to *Jubilees*, and in what ways it falls short. The book of Deuteronomy recasts a large portion of the laws in Exodus with its own perspective and focus, as the writer of *Jubilees* recasts the biblical narratives in Genesis and Exodus to solve some of their problems and speak to his own set of concerns. Thus, we might call Deuteronomy an early example of "rewritten Bible"—although it is not, in fact, rewriting Exodus and Numbers *as we have it*, since it is widely agreed that the base of Deuteronomy was not aware of the P-source.[79]

Deuteronomy is indeed a new text that recasts existing authoritative traditions to speak to a new audience.[80] But when we consider the narrative frameworks of each text, an important difference emerges between the way Deuteronomy and *Jubilees* are framed. Deuteronomy presents itself explicitly as a *recapitulation* of past revelation—Moses's farewell speech at the end of the wilderness wandering that couches itself as a review or reminder of what God had revealed earlier, on Sinai. This is, as we have seen, reflected in the Greek title *deuteros nomos*: repeated or second law.

But *Jubilees* does not position itself as an echo. Instead, it places itself with Moses on Sinai, within earshot of the angels, and claims to transmit freshly revealed material. Indeed, it is *prior* to the revelation of the Torah of Moses, pitching itself as, in David Lambert's term, *prewritten*, not rewritten.[81] This does not mean that it denies other revelations have happened before it: on the contrary, it situates itself in a long line of revealed texts that date back to Enoch. But unlike Deuteronomy, *Jubilees* does not claim to be *based on* or *derived from* the memory of earlier revelation. It presents itself as a report of immediate revelatory events, newly dictated to Moses by the Angel of the Presence, and based not on any earthly writing, but derived directly from angelic revelation and the heavenly tablets.[82] In *Jubilees'* epistemology, as Annette Reed notes, "heaven [is] the ultimate source for all true knowledge."[83]

Jubilees begins with this prologue:

> These are the words regarding the divisions of the times of the law and of the testimony, of the events of the years, of the weeks of their jubilees throughout all the years of eternity as he related (them) to Moses on Mt. Sinai when he went up to receive the stone tablets—the law and the

commandments—on the Lord's orders as he had told him that he should come up to the summit of the mountain.[84]

Jubilees, then, places itself on Sinai, where other revelations—the law and the commandments on stone tablets—were also given. Scholars have long debated about what precisely *Jubilees* means by these different categories of revelation—the torah, the testimony, and the law and the commandments on Moses's stone tablets, as well as the precise contents of the heavenly tablets invoked later in the chapter and throughout the narrative. I will not relate the details of these debates here.[85] But it is important to note that the idea of testimony—witness or warning—is a key function of the purpose *Jubilees* states for itself. The Angel of the Presence later tells Moses that he must write everything down—the entire history of the world—as written proof that humans have been duly instructed about the law, and cannot claim ignorance when they are punished for transgressing it.

If *Jubilees* claims direct angelic revelation and the heavenly tablets as its sources, how do we understand its relationship to its actual precursors, Genesis and Exodus? *Jubilees* does not seek to replace the texts that are now part of the Pentateuch, but neither does it merely seek to interpret them.[86] It refers explicitly to the "first law" (6:22 and 30:12), but it does not present this first law as its own source, or as the pinnacle of revelation. Indeed, the first law cannot be properly understood without *Jubilees*, which provides its primordial matrix. Anders Klostergaard Petersen shows this with the laws for observing Shavuot, which the Angel of the Presence says can be found "in the book of the first law in which I wrote for you that you should celebrate it at each of its times one day in a year. I have told you about its sacrifice so that the Israelites may continue to remember and celebrate it throughout their generations during this month — one day each year" (6:22). The first law is affirmed, but "did not suffice";[87] according to the perspective of *Jubilees*, people were following the wrong calendar, and needed correction based on what had always been written on the heavenly tablets.

Thus, *Jubilees*' relationship to its historical precursors, to the "first law," is neither subservient nor hostile. To ask the question about whether a new text intends to *replace* or merely *interpret* the Torah of Moses is already to assume a particular way of imagining the shape of sacred literature: the idea that it must be arranged around a single center. In this model, a nonbiblical text can either claim to take over the central, preeminent place or it can place itself in a derivative position in the service of the central text, as interpretation. But the prebiblical imagination was not structured this way. Scriptures took their place alongside other scriptures; proliferation was a value. And we can see this most clearly from the narrative presentation of *Jubilees* itself.

Jubilees as a Native Theory of Sacred Literature

As we have seen, *Jubilees* uses both canonical texts (Genesis and Exodus) and noncanonical works (*1 Enoch*) as sources. It recognizes the existence and authority of the "first Torah." But though *Jubilees'* author had these texts at hand, his imagined library is far larger. *Jubilees* does review past revelations: but unlike Deuteronomy, the revelations that *Jubilees* reviews cannot be identified with the texts found in our Bible.[88]

Instead, *Jubilees* presents us with a parade of "bookish heroes,"[89] from the first human writer, Enoch, through Moses's writing on Sinai. Revealed books of different genres populate the narrative. The focus on writing in *Jubilees* is strategic, because writing functions as testimony that vindicates the judgments of God. A statement of what writing is *for* can be found near the very beginning of the book, when the angel says to Moses:

> 1 [5] Pay attention to all the words which I tell you on this mountain. Write (them) in a book so that their offspring may see that I have not abandoned them because of all the evil they have done in straying from the covenant between me and you which I am making today on Mt. Sinai for their offspring. [6] So it will be that when all of these things befall them they will recognize that I have been more faithful than they in all their judgments and in all their actions. They will recognize that I have indeed been with them.

Moses's writing is to serve as evidence of God's continuous attention to Israel. What Moses must write includes narratives about all the other ancient writing heroes—Enoch, Noah, Abraham, and Jacob—and the written sources each figure transmitted to future generations. This way *Jubilees* makes an unshakable case that God had been communicating with Israel in writing since the beginning of the world, and continuously through the ages. Given the text's focus on who wrote what, when, and why, it seems that one of this author's goals is to gather, put into order, and describe all the written texts he knows, has heard of, or imagines must once have existed.

In this way, one of the many kinds of work that *Jubilees* does is the work of bibliography—listing and describing all the written texts that might be relevant to the author's subject matter. The writer is recognizable in D. F. McKenzie's description of the modern bibliographer or book historian, who is occupied with "texts as recorded forms, and with the process of their transmission, including their production and reception."[90] To be sure, the modern category of "bibliography" is hardly what we find in *Jubilees*. But historically, there have been different ways of thinking about recorded form and transmission, from Mesopotamian catalogs of authors[91] to the cryptic references to a *sefer ha-yashar*, "book of Jashar" or "Book of the Upright" in the books of Joshua and Samuel (Josh 10:13, 2 Sam 1:18). References to recorded texts and their transmission populate the narrative of *Jubilees*; but many are vague, and cannot easily be identified with specific books now available to us. While some perhaps refer to books now lost (like writing associated with Noah), others (like the visionary writing of Jacob) may refer to legendary texts that never existed, or represent *Jubilees'* own addition to the imagined library of Israel.[92] And *Jubilees'* brand of bibliography does not come in the form of a list or catalog: rather than a separate genre, it is woven tightly into the plot. The history that Moses must write down in a book is itself, in part, a history of books.

In the final pages of this chapter, I read *Jubilees* as a native "book history," a "historical bibliography" as presented from the perspective of a second-century BCE writer. To take *Jubilees'* own self-presentation seriously, I argue, is not only to recognize that it claims revelation, rather than derivative status, for itself; it is also to recognize that it presents us with its own theory of its literary context and heritage.

This means setting aside some common driving questions of our field. The story about the origins of the Bible has been told and retold by scholars. In those narratives, we take the canonical collection as our point of departure, and we ask how the texts that are now biblical were created and gained authority, and how they were interpreted and collected in a corpus. Nonbiblical texts are considered part of *that* story because they testify to the biblical texts' earliest reception. But Second Temple writers themselves tell us a different history of sacred literature. If we set aside our modern, theologically and historically determined questions about the origins of biblical texts and their interpretation, we can attend to *Jubilees* as a guide to what the literary world of early Judaism *seemed like* to its author(s) and to those readers who found this work compelling. What idea of the origins, shape, and transmission of sacred writings does this text present? And how might this native theory inform the way we ourselves tell the story of early Jewish literature?

Jubilees' Book History: Enoch

Sacred writing begins with Enoch, the first human to learn to write:

> 4 17 He was the first of mankind who were born on the earth who learned (the art of) writing, instruction, and wisdom and who wrote down in a book the signs of the sky in accord with the fixed pattern of their months so that mankind would know the seasons of the years

according to the fixed patterns of each of their months. [18] He was the first to write a testimony. He testified to mankind in the generations of the earth: The weeks of the jubilees he related, and made known the days of the years; the months he arranged, and related the sabbaths of the years, as we had told him. [19] While he slept he saw in a vision what has happened and what will occur—how things will happen for mankind during their history until the day of judgment. He saw everything and understood. He wrote a testimony for himself and placed it upon the earth against all mankind and for their history.

We can see that one patriarch's writing is already multiform in nature. In this report, the first piece of human writing in the history of the world is astronomy, which teaches the proper calendar. The movement of the heavenly bodies is, of course, the focus of the Enochic *Astronomical Book*, now *1 Enoch* 72–82, which is introduced as a book based on what the angel Uriel showed Enoch.[93] Enoch's writing is also called a "testimony," *te'udah*, from the word for "witness," which is to serve as an indictment of human sins in the future—including, it seems, following the wrong calendar, which transgresses the divinely revealed structure that Enoch wrote down and left on earth. The writing of Enoch, then, includes not only the cosmic revelation he was shown by the angels but also an account of the future, which he sees in a dream vision. All this is part of the written "witness" he leaves behind.

But Enoch's writing does not end there—and for the writer of *Jubilees*, it has still not come to an end. Enoch, as we read in Gen 5:24, did not die, but was taken—and *Jubilees* relates this in greater detail:

> 4 [23] He was taken from human society, and we led him into the Garden of Eden for (his) greatness and honor. Now he is there writing down the judgment and condemnation of the world and all the wickedness of mankind. [24] Because of him the flood water did not come on any of the land of Eden because he was placed there as a sign and to testify against all people in order to tell all the deeds of history until the day of judgment.

Enoch is a human testimony, and his writing is perpetual. Later in the narrative, *Jubilees* relates that only Enoch lived longer than Noah, "because Enoch's work was something created as a testimony for the generations of eternity so that he should report all deeds throughout generation after generation on the day of judgment" (10:17).[94] In the imagined world of *Jubilees*, Enoch's writing was first—and it will also be last: his writing is an unfolding process that must march together with history, remaining unfinished until history itself comes to an end.

Enochic and Mosaic: Multiple Mediating Figures in *Jubilees*

How do we think about the multiple mediating figures in *Jubilees*—especially the elevation of Enoch in a text framed as Mosaic revelation? There has been significant debate over the social location of the textual traditions related to Enoch, since they seem to be unrelated to the Torah of Moses. Gabriele Boccaccini famously suggests that the literature related to Enoch came from a separate social formation, which he calls "Enochic Judaism," which was in tension and polemic with "Mosaic Judaism," for whom Moses was the major mediating figure and the Torah was the central textual authority. Boccaccini argues that the book of *Jubilees*, which draws heavily on Enochic traditions and sets up Enoch as the first writer, but within a Mosaic framework, was trying to reconcile two ideologically opposed movements into a new blended form of Judaism.[95]

But there is little evidence that would suggest that *literature* about Enoch necessarily came from a separate social group that revered that figure and textual tradition while rejecting others. Proponents of such a theory do not think that these groups were isolated from each other: they recognize the shared terms, for example, in which different mediating figures are described. These descriptions are presented as evidence of deliberate polemic, a kind of one-upmanship: communities set their own figure as the superior revealer and mediator by appropriating the terms used for a competing figure.[96] But why is shared descriptive language indicative of polemic between separate groups? The way in which, for example, David in 11QPsalms[a] is described in similar terms to Enoch—as an illuminated sage with calendrical knowledge—does not indicate the existence of a Davidic community polemicizing against the competing Enochic one.

There is a further issue here that has to do with deeper methodological presuppositions about what an interpretive community looks like: the model that it must be unified around a single, central textual core. This, as I have already shown, is also what the dominant picture of early Judaism as centered around "the Bible" or "the Torah" presupposes: a community that must have a unique textual fountainhead, which forms the source, goal, and touchstone for all other traditions. This unitary structure seems to be behind presuppositions of an "Enochic" Judaism that would be Mosaic Judaism's counterpart. According to such a model, the unitary and centralized traditions, focused around Enochic and Mosaic texts, come first, and then are subsequently blended together into a kind of hybrid in the book of *Jubilees*, which is able to integrate multiple figures into its tradition.[97] Indeed, the idea that Enochic traditions, since they do not mention Torah, must therefore come from a competing kind of Judaism presupposes that this competing Judaism already had its own unique and exclusive textual center.

While *Jubilees* does integrate literary figures and strands of tradition that do not typically appear together in other texts, this seems to be a factor of its literary strategy and scope.[98] What the author presents as impressive is the very multiplicity of books in the history he tells, and their constant rerevelation and renewal over time.[99] There is no focused center in this description of this bookish world; if anything can be considered the unique fountainhead of tradition and authority, it is the heavenly tablets, which serve as the anchoring authority of many (although not all) human writings, but contain more than any of those writings transmit on their own.

The model of competing communities focused around single figures is, then, dependent on a projection of postcanonical thinking on precanonical Jewish culture. I do not mean that the proponents of such a model believe the canon of the Bible already existed. Instead, I am suggesting that their model presupposes that revelation can only be conceived as embodied in a single, central location—in the persona of one inspired figure, if not one unified corpus of texts. But the idea of a revelatory body that is unified and centralized is a postcanonical one. Before the gathering of sacred texts into a corpus—a body—written revelation inhabited many locations, on earth and in heaven, and in lore about multiple heroes' lives. This includes not only the material dictated to Moses on Sinai but also the cosmic knowledge shown to Enoch and—as we will see—Noah's priestly and medical lore, Abraham's recovery of Hebrew books, the future as revealed to Jacob, and the books he passes down to his sons. Let us now move on to these other writing heroes.

Jubilees' Book History: Noah

Jubilees' next writing figure is Noah, who becomes a writer after the flood. First, he divides the earth between his three sons, recording their territories in a written document.[100] His sons "reached out their hands and took the book from the bosom of their father Noah" (8:11), and then *Jubilees* relates in great detail the precise geographical areas assigned "in the book" (8:12) to Shem, Ham, and Japhet. Writing ensures an "authoritative and lasting division of the land, forestalling future disputes,"[101] another kind of testimony for the future.

But an even more striking example of Noachic writing is enmeshed with the story of the fallen Watchers, although its genre and purpose is different from the writing of Enoch. According to *Jubilees*, after the flood the evil spirits are to be bound up (cf. *1 Enoch* 10:11–14 and 13:1–2), in keeping with Noah's request, but the wicked angel Mastema asks that God leave some demons free and at his command. One-tenth, then, are left unbound, free to roam the earth and threaten humanity. To counteract this danger, God asks one of the good angels to teach Noah the secrets of healing:

> 10 [10] He told one of us that we should teach Noah all their medicines
> because he knew that they would neither conduct themselves properly

nor fight fairly. [11] We acted in accord with his entire command. All of the evil ones who were savage we tied up in the place of judgment, while we left a tenth of them to exercise power on the earth before the satan. [12] We told Noah all the medicines for their diseases with their deceptions so that he could cure (them) by means of the earth's plants. [13] Noah wrote down in a book everything (just) as we had taught him regarding all the kinds of medicine, and the evil spirits were precluded from pursuing Noah's children. [14] He gave all the books that he had written to his oldest son Shem because he loved him much more than all his sons.

Here again, the source of an ancient figure's book is angelic knowledge. Just as astronomical knowledge was revealed to Enoch by angels, so here, too, angels teach Noah about the medicinal use of plants. This knowledge is protective: it is meant to keep Noah's descendants safe from the "diseases" and "deceptions" of the evil spirits. Noah writes what he is taught "in a book," but in the following verse we see that Noah has apparently written multiple volumes, for he gives "all the books that he had written" to his son Shem.[102]

Jubilees is not the only place where written texts are ascribed to Noah.[103] As we have seen, the *Genesis Apocryphon* has a reference to the "book of the words of Noah" that introduces a section where Noah, in first-person speech, relates the story of his life.[104] In the *Aramaic Levi Document*, the ritual rules that Isaac passes down to Levi are ascribed to "the book of Noah concerning the blood."[105] While these ritual laws are of a different genre than the medical and magical lore ascribed to Noah in *Jubilees* 10, later in *Jubilees* Abraham refers to books of Enoch and Noah as sources for priestly instruction (21:10).[106]

One important witness to Noah traditions is found in a much later manuscript—a medieval medical work, *Sefer Asaph ha-Rofe*, "The Book of Asaph the Physician."[107] Its introductory passage about medical revelation to Noah is quite reminiscent of *Jubilees*: here, too, one-tenth of Mastema's evil spirits are left to roam free and afflict human beings. The angel Raphael teaches Noah herbal remedies, and sends "the princes of the spirits who remained" (the evil spirits!) to show him medicinal plants "and to teach him all their curative properties for healing and for life" (10). Then, as in *Jubilees*, Noah "wrote these words in a book and gave them to Shem, his oldest son." According to this version of the text, Noah's revealed medical text becomes the source for subsequent knowledge: "ancient wise men copied from this book and wrote many books, each one in his own language" (11).[108] The precise relationship between *Jubilees* and *Sefer Asaph ha-Rofe*, dated centuries apart, is not clear; they may have drawn on a common source.[109]

Scholars are divided as to whether an ancient book of Noah really existed or is a literary fabrication.[110] A common argument against seeing references to a real book of Noah in these sources is the diverse kinds of material—ritual, medical, antidemonic, autobiographical, and geographical—that various sources ascribe to such a book.[111] But as Michael Stone has argued, there is no reason why only a single Noachic book could have existed, and at any rate existing works often do contain diverse kinds of material (Stone offers Deuteronomy and the *Book of the Watchers* as examples of such internally diverse texts).[112]

What we know for certain is that Noachic writing, in multiform genres, was part of the imagined library of some Second Temple writers, regardless of whether such a text had ever really been available. The idea that there were texts associated with a biblical figure that seem otherwise unrelated to the Bible, and that they were both divinely revealed and transmitted through the generations, is persistent and pervasive in the literary imagination.

But another part of Noah's story shows that writing can be found in unexpected places—and that it can be dangerous. One of the sons of Shem, Arpachshad, had a son named Kainan:

> 8 ² When the boy grew up, his father taught him (the art of) writing. He went to look for a place of his own where he could possess his own city. ³ He found an inscription which the ancients had incised in a rock. He read what was in it, copied it, and sinned on the basis of what was in it, since in it was the Watchers' teaching by which they used to observe the omens of the sun, moon, and stars and every heavenly sign. ⁴ He wrote (it) down but told no one about it because he was afraid to tell Noah about it lest he become angry at him about it.

Kainan comes upon writing by accident—ancient writing inscribed onto a rock, containing, it seems, the forbidden knowledge of the Watchers. He copies it and is led astray. Why is he afraid to tell Noah? Noah is that generation's keeper of sanctioned writing, passed down from the ancestors or revealed by angels.[113] But this bibliographically rich world contains dangerous texts as well, secrets inscribed long ago, waiting to draw unwary readers into their ancient power.

Jubilees' Book History: Abraham

After the oldest writings—the astronomical knowledge and testimony of Enoch and the medical and antidemonic work of Noah—the next figure in *Jubilees'* history of books is Abraham, or rather, Abraham's father, Terah. Thanks to the influence of Mastema and the demons who had not been bound up, humanity had again gone astray and the land was unfruitful. Abraham's grandfather Nahor settles in Ur of the Chaldeans, the land known for astrology. *His* father, Serug, teaches him "the studies of the Chaldeans: to practice divination and to augur by the signs of heaven" (11:8), which Nahor, in turn, passes down to Terah. Three generations of Abraham's ancestors are all presented as idol worshippers, but Abraham is perceptive:

> 11 [16] The child began to realize the errors of the earth—that everyone was going astray after the statues and after impurity. His father taught him (the art of) writing. When he was two weeks of years [=fourteen years], he separated from his father in order not to worship idols with him. [17] He began to pray to the creator of all that he would save him from the errors of mankind and that it might not fall to his share to go astray after impurity and wickedness.

Despite the writer's vehement condemnation of Abraham's entire family, it seems that Terah's divinatory and astrological education, at least, has its benefits: Terah is able to teach his son writing (11:16). While Enoch learns writing presumably from angels, Abraham is taught by an idolater. Later in *Jubilees*, Abraham draws on his ancestral education in observing the skies to predict rainfall, but his study of the heavenly bodies generates a realization unmediated by any revelatory experience: "All the signs of the stars and signs of the moon and the sun — all are under the Lord's control. Why should I be investigating (them)? If he wishes he will make it rain in the morning and evening; and if he wishes, he will not make it fall. Everything is under his control" (12:17–18).

How does Abraham make use of this skill in writing? After his realization of divine control, Abraham utters his first prayer to God, who answers with the promise of land, descendants, and blessing, as in Genesis. But then *Jubilees* adds a remarkable paragraph, narrated by the Angel of the Presence:

> 12 [25] Then the Lord God said to me: 'Open his mouth and his ears to hear and speak with his tongue in the revealed language'. For from the day of the collapse it had disappeared from the mouth(s) of all mankind. [26] I opened his mouth, ears, and lips and began to speak Hebrew with him—in the language of the creation.[27] He took his fathers' books (they were written in Hebrew) and copied them. From that time he began to study them, while I was telling him everything that he was unable (to understand). He studied them throughout the six rainy months.

The Angel of the Presence teaches Abraham Hebrew, the holy language of creation, which had been forgotten since the collapse of the Tower of Babel. It is only then that he can read, study, and copy the books of his father, Terah, who had apparently kept ancestral texts that nobody had been able to decode since the confusion of tongues.

In *Jubilees'* history of books, then, the recovery of Hebrew is a new revelation of scripture: the ancestral writings are, in a very concrete sense, revealed anew through the teaching of a lost language. Here, access to books is unlocked by angelic instruction, but not in an instant transformation, a wave of a magic wand. The renewed revelation is a process where both human agency and ongoing divine intervention are key: Abraham studies the books, legible now for the first time in generations, for a period of six months, while the Angel of the Presence stands by to explain what he cannot understand.

The time before the recovery of Hebrew—when the books were illegible—was a rupture in *Jubilees'* story of divine guidance through the repeated revelation and continuous transmission of texts. And the time when the books were unreadable—when they were, in the literal sense, "apocryphal," concealed in a lost language—was coextensive with violent and terrifying times, a world of blood, war, and idolatry. Thus, part of what the author of *Jubilees* claims to reveal in his new text is what can happen when ancestral texts are forgotten, when they remain unread.

But he also presents the possibility of recovery. The ancient writings were not given once and for all, but may be renewed through direct divine interaction: the Angel of the Presence not only teaches Abraham Hebrew but also becomes Abraham's guide as he studies the new, although ancient, texts.

Abraham's final testamentary speech invokes the written legacy of Enoch and Noah in the context of sacrificial law. Sacrificial meat is to be eaten on the day of the sacrifice and the next day, but on the third day, it is no longer acceptable: "[a]ll who eat it will bring guilt on themselves because this is the way I found (it) written in the book of my ancestors, in the words of Enoch and the words of Noah" (21:10).[114]

Priestly instructions are found in ancestral writings associated with Enoch and Noah, Abraham invokes them orally as he instructs his own descendants on his deathbed, and all this is found in the story the Angel of the Presence dictates for Moses to write down on Sinai. *Jubilees* becomes a metatext, crafting a recursive story of written transmission that constantly reamplifies divine script. Stories about writing testify to the constant renewal of divine communication with Israel's ancestors.

Jubilees' Book History: Jacob

The bibliographic history of Israel skips a generation: just as there are fewer Isaac traditions in Genesis, so too, in *Jubilees,* Isaac is a less prominent figure, and does not become a transmitter of sacred writing. Written revelation is next entrusted to Jacob.

The occasion for his revelatory scribal experience is his second visit to Bethel in *Jubilees* 32. In Genesis, Bethel is the place where Jacob has his iconic dream of

angels ascending and descending a ladder to heaven (Gen 28) and where he receives his patriarchal promise of land and descendants. He calls it the "house of
God" and the "gate of heaven," terms that must have been troubling to later readers from the perspective of deuteronomistic theology, in which only Jerusalem
was the proper site of the "house of God," the Temple, and Bethel was associated
with the temple of Jeroboam, which is depicted as idolatrous in the books of
Kings. *Jubilees* retells Jacob's Bethel saga in a way that solves this problem: Bethel
remains central to the Jacob cycle as a site of theophany and promise, and becomes the site of Levi's priestly investiture as well. But Jacob is explicitly prohib-
ited from building a sanctuary there through divine revelation.[115]

The multipart revelation comes immediately after we are told Jacob planned
to build at Bethel:

> 32 [16] During the next night, on the twenty-second day of this month,
> Jacob decided to build up that place and to surround the courtyard with
> a wall, to sanctify it, and make it eternally holy for himself and for his
> children after him forever. [17] The Lord appeared to him during the
> night. He blessed him and said to him: 'You are not to be called Jacob
> only but you will (also) be named Israel'. [18] He said to him a second
> time: 'I am the Lord who created heaven and earth. I will increase your
> numbers and multiply you very much. Kings will come from you, and
> they will rule wherever mankind has set foot. [19] I will give your descen-
> dants all of the land that is beneath the sky. They will rule over all the
> nations just as they wish. Afterwards, they will gain the entire earth, and
> they will possess it forever'. [20] When he had finished speaking with him,
> he went up from him, and Jacob kept watching until he had gone up
> into heaven.

The patriarchal promise, in this iteration, is a universal royal one. In addition, it
is here that Jacob is renamed Israel, the moment that he becomes the epony-
mous ancestor of a nation. This is a major difference from the version we see in
the book of Genesis, where Jacob's transformation into Israel happens when he
wrestles with the mysterious stranger at the Jabbok ford (Gen 37). This episode
is entirely missing from *Jubilees*.

While the first vision was a reiteration of the patriarchal promise, the second
part of the dream vision explicitly prohibits the construction of a sanctuary at
Bethel. It is here that we see Jacob's connection with writing:

> 32 [21] In a night vision he saw an angel coming down from heaven with
> seven tablets in his hands. He gave (them) to Jacob, and he read them.
> He read everything that was written in them—what would happen to

him and his sons throughout all ages. [22] After he had shown him every-thing that was written on the tablets, he said to him: 'Do not build up this place, and do not make it an eternal temple. Do not live here be-cause this is not the place. Go to the house of your father Abraham and live where your father Isaac is until the day of your father's death. [23] For you will die peacefully in Egypt and be buried honorably in this land in the grave of your fathers—with Abraham and Isaac. [24] Do not be afraid because everything will happen just as you have seen and read. Now you write down everything just as you have seen and read'. [25] Then Jacob said: 'Lord, how shall I remember everything just as I have read and seen?' He said to him: 'I will remind you of everything'. [26] When he had gone from him, he awakened and remembered everything that he had read and seen. He wrote down all the things that he had read and seen.

Jacob cannot build because Bethel is not the right place for a sanctuary. But this prohibition from temple building comes with a reward for Jacob: he gets to see the future of his descendants written on angelic tablets, and becomes a tradent of divine writing. As with Abraham's angelic Hebrew lessons that give him access to his father's books, the revelation of text to Jacob occurs in complex layers of divine and human activity. Jacob first sees the tablets in a night vision, but is told to write down everything he has "seen and read." Worried that he won't be able to remember everything he saw on the tablets, Jacob is assured that he can depend on a divine reminder, and indeed, he remembers everything when he wakes up.[116]

Jacob and his revelation of the future at Bethel stands as another episode in *Jubilees'* sacred bibliography. The evidence for Jacob as a transmitter of writing is not as rich in early Jewish sources as it is for Enoch, Noah, or Moses. But a few texts besides *Jubilees* may be aware of such a tradition.[117] One is the *Testament of Jacob*, a fragmentary Qumran manuscript in Aramaic (4Q537), which refers to reading tablets ("take the tablets and read everything"), revelations of the future, and priestly sacrifice. While Jacob is not explicitly named—the beginning of the text, which would presumably have included the name of the visionary, is missing—these themes overlap with *Jubilees'* portrayal of Jacob. Another hint of such a tradition is the *Prayer of Joseph*,[118] a text that likely dates to the first cen-tury CE but is known only from quotations by Origen. One of the fragments has Jacob saying, "I have read in the tablets of heaven all that shall befall you and your sons." Jacob is a visionary of heavenly written knowledge about the future.[119]

Jacob's relationship to writing in *Jubilees* is not limited to his own separate vision of the seven tablets. *Jubilees* takes care to place Jacob in continuity with his ancestors' writings. In its version of the story of Joseph, *Jubilees* relates that when Potiphar's wife tried to seduce young Joseph, he was able to resist because he remembered the Lord and the words which Jacob, his father, used to read, which were from the words of Abraham, that there is no man who (may) fornicate with a woman who has a husband (and) that there is a judgment of death which is decreed for him in heaven before the Lord Most High. And the sin is written (on high) concerning him in the eternal books always before the Lord (39:6).

Here, Jacob reads the words of Abraham, which reflect the "eternal books" of heaven, to his children. And Jacob's work of textual transmission, like Abraham's, continues even to his deathbed, when he passes on his books to Levi: "He gave all his books and the books of his fathers to his son Levi so that he could preserve them and renew them for his sons until today" (45:16).

Conclusion: Bibliography and Totality

Moses, too, must be part of the story of writing, since he is the one to write it. The Angel of the Presence tells Moses his own life story: though he is raised by Pharaoh's daughter, his father, Amram, teaches him to write (47:9).

But Mosaic writing on Sinai becomes the frame in which a wider world of written revelation, beside and beyond Moses, becomes visible. Genesis and Exodus form much of *Jubilees'* source material, but this matrix is used to tell the story of other writings. Scribal heroes populate the narrative, leaving behind texts that are divinely revealed and meant to last. Does *Jubilees* have a native theory of scriptures—a sense of how they are revealed and transmitted, and an idea of what they are for?

Divine mediation is inherently heterogeneous, taking various pathways through people and language, and ending up as written documents; once inscribed, these documents have their own lives as they are taught, invoked, and transmitted through time. While there is an emphasis on continuity from generation to generation, the precise origin and mode of transmission of revealed writing is different every time it is described. Angelic dictation and instruction, dream visions, inheritance, and learning a forgotten language all play a part in *Jubilees'* history of how scriptures are revealed and how they travel through time. Angels are the scholarly class: they instruct Enoch in astronomy and Noah in magic and medicine, teach Abraham Hebrew, show Jacob the tablets of history and ensure he remembers what they say, and dictate what Moses must write down. Many references to written texts lend authority to specific rules of purity and sacrifice (e.g. when sacrificial meat can be eaten, *Jubilees* 21:10). But when read together across the narrative, the story of writing in *Jubilees* makes a larger point: it highlights the multiple and multiform ways that God has communicated with Israel.

Thus, *Jubilees'* "book history" is key to the work's purpose. It serves as proof that God has been talking to Israel—in writing—forever. Moses must write this bibliographic history "in a book so that their offspring may see that I have not abandoned them because of all the evil they have done" (1:6); "this testimony will serve as evidence" (1:8) of Israel's guilt and God's continuous righteousness and constant communication—broken only when Hebrew was forgotten and the earth plunged into bloodshed, but reestablished again through Abraham's linguistic renewal and textual study. *Jubilees'* history is in large part a historical bibliography: the relationship between God and Israel is embodied in the writings that make up its imagined library.

This library is not biblical, and it does not claim totality. Instead, *Jubilees* presents a world of bibliographic mystery: not all the texts are easily identifiable, and none claim to be the entirety of what has ever been revealed. None transmit the entire contents of the heavenly tablets. Enoch's writing in heaven continues even to this day. And might more texts still be found, by chance, inscribed on rocks a long time ago? *Jubilees* tells of a long history of books, but gives only hints of what they say. The bibliographically enchanted world is full of writing that proves God's constant, multiform, and renewing communication, but the totality of that writing is only indexed, not collected as a central corpus. One thing that *Jubilees'* bibliography shows is that no library has collected "all the books in the world."

This chapter has shown that the mental architecture through which we understand the literary world of early Judaism is constructed by our ideas about the Bible as a complete and unified corpus, but also by the way our nonbiblical sources have been published—always framed in relationship to the Bible. But we can visit and learn to inhabit other structures, imagining our way into a world where sacred writing was shaped differently. What did the ancient authors' literary heritage seem like to them? We can see a world where revealed writing was not centralized in a single corpus but found in various locations, and where the history of inscription was a key part of the history of Israel's ancestors.

This was a time before sacred writing was conceived as a unified compilation with set contents and boundaries. The imagined library of sacred writing was vast and its catalog somewhat vague, with no established list or particular number of works that it could accommodate. But what happens when such lists and numbers emerge—that is, when we begin to see an awareness of what looks, to us, like a scriptural canon? When texts are gathered into a unity—when the Bible is finally complete—what happens to those texts that are left out of bounds? We will explore this question in the next chapter.

Outside the Number

Counting, Canons, and the Boundaries of Revelation

> The Sages said about David, King of Israel, that when he completed the
> Book of Psalms, he became proud. He said before the Holy One,
> Blessed be He, "Is there any creature in Your world that recites more
> songs and praises than I?" At that moment a frog appeared and said to
> him: "David! Do not become proud, for I recite more songs and praises
> than you. Furthermore, for each song I recite, I utter three thousand
> proverbs, as it says, 'And he spoke 3000 proverbs and his songs were
> 1005.'" (1 Kgs 5:12)
>
> —Pereq Shirah, *Introduction*

Introduction: When Haile Selassie Finished the Bible

Haile Selassie, besides being the emperor of Ethiopia, Conquering Lion of the
Tribe of Judah, and Elect of God, is also credited with completing the Bible.
Having asked church scholars to study the canon and write out the texts by hand,
he then reportedly pronounced the result "the complete Bible of Ethiopia."

This is no small claim: in the history of the Ethiopian Orthodox Tewahido
Church, Haile Selassie is the only authority on record to say any biblical collection was complete.[1] Did it take the messianic descendant of King Solomon to
finally close the Ethiopian canon?

The Ethiopian church is well known for recognizing a uniquely broad collection
of Scriptures. It is thanks to translations into Ge'ez that the books of *Enoch* and
Jubilees have survived intact, and these are included in the four-volume Ge'ez and
Amharic diglot that the emperor pronounced complete.[2] Also included in that
diglot are three books of *Meqabyan*, not to be confused with the books of
Maccabees. But Selassie's canon making is not binding for the church. No council has never officially defined exactly what texts constitute its Bible, and church
authorities have never followed the emperor's lead in ascribing completeness to
any existing Bible.[3]

And yet Ethiopian Christians universally recognize that there are eighty-one
books in the Bible. The most binding statement on the subject seems to be the

medieval Ge'ez canon law code, *Fetha Nagast, the Law of the Kings*.[4] *Fetha Nagast* cites the earlier collection *Sinodos*, which claims the authority of the apostles and early church councils. The code's second section is unequivocal: it presents the "Divine Books which must be accepted by the Holy Church and which are Eighty-One in Number." It lists only seventy-three.

What are we to make of this contradiction—the legal exhortation to accept a set number of books, with a list that doesn't add up? If the number eighty-one does not signify eighty-one items, what does it mean?

R. W. Cowley describes a number of later traditions that attempt to account for this discrepancy by enumerating some additional texts and dividing others into separate books. These attempts result in a "narrower canon"—found in "The Prayers of the Church" and printed in the diglot and Amharic Bibles commissioned by Haile Selassie—and a "broader canon"—found in an Amharic commentary on the Ge'ez *Fetha Nagast*. Most lists include *Enoch* and *Jubilees*—while the *Fetha Nagast* omits them, the commentary on the code defends their authority and explains their omission. The Ethiopian *Andemta* commentaries to *Jubilees* and *Enoch* both say that when the apostles gave the eighty-one books to Clement, they counted these books "in their hearts, but with their mouths they omitted to count [them]."[5]

To get to the sum of eighty-one, the narrower canon also divides Proverbs into two and counts Susannah as a separate book. This count is not standardized, and although the Ethiopian New Testament is the universal twenty-seven books, the "narrow canon" editions all have variations in how they divide texts to make the Old Testament add up to fifty-four. The "broader canon" arrives at the correct number of books by listing forty-six Old Testament books; the contents are essentially the same as the "narrow canon" Old Testament, but less fragmented, and including the work of Pseudo-Josephus (*Yosef Walda Koryon*). The New Testament, then, must add up to thirty-five. The eight books beyond the standard twenty-seven are *Sinodos*, comprising four books of ecclesiastical rules; the book of the Covenant in two parts; Clement; and the Ethiopian Didascalia (not the same as the *Didascalia Apostolorum*) to make up thirty-five New Testament books—although by another count, the necessary total of thirty-five is also reached by counting the eight parts of Clement as separate books, and omitting the rest.[6] These long texts are not included in printed Bibles and were, for a long time, barely available in Ethiopia at all.[7]

Such pious attempts to arrive at the correct number of books may seem arcane, but the same phenomenon persists in recent scholarship. Similar maneuvers have been attempted to arrive at Josephus's famous twenty-two-book canon. There, too, diverse lists have been suggested for what Josephus meant and what books, in what divisions, the first-century Jewish canon actually contained. In the Ethiopian example, however, it would be a mistake to say that any of the lists that add up to eighty-one is a representation of what the codifiers of the *Fetha Nagast originally meant*, or even more, what the actual Ethiopian canon *really was*. The number is its own entity—not the result of empirical counting of a preexisting set. Perhaps what this modern analogy can tell us, then, is that a fixed number of books, even one presented as legally binding, and the existence of a fixed canon do not necessarily coincide. What, then, do we do with these sources? If the number eighty-one and the legal exhortation denote closure, and the ambiguity about the identity of the eighty-one denotes openness, is the Ethiopian canon open or closed? And what might this suggest about the limitations of our concepts?

Attempting a study of the formation and contents of the Ethiopian canon in 1974, Cowley writes that he encountered several difficulties that stood in the way of answering his research question. Besides describing how the iconic number of eighty-one is reached in various ways, he also mentions that some of the texts on the various lists had never been printed in Ge'ez and are difficult to obtain, some of the listed titles do not uniquely identify particular books, and no church authority had ever called a Bible complete.[8]

More recently, interviews conducted separately by Leslie Baynes[9] and Bruk Asale[10] in the United States and Ethiopia have revealed more about how people involved with the contemporary Ethiopian Orthodox Tewahido Church understand this ambiguity. Baynes reports that Daniel Assefa of the Franciscan Institute of Philosophy and Theology in Addis Adaba says that "[y]ou have various lists and no one seems to be worried or to be preoccupied to have something definitive and normative."[11] Another informant, Emmanuel Fritsch, expert on Ethiopian liturgy, says that "there is no canon in the generally received sense; rather, there are various codices which include various books, not always the same, and the same names do not always indicate the same contents. It follows that I would not speak of a canon but of lists of books, lists which do not point in themselves of [*sic*] the nature of the reception of the various writings listed."[12] How, then, *are* the lists related to the reception of the actual texts enumerated there? Baynes reports that everyone she interviewed confirmed that *Enoch* and *Jubilees* were in the canon. But "no one, even those who described themselves as devout, could express further knowledge of them other than that fact."[13] There is evidence that these texts were used in the Ethiopian Church, but generally, the *fact* of their inclusion in a list seems to hold more significance than their contents.

"Most of my informants from the EOTC," Bruk writes, "couldn't exactly say whether the church has a closed or an open canon."[14] And no council or other authority has made a decision about which list—the narrow canon, the broader canon, or the variations of each—is correct. Bruk writes that

> in principle, any ancient scriptural book, which is coherent with the dogma of the church, can be part of the "canon." However, in practice,

the list of books which have potential to be part of the "canon" of scriptures, is limited to only those which are mentioned in the various traditional lists and the symbolic number 81. As a result, the church has never officially defined what constitutes a "canon" of scriptures nor fixed which books comprise this list. It is satisfied with the tradition of 81 books of "canon" as binding without interrogating the number or the value of the 81 and without worrying whether this number is either unambiguous or definitive.[15]

Counterintuitively for bibliographers, perhaps *all* the available ways of counting to eighty-one can be "correct." After all, don't they all reach the right number?

But this way of understanding numbers and imagining the contents of the Bible suggests a fundamentally different morphology of scripture from the one scholars take as given. Thus, what for Cowley was a "difficulty" in answering his research question seems to pose no problem for the people he sought to study. How might we use this example of a scriptural imagination, for which we have living informants, to illuminate the scriptural world of early Judaism? The Ethiopian example tells us that even our most basic questions about the shape of scriptural collections may rest on presuppositions alien to our sources. "What is in the canon?" and "is the canon open or closed?" are questions that the evidence—both the texts and the living informants—is literally unable to answer.

The concept of canon as a strict list of books is foreign to the scriptural imagination of the Ethiopian tradition. And so, Bruk argues, even if we agree that the "canon" of the Ethiopian church is fluid, "such a conclusion remains meaningless if it does not consider the deeper understanding of the canon by the EOTC. It represents no more than an understanding of the external appearance of the canon of the EOTC, but it does not include the historical and pragmatic position of the church itself."[16]

For the study of early Judaism, such claims, while perhaps not meaningless, are perhaps equally insufficient. A canon is not like a door that is either open or closed; in either state, the door is a stable, recognizable object. Not so with canons. But still, the major question in scholarship on canon formation has long been a chronological one: when was the Jewish canon closed? And before the canon, during the "canonical process," what books were authoritative?

In his thorough study *The Formation of the Jewish Canon*, Timothy Lim synthesizes the scholarship on these questions, evaluating arguments for when the canon was fixed. But he pays less attention to what the ancient sources would have recognized or not recognized about the question, and, when the concept of a fixed number of books *does* arise, what such a number might have meant to its creator and its audiences.[17] Josephus refers to twenty-two books; *4 Ezra* mentions twenty-four. This is the external appearance of a "canon." But what kind of limits do these numbers set, and what were their semiotic possibilities? How do they function in the context of the literary imagination and connect to the function of numbers in the ancient culture?

Intuitively, numbers mean precision and fixity, a certain *factness*—but this has not always been so obvious. For example, Mary Poovey, in *A History of the Modern Fact*, discusses how the connection between enumeration and factual knowledge emerged in history.[18] It was with bookkeeping and economic discourse in modern Britain, she argues, that numerical reporting became the privileged way of representing knowledge.

But this modern use of enumeration as fact—as neutral reports of observed particulars—is alien to the way numbers are used in discourses about sacred literature. The Ethiopic example shows that it is possible for a religious community to have a fixed number of books, even a sense of "the Bible," but not a set canon—instead, different lists that disagree with one another but still somehow coexist. But this is not only marginal trivia or a quaint exception. Indeed, in early Jewish sources that count revelation, I suggest that ambiguity and imprecision are the usual characteristics of such numbers. When they are counting sacred texts, numbers are not quantitative, but qualitative.

This numerical synesthesia forces us to radically rethink how we narrate the formation of the canon. What kind of evidence do references to numbers really give us about bibliographic history, if they are not necessarily at the service of an actual set? And whatever happened to Haile Selassie's pronouncement that the Bible was complete?

In the rest of this chapter, I investigate what numbers can do for our understanding of the ancient literary imagination, how counting books and compositions is related to establishing the boundaries of canon, and what those boundaries signify. This is not the same as asking what evidence we have for a fixed number of books and when. Rather, I begin with the literary resonance of how numbers are used in Josephus and in *4 Ezra*. In both cases, scholars widely recognize the typological nature of the numbers twenty-two and twenty-four, but for the most part, still continue to see them as a counting or identifying a precise set of items. I situate these so-called canonical notations in the context of other uses of numbers or quantities in these texts, such as Josephus's references to the "many hymns" of David or his praise of Solomon's 4,005 *books* of songs and sayings—instances that are less privileged, and sometimes made invisible, because they do not assimilate neatly into the history of the Bible. These numbers, however, have their own poetics, one that helps us see that a precise enumeration of books that comprise the complete divine word tends to be neither precise nor complete.

I then return to the case study that began this book, and consider the enumeration of psalms. While there are 150 psalms in the Masoretic canon, other reckonings exist, and help shed light on how textual unities and scriptural boundaries were imagined in antiquity. I present three snapshots: the 4,050 psalms of Qumran; the 151 psalms of the Septuagint, which names Ps 151 "idiographos" of David but "outside the number"; and Pss 151–55 in Syriac, which are also considered "outside the number," but certainly not outside the realm of revelation and authenticity. In the latter two examples, the numbers do enumerate specific texts, but the function of this enumeration is not to draw a boundary around divine inspiration—they do not signify completeness.

What is the payoff of studying the way people have counted holy texts? The existence of a strict number of books has long been one of the touchstones for determining when the canon was set. But Michael E. Stone identifies a tension "between the implications of the fixed numbers of books that appear about 100 CE (in Josephus and 4 *Ezra*) and the apparent fluidity of scriptural texts and collections." For Stone, this tension might be illuminated by asking whether, once there was an established collection, that corpus alone was "considered to contain authentic revelation from which all knowledge about the divinity derived, or were there other works that were considered also to be divinely inspired but were not in this special collection? In other words, does fixedness also imply exclusiveness of inspiration?"[19] Stone writes that this does not always seem to be the case, but that "writings could be viewed as venerated and even inspired and not be 'biblical.'"

But Stone does not go as far as showing how this dialectic between openness and closure might work, and it is not entirely clear whose definition of "biblical" he has in mind. I suggest that looking through the lens of counting and numbers, and their range of cultural meanings, might give us one good way into these questions. Rather than asking when the canon was closed or what it contained— questions that are raised for our own sake—I ask what these concepts or developments might have meant to ancient writers. When we ask when the canon was closed and what was in it, we are already presupposing a certain notion of what canon is, and what its closure implies for a literary culture—most often, that it fixes once and for all exactly what is scriptural, and that it is a stable and self-sufficient corpus. But this is not necessarily the case. Numbers do not limit revelation; the categories of "canon" and "inspired writing" are not identical, and— despite Haile Selassie—"the Bible" has rarely been complete.

Qualitative Numbers: Twenty-Two and Twenty-Four Books in Josephus and 4 *Ezra*

In the first century CE, a new phenomenon emerges in Jewish literature: a corpus of Jewish texts begins to be identified with a set number. Josephus refers to twenty-two books, and *4 Ezra,* roughly contemporary, mentions twenty-four; the traditional number of books in the rabbinic canon is indeed twenty-four, but both numbers appear in patristic reports of the sacred books of the Old Testament. Origen reports twenty-two, mentioning that this is the number of letters in the Hebrew alphabet (Eusebius, *Hist. eccl.* 6.25). In the preface to his Latin translation of Samuel and Kings, Jerome also writes that there are twenty-two books to reflect the Hebrew letters, but he knows the number twenty-four as well, where Lamentations is separate from Jeremiah and Ruth is separate from Judges. Jerome links that number typologically to the twenty-four elders in the book of Revelation. Another alternative is known to Jerome, but presented more explicitly by Epiphanius (*Weights and Measures,* 4): in addition to the twenty-two book reckoning, the Hebrew Scriptures can also add up to twenty-seven. This is also alphabetic, because it reflects the number of Hebrew letters if the five final letter forms are counted separately. The actual contents of patristic canonical lists vary from source to source. And even in the work of a single writer, the books can be rearranged and redivided to create various meaningful numerical patterns.

Clearly, the numbers that structure lists of sacred books are typological, which the patristic authors—but not their Jewish precursors—tell us explicitly. In what follows, I return to their earlier instances in first-century CE Jewish texts, generations before Origen and Jerome. Where the late antique Christian writers had specific lists of titles, albeit in differing versions, the earlier Jewish examples do not precisely enumerate which texts were supposed to add up to their iconic numbers. I will consider what these numbers signify in their earliest known contexts, and what this apparent evidence for the fixing of a set canon means when we consider it in the larger context of these writers' literary imaginations.

Josephus's Twenty-Two Books

At the beginning of *Against Apion,* Josephus criticizes Greek history and historiography: the Greeks are a recent people, and their record keeping has been broken and unreliable; the Jews, on the other hand, can trace their history much further back in time, through the unbroken historical records written down by prophetic eyewitnesses. He writes:

> [37] [T]he prophets alone learned, by inspiration from God, what had happened in the distant and most ancient past and recorded plainly events in their own time just as they occurred— [38] among us there are not thousands of books in disagreement and conflict with each other, but only twenty-two books, containing the record of all time, which are rightly trusted. [39] Five of these are the books of Moses, which contain

both the laws and the tradition from the birth of humanity up to his death; this is a period of a little less than 3000 years. [40] From the death of Moses until Artaxerxes, king of the Persians after Xerxes, the prophets after Moses wrote the history of what took place in their own times in thirteen books; the remaining four books contain hymns to God and instructions for people on life. [41] From Artaxerxes up to our own time every event has been recorded, but this is not judged worthy of the same trust, since the exact line of succession of the prophets did not continue.[42] It is clear in practice how we approach our own writings. Although such a long time has now passed, no one has dared to add, to take away, or to alter anything. (*Ag. Ap.* 1.37–42)[20]

But does this number mean that the Jewish canon was "fixed" in the first century CE, and if so, what are the implications of the existence of a canon for cultural ideas about writing and divine revelation?

While essentially all treatments of this passage mention that there is a typological quality to the number twenty-two, scholars nevertheless continue to debate about *which* twenty-two books these are. No consensus exists on exactly which books Josephus meant to reference, and how he counted them to reach his number twenty-two. The five books of Moses seem clear enough, although earlier references to Torah, while often identified with Pentateuch, do not seem to specifically imagine a five-book collection.[21] Three other genres—prophets, hymns, and instruction—bring the count up to twenty-two volumes, presented as ancient and unaltered, but Josephus himself does not seem particularly interested in telling us exactly which ones he means.

But what do we assume when we ask the question about which books Josephus meant? Presumably, behind this question is the desire to determine which books were *in the actual canon* of first-century Judaism. The idea that numbers must determine exact contents, however, is a misunderstanding. As the Ethiopic example makes clear, the number does not necessarily arise from a specific and fixed number of books—the number itself serves as an icon for completeness and structure, but does not necessarily reflect and identify an already existing set of specific items; that specific list may well be a secondary development, a response to the number itself.

Thus, the various attempts to count and redivide books of the Ethiopic corpus so that they add up to the correct canonical number do not uncover the "real" canon "behind" the Ethiopic *Fetha Negast*'s reference to eighty-one. Few people would make this claim. Why, then, are attempts to parse the Josephan number understood, on the contrary, as scholarly investigations to discover underlying historical facts? Perhaps because Josephus—and the number twenty-two, close to the eventual rabbinic canon of twenty-four and found in Christian patristic sources—stands in a direct line to "our" Bible, as it is understood by most Western scholars. There is more at stake for scholars in tracing the origins of "our" Bible in a historically precise way, while we feel more comfortable ascribing less "scientific" enumerative practices to a non-Western culture with an unfamiliar biblical tradition—and more comfortable remaining content with less "scientific" answers about the extent and contents of its corpus.

And thus, many scholars have taken Josephus's claim of the Jews' twenty-two books more or less at face value. For Steve Mason, the evidence of *Against Apion* seems unequivocal: Josephus "insists that the Judaean records have long since been completed in twenty-two volumes,"[22] and Josephus would not declare this publicly if it were not true. Mason, however, warns that there are too many variables and not enough evidence to exactly determine the shape and contents of Josephus's Bible. Indeed, Mason rightly says that we should not try to figure this out based on *Against Apion*: Josephus's remarks there "cannot be made, no matter how long we gaze at them, to designate standard enumerations of divisions within the first-century canon." Rather than specific divisions, they sketch, for Gentile readers, the genres of material that are found in the twenty-two books.[23]

For Menahem Haran, the reason why Josephus writes that there were only twenty-two Jewish books is because there actually *were*—perhaps not exactly twenty-two, but at any rate very few. "[I]t would be rather puzzling," he writes, "to reckon what would have motivated Josephus to claim that the Jewish books are few, had they in fact been many in number."[24] And there is no need for more: "In these twenty-two books," Haran writes, "the Jews find everything."[25] This is a classic understanding of canonicity—canon as an embodiment of all revelation, the source and the goal, and the self-contained repository of all sacred writing.

But Josephus himself presents evidence against such an understanding. Across his oeuvre, it is abundantly clear that he did not find everything in twenty-two books. He draws on a great variety of extrabiblical traditions in his writing, particularly the retelling of Israel's history in the *Jewish Antiquities*. But he also references a proliferation of other divinely inspired writings. In *Ant.*VIII.44, for instance, he describes a vast collection of Solomon's works. Drawing on the tradition in 1 Kgs 5, where Solomon "spoke three thousand proverbs, and his songs were one thousand and five" (v. 12), Josephus redefines Solomon's corpus to epic proportions: in this version, "Solomon composed *one thousand and five books* of odes and songs, and *three thousand books* of 'parables and similitudes'" (συνετάξατο δὲ καὶ βιβλία περὶ ᾠδῶν καὶ μελῶν πέντε πρὸς τοῖς χιλίοις καὶ παραβολῶν καὶ εἰκόνων βίβλους τρισχιλίας). Josephus also speaks of Daniel's "books" in the plural (*Ant.* X.267). While no parallel reference exists to David's "books," Josephus does say he "composed songs and hymns to God in varied meters; some he made in trimeters, others in pentameters" (*Ant.* VII.305), once again showing that Josephus's imagined literary world is densely populated.

The rejoinder to these examples seems obvious: these are hyperbolic, imaginative numbers, not referring to real texts. And so there is no real tension between the limited twenty-two books in *Against Apion* on the one hand, and on the other, Josephus's own use of noncanonical scriptures and his references to a myriad of other inspired writings. *Against Apion* takes precedence in our assessment of the facts on the ground, and it clearly stakes a claim for an established canon. Mason writes: "If we lacked the *Against Apion*, Josephus himself would offer a clear case for an open canon. But we *do* have the *Against Apion*, in which this same Josephus emphatically, and matter of factly, insists that the Judean records have long since been completed in twenty-two volumes."[26] Josephus's readers either did not notice or were not bothered by the apparent contradiction between the limited twenty-two books and the evidence that he imagined many others, some of which he may have known and drawn on in his work, and thousands more besides, somewhere beyond reach. Those numbers are imagined and hyperbolic, while *Apion* is matter-of-fact. For Mason, the scholarly concern with these apparent discrepancies says more about modern presuppositions about academic precision than about Josephus's point of view.

But in the question of what Josephus really thinks about the canon, there are other kinds of academic presuppositions at play—in particular, the difference in genre between the different kinds of numbers Josephus uses to enumerate revealed writing. Indeed, I do not think there is an irreconcilable contradiction between the twenty-two and the thousands of other books. But this is not because one is matter-of-fact and the other is imaginary. As Jonathan Campbell astutely points out, if we take Solomon's 1,005 and 3,000 books as hyperbolic, "it must then be asked why twenty-two in *Against Apion* 1.38 cannot be seen as symbolic,"[27] since it reflects the number of letters in the Hebrew alphabet. And yet twenty-two holds a privileged place, something that we might call "matter-of-fact"—it is a smaller number, therefore more realistic; and it is close to our actual enumeration of canonical texts.

But Josephus does not seem particularly concerned with precision, to the chagrin of generations of scholars struggling to make specific books add up to fit his number. The vague reference to "hymns to God and instructions for people on life" seems to suggest that the precise inventory is less significant than what the number represents. Perhaps Josephus had a specific list of texts in mind that matched his enumeration: we cannot know. Either way, he, like later writers, is one of many interpreters working to make sense of an iconic number that is conceptually prior to any specific list of books.[28] As with the symbolic number eighty-one in the Ethiopic example, it is the number itself, not what it counts, that reflects Josephus's textual values.

This number is rhetorically and poetically powerful in several ways. Its relationship with the letters of the alphabet is taken up in the book of *Jubilees*, where it is a principle both of the order of creation and of Israel's primeval narrative: "There were twenty-two chief men from Adam until Jacob, and twenty-two kinds of works were made before the seventh day. The former is blessed and sanctified, and the latter is also blessed and sanctified. One was like the other with respect to sanctification and blessing" (*Jubilees* 2:23–24).[29] The number twenty-two not only counts the letters of the alphabet but also structures nature and history; these are identical in "sanctification" and "blessing." In a world where twenty-two represents a perfect symmetry of the temporal and the material—different aspects of divine wholeness—it is an appropriate cipher for Josephus's claim about the written records of Jewish history. They are ancient, complete, exactly reflective of history, and sacred, identical "to the highest and oldest matters" (*Ag. Ap.* 1.37) revealed by God, "containing the record of all time" (*Ag. Ap.* 1.38), a perfect embodiment of these "with respect to sanctification and blessing."

And in even more perfect symmetry, the number helps Josephus argue for how "his own culture fulfills a cultural value of the opponent culture better."[30] Jonathan Campbell argues that his insistence on accuracy, antiquity, and a limited number reflects the values of Alexandrian scholarship, where textual stability was becoming important. Josephus presents a caricature of Greek literature as sprawling and contradictory, and sets up the limited list of twenty-two as a rhetorical weapon, without particular concern for its detailed contents. Guy Darshan goes further, connecting the number to Alexandrian practices of dividing the *Iliad* and the *Odyssey* into twenty-four books according to the Greek alphabet, alpha to omega.[31] Here, the division is typological, and is not dependent on actual practical requirements for dividing books, as, for example, the *Iliad* has far longer books than the *Odyssey*, but both are divided into twenty-four. Darshan explains how the two modes of counting twenty-two and twenty-four, in Josephus, *4 Ezra*, rabbinic literature, and church fathers, are adapted from the Alexandrian model for dividing the Homeric corpus. The difference, of course, is that the Homeric corpus exists *as* a corpus to be divided. In the Jewish case, it seems that it is the number as a symbol that comes first, only then, like the Ethiopian eighty-one, to be populated with specifics by other writers who are concerned with such precision.

For Josephus, the flavor of the number twenty-two is one of completion and coherence, a quantitative expression that is qualitative in meaning. How, then, is this number related to Josephus's assumptions or direct claims elsewhere about many more scriptures? To review some terms of the debate: for Mason, twenty-two is a matter-of-fact statement about what Josephus thought the Jewish canon was like, while the other numbers, like Solomon's 4,005 books, are imaginative and hyperbolic, and there is no real contradiction.[32] Campbell, against Mason, writes that both sets of claims are symbolic, and attempts to determine how they are related. His solution is that they simply do not represent two parts of a coherent system that need to be somehow reconciled: the claim in *Against Apion* is peculiar only to Josephus's last work, and is formulated as a rhetorical, not factual, statement that is directly in conversation with Alexandrian scholarship. He writes that

> it is unnecessary to conflate all Josephan statements about Scripture on the assumption they constitute a coherent whole devoid of hyperbole or inaccuracy for fear of contradiction.... [I]f so, the need to appeal to excessive contrasts between ancient and modern sensibilities to reconcile the irreconcilable within the primary data is removed. We are not constrained to maintain that Josephus believed in a twenty-two book canon that somehow contained thousands of works or in a long-fixed text that he or others nevertheless felt free substantially to alter.[33]

Campbell's point about Josephus's apparent inconsistency is important, and we can go even further to explain it from the point of view of rhetoric and poetics. The tensions he presents are more comprehensible if we think of the synesthetic possibilities of what numbers can do. If the numbers are performing a poetic, not a bibliographic, function, both 22 and 4,005 can coexist in the mind of the same author, because they are expressing different values. Twenty-two means completion, organization, symmetry with creation, and coherence with Greek values. Four thousand and five means a profusion of revelation, the overwhelming productivity of an ancient sage. They are aesthetic and poetic, not bibliographic statements, and so do not need to "add up." The two kinds of numbers illustrate a tension that Roger Chartier has identified at the heart of text collecting: the tension between the exhaustive and the essential—between the value of comprehensiveness and the value of selectivity.[34]

Josephus gives us a sense of closure and enumeration as an expression of values, but this closed corpus does not contain everything within in. Revelation exists, or at least once existed, outside the boundaries of a closed corpus. While the criteria of self-sufficiency and totalization seem to be key features of canonicity,[35] we must now think about a wholly new way of understanding canon—as an entity that is *not* necessarily defined as a self-sufficient corpus that contains everything within it, that embodies the fullness of revelation. This question of what exactly canonical boundaries are supposed to contain or limit is the subject of the rest of this chapter.

4 *Ezra's* Twenty-Four and Seventy Books

The other source universally cited as evidence for a canon around 100 CE is *4 Ezra*, an apocalyptic text written in the aftermath of the Roman destruction in

70 CE, but set in the Babylonian Exile. Where Josephus has twenty-two books, 4 *Ezra* mentions twenty-four.[36] But what does this number mean for the scriptural imagination and the meaning of the canon in early Judaism?

The narrative is set in the aftermath of the Babylonian destruction in 586 BCE, and features seven visions revealed to the character Ezra, who both builds on and reimagines the biblical Ezra first known from the books of Ezra-Nehemiah. In that earlier incarnation, Ezra is a scribe and specialist in the law authorized by the Persian Empire to lead the community returning from exile, reestablish them in Judah, and rebuild the Temple. In a key passage that illustrates the textual reconstitution of the community (Neh 8), Ezra acts as a new Moses: he stands up on a wooden platform, high above all the men, women, and children—"all who could understand what they heard" (v. 2)—and he reads all day long from a "scroll of the law," which his assistants go around explaining to the entire community. The Torah—whatever precisely that meant for the writer of Ezra-Nehemiah—is presented here as an authoritative and interpretable text, serving as a symbol of both divine and imperial authority, an icon of continuity with an ancient past, and a blueprint for a community's future.

But the reimagined post-70 CE Ezra is more complex, and his relationship to textual tradition more ambivalent. Rather than appearing fully formed as the Persian-backed leader of the returnees, this Ezra undergoes a spiritual transformation, from the pit of despair to heavenly ascent. Ezra appears in the first chapter, set thirty years after the destruction, lying alone in his bed in distress; Job-like, he laments the injustice of God and the suffering that has befallen his city. Significantly, he despairs that in the wake of the Babylonian destruction—a cipher, of course, for the Roman destruction in 70 CE—and the ensuing loss of meaning, the older textual traditions no longer seem relevant or accessible: "the Torah of our fathers has been made of no effect and the written covenants no longer exist" (4:23).[37] Indeed, "thy law has been burned" (14:21); God's plan for the people is inscrutable, and there is no more basis for communal existence.[38]

Ezra's divine interlocutor, the angel Uriel, never quite answers his questions of theodicy, and barely engages Ezra's inquiries into the nature and meaning of the Torah. But gradually, as Ezra is told to fast and isolate himself and experiences a series of apocalyptic visions, he is steered away from his lonely despair. A major turning point in the narrative is Ezra's dialogue with a mourning woman, who is then transformed before his eyes into a dazzling heavenly city. The overwhelmed seer then enters a liminal, deathlike state, and by the end, his interlocutor is no longer a mediating angel but God himself. God tells Ezra that he will be "taken up" to be with "those who are like [him]" (14:9)—apparently other enlightened, angelified beings.

But there is a final vision before Ezra's ascent: the rerevelation of the holy books that had been burned in the destruction. Ezra drinks a cup of fire, and in forty days of ecstatic speech, dictates to five scribes who write "in characters they did not know" (v. 42):[39]

> 14 [44] So during the forty days, ninety-four books were written. [45]And when the forty days were ended, the Most High spoke to me, saying, "Make public the twenty-four books that you wrote first and let the worthy and the unworthy read them; [46] but keep the seventy that were written last, in order to give them to the wise among your people. [47] For in them are the springs of understanding, the fountains of wisdom, and the river of knowledge."

This reference to twenty-four books, the actual number of books in the rabbinic canon and a number that appears in many patristic sources as well, is taken as the other piece of explicit evidence for a closed canon of the Bible in the first century CE. But once again, "neither system—twenty-four or twenty-two—reflects the *precise* number of the biblical compositions."[40] The number twenty-four—the number of the public books, for the worthy and the unworthy—may reflect the Greek alphabet rather than the Hebrew. And seventy, the number of the secret books meant only for the wise, is a typological number that represents completion. Neither twenty-four nor seventy, writes Bruce Longenecker, should be "understood as a literal signifier of the accumulated texts."[41] The number seventy is used also in the narrative of the translation of the Septuagint—and earlier, for the number of nations and languages (Gen 10–11), the members of Jacob's family who went to Egypt (Gen 46:27), and the elders who accompanied Moses (Num 11:16). As Hindy Najman writes, "[i]f twenty-four represents the minimal number of units with which every meaningful utterance may be formed, then seventy represents the totality of the world."[42]

Leaving aside the typological quality of the numbers, what, according to this writer, is the ontological status of this putative canon of twenty-four books? One way to read *4 Ezra* is to see the rerevelation of the Scriptures as the culmination of the narrative: it is, after all, the final vision, and the rewriting of the Scriptures happens in dramatic fashion, with liquid fire, ecstatic speech, and forty wakeful nights. And Ezra, in other traditions—biblical, rabbinic, and patristic—is prominently identified as the promulgator of Torah in a way that is second only to Moses,[43] so it seems natural to think of the rerevelation of the holy books to Ezra as the pinnacle of *4 Ezra* as well.

But such an absolute privileging of Scripture does not seem to fully reflect this writer's ideas. The twenty-four books of Scripture are only one part of *4 Ezra*'s revelatory world. If we no longer assume that everyone had always found the biblical to be the full embodiment and pinnacle of revelation, things begin to look somewhat different: indeed, the twenty-four books emerge as a basic form of revealed text, but not as the culmination or fullness of divine communication. First, the revelation of Scripture happens not on God's initiative, but on Ezra's, who asks for it as his final request. As he is about to be taken up to be with "those who are like [him]," he asks:

14 [20] "[B]ut who will warn those who will be born hereafter? For the world lies in darkness, and its inhabitants are without light. [21] For thy law has been burned, and so no one knows the things which have been done or will be done by thee. [22] If then I have found favor before thee, send the holy spirit into me, and I will write everything that has happened in the world from the beginning, the things which were written in thy law, that men may be able to find the path, and that those who wish to live in the last days may live.

God accepts Ezra's request and the burned books are revealed again. But this is not the culmination of the narrative, but a favor God grants to make the world livable in its remaining days. These books are meant as a testimony for those who are left behind—not as the embodiment of divine truth or the height of revelation, but as a life raft for the remaining community before the approaching end.

Thus, when we move on from considering *only* what the number twenty-four indicates for the closure of the biblical canon, and consider the meaning and status of these twenty-four books in the textual imagination of *4 Ezra*, a new landscape of writing and revelation emerges. The locus of the highest revelation is not textual: it is Ezra's discourses with the angel Uriel, then directly with God, and finally his ascent to heaven. Writing comes next: in chapter 12, Ezra has already been instructed to write his revelatory dreams and their angelic interpretations in a book that he is to teach to the wise. Then there are the seventy secret books revealed to Ezra in the final vision—"For in *them* are the springs of understanding, the fountains of wisdom, and the river of knowledge" (14:47); and last, the twenty-four, for the worthy and the unworthy.

While Ezra retains his identity here as the postdestruction revealer of Torah, this Torah is not an object of interpretation. The revelation of the Scriptures is indeed an ecstatic, inspired process and makes Ezra an even more exalted figure, but it does not go hand in hand with an interest in communicating or interpreting their textual contents. In fact, quite the opposite is true. Amid the crowded interpretive landscape of *4 Ezra*—interpretation of visions, of dreams, and of angelic speech—the exegesis of Torah is absent. While Ezra asks many questions about the Torah, none of them receive answers; in the first few visions, the Torah is unintelligible. And the fourth vision—the mourning woman who becomes a heavenly city and marks the turning point in Ezra's transformation—begins with Ezra fretting about the problems of the Torah; but then he "turns away from the thoughts with which [he] had been occupied" in order to interact with the woman in the vision (9:39). This, it seems, is what occasions Ezra's transformation into a different kind of religious subject, one who turns away from trying to untangle the problems of the Torah and stops asking unanswerable questions, in order to acquire a different kind of divine knowledge.

Scholars of religion have written widely about the dialectic between tradition and innovation, between the desire to claim eternal truths and ancient pedigree and the challenge of changing historical circumstances. This is particularly salient in the study of canons, which claim unchangeability but must nevertheless adapt to changing needs in order to remain viable. One model, which I discuss further below, is that the finite contents of a religious canon can adapt to new contexts through exegetical creativity. At times when "the scriptural canon was faced with historical circumstances that threatened its viability,"[44] exegesis makes it possible for the canon to be revived and adapted. But in *4 Ezra*, where the Torah had become unavailable or unintelligible, it is not exegesis that is the solution, but entirely new revelation, beside and far beyond any established canonical corpus.

Beyond Psalm 150: When King David Finished the Psalter

Both Josephus and *4 Ezra* do present us with a limited, enumerated corpus of scriptural texts, twenty-two or twenty-four books. But in neither text is it clear which texts are meant; in fact, it does not seem as if these writers are particularly interested in such bibliographic information. Both numbers are typological, reflecting certain qualities, rather than quantities of precise and preexisting texts. But even more significantly, neither text understands this "canon" to be the fullness of revelation, and neither works within its limits.

My final major example of textual limits and enumeration returns us to the case of psalms transmission, and shows another way to challenge our typical understanding of canonicity and the so-called canonical process. How does the enumeration of psalms, and the emergence of a standard collection of 150 compositions, fit into our story?[45]

In one sense, both Jewish and Christian tradition indicates that the canonical psalter ends with Ps 150. The canons of the Council of Laodicea (363–64) are often said to have defined and limited the canonical psalms to 150, but this is misleading. Canon 59 reads Ὅτι οὐ δεῖ ἰδιωτικοὺς ψαλμοὺς λέγεσθαι ἐν τῇ ἐκκλησίᾳ, οὐδὲ ἀκανόνιστα βιβλία, ἀλλὰ μόνα τὰ κανονικὰ τῆς καινῆς καὶ παλαιᾶς διαθήκης ("Let no private psalms nor any uncanonical books be read in the church, but only the canonical ones of the New and Old Testament"). Canon 60 then provides a catalog of these canonical books (it lists Baruch and the Epistle of Jeremiah, but excludes Revelation), and includes a note on the number of psalms—Βίβλος ψαλμῶν ρν', "the book of 150 psalms." But Canon 60 is absent from various early witnesses and from Syriac translations, suggesting that the catalog was not original to the council, but rather appended later.[46]

Our witnesses to a standard collection of 150 psalms in late antique Christianity are not official conciliar pronouncements, but the evidence of early Septuagint codices themselves. As I discuss in detail below, these manuscripts recognize the number 150, but in fact include 151 compositions; the variations in how scribes handled this discrepancy shows that the nature of the Psalter's boundary was not completely settled.

Even in the fairly standardized Masoretic tradition, where the text and sequence of the Psalter are uniform, there is variation in how the psalms are counted. The Codex Leningradensis, the oldest complete biblical codex and the basis for the BHS, presents Pss 114 and 115 as one, and counts 149 psalms, numbered up to קמט in the middle of the column above each composition.[47] This variation is easily visible in our printed Bibles, which print the "standard" number 150 in Arabic numerals next to the final psalm, placing it in obvious tension on the page with the "anomalous" Hebrew number 149.

But the evidence from medieval manuscripts shows that this may not be anomalous after all. In a study of over four hundred medieval Psalters, William Yarchin traces a surprising flexibility in how psalms were divided and numbered.[48] He shows that, in fact, the majority of the manuscripts do *not* reflect our familiar division into 150 psalms, but configure the compositions in a variety of ways, with counts ranging between 144 and 156 textual units. Yarchin does not see standardization until the advent of movable type—the print publication of the Mikraot Gedolot, the Rabbinic Bible, in 1525, and with it the beginning of mechanical reproduction of the Psalter. The number 150 itself, then, was not always the gold standard.

But to return to antiquity: one scroll from Masada, MasPsalms[b], does end with Ps 150, suggesting that a collection with an ending (but not necessarily a size) matching the later Masoretic Psalter did exist around the turn of the eras, although it was far from the only option. I have already discussed the unbounded nature of psalms collections in the Second Temple period, based primarily on the finds from Qumran. As I demonstrated in chapter 1, the Qumran manuscripts do not preserve a "Psalter," but a variety of psalms collections with diverse extents, inventories, and arrangements, and there is no evidence of an established number of 150 psalms. The longest psalms scroll, 11QPsalms[a], contains about 50 compositions, including 10 noncanonical pieces, and presents them in a radically different order from the biblical Psalter. What is now known as Ps 150 does not close the collection, but is followed by Ps 134, Ps 140, several nonbiblical compositions, and a version of the Hebrew *Vorlage* of Ps 151—a composition about David as the least of his brothers, and his praise with musical instruments, previously known in several languages, including Greek, Syriac, and Arabic, but not in Hebrew.[49] There is no counting of psalms to define their boundaries— rather, an organically expanding and morphing collection.

I have already discussed "David's Compositions" in 11QPsalms[a], which uses numbers in a different way. David, scribe, sage, and psalmist, writes 3,600 psalms, 364 songs for every day of the year, 52 songs for the Sabbath, 30 songs for special festivals, and 4 songs for exorcisms, for a total of 4,050. This reckoning does not place limits on collections or try to enumerate specific compositions. Instead, it presents us with an array of numbers that at once represent two ideals: over- whelming proliferation and cosmic precision. These numbers are typological— they reflect the days, weeks, and months according to the solar calendar, and they link David to an earlier tradition about Solomon's 4,005 sayings and songs (1 Kgs 5:12; David, with 4,050 compositions, comes out ahead).

Here, like the twenty-two created things and the twenty-two patriarchs in *Jubilees*, numbers are means of tapping into both the structure of the universe and the history of Israel. Far from drawing boundaries around specific collec- tions, the huge number of songs ascribed to David throws open the scope of possible revelation. The profusion of divinely inspired psalms is *almost* beyond number—a vast heavenly archive that may be reflected in only piecemeal, partial ways in whatever collections communities might actually know and have. The text praises David for his character and his acts, which include writing num- bered, but effectively countless, compositions. In this quantitative poetics, number is a cipher for innumerability.

Things change when we move to the Greek tradition, where we find aware- ness of a limited psalms collection of 150 compositions. That number draws boundaries, and—unlike the Ethiopic canon of 81, Josephus's 22, or *4 Ezra's* 24 books—actually refers to identifiable, specific compositions that are numbered using Greek letters in the margins of the manuscripts. But even as 150 is the es- tablished number, Greek Psalms manuscripts actually contain 151, including the composition about David's musical instruments also found in Hebrew in 11QPsalms[a]. And the Greek superscription to Ps 151 presents us with a puzzle:

οὗτος ὁ ψαλμὸς ἰδιόγραφος εἰς δαυιδ
καὶ ἔξωθεν τοῦ ἀριθμοῦ
ὅτε ἐμονομάχησεν τῷ γολιαδ.

This is the version in the fourth-century Codex Sinaiticus, and shared, with minor variation, across the Greek manuscript tradition. In some other manu- scripts, the notation that the psalm is "outside the number" is followed by a fur- ther clarification—"outside the number of 150 psalms." Another variation occurs in the phrase οὗτος ὁ ψαλμὸς ἰδιόγραφος εἰς Δαυιδ. Most standard interpretations of this line translate comparably to the NRSV—"This psalm is ascribed to David as his own composition."[50] Albert Pietersma, however, translates more faithfully to the literal Greek: "This psalm is autographical. Regarding David,"[51] reflecting the ambiguity of the preposition εἰς, whose basic meaning is "for" or "to." In Codex Alexandrinus, εἰς is replaced with the genitive τοῦ, seemingly to clarify a possessive, authorial relationship—a writing *of* David.[52]

Despite these variations, the ἰδιόγραφος and ἔξωθεν τοῦ ἀριθμοῦ superscription is a shared paratextual layer that *both* signals Ps 151 as a Davidic writing *and* explicitly excludes it from a standard collection. In other words, the scribe who wrote this superscription recognizes an established number of 150 psalms— here, a specific set, not an ideal number; at the same time, he pointedly asserts the presence of an authentic Davidic composition beyond that corpus.

But there is a second layer of variable paratextual features in the manuscripts that shows how scribes negotiated this psalm's ambiguous status: the actual marginal numbering of the psalm, and the brief colophons that follow the Psalter. The major Septuagint codices—the Vaticanus, Sinaiticus, and Alexandrinus— each present these features differently.

While the other psalms are numbered in the margins, both the Codex Vaticanus and the Sinaiticus stop their numbering at Psalm 150, without giving a number to what we call Ps 151. Vaticanus (fourth century) includes a notation after Ps 150, which says Βίβλος ψαλμῶν ρν'—the Book of 150 Psalms. The scribe of Codex Sinaiticus (fourth century; figure 5.1) gives us a different presentation: while he, too, omits the number 151 from the margin, it does appear after the composition, in the colophon to the Psalter: "the 151 psalms of David."

Interestingly, we find the opposite combination of features in the Codex Alexandrinus (fifth century; figure 5.2). There, the colophon asserts the primacy of the 150-psalm collection, reading "150 psalms and the idiograph." But this manuscript numbers the "idiograph" with the same scribal system as the rest of the psalms, continuously from 1 through 151. It also contains a letter of Athanasius, who speaks unequivocally about this psalm as a Davidic composition that should be recited in times of strife. What is the relationship between this psalm and the canonical ones? It is clearly labeled a Davidic writing; it is attached to an event in the authoritative figure's life; it is worthy of copying in luxury biblical manuscripts, and recommended for prayer by a patristic authority. But yet it is clearly outside the number.[53]

In the Syriac tradition, not only Ps 151 but also four more compositions fit the category of authentically Davidic, but outside the pale. Conventionally titled the "five Syriac apocryphal psalms," these compositions have long been known from medieval manuscripts, both biblical and pedagogical. With the discovery of 11QPsalms[a], Ps 151 and two more of these five Syriac compositions turned

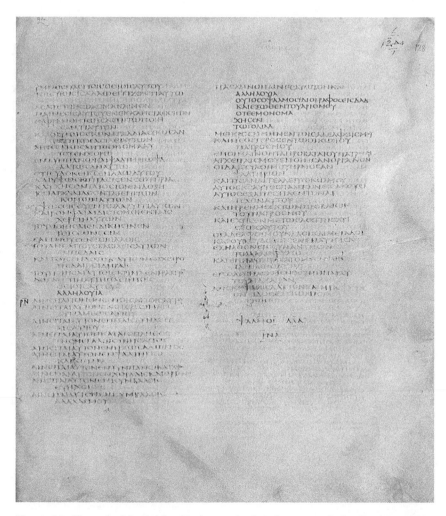

Figure 5.1 The end of the Book of Psalms in the fourth-century Codex Sinaiticus. The colophon to the Psalter reads "the 151 psalms of David," although the numbering of each psalm in the margin ends at Ps 150, with Ps 151 left unnumbered. (c) The British Library Board, Codex Sinaiticus, folio 128 r.

up in Hebrew originals, which had been lost for centuries. In the Qumran manuscript, these compositions do not appear as a unit. They have nothing in particular in common, and are in no way distinguished from the other psalms, either scribally or thematically, but are simply collected, undifferentiated, with other psalmic compositions. But Syriac scribes, working with a model of a 150-psalm collection, invariably consider the five compositions as a separate group.

While the Septuagint gives us only a laconic statement about a Davidic idiograph that is outside the number, some Syriac scribes are more forthcoming about how they understand these inspired-but-not-canonical compositions. Most

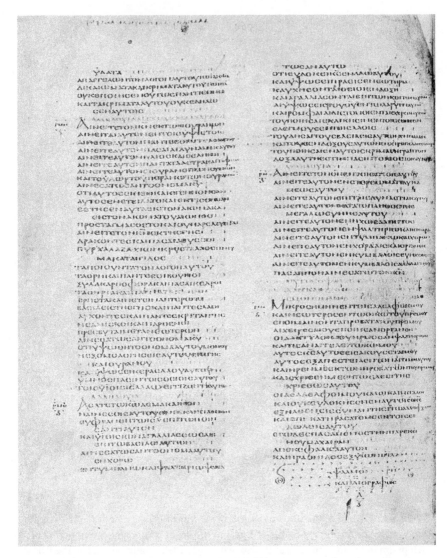

Figure 5.2 The end of the Book of Psalms in the fifth-century Codex Alexandrinus. The psalms are numbered in the margins through Ps 151, but the colophon reads "150 psalms and the 'idiograph.'" (c) The British Library Board, facsimile of Codex Alexandrinus, MS Royal 1 D vi–viii.

manuscripts introduce the psalms as a unit, saying: "Again, five Psalms of David that are not written in the series [or 'order'] of the Psalms."[54] One twelfth-century manuscript, 12t4, appends these texts as a "sequel"[55] to the 150 biblical psalms, and provides longer introductions to each. The introduction to Ps 151 reads:

> The one hundred and fifty first. It does not occur in the Hebrew. Neither is there an introduction to the Psalm in the work of Eusebius. And in

Athanasius, who makes known the words of the glory in the Lord: But when you were the smallest, you were chosen to be of some use to your brothers. You were not raised above them. But sing, while giving the glory to God who chose you. The blessed lord Theodore the commentator did not write an introduction either. In the Syriac manuscripts this is its notation.[56]

After Ps 155 we find a colophon: "With the help of our Lord the book of Psalms of the blessed David, prophet and king, is completed, together with five Psalms, not of the number, Greek or Hebrew, but, as they say, they are found in Syriac and we wrote them for the one who asked." Although the additional psalms— apparently copied here by request—are "not of the number," they are not beyond numbering. After the "final" Ps 150, the numbering picks up where it left off, each psalm enumerated in words, consecutively and clearly—one hundred and fifty-one through one hundred and fifty-five. Here, we have a postcanonical example of a collection spilling beyond its ending, continuing outside its borders.

What, then, do these borders define? It is abundantly clear that there *is* a distinction between the canonical and apocryphal psalms. But these apocryphal psalms are presented as no less authentic, no less Davidic, than the rest: there are legitimate writings ascribed to a biblical figure, but nevertheless beyond the boundaries of the biblical canon. So what are these boundaries, and what *does* distinguish the "outside" texts from the "inside" ones? Syriac scribes differentiate these psalms from the Psalter "proper" in several ways. The common brief introduction gives pragmatic information about scribal convention and the manuscript tradition, saying simply that these five psalms of David are "not written in the series [or 'order'] of the psalms"—a distinction based most likely on liturgical usage. MS 12t4 gives more distinguishing features:

1. *Language*: Ps 151 does not exist in Hebrew (but "in the Syriac...this is its notation"); the other four are found in neither Hebrew nor Greek, but "they are found in Syriac."
2. *Availability of patristic commentaries*: no major commentators introduce Ps 151 except Athanasius, who recommends it for recitation; the other four are not discussed by Athanasius, Eusebius, or Theodore.
3. *Number in excess of the accepted 150*: just as 151 is "outside the number" in the LXX, so the subscription in 12t4 ascribes this outsider status to all five apocryphal compositions.

The distinction between canonical and noncanonical compositions is not presented as theological, and is completely free of any value judgment. Rather, it is based on scholarly observations—where and in what languages the compositions

are found, commentators' attention, and number.[57] None of these considerations seem to have any bearing on the assessment of their Davidic authenticity,
antiquity, and inspiration. On the contrary, those value-laden features are shared
with the rest of the Davidic psalms, across canonical boundaries.

While the number 4,050 in 11QPsalms[a] serves to throw open the imagined
corpus of psalms beyond any realistic, identifiable collection, in the Septuagint
and the Syriac manuscripts, numbers set boundaries. But even when there is a
sense of closure of a canonical collection, this does not imply that the canon and
revelation are coextensive, or that ascription of authorship to a biblical figure is
the criterion for inclusion in such collections: texts can be Davidic but not canonical. The boundaries of canon are not the boundaries of divinely inspired,
ancient, and authentic text, and do not necessarily imply that what is outside
those boundaries is spurious. Perhaps the category of canon is more formal and
conventional, and less theologically meaningful than we might expect.

Who Sings More Songs and Praises than I?

These apocryphal Davidic psalms have not survived in normative Jewish sources.
And while David is the Psalmist in rabbinic tradition, the tradition of 4,050
psalms appears only in the manuscript from Qumran. But one later text—from a
time long after Qumran—gives us another echo of this tension between numbered
limits and numerical proliferation. This is the late antique *Pereq Shira*, "Chapter
of Song,"[58] a collection of eighty-five sections in which parts of creation—earth,
sea, plants, and animals, from sheep to sea monster—each sing a verse of praise,
taken mostly from the Psalms. But the text begins with David:

> The Sages said about David, King of Israel, that when he completed the
> Book of Psalms (בשעה שסיים ספר תהלים), he became proud. He said
> before the Holy One, Blessed be He, "Is there any creature in Your
> world that recites more songs and praises than I?" At that moment
> a frog appeared and said to him: "David! Do not become proud, for
> I recite more songs and praises than you. Furthermore, for each song
> I recite, I utter three thousand parables, as it says, "And he spoke 3000
> proverbs and his songs were 1005."" (1 Kgs 5:12)

Here, the Psalter is a *book* that is *completed* (*siyyem*). But this closed corpus is
dwarfed by a prolific frog, who beats the king at his own game.

The frog appropriates the count of 4,005 sayings and songs of Solomon—and
expands it: for each song, it recites 3,000 proverbs, similarly to Josephus's enormous magnification of Solomon's corpus to 4,005 books. At Qumran, David
overtakes the Solomonic number with 4,050 songs. But in *Pereq Shirah*, David's

slimmer Psalter is finished—and the frog takes over a profusion of praise that is not contained in the completed corpus.

We cannot demonstrate that there is a genetic link between 11QPsalms[a] and *Pereq Shirah*. But if there is no direct influence between them, this makes their thematic connection all the more significant: there is a deep shared topos expressed in texts that are not copying from one another. A shared set of ideas persists across precanonical and postcanonical Judaism; in *Pereq Shirah*, the value of a vast proliferation of thousands of songs is in tension with, and even a challenge to, the available canon, complete at a manageable and collectable 150.

Concepts of Revelation and the "Canonical Process"

I began with Haile Selassie, who pronounced the Bible complete, and ended with the original messianic king, David, proudly completing the Psalter. Two inspired monarchs "close" a scriptural corpus. But neither can fix or contain everything—even after Scriptures are counted and boundaries set, their contents won't come into precise focus, and they can't keep all of inspiration within their borders.

I have shown in this chapter that even when canonical boundaries are erected, the "canon of Scripture" was still not identical with "divinely inspired writing." Rather, they are overlapping but not isomorphic categories. This deconstruction of the identity between canon and revelation forces us to rethink the story of how the canon of Scripture came to be. Scholars who try to uncover how the canon developed must find ways to talk about the protocanonical—something *like* canon before canon existed. In order to begin telling this story, then, we ask: what did ancient communities consider divinely inspired or ascribed to authoritative figures? These features, in the standard narrative, are the precursors to canonicity; authoritative and authentic, logically, seems to equal "protocanonical"—the tadpole that develops into the frog.

But authenticity and inspiration are not necessarily what canonical boundaries define. And so, tracing the story of divinely inspired text and authorial attribution is part of the story of *scripturalization,* but it is not the same as tracing the evolution of *canonization.* Clearly, the boundaries of standard collections do not contain all of revelation; and so, asking how these texts emerged as bounded collections is not the same thing as asking what texts communities considered divinely inspired. Texts outside the canon—imagined or real—can still be attributed to biblical figures and can still be considered the fount of wisdom, even after such boundaries have been set. Noncanonical texts are not always seen as spurious, and canonical judgments are not always value judgments. Recognition of inspiration and authenticity on the one hand and the establishment of set collections on the other are not necessarily different chronological stages in the same process. Determining what was considered divinely inspired, ancient, or authentic may not be the most meaningful criterion for determining how and why texts became canonical in antiquity.

Canons, Closure, and the Insufficiency of Scripture

Jonathan Z. Smith describes the phenomenon of canon, "the arbitrary fixing of a limited number of 'texts' as immutable and authoritative,"[59] as "one form of a basic cultural process of limitation and of overcoming that limitation through ingenuity."[60] This ingenuity, for Smith and others, is the innovative exegesis of a corpus that is deemed to be, in itself, complete and sufficient. The formal characteristic of canon, as opposed to a list or a catalog, is

> that the list be held to be complete. This formal requirement generates a corollary. Where there is a canon, it is possible to predict the *necessary* occurrence of a hermeneute, of an interpreter whose task it is continually to extend the domain of the closed canon over everything that is known or everything that exists *without* altering the canon in the process. It is with the canon and its hermeneute that we encounter the necessary obsession with exegetical totalization.[61]

The hermeneute must "develop exegetical procedures that will allow the canon to be applied without alteration or, at least, without admitting to alteration."[62] This dialectic between fixity, closure, and totality on the one hand, and on the other, the vital processes of exegetical innovation that continues to pump new blood into a closed repository of traditions, is for Smith the "most characteristic, persistent and obsessive religious activity."[63]

Bernard Levinson has taken up Smith's challenge in a study of cuneiform and biblical law, where the "canon formula" that prohibits texts from being altered or added to nevertheless leaves room for legal innovation over time.[64] Levinson nuances Smith's framework in two ways: first, one aspect of the dialectic between exegetical ingenuity and canon is that the exegesis is rendered invisible through the claim that no innovation has happened at all—"the interpreter merely elucidates the plenitude of truth already latent in the canon." Second, exegetical ingenuity does not require a closed canon. Authoritative texts seem to project the same kind of constraints and challenges on the innovative exegete even before the closure of a literary canon, and the canonical process and the kind of interpretive ingenuity that must work within the bounds of textual authority can happen simultaneously. Canon, even before canon, is the "sponsor of innovation."[65]

Indeed, Levinson's critique from the perspective of biblical studies makes it clear that Smith's model of closure, totalization, and exegetical ingenuity seem to work best as a description of the way we have come to imagine rabbinic hermeneutics, where practices of interpretation fold in upon a canon within which, in rabbinic myth, everything is to be found. The instruction to "turn it and turn it, for everything is in it" (*Pirqe Avot* 5.21) is read in terms of midrashic practices that take a closed text—complete and self-contained—and "open" it, revivify its meaning, through exegesis that takes Scripture as a complete and bounded world unto itself. "There is no meaning apart from the letters," writes Susan Handelman; they cannot be altered, and "they are not transcended, but turned again and again, always remaining."[66] Here, we see a fixed and bounded canon, "exegetical totalization," and the claim that nothing is new but all had already been revealed on Sinai—together with irrepressible exegetical ingenuity that makes the aggressively finite text infinitely generative.

This model of scripturally bounded hermeneutics does not always hold up to critical scrutiny of the rabbinic sources, which reveal more variety in how the text of Scripture is regarded and the extent to which it is used.[67] But, as Levinson points out, such a concept of canon-bound innovation has been romanticized by literary critics, and has become a sort of ambassador from the general realm of biblical and Jewish studies to interdisciplinary conversations about canonicity. Levinson, wishing to expand the interdisciplinary conversation, contributes the Mesopotamian and biblical case study and uses it to complicate and extend Smith's canon-innovation dialectic. Here, I have offered a different set of sources and a new set of possibilities for thinking about canonical limits and their transcendence in religious discourse. Each of the cases I have discussed—from the Ethiopic canon, Josephus and *4 Ezra*, the Greek and Syriac psalms—presents us with a notion of canon, in Smith's definition, "the arbitrary fixing of a limited number of 'texts' as immutable and authoritative." Eighty-one, twenty-two, twenty-four, and one hundred fifty—the numbers set limits. But the difference between these canons and Smith's is that, to the people who reflect on them, these canons do not seem complete, or at least they are not sufficient. And it is not exegesis that becomes the way their limits can be overcome. Instead, these canons *are* transcended, even altered, for *not* everything is in them.

In some of the examples, the canon exists as an idea, but not as a stable list, a fixed set of texts, or an accessible object. "Exegetical totalization" is not available when the body of interpretable text is a shapeshifter. The canon exists as an icon, but not as an identifiable set. In the Ethiopic canon, two different lists—or three or more—transcend the limitations of a closed set; the parts that make up the fixed number of 81 reconfigure and refocus like a kaleidoscope, depending on which list you read. In *4 Ezra*, the canon that is limited by the number 24 is far from sufficient and self-contained, but is cast in the role of the most basic kind of written revelation. In other examples, a limited number defines actual texts, like 150 psalms; but they do not limit other compositions that seem equally authoritative from thriving somewhere outside the walls.

From these examples, it seems clear that canonical limitations are not overcome through *exegetical* practices that have canon itself as their source and goal, but by imagining the possibility of larger bodies of revelation, accessible or not. And it seems equally clear that canonical consciousness does not necessarily coincide with a sense of completion and self-sufficiency. There is no question, for Josephus and *4 Ezra*—as for Bishop Timothy, hundreds of years later—that the biblical canon is not enough, that it is not a world unto itself.

Conclusion: Revelation Out of Reach

The tension between canon and interpretive innovation is a familiar scholarly model. A closed canon sets limits, but those limits are transcended through exegetical ingenuity; finite text is infinitely interpretable, and therefore continuously vital. This might be a good description of rabbinic midrash—or, perhaps more accurately, of some scholarly presuppositions *about* rabbinic midrash. But it cannot be universalized. The dialectic is not always between canonical limits and their overcoming through ingenious exegesis. It is also between canonical limits and a sense of canonical limitations—a consciousness of the canon's own incompleteness or insufficiency. There must be, or must have been, or one day might be, more than this.

This dissatisfaction and desire is sometimes expressed explicitly and disarmingly—by people we might have reasonably expected to be convinced by the authority and unity of Scripture. Timothy of Baghdad—author of the letter that began this book—is a bishop and a biblical scholar. But in his reflections in 800 CE about the discovery of Hebrew manuscripts in the desert, which may contain not only lost passages but also "over two hundred psalms of David," he expresses a near certainty that the canon *he* has is not self-contained.

The new discovery is less threatening to Timothy than the Dead Sea Scrolls have been to some modern scholars. On the contrary, Timothy is all but convinced that his own Bible is not complete: it does not have all the psalms of David, and is not as reliable as the texts in a desert cave that he has never seen. Those new discoveries must be used to emend and expand his own Bible.

Having presented his theory that it was Jeremiah or Baruch who hid the manuscripts to keep them from being burned, he laments that the texts remain unavailable: "[W]hat I have written about this has generated no response from them, and I have no competent envoy whom I can send. This is in my heart like a fire that burns and inflames my bones." In the desire to use Timothy's letter as a certain kind of historical source—evidence for an ancient discovery of Jewish manuscripts, which can explain some incomplete histories of textual transmission from ancient Judaism to the medieval world—scholars have not taken account of his letter's subtle literary texture. Having praised Jeremiah from saving books from burning, he then looks to Jeremiah for words to express the burning absence of books. The fire in his heart that burns and inflames his bones is a direct quotation from Jer 20:9 in the Syriac Peshitta version. In context, the verse is part of Jeremiah's lament about having the word of God forced upon him—or better, forced into him. Jeremiah describes his invasive prophetic commission in the language of bodily violation:

> 20⁷ O Lord, you have enticed me, and I was enticed;
>
> you have overpowered me, and you have prevailed.
>
> I have become a laughingstock all day long; everyone mocks me.
>
> ⁸ For whenever I speak, I must cry out,
>
> I must shout, "Violence and destruction!"
>
> For the word of the LORD has become for me
>
> a reproach and derision all day long.
>
> ⁹ If I say, "I will not mention him, or speak any more in his name,"
>
> then within me there is something like a burning fire inflaming[68] my bones;
>
> I am weary with holding it in, and I cannot.

For Jeremiah, the word of God is an unwanted and undeniable violation that burns him from the inside. But later in the book of Jeremiah, the prophet's words, written on a scroll, are themselves subject to burning, before they are written anew. And in the later history of interpretation, Jeremiah and his scribe are the saviors of manuscripts from destruction and loss.

Timothy's quotation reverses its biblical sense: it is not the constant violating presence of the unwanted word, but the absence of words much desired, that inflames his bones. Timothy, who can't get across the desert to the hidden manuscripts, becomes Jeremiah's mirror image. Using the very words of Scripture, he expresses not the overwhelming closeness of divine words, but the burning awareness that they are absent, distant, incomplete.

Conclusion

In the strands of the literary imagination I have discussed in this book, divine words and sacred texts are not always close at hand. They are found in multiple locations. Bishop Timothy's yearning for better manuscripts and unknown psalms evokes an earlier sense of sacred writing that can neither be completely possessed nor fully accounted for: psalms that exist in staggering numbers, only partially available in actual manuscripts; wisdom that overflows beyond the work of individual tradents, always larger than they can grasp in any one collection; ancient tracts that had once been revealed to legendary figures—but that now exist only in legends, not in libraries.

What I have described here seems at odds with some other modes of thinking about the location and accessibility of revelation in ancient Hebrew texts. There is a tradition, inspired by the book of Deuteronomy, of written revelation as eminently available to and graspable by human beings. In an iconic passage (Deut. 30:11–14), the law that Moses is giving to the people is

> not too hard for you, nor is it too far away. [12] It is not in heaven, that you should say, "Who will go up to heaven for us, and get it for us so that we may hear it and observe it?" [13] Neither is it beyond the sea, that you should say, "Who will cross to the other side of the sea for us, and get it for us so that we may hear it and observe it?" [14] No, the word is very near to you; it is in your mouth and in your heart for you to observe.

This description of the location of divine law—"it is not in heaven," but "near to you"—has been influential in rabbinic conceptions of the location of revelation. In the famous Talmudic story of the Oven of Akhnai (B. Baba Metzia 59b), a halakhic dispute about whether an oven is pure gives way to a broader statement about where the authority to make legal rulings is to be found. In other words, the real question is not about the purity of the oven, but about how we are to decide such questions. On what basis shall halakhic disputes be resolved?

In the story, Rabbi Eliezer calls on signs from heaven to confirm his minority opinion: a carob tree uproots itself and moves, a channel flows backward, and the walls of the study house tilt. The other sages are still not convinced: no proof can be found in such signs. Finally the divine voice, the *bat qol*, cries out from heaven to express support for Rabbi Eliezer's position. Should a divine voice from heaven not settle the matter? But not even this revelation can convince the other sages to accept his ruling.

Finally, it is a quotation from our passage in Deuteronomy that puts the question to rest: "R. Joshua stood up and protested: 'The Torah is not in heaven!' (Deut. 30:12). We pay no attention to a divine voice because long ago at Mount Sinai You wrote in your Torah at Mount Sinai, 'After the majority must one incline' (Ex. 23:2)." In this rabbinic context, it is not signs from heaven or divine voices that prove the validity of halakhic rulings. What makes a ruling valid is the consensus of the rabbinic leadership. All the revelation that is needed is contained in the Torah from Sinai, a Torah that is now in human hands, "not in heaven." Whatever voices do come from above are irrelevant, since all the revelation that matters has been revealed on Sinai, and is contained in Scripture. Other revelations might be possible, even unsurprising: none of the sages in the story dispute that the miracles are real or that the *bat qol* is really divine—but they are not impressed. These signs do not trump the interpretation of the fixed corpus of Scripture, now in the possession of the rabbinic sages.

In one important sense, the Talmudic story means to make a point about the human authority to derive legal rulings from Torah. But it also illustrates a larger idea about where divine revelation now resides. The Torah is "not in heaven"— not, for example, in the celestial storeroom of the heavenly tablets, parts of which various enlightened figures get to glimpse over time. It has been brought down to earth as Scripture, revealed once and for all, finite and sufficient in itself.

This idea, that the Torah is available to human beings on earth to possess and interpret, and that revelation is contained in a scriptural corpus, is related to a broader trajectory of textualization that scholars have identified in the book of Deuteronomy itself. Framed as Moses's farewell speech before to the people before he dies, Deuteronomy becomes at once the text that replaces Moses in the community and the story of that transition between the presence of the figure and the text he leaves behind. It is "this torah," inscribed in a text, that will now stand in for the living lawgiver; it, and not the presence or persona of the figure, becomes the source and embodiment of divine instructions. Through some rabbinic lenses, this rhetorically applies to Scripture as a corpus—the embodiment of revelation in a limited written text, the Bible, once revealed to inspired prophets, but now completed, and given into the hands of the sages.

This is one of the major differences interpreters have identified as a dividing marker between Jewish and Christian theologies as they emerge in late antiquity: in Jewish theology the divine is contained in Scripture, and in Christian, God is incarnate in the person of Jesus Christ—although, as scholars from Daniel Boyarin[1] to Shaul Magid[2] have shown, strands of incarnational thinking are never completely absent from Judaism. But the idea of Scripture as the full embodiment of divine self-revelation is one aspect of a postcanonical, rabbinic imagination (although, as scholars like Rebecca Wollenberg and Azzan Yadin-Israel have stressed, the centrality of the scriptural text in rabbinic theology cannot always be assumed either; it is one scholarly construction of a more complex and ambivalent rabbinic tradition).[3] The transition from the inspired person to the revealed text that we read about in Deuteronomy can only be read in terms of Scripture as a whole from the perspective of a much later scriptural world— through the lens of the rabbinic canon.

As this book has demonstrated, before the emergence of a bounded canon of Scripture in Judaism and Christianity in late antiquity, we must allow ourselves to imagine that sacred writings took fundamentally different shapes. This is stronger than conceding that the canon had not yet been fully fixed. It is not that, in Second Temple Judaism, there was a proto-Bible—a literary concept similar to the Tanakh, only with fuzzier edges. Instead, there is a different morphology of text, a different imagined sense of where revelation is to be found and how it is related to the figures who transmit it.

The literary imagination includes both sacred writings in multiple scopes, locations, and levels of accessibility and lore *about* writings taught to a varied cast of enlightened figures who had transcended their humanity. Thus, in the Second Temple period, we have neither a single central textual corpus, as in our dominant picture of later Judaism, nor a single ideal divinized figure, as in Christianity, that embodies the fullness of revelation. Rather, we have many texts that contain divine words, available or not, and several inspired heroes who had once heard and written them. Enoch, Jacob, and Ezra are all imbued with divine power. Each, in some way, has received and transmitted divine text, even if that text is contained in multiple locations, or only known in legend.

Their writing is part of—but not a replacement for—their inspired personalities, which continue to generate new traditions about their lives and characteristics. Many of the ancient figures credited with writing sacred texts are transformed into angelic or divine beings as the traditions about them develop— and many of them, in one source or another, dwell in heaven. Far from being replaced by the text of Deuteronomy, Moses takes on new roles as a scribe of *more* revelation beyond the Torah (*Jubilees*), but also as an angelic figure (Qumran); an ascended hero who never died, even though he claimed he did (Josephus); mind or soul alone (Philo); and a transfigured being who appears together with

Elijah and Jesus. Enoch and David are divinely enlightened heroes who have prolific writing as part of their repertoires; in Jewish texts of late antiquity, both have become cosmic beings enthroned on high, continuing their mandates in heaven. Ezra leaves Torah for his community, but he himself receives not only greater writings reserved only for the wise but also greater rewards for himself, as a transformed being taken up to the heavenly world. None of these writing heroes are replaced or subsumed by their textual products.

This project has emphasized the perpetually unfinished nature of writing as it seemed to some of its ancient creators. And so, writing its own ending is a strange endeavor. If a book's conclusion is meant to offer a summation or to close a project, this one will not quite do that. Qohelet's warning that there is no end to making many books is true now as it was then. Hellenistic and early Roman period writers did not understand themselves to be in full possession of all the writing ever revealed, and neither does this book pretend to give a complete picture of their literary imaginations.

Here, as in the ancient library, the dream of comprehensiveness is impossible, and I have instead been selective and exploratory. There is a great deal more to be said, and different principles for selecting our sources are possible. A focus on only documents written by Greek-speaking Jews in the shadow of Alexandrian scholarship, or only the traditions related to Enoch, cosmology, and apocalyptical speculation, gives us other views on how ancient people envisioned scriptures before the Bible. Other sources are more elusive, or more mediated: single fragments of Aramaic visionary texts from the Dead Sea Scrolls, or works that have survived in secondary or tertiary translations in medieval manuscripts— removed by centuries, languages, and theologies from the world of the Second Temple Jewish writers responsible for some form of their oldest layers—can enrich and complicate the picture.

But even the sources that are more familiar to us can become strange when seen outside of our most naturalized categories and our most pressing teleological interests. The sources on which I have focused most closely are well known and widely studied—Psalms, Ben Sira, and *Jubilees*. Each originates in Hebrew, is widely attested, and enjoyed broad popularity. And each seems to fit rather neatly into a bibliographic category: a biblical text with a legendary author, an apocryphal book whose author has identified himself, and an interpretive rewritten Bible composition.

But these textbook classifications, while conventional to us, were not obvious to their producers and Second Temple period audiences. They did not have our powerful categories of "book" and "Bible" available to think with. But they had other ways of imagining their textual world. Putting aside our own teleological interests, we have listened to the moments in which they reflect on the sources, shapes, locations, and inventories of written tradition, to the metaphors and images they choose to describe it.

When not read as players in a story about the Bible, these sources take on different roles and hierarchies, and—like pieces of glass in a turning kaleidoscope—arrange themselves into new patterns. What once looked like books, or protobooks, expand and scatter into archipelagos of textual fragments, pieces of a prolific divine cache only partially reflected in heterogeneous scribal collections. Texts neither begin nor end with the creative activity of their authorial figures. Instead, written revelation becomes part of their broader and developing biographies, and they themselves become characters in a larger story about divine writing as it moves through people and through time. Without a single center or corpus to contain it, writing can be found at different times and locations, only some of it currently identifiable and accessible.

We can thus imagine that the literary world of early Judaism was not a library, but a story. It was a story about writing as it traveled from its divine origins, and became—in Robert Kraft's term—"earthbound,"[4] partially instantiated in concrete scribal projects. It was a story about its divinely favored revealers, who traveled across new textual territories. Thinking of it in this way—as a story, not a library—helps us see how texts that do not stand still or cannot be identified are not conundrums to be explained, but actors in an unfolding narrative, where the history of Israel is intertwined with the history of its writing.

In the *Testament of Moses*, Moses gives Joshua a piece of writing and instructs him how to preserve and conceal other documents:

> I am going to sleep with my fathers. But (you) take this writing so that later you will remember how to preserve the books which I shall entrust to you. You shall arrange them, anoint them with cedar, and deposit them in earthenware jars in the place which (God) has chosen from the beginning of the creation of the world, (a place) where his name may be called upon until the day of recompense when the Lord will surely have regard for his people (1:15–18).[5]

As Enoch was the first human writer and will still be writing the deeds of humanity until Judgment Day, Moses's books will dwell in a place God has chosen from the beginning of creation, a place set apart until the end times. As in the writings that appear in *1 Enoch* and *Jubilees* and the thousands of Davidic psalms, the texts in question are not quoted or precisely defined. This world of bibliographic mystery—where more has been revealed than has ever been collected or read—recurs in the literary imagination.

An awareness of textual proliferation, incompleteness, and inaccessibility produces both anxiety and a sense of potential. As I conclude this book, I am thinking of all the things that it does not contain. I am also thinking about the ancient scholar I have sometimes imagined looking over my shoulder since this book's first words: Bishop Timothy, patriarch of Baghdad, whose enthusiasm about the possibility of new scriptures kindled a "fire in his bones" when he could not access them. But I imagine, too, the possibility of a different lost text. Maybe, from some later letter that has not survived, we would have learned that Timothy did receive a reply to his inquiries. Maybe he did get to read hundreds more psalms of David. It is not impossible: the end of the story has not been written, but is sealed for a future time.

NOTES

Introduction

1. The report of the manuscript find comes from a letter of Timothy I to Sergius, metropolitan of Elam, first published by O. Braun, "Ein Brief des Katholikos Timotheos I über biblische Studien des 9 Jahrhunderts," *Oriens Christianus* 1 (1901): 299–313. See also R. J. Bidawid, *Les lettres du patriarche nestorien Timothée I* (Vatican City: Biblioteca Apostolica Vaticana, 1956), and J. C. Reeves, "Exploring the Afterlife of Jewish Pseudepigrapha in Medieval Near Eastern Religious Traditions: Some Initial Soundings," *JSJ* 30 (1999): 175–77; Reeves provides the Syriac text from Braun with an English translation, which I have adapted here. On Timothy, see also B. ter Haar Romeny, "Biblical Studies in the Church of the East: The Case of Catholicos Timothy I," *SP* 34 (2001): 503–10. Timothy's quotation about the fire in his bones is from Jer 20:9; I discuss this allusion in chapter 5.
2. The scholarly consensus is that most of the texts found among the Scrolls did not originate with the sectarian group or groups that settled Qumran. Even those that do seem to originate with the group show many points of contact with a much broader culture. Thus, the Scrolls can tell us a great deal about the broader culture of Hellenistic and early Roman Judaism, not only about a marginal group.
3. See B. W. Breed, *Nomadic Text: A Theory of Biblical Reception History* (Indiana Studies in Biblical Literature; Bloomington: Indiana University Press, 2014), who presents the fluid and developing texts as dynamic processes, not fixed and finished products.
4. D. M. Carr, *Writing on the Tablet of the Heart: Origins of Scripture and Literature* (New York: Oxford University Press, 2008), and K. van der Toorn, *Scribal Culture and the Making of the Hebrew Bible* (Cambridge, Mass.: Harvard University Press, 2007).
5. J. Barton, *Oracles of God: Perceptions of Ancient Prophecy in Israel after the Exile* (New York: Oxford University Press, 1986; F. García Martínez, "Rethinking the Bible: Sixty Years of Dead Sea Scrolls Research and Beyond," in *Authoritative Scriptures in Ancient Judaism* (ed. M. Popović; Leiden: Brill, 2010), 19–36, and "Beyond the Sectarian Divide: The 'Voice of the Teacher' as an Authority-Conferring Strategy in Some Qumran Texts," in *The Dead Sea Scrolls: Transmission of Traditions and Production of Texts* (ed. S. Metso, H. Najman, and E. Schuller; Leiden: Brill, 2010), 227–44; R. A. Kraft, "Para-mania: Before, beside and beyond Biblical Studies," *JBL* 126 (2007): 5–27, and "Scripture and Canon in the Commonly Called Apocrypha and Pseudepigrapha and in the Writings of Josephus," in *Hebrew Bible/Old Testament: The History of Its Interpretation*, vol. 1: *From the Beginnings to the Middle Ages (until 1300). Part 1: Antiquity*, (ed M. Sæbø; Göttingen: Vandenhoeck & Ruprecht, 1996), 199–216; H. Najman, *Seconding Sinai: The Development of Mosaic Discourse in Second Temple Judaism* (Leiden: Brill, 2003), "The Vitality of Scripture within and beyond the 'Canon,'" *JSJ* 43 (2012): 497–518, and *Losing the Temple and Recovering the Future: An Analysis of* 4 *Ezra* (Cambridge: Cambridge University Press, 2014), and other

work on *Jubilees, 4 Ezra,* and notions of authorship, cited in subsequent chapters; A. Y. Reed, "The Modern Invention of 'Old Testament Pseudepigrapha,'" *JTS* 60 (2009): 403–36, "Pseudepigraphy, Authorship and the Reception of 'the Bible' in Late Antiquity," in *The Reception and Interpretation of the Bible in Late Antiquity: Proceedings of the Montréal Colloquium in Honour of Charles Kannengiesser, 11–13 October 2006* (ed. L. DiTommaso and L. Turcescu; Leiden: Brill, 2008), 467–90, and her forthcoming *Demons, Angels, and Writing in Ancient Judaism* (New York: Cambridge University Press); J. E. Bowley and J. C. Reeves, "Rethinking the Concept of 'Bible': Some Theses and Proposals," *Henoch* 25 (2003): 3–18; Reeves, "Problematizing the Bible…Then and Now," *JQR* 100 (2010): 139–52; M. E. Stone, "The Book of Enoch and Judaism in the Third Century B.C.E.," *CBQ* 40 (1978): 479–92, *Ancient Judaism: New Visions and Views* (Grand Rapids, Mich.: Eerdmans, 2011), and his other work on Enoch traditions, literature about Adam and Eve, and *4 Ezra.* For an exemplary discussion of such problems in the field of early Christianity, see D. Brakke, "Scriptural Practices in Early Christianity: Towards a New History of the New Testament Canon," in *Invention, Rewriting, Usurpation: Discursive Fights over Religious Traditions in Antiquity* (ed. J. Ulrich, A. C. Jacobsen, and D. Brakke; Early Christianity in the Context of Late Antiquity 11; New York: Peter Lang, 2012), 263–80.

6. T. M. Law, *When God Spoke Greek: The Septuagint and the Making of the Christian Bible* (New York: Oxford University Press, 2013), 19.

7. See, prominently, W. Schniedewind, *How the Bible Became a Book: The Textualization of Ancient Israel* (New York: Cambridge University Press, 2004); S. Niditch, *Oral World and Written Word: Ancient Israelite Literature* (Library of Ancient Israel; Louisville, Ky.: Westminster John Knox Press, 1996); and Carr, *Writing on the Tablet of the Heart.*

8. Concepts of textuality and Scripture have been widely studied for subsequent periods, i.e., rabbinic and later forms of Jewish tradition and hermeneutics, where the closed canon is presupposed. See especially the book-length study of the centrality of text and the significance of a "sealed" canon by M. Halbertal, *People of the Book: Canon, Meaning, Authority* (Cambridge, Mass.: Harvard University Press, 1997). An incisive recent critique of the tendency to assume rabbinic Judaism was dominated by the text of the Bible is found in R. S. Wollenberg, "The People of the Book without the Book: Jewish Ambivalence toward Biblical Text after the Rise of Christianity" (PhD diss., University of Chicago, 2015). See also the collected essays in B. D. Sommer, ed., *Jewish Concepts of Scripture: A Comparative Introduction* (New York: New York University Press, 2012).

9. M. Satlow, *How the Bible Became Holy* (New Haven, Conn.: Yale University Press, 2014). Satlow outlines three kinds of authority that texts could have: literary (they were used as models or sources for new writings), oracular (they carried divine messages), and normative (they dictated behavior); 4–5.

10. Satlow argues that it was the Sadducees who first insisted on the authority of scriptural texts to guide religious practice in order to oppose the established priestly aristocracy in the Hasmonean period, and whose ideology "posthumously won" in the rabbinic era; *How the Bible Became Holy,* 136–53, 275.

11. Satlow writes that as late as "the third century CE, 'the Bible' as we know it still did not exist. There was, to our knowledge, no single codex or composition that combined all or most of the writings that comprise either the Jewish Bible (Old Testament) or the New Testament, and all the more so both together" (276).

12. Stone, "The Book of Enoch and Judaism," 489, and *Ancient Judaism.*

13. S. J. D. Cohen, *From the Maccabees to the Mishnah* (2nd ed.; Louisville: Westminster John Knox, 2006), 9.

14. M. Fishbane, "Use, Authority and Interpretation of Mikra at Qumran," in *Mikra: Text, Translation, Reading and Interpretation of the Hebrew Bible in Ancient Judaism and Early Christianity* (ed. M. J. Mulder and H. Sysling; Assen: Van Gorcum; Philadelphia: Fortress, 1988), 339–77, at 375, 377.

15. J. L. Kugel, *How to Read the Bible: A Guide to Scripture, Then and Now* (New York: Free Press, 2007), xiv.

16. G. Vermes, *Scripture and Tradition in Judaism: Haggadic Studies* (2nd ed.; Leiden: Brill, 1973), first published in 1961. The literature on rewritten Bible is extensive. For excellent

recent assessments of the issues, see S. W. Crawford, *Rewriting Scripture in Second Temple Times* (Grand Rapids, Mich.: Eerdmans, 2008), and her concise summary of North American scholarship in "'Rewritten Bible' in North American Scholarship," in *The Dead Sea Scrolls in Scholarly Perspective: A History of Research* (ed. D. Dimant; Leiden: Brill, 2012), 75–78; and M. M. Zahn, *Rethinking Rewritten Scripture: Composition and Exegesis in the 4QReworked Pentateuch Manuscripts* (*STDJ* 95; Leiden: Brill, 2011), and a shorter account of the issues in "Rewritten Scripture," in *The Oxford Handbook of the Dead Sea Scrolls*, ed. T. H. Lim and J. J. Collins (Oxford: Oxford University Press, 2010), 323–36. See also scholarship cited in chapter 4.

17. This goes beyond a convenient scholarly periodization: not only is the Second Temple period considered "postclassical," but some scholarship seems to assume writers of the period were *aware* of their status as latecomers on the scene, in a way that was somehow different or at least more acute than in other literary periods. But the burden of an already ancient cultural past weighs on every age, and the emphasis on this anxiety as a particularly salient feature of Second Temple literary consciousness is a result of our own privileging of the biblical. See analogous work done by Mark Payne on Hellenistic poetry, which he argues it is not as dominated by the anxiety of classical influence as our standard periodization of literary history would have it. See Payne, "Aristotle on Poets as Parents and the Hellenistic Poet as Mother," in *Classical Myth and Psychoanalysis: Ancient and Modern Stories of the Self* (ed. E. O'Gorman and V. Zajko; Oxford: Oxford University Press, 2013), 299–313.

18. R. Chartier, *The Order of Books: Readers, Authors, and Libraries in Europe between the Fourteenth and Eighteenth Centuries* (trans. L. G. Cochrane; Stanford, Calif.: Stanford University Press, 1994), vii.

19. See L. Howsam, *Old Books and New Histories: An Orientation to Studies in Book and Print Culture* (Toronto: University of Toronto Press, 2006). "Book history," then, combines three disciplines: bibliography (the study of books as material objects), literature (the study of the text), and history (the study of the social and cultural context in which texts were created and used). For these book-historical concepts as they relate to the Dead Sea Scrolls, see the work of L. S. Schiffman, "Memory and Manuscript: Books, Scrolls, and the Tradition of the Dead Sea Scrolls," in *New Perspectives on Old Texts: Proceedings of the Tenth International Symposium of the Orion Center for the Study of the Dead Sea Scrolls and Associated Literature, 9-11 January 2005* (ed. E. G. Chazon and B. H. Amaru, in collaboration with R. Clements; STDJ 88; Leiden: Brill, 2010), 133–50, and "The Dead Sea Scrolls and the History of the Jewish Book," *AJS Review* 34.2 (2010): 359–65.

20. See my discussion in "Thinking Digitally about the Dead Sea Scrolls: Book History before and beyond the Book," *Book History* 13 (2011): 235–63, where I apply this concept to ancient Jewish texts. Now-classic discussions of the impact of the digital on our textual concepts include N. K. Hayles, "Translating Media: Why We Should Rethink Textuality," *Yale Journal of Criticism* 16 (2003): 263–90; R. Chartier, "Languages, Books, and Reading from the Printed Word to the Digital Text," trans. T. L. Fagan, *Critical Inquiry* 31 (2004): 133–51; J. J. McGann, *Radiant Textuality: Literature after the World Wide Web* (New York: Palgrave, 2001); and K. Sutherland, ed., *Electronic Text: Investigations in Method and Theory* (Oxford: Clarendon, 1997).

21. Chartier, "Languages, Books, and Reading," 141.

22. See Law, *When God Spoke Greek*.

23. Here I am inspired by the new work on manuscript materiality and media culture by L. I. Lied, "Manuscript Culture and the Myth of Golden Beginnings," in *Religion across Media: From Early Antiquity to Late Modernity* (ed. K. Lundby (New York: Peter Lang, 2013), 54–70.

24. See, for example, the crucial new work of Reed, *Demons, Angels, and Writing in Ancient Judaism*.

25. R. A. Kraft has done extensive work to show how the later Christian contexts of transmission of many of the Pseudepigrapha deeply complicates the possibility of using them to reconstruct Second Temple Jewish traditions. See e.g. the essays collected in Kraft, *Exploring the Scripturesque: Jewish Texts and Their Christian Contexts* (JSJSup 137; Leiden: Brill, 2009).

Chapter 1 The Mirage of the Bible

1. D. F. McKenzie, "The Broken Phial: Non-Book Texts," in *Bibliography and the Sociology of Texts* (Panizzi Lectures, 1985; Cambridge: Cambridge University Press, 1999), 31–54, at 31; first pub. by the British Library, 1986. Milton's reflections on the nature of text have caught the attention of other scholars of literary ideas in Jewish antiquity: see B. W. Breed's discussion of "The Miltonesque Concept of the Original Text," chapter 1 of his *Nomadic Text: A Theory of Biblical Reception History* (Indiana Studies in Biblical Literature; Bloomington: Indiana University Press, 2014), 15–51.

2. McKenzie, "The Broken Phial," 35.

3. See G. J. Brooke, *Reading the Dead Sea Scrolls: Essays in Method* (Early Judaism and Its Literature 39; Atlanta: Society of Biblical Literature, 2013), chapters 1–5; and Eugene Ulrich, *The Dead Sea Scrolls and the Origins of the Bible* (Grand Rapids, Mich.: Eerdmans; Leiden: Brill, 1999).

4. A version of part of this chapter was first published as "The Hegemony of the Biblical in the Study of Second Temple Literature," *Journal of Ancient Judaism* 6 (2015): 2–35.

5. R. A. Kraft, "Para-mania: Beside, before and beyond Bible Studies," *JBL* 126 (2007): 5–27, at 17–18, 22.

6. M. E. Stone, "The Book of Enoch and Judaism in the Third Century B.C.E.," *CBQ* 40 (1978): 479–92, at 489.

7. Stone, "Book of Enoch," 490–91.

8. E.g., D. Boyarin, *Border Lines: The Partition of Judaeo-Christianity* (Philadelphia: University of Pennsylvania Press, 2004); H. Najman, "The Vitality of Scripture within and beyond the 'Canon,'" *JSJ* 43 (2012): 497–518; F. García Martínez, "Parabiblical Literature from Qumran and the Canonical Process," *RevQ* 25 (2012): 525–56; A. Y. Reed, "The Modern Invention of 'Old Testament Pseudepigrapha,'" *JTS* 60 (2009): 403–36; J. E. Bowley and J. C. Reeves, "Rethinking the Concept of 'Bible': Some Theses and Proposals," *Henoch* 25 (2003): 3–18; Reeves, "Problematizing the Bible... Then and Now," *JQR* 100 (2010): 139–52; and M. Satlow, *How the Bible Became Holy* (New Haven, Conn.: Yale University Press, 2014); see also the contributions to the volume *What Is Bible?*, ed. K. Finsterbusch and A. Lange (Leuven: Peeters, 2012), especially G. Boccaccini, "Is Biblical Literature Still a Useful Term in Scholarship?" (41–52), and S. W. Crawford, "Biblical Text: Yes or No?" (113–19), where she distinguishes between fixed canon, established shapes of books, and fixed texts.

9. S. J. D. Cohen, *From the Maccabees to the Mishnah* (2nd ed.; Louisville: Westminster John Knox, 2006), 11.

10. J. L. Kugel, *How to Read the Bible: A Guide to Scripture, Then and Now* (New York: Free Press, 2007), xiv.

11. M. Fishbane, "Use, Authority and Interpretation of Mikra at Qumran," in *Mikra: Text, Translation, Reading and Interpretation of the Hebrew Bible in Ancient Judaism and Early Christianity* (ed. M. J. Mulder and H. Sysling; Assen: Van Gorcum; Philadelphia: Fortress, 1988), 339–77, at 375, 377.

12. M. E. Stone, *Ancient Judaism: New Visions and Views* (Grand Rapids, Mich.: Eerdmans, 2011), 11.

13. Stone, *Ancient Judaism*, 12.

14. See J. Finkel, "The Author of the Genesis Apocryphon Knew the Book of Esther," in *Essays on the Dead Sea Scrolls in Memory of E. L. Sukenik* (ed. C. Rabin and Y. Yadin; Jerusalem: Hekhal Ha-Sefer, 1961), 163–82 (Hebrew); R. H. Eisenman and M. O. Wise, *The Dead Sea Scrolls Uncovered* (Shaftesbury: Element, 1992); J. T. Milik, "Les modèles araméens du livre d'Esther dans la grotte 4 de Qumran," *RevQ* 15 (1992): 321–99; S. Talmon, "Was the Book of Esther Known at Qumran?" *DSD* 2 (1995): 249–67; S. W. Crawford, "Has *Esther* Been Found at Qumran? 4QProto-Esther and the *Esther* Corpus," *RevQ* 17 (1996): 307–25; and K. De Troyer, "Once More, the So-Called Esther Fragments of Cave 4," *RevQ* 19 (2000): 401–22.

15. The other exception was long thought to be Nehemiah, although Ezra is attested, and Ezra-Nehemiah may have circulated as one. However, Torleif Elgvin recently announced the discovery of a Qumran fragment of Nehemiah in the Schøyen collection, to be published

in *Gleanings from the Caves: Dead Sea Scrolls and Artifacts from the Schøyen Collection* (ed. T. Elgvin; Library of Second Temple Studies 71; London: Bloomsbury T&T Clark, 2016).

16. Many biblical scholars are sensitive to the historical multiformity of Psalms traditions and their development over time. For work that traces the development of the collections over the *longue durée*, See W. Holladay, *The Psalms through Three Thousand Years: Prayerbook of a Cloud of Witnesses* (Minneapolis: Fortress, 1993), esp. chapters 5, 6, and 7, on the development and use of psalms from the beginning of the Second Temple period through Qumran; and S. Gillingham, *Psalms through the Centuries*, vol. 1 (Oxford: Blackwell, 2008). G. H. Wilson studies the editorial shaping and compilation of both the biblical book of Psalms and the Qumran psalms collections as part of the same cultural practice; see *The Editing of the Hebrew Psalter* (SBLDS 76; Chico, Calif.: Scholars Press, 1985), and "The Qumran Psalms Scroll (11QPs^a) and the Canonical Psalter: Comparison of Editorial Shaping," *CBQ* 59 (1997): 448–64. G. J. Brooke offers an excellent analysis of the early Jewish situation in "The Psalms in Early Jewish Literature in Light of the Dead Sea Scrolls," ed. S. Moyise and M. J. J. Menken, *The Psalms in the New Testament* (The New Testament and the Scriptures of Israel; London: T & T Clark, 2004), 5–24. Recently, see the important study of psalms from the perspective of noncanonical manuscripts by M. S. Pajunen, *The Land to the Elect and Justice for All: Reading Psalms in the Dead Sea Scrolls in Light of 4Q381* (JAJSupp 14; Göttingen: Vandenhoeck & Ruprecht, 2013).

17. See the excellent summary of the debate between James Sanders, the scroll's editor, who thought the scroll was scriptural, and his critics in P. W. Flint, *The Dead Sea Psalms Scrolls and the Book of Psalms* (STDJ 17; Leiden: Brill, 1997), 204–17. Flint also argues for a non-Qumranic origin for the collection (but not the physical manuscript, which he still believes could have been copied at Qumran for community use); *Dead Sea Psalms Scrolls*, 200–201.

18. E.g. J. C. VanderKam, *The Dead Sea Scrolls Today* (Grand Rapids, Mich.: Eerdmans, 1994), 31: "The book of Psalms is present in the largest number of copies (36)"; in his new 2010 edition this has been revised to "34 or 36"; K. van der Toorn, *Scribal Culture and the Making of the Hebrew Bible* (Cambridge, Mass.: Harvard University Press, 2007), 102: "The three books represented by the most manuscripts are Psalms (thirty-nine in total, including twenty-two manuscripts from Cave Four)…"; E. Tov, "The Text of Isaiah at Qumran," in *Writing and Reading the Scroll of Isaiah: Studies of an Interpretive Tradition* (vol. 2; ed. C. C. Broyles and C. A. Evans; VTSup 70; Leiden: Brill, 1997), 491–511, at 491: "Other books represented at Qumran in large numbers are Deuteronomy, of which twenty-six copies are known, and Psalms with thirty-six copies."

19. See F. García Martínez, "Les manuscrits du désert de Juda et le Deutéronome," in *Studies in Deuteronomy in Honour of C. J. Labuschagne on the Occasion of His 65th Birthday* (ed. F. García Martínez et al.; VTSup 53; Leiden: Brill, 1994), 63–82.

20. Tov, "The Text of Isaiah." Tov recognizes the conjectural nature of establishing the number of manuscripts for each book.

21. On these misleading statistics see the conclusions reached by M. S. Pajunen, "Perspectives on the Existence of a Particular Authoritative Book of Psalms in the Late Second Temple Period," *JSOT* 39 (2014): 139–63. Pajunen presents an excellent statistical analysis of the contents and scope of the Qumran manuscripts. See now the new publication of the Qumran psalms manuscripts by E. Jain, *Psalmen oder Psalter? Materielle Rekonstruktion und inhaltliche Untersuchung der Psalmenhandschriften aus der Wüste Juda* (Leiden: Brill, 2014).

22. Armin Lange underscores that several collections existed, and combined the inventory of psalms in different ways; Lange, "Collecting Psalms in Light of the Dead Sea Scrolls," in *A Teacher for All Generations: Essays in Honor of James C. VanderKam* (2 vols.; ed. E. F. Mason et al; Leiden: Brill, 2011), 1:297–308. In his analysis of textual fluidity in the manuscripts, Lange wisely considers only eleven of the thirty-six identified "psalms manuscripts," because the other twenty-five cannot be conclusively identified as psalm collections (299). Lange compares the collection of psalms to that of *hodayot*, arguing that both psalms and *hodayot* were considered independent units and collected more or less randomly depending on need and affordability. While I see some evidence of deliberate editorial choices in combining psalms, these seem to apply to smaller units of a few compositions, rather than to entire, deliberately shaped collections.

23. For his survey, see P. W. Flint, *The Dead Sea Psalms Scrolls and the Book of Psalms*, 27–47.
24. 4QPs^a, 4QPs^b, 4QPs^c, 4QPs^e, 11QPs^d, and 11QPs^a.
25. See Pajunen, *Land to the Elect*, 55–62. See also J. P. M. van der Ploeg, "Un petit rouleau de psaumes apocryphes (11QPsAp*)," in *Tradition und Glaube: Das frühe Christentum in seiner Umwelt: Festgabe für Karl Georg Kuhn zum 65. Geburtstag* (ed. G. Jeremias et al.; Gottingen: Vandenhoeck & Ruprecht, 1971), 128–39; and É. Puech, who identifies 11Q11 with the four compositions mentioned in col. 27 of 11QPsalms^a in "Les Psaumes davidiques du rituel d'exorcisme (11Q11)," in *Sapiential, Liturgical and Poetical Texts from Qumran: Proceedings of the Third Meeting of the International Organization for Qumran Studies, Oslo, 1998: Published in Memory of Maurice Baillet* (ed. D. Falk et al.; STDJ 35; Leiden: Brill, 2000), 160–81.
26. See the discussion of David as exorcist in the next chapter.
27. On this text and other Joshua traditions at Qumran, see E. Tov, "The Rewritten Book of Joshua as Found at Qumran and Masada," chapter 7 in E. Tov, *Hebrew Bible, Greek Bible, and Qumran: Collected Essays* (TSAJ 121; Tübingen: Mohr Siebeck, 2008), 71–91.
28. É. Puech, "Fragments du Psaume 122 dans un manuscrit hébreu de la grotte IV," *RevQ* 9 (1978): 547–54, and, "La pierre de Sion et l'autel des holocaustes d'après un manuscrit hébreu de la grotte 4 (4Q522)," *RB* 99 (1992): 676–96; E. Qimron, "Concerning 'Joshua Cycles' from Qumran" (Hebrew), *Tarbiz* 63 (1994): 503–8; E. Tov, "The Rewritten Book of Joshua as Found at Qumran and Masada," in *Biblical Perspectives: Early Use and Interpretation of the Bible in the Light of the Dead Sea Scrolls: Proceedings of the First International Symposium of the Orion Center, 12–14 May 1996* (ed. M. E. Stone and E. G. Chazon; STDJ 28; Leiden: Brill, 1998), 233–56.
29. Flint, *Dead Sea Psalms Scrolls*, 38.
30. See edition and notes by P. W. Flint, in *The Dead Sea Scrolls: Hebrew, Aramaic, and Greek Texts with English Translations: Pseudepigraphic and Non-Masoretic Psalms and Prayers* (ed. J. A. Charlesworth; Tübingen: Mohr Siebeck, 1997), 40–45.
31. A Hasmonean dating (175–125 BCE) was suggested by J. T. Milik, "Fragment d'une source du Psautier (4QPs89) et fragments des Jubilés, du Document de Damas, d'un phylactère dans la Grotte 4 de Qumran," *RB* 73 (1966): 94–106; J. P. M. van der Ploeg, "Le sens et un problème textuel du Ps LXXXIX," in *Mélanges bibliques et orientaux en l'honneur de M. Henri Cazelles* (ed. A. Caquot and M. Delcor; AOAT 212; Neukirchen-Vluyn: Neukirchener, 1981), 471–81, at 475, disagrees, dating it to late in the first century BCE.
32. P. Skehan, "Gleanings from Psalms Texts from Qumrân," in *Mélanges bibliques et orientaux en l'honneur de M. Henri Cazelles* (ed. A. Caquot and M. Delcor; AOAT 212; Neukirchen-Vluyn: Neukirchener, 1981), 439–45, at 439.
33. It seems that the scribe began the passage with the chosenness of David, Ps 89:20b, "I have exalted one chosen from the people," and a variant version of 89:20a—"you will speak in a vision to your chosen ones" (cf. MT "you spoke")—was inserted in smaller letters in the space above the text, probably in the top margin of the fragment.
34. Milik, "Fragment."
35. Van Der Ploeg, "Le sens," 475, 481.
36. Skehan, "Gleanings," 439.
37. 4QPs^h makes this fairly clear, since the extant fragment is from the first column of the scroll.
38. P. W. Skehan, E. Ulrich, and P. W. Flint, "Two Manuscripts of Psalm 119 from Qumran Cave 4," *RevQ* 16 (1995): 477–86. See also the analysis in E. M. Schuller, "Some Reflections on the Function and Use of Poetical Texts among the Dead Sea Scrolls," in *Liturgical Perspectives: Prayer and Poetry in Light of the Dead Sea Scrolls: Proceedings of the Fifth International Symposium of the Orion Center, 19–23 January, 2000* (ed. E. G. Chazon; STDJ 48; Leiden: Brill, 2003), 173–89, at 184.
39. K. A. Reynolds, *Torah as Teacher: The Exemplary Torah Student in Psalm 119* (VTSup 137; Leiden: Brill, 2010).
40. 1QPs^c—Ps 44; 3QPs—Ps 2:6–7; pap6QPs—some words probably from Ps 78:36–37; 4QPs^l—Ps104; 4QPs^p—Ps 104:3–4, 6–8; 4QPs^t—two words from Ps 42:5; 4QPs^u—two words from Ps 99:1; 4QPs^v—part of Ps 18:26–29.

41. The manuscript comprises four fragments containing Pss 101, 102, and 109 and an intact scroll with the rest of the compositions. While the ending is preserved (Ps 151 followed by a blank final column), the fragments from the beginning are not complete. But as Skehan first argued in detail, it seems likely that Psalm 101 was indeed the first composition in the original scroll based on the unique placement of the text on the parchment. The top of the manuscript is preserved, and Ps 101 begins on the right margin. See Skehan, "Qumran and Old Testament Criticism," in *Qumrân: Sa piété, sa théologie et son milieu* (ed. M. Delcor; BETL 46; Leuven: Leuven University Press, 1978), 163–82, at 169–70. B. Z. Wacholder posits that Ps 100 was the first composition, but this is unlikely: Ps 101 begins on the top of the sheet, and Ps 100 would not have filled up the entire column before it, if one had existed; "David's Eschatological Psalter: 11QPsalms^a," *HUCA* 59 (1988): 23–72. On this see first Skehan, "Qumran and Old Testament Criticism," 163–82. One notable exception to this understanding is M. Chyutin, who argues that the scroll originally contained most of the first part of what became the Masoretic Psalter in "The Redaction of the Qumranic and the Traditional Book of Psalms as a Calendar," *RevQ* 16 (1994): 367–95. Chyutin's proposal is not based on material considerations, but required by his theory that the Psalms Scroll is rigidly calendrical and comprises a representative sampler of the compositions listed in "David's Compositions"— elaborate reconstruction of the Scroll is based on a strict understanding of its structure in line with the text of "David's Compositions," which lists, in addition to 3,600 psalms, 364 songs for each day of the year, 52 Sabbath songs, 30 songs for the new moons and festivals, and 4 songs for exorcism. For a discussion of this proposal, see E. Mroczek, "Psalms Unbound: Ancient Concepts of Textual Tradition in 11QPsalms^a and Related Texts" (Ph.D. diss., University of Toronto, 2012), 51–53.
42. J. A. Sanders, *The Psalms Scroll of Qumrân Cave 11 (11QPs^a)* (DJD 4; Oxford: Clarendon, 1965), 4; Flint, *Dead Sea Psalms Scrolls*, 40, 40 n. 85. Two scrolls are substantially longer: 1QIsa^a (nearly 7.5 meters) and 11QT (originally about 9 meters). See E. Tov, "The Dimensions of the Qumran Scrolls," *DSD* 5 (1998): 69–91.
43. On this, see the assessment of Pajunen: "In practical terms, in order to fit all 150 MT Psalms into a single scroll it would have to be a tall scroll of 30+ lines in a column, with broad columns written in prose format, and even then the resulting book of psalms would probably be close to ten meters long, i.e., comparable to the longest extant scroll from the Judean desert, *viz.* the Temple Scroll. It is not self-evident that any of the preserved Qumran psalms manuscripts were originally of such size in column width and height." Pajunen, "Perspectives," 143–44.
44. D. Barthélemy and J. T. Milik, *Qumran Cave 1* (DJD 1; Oxford: Clarendon, 1955), 71; Flint, *Dead Sea Psalms Scrolls*, 31.
45. See P. W. Skehan et al., "4QPs^b," in *Qumran Cave 4, XI. Psalms to Chronicles* (ed. E. Ulrich et al.; DJD 16; Oxford: Clarendon, 2000), 23–48; Flint, *Dead Sea Psalms Scrolls*, 34.
46. 120 is conjectured, but 121–132 are extant. The remaining Psalms of Ascent, 133 and 134, appear later in the collection.
47. The Passover Hallel, Psalms 113–18, may be another shared sequence, although only part of 118 remains, with the rest reconstructed. See Flint, *Dead Sea Psalms Scrolls*, 135–49, 238–39, 254; Wilson, *The Editing of the Hebrew Psalter*, esp. 116–21, and "The Qumran Psalms Scroll (11QPs^a) and the Canonical Psalter: Comparison of Editorial Shaping," *CBQ* 59 (1997): 448–64.
48. Scrolls 1QPs^a, 4QPs^e, 4QPs^f, 11QPs^b, and 11QPs^d.
49. Scrolls 4QPs^e, 4QPs^f, 11QPs^b, respectively.
50. Scrolls 11QPs^a, 4QPs^f, 4Q522, 11QPs^b, and 11QPsAp^a. Flint, *Dead Sea Psalms Scrolls*, 243–51 ("Appendix 1: 'Apocryphal' Psalms and Other Compositions").
51. P. Flint, "Psalms, Book of: Biblical Texts," in *Encyclopedia of the Dead Sea Scrolls*, 2:702–7, at 702 and 706–7.
52. See Lange, "Collecting Psalms in Light of the Dead Sea Scrolls."
53. See, e.g., J. A. Sanders, "Cave 11 Surprises and the Question of Canon," *McCormick Quarterly* 21 (1968): 284–98. Flint discusses two-stage stabilization in *Dead Sea Psalms Scrolls*, 149, 150–71.

54. On the nonexistence of a book of Psalms as a concept and the inadequacy of book language for early Jewish traditions, see Mroczek, "Psalms Unbound," esp. 32–35, and "Thinking Digitally about the Dead Sea Scrolls: Book History before and beyond the Book," *Book History* 14 (2011): 235–63. See now also the thorough statistical analysis of the manuscripts in Pajunen, "Perspectives."

55. See, e.g., B. Baba Bathra 14b. Also Genesis Rabbah 68 and 74, B. Soferim 16:17, Y. Baba Bathra 13a (cf. Jastrow, 1649).

56. 4Q491 frag 17 line 4. M. Baillet, *Qumrân Grotte 4 III (4Q482–4Q520)* (DJD 7; Oxford: Clarendon, 1982), 40–41.

57. F. García Martínez and E. J. C. Tigchelaar, *The Dead Sea Scrolls Study Edition* (2 vols.; Leiden: Brill, 1997–98), 2:979.

58. "S'il s'agit vraiment du livre biblique des Psaumes, nous avons ici la plus ancienne attestation de son titre, tel qu'il a été conservé par la tradition juive." Baillet, *Qumrân Grotte 4 III*, 7, 41.

59. As translated in García Martínez and Tigchelaar, *The Dead Sea Scrolls Study Edition*, 1.135 and 1.119.

60. Communication reported in Flint, *Dead Sea Psalms Scrolls*, 23 n. 56; and see F. García Martínez, "Old Texts and Modern Mirages: The 'I' in Two Qumran Hymns," in *Qumranica Minora I: Qumran Origins and Apocalypticism* (ed. F. García Martínez; STDJ 63; Leiden: Brill, 2007), 105–28, at 118, n. 54. The references are translated as "hymn of the return" and "praise of God" in J. Duhaime, "War Scroll," in *The Dead Sea Scrolls*, vol. 2: *Damascus Document, War Scroll and Related Documents* (ed. J. A. Charlesworth; PTSDSSP 2; Louisville: WJK Press and Tübingen: Mohr Siebeck, 1995), 80–203, at 124 and 107.

61. K. Davis, "'Self-Glorification Hymn(s)' and the Usage of 'Scripture' in the Context of War: A Study of ספר התהלים in 4QM^a (4Q491) Frg. 17," forthcoming in *Text and Interpretation of the Hebrew Bible* (provisional title; ed. D. K. Falk et al.; Atlanta: SBL Press).

62. Baillet, *Qumrân Grotte 4 III*, 7, 41 (Hippolytus: ed. deLagarde, 188; hexaplaric palimpsest: Mercati, *Un Palimpsesto Ambrosiano dei Salmi Esapli*, Turin, 1898; Eusebius, *Hist. eccl.* 6.25).

63. I discuss this text in detail in chapter 2.

64. Trans. C. Begg, *Flavius Josephus: Translation and Commentary*, vol. 4: *Judean Antiquities Books 5–7* (ed. S. Mason; Leiden: Brill, 2005), 288.

65. Josephus does not use the word "psalm" for David's compositions; this term is also lacking from his vague list of scriptural texts in *Against Apion* (I.40), where he presents the law of Moses, thirteen prophetic books, and "the remaining four books [which] contain hymns to God and instructions for people on life."

66. Flint, "Psalms, Book of: Biblical Texts," 207.

67. Flint, *Dead Sea Psalms Scrolls*, 26.

68. J. M. Allegro, *Qumrân Cave 4*, vol. 1, *4Q158–4Q186* (DJD 5; Oxford: Clarendon, 1968), 42–53; J. Strugnell, "Notes en marge du volume V des 'Discoveries in the Judaean Desert of Jordan,'" *RevQ* 7 (1970): 211–20; Barthélemy and Milik, *Qumran Cave 1*.

69. The *pesharim* are so heavily fragmented that any attempt to determine how their lemmata were selected would be mere speculation; but at least from the one fairly extensive manuscript, 4Q171, the appeal of Ps 37 to sectarian concerns seems obvious. Psalm 37 is an acrostic wisdom psalm that sets up a duality between the righteous and the wicked, is concerned with the affliction of the righteous, exhorts them to turn away from sin, and promises them ultimate salvation. These concerns lend themselves well to reinterpretation in sectarian theological terms in the *pesher*, which predictably connects the righteous and the wicked to the community and its enemies, and, as Jutta Jokiranta writes, exhorts the addressee to "return to the Law and submit to the community—and avoid the fate of the wicked." See Jokiranta, *Social Identity and Sectarianism in the Qumran Movement* (STDJ 105; Leiden: Brill, 2013), 122–40, at 134.

70. M. Haran, "Archives, Libraries, and the Order of the Biblical Books," *JANES* 22 (1993): 52–61, at 58.

71. J. Barton, *Oracles of God: Perceptions of Ancient Prophecy in Israel after the Exile* (New York: Oxford University Press, 1986), 57. On the "library" of Nehemiah as a royal archive, see S. Schorch, "The Libraries in 2 Macc 2:13-15," in *The Books of the Maccabees: History,*

Theology, Ideology: Papers of the Second International Conference on the Deuterocanonical Books, Pápa, Hungary, 9–11 June, 2005 (ed. G. G. Xeravits and J. Zsengellér; JSJS 118; Leiden: Brill, 2007), 169–80.

72. S. J. DeVries, "Moses and David as Cult Founders in Chronicles," *JBL* 107 (1988): 619–39; and S. Japhet, *The Ideology of the Book of Chronicles and Its Place in Biblical Thought* (trans. A. Barber; BEATAJ 9; Frankfurt am Main: Lang, 1989), 236–38.

73. S. Japhet, *I and II Chronicles: A Commentary* (Louisville: Westminster John Knox, 1993), 1049.

74. Biblicizing distorts our sense of what kind of information 2 Macc 2 can provide, since the automatic identification of David with Psalms has been the basis for further-reaching conclusions. Y. Miura, for example, writes that it tells us "how the Psalms are employed in the final 150 years BCE," namely that

> [a]ll the Psalms are read in the Davidic context. Unlike Sirach, 2 Maccabees indicates Davidic attribution of the Psalter.... The Psalms in the Davidic context are easily applied to the Jew's individual life. David's life gives the dispersed Jews great encouragement.... The authority of the Psalms is necessary so they might be able to give the Jews in [sic] instruction the ways of the Jewish festival (*David in Luke-Acts: His Portrayal in the Light of Early Judaism* [Tübingen: Mohr Siebeck, 2007], 54).

This circular argument assumes that "David" means all the Psalms, and based on this, concludes that all the Psalms were now Davidic, speculating further on the reception of the Psalter in Maccabean times—based on a text that never mentions psalms at all. The reference to David is taken for granted as biblical, and molded into evidence for the development of canon, attribution, and exegesis.

75. E. Qimron and J. Strugnell, *Qumran Cave 4. 5, Miqsat Ma'ase Ha-Torah* (DJD 10; Oxford: Clarendon, 1994); M. L. Grossman, "Reading 4QMMT: Genre and History," *RevQ* 20 (2001): 3–22; H. von Weissenberg, *4QMMT: Reevaluating the Text, the Function, and the Meaning of the Epilogue* (STDJ 82; Leiden: Brill, 2009); M. J. Bernstein, "The Employment and Interpretation of Scripture in 4QMMT: Preliminary Observations," in *Reading 4QMMT: New Perspectives on Qumran Law and History* (ed. J. Kampen and M. J. Bernstein; SBLSymS 2; Atlanta: Scholars Press, 1996), 29–51.

76. Qimron and Strugnell, DJD 10, 59.

77. See, among many others, S. Z. Leiman, *The Canonization of Hebrew Scripture: The Talmudic and Midrashic Evidence* (Hamden, Conn.: Archon Books, 1976), 28–30; A. van der Kooij, "The Canonization of Ancient Books Kept in the Temple of Jerusalem," in *Canonization and Decanonization* (ed. A. van der Kooij and K. van der Toorn; Studies in the History of Religions 82; Leiden: Brill, 1998), 17–40; H. Eshel, "4QMMT and the History of the Hasmonean Period," in *Reading 4QMMT: New Perspectives on Qumran Law and History* (ed. J. Kampen and M. J. Bernstein; SBLSymS 2; Atlanta: Scholars Press, 1996), 53–65, esp. 59; and L. H. Schiffman, "The Place of 4QMMT in the Corpus of Qumran Manuscripts," in Kampen and Bernstein, *Reading 4QMMT*, 81–98; and G. J. Brooke, "The Explicit Presentation of Scripture in 4QMMT," in *Legal Texts and Legal Issues: Proceedings of the Second Meeting of the International Organization for Qumran Studies, Published in Honour of Joseph M. Baumgarten* (ed. M. Bernstein et al.; STDJ 23; Leiden: Brill, 1997), 85–87. Other proof texts are Luke 24:44, Philo's *Contempl.* 25, and the prologue to Sirach.

78. The original editors, Elisha Qimron and John Strugnell, write that ובדוי[ד] "probably refers not only to the Psalms of David, but rather to the Hagiographa. This is a significant piece of evidence for the history of the tripartite division of the Canon" (*Qumran Cave 4. 5*, 59 n. 10).

79. See, e.g., K. Berthelot, "4QMMT et la question du canon de la Bible hébraïque," in *From 4QMMT to Resurrection: Mélanges qumraniens en hommage à Émile Puech*, eds. F. García Martínez et al.; STDJ 61 (Leiden: Brill, 2006), 1–14; H. von Weissenberg, "4QMMT— Some New Readings," in *Northern Lights on the Dead Sea Scrolls: Proceedings of the Nordic Qumran Network 2003–2006* (ed. A. Klostergaard et al.; STDJ 80; Leiden: Brill, 2009), 217–21; see also E. C. Ulrich, "The Non-Attestation of a Tripartite Canon in 4QMMT," *CBQ* 65 (2003): 202–14, and T. H. Lim, "The Alleged Reference to the Tripartite Division of the Hebrew Bible," *RevQ* 20 (2001): 23–37.

80. After careful examination of each fragment, Ulrich concludes that it is not certain that the word "Moses" or the "books of the prophets" occur here, and that the word "David" is also uncertain (ובדור is an equally likely reading). Ulrich's last point is that "if the word were David, there would be no basis for suggesting that it is intended to signify anything more than the Psalms" (Ulrich, "Non-Attestation," 211). I would add another point of uncertainty: If the word were "David," there would be no basis for assuming it signifies the Psalms; in fact, more likely possibilities exist.

81. G. J. Brooke, "The Psalms in Early Jewish Literature in the Light of the Dead Sea Scrolls," in *The Psalms in the New Testament*, eds. S. Moyise and M. J. J. Menken; (London: T&T Clark, 2004), 14; Lim, "The Alleged Reference to the Tripartite Division," 35–36. Lim's argument is stronger than he presents it. In his view, the *"Psalms* [sic] have certainly been collected, even if the latter part of the Psalter is still in a state of flux" ("Tripartite Division," 35); but since there is no recognizable concept of a coherent "Psalter," the identification of "David" with such a collection is even less likely.

82. Scroll 4QMMTe frag. 14 II 1–2.

83. See, e.g., 4Q398 frags. 11–13, lines 1–2; Lim, "Tripartite Division," 36.

84. Kraft, "Para-Mania," 22.

85. An intriguing analogy comes from the study of medieval manuscripts, particularly kabbalistic texts. Daniel Abrams presents a similar argument about the Zohar to my contention about the book of Psalms:

> All the facts demonstrate that the 'Book of the *Zohar*', or the *Zohar as a book, is a late invention* that should not be attributed to the process or intention of its composition at the end of the thirteenth century and the beginning of the fourteenth century. *In other words, the Zohar was neither written, nor edited, nor distributed as a book by the various figures who produced the literary units that were later known by the name 'Zohar.'* (*Kabbalistic Manuscripts and Textual Theory: Methodologies of Textual Scholarship and Editorial Practice in the Study of Jewish Mysticism* [2nd rev. ed.; Jerusalem: Magnes Press, 2013], 227; italics in the original)

86. Barton, *Oracles of God*, 58.

87. For issues related to editing the texts of the Hebrew Bible, see R. S. Hendel, "The Oxford Hebrew Bible: Prologue to a New Critical Edition," *VT* 58 (2008): 324–51; and E. J. C. Tigchelaar, "Editing the Hebrew Bible: An Overview of Some Problems," in *Editing the Bible: Assessing the Task Past and Present* (ed. J. S. Kloppenborg and J. H. Newman; Atlanta: Society of Biblical Literature, 2012), 41–68. For a vibrant recent discussion of the idea of text as process, not finished product, as a challenge to traditional textual criticism in biblical studies, see Breed, *Nomadic Text*. For this problem in the study of Jewish pseudepigrapha—which are usually preserved in much later Christian manuscripts—the work of Liv I. Lied is especially instructive. See, e.g., her *"Nachleben* and Textual Identity: Variants and Variance in the Reception History of 2 Baruch," in *Fourth Ezra and Second Baruch: Reconstruction after the Fall* (ed. M. Henze and G. Boccaccini; JSJSup 164; Leiden: Brill, 2013), 403–28. Much work has also been done on this in the context of later Jewish manuscripts, esp. the Heikhalot literature; see P. Schäfer, *The Hidden and Manifest God: Some Major Themes in Early Jewish Mysticism* (trans. A. Pomerance; Albany: State University of New York Press, 1992); and R. Boustan, "The Study of Heikhalot Literature: Between Mystical Experience and Textual Artifact," *Currents in Biblical Research* 6 (2007): 130–60. See more on the issue of textual identity and editorial practice in chapter 3.

88. McKenzie, "The Broken Phial," 37.

89. McKenzie, "The Broken Phial," 37.

90. R. Chartier, "Languages, Books, and Reading from the Printed Word to the Digital Text," trans. T. L. Fagan, *Critical Inquiry* 31 (2004): 133–51, at 145.

91. R. Chartier, "Representations of the Written Word," in *Forms and Meanings: Texts, Performances and Audiences from Codex to Computer* (Philadelphia: University of Pennsylvania Press, 1995), 6–24, at 18.

92. See Mroczek, "Thinking Digitally," 238 and notes.

93. N. K. Hayles, "Translating Media: Why We Should Rethink Textuality," *Yale Journal of Criticism* 16 (2003): 263–90, at 277.

94. Hayles, "Translating Media,"278.
95. For a different context where the analogy of a "database" is helpful, see Israel Ta-Shma's work on the concept of the "open book" in medieval Hebrew writing, that is, texts that were not intended by their creators to be final or fixed, but "as presentations of an interim state of knowledge or opinion, somewhat like our computerized databases, which are constantly updated"; I. M. Ta-Shma, "The 'Open' Book in Medieval Hebrew Literature: The Problem of Authorized Editions," *BJRL* 75 (1993): 17–24, at 17. I discuss this concept further in chapter 3.
96. See Abrams, *Kabbalistic Manuscripts*, which draws on the concept of the "open book" developed by Ta-Shma and by M. Beit-Arié, *Hebrew Manuscripts of East and West: Towards a Comparative Codicology* (Panizzi Lectures; London: British Library, 1993), 79–124; see further chapter 3.
97. Translation adapted from García Martínez and Tigchelaar, *The Dead Sea Scrolls Study Edition*, 2:1179.
98. J. L. Kugel, "David the Prophet," in *Poetry and Prophecy: The Beginnings of a Literary Tradition* (ed. J. L. Kugel; Ithaca, N.Y.: Cornell University Press, 1990), 45–55, at 54.
99. Begg, *Flavius Josephus*, 288.
100. On heavenly books as a motif and a life-and-death metaphor in apocalyptic literature, see L. Baynes, *The Heavenly Book Motif in Judeo-Christian Apocalypses, 200 B.C.E.–200 C.E* (JSJSup 152; Leiden: Brill, 2012).
101. L. T. Stuckenbruck, "The Epistle of Enoch: Genre and Authorial Presentation," *DSD* 17.3 (2010): 387–417, at 398.
102. W. Yarchin, "Was 11Q5 a True Psalter?," paper presented at the Annual Meeting of the Society of Biblical Literature, November 23, 2013. I thank the author for sharing the prepublication version of this paper with me. It has since been published as "Were the Psalms Collections at Qumran True Psalters?" *JBL* 134 (2015): 775–89. His research on the flexible shaping of medieval Hebrew psalms manuscripts is also discussed in N. L. deClaissé-Walford et al., *The Book of Psalms* (New International Commentary on the Old Testament; Grand Rapids, Mich.: Eerdmans, 2014), 3–4. See further chapter 5.
103. See the essays collected in *The Old Greek Psalter: Studies in Honour of Albert Pietersma* (ed. R. J. V. Hiebert, C. E. Cox, and P. J. Gentry; Sheffield: Sheffield Academic Press, 2001).
104. See Flint, *Dead Sea Psalms Scrolls*, 228–36, and "Variant Readings of the Dead Sea Psalms Scrolls against the Massoretic Text and the Septuagint Psalter," in *Der Septuaginta-Psalter und seine Tochterübersetzungen* (ed. A. Aejmelaeus and U. Quast; Göttingen: Vandenhoeck & Ruprecht, 2000), 337–65.
105. Rahfls 2014, 2019, 2051.
106. Rahfls 2110; see A. Pietersma, "Ra 2110 (P. Bodmer XXIV) and the Text of the Greek Psalter," in *Studien zur Septuaginta—Robert Hanhart zu Ehren* (ed. D. Fraenkel, U. Quast, and J. W. Wevers; MSU 20; Göttingen, Vandenhoeck & Ruprecht, 1990), 262–86.
107. See Brooke, "The Psalms in Early Jewish Literature," 7 n. 8.
108. Origen, prologue to his *Commentary on Psalms, Patrologia Graeca* 12:1056.
109. K. Davis, *The Cave 4 Apocryphon of Jeremiah and the Qumran Jeremianic Traditions: Prophetic Persona and the Construction of Community Identity* (STDJ 111; Leiden: Brill, 2014). See G. J. Brooke, "The Book of Jeremiah and Its Reception in the Qumran Scrolls," in *The Book of Jeremiah and its Reception* (ed. A. H. W. Curtis and T. Römer; BETL 128; Leuven: Peeters, 1997), 183–205; and E. J. C. Tigchelaar, "Classification of the Collection of Dead Sea Scrolls and the Case of Apocryphon of Jeremiah C," *JSJ* 43 (2012): 519–50.
110. Davis, *The Cave 4 Apocryphon of Jeremiah*, 302–3.
111. Davis, *The Cave 4 Apocryphon of Jeremiah*, 7.
112. Davis, *The Cave 4 Apocryphon of Jeremiah*, 303.
113. On this text as a locus classicus of inner-biblical interpretation, see M. Henze, "The Use of Scripture in the Book of Daniel," in *A Companion to Biblical Interpretation in Early Judaism* (ed. M. Henze; Grand Rapids, Mich.: Eerdmans, 2012), 279–307.
114. Henze, "The Use of Scripture," 301.
115. Henze, "The Use of Scripture," 300.
116. S. L. Sanders, "Daniel and the Origins of Jewish Biblical Interpretation," *Prooftexts,* forthcoming.
117. Sanders, "Daniel and the Origins."

118. M. Fishbane, *Biblical Interpretation in Ancient Israel* (Oxford: Clarendon, 1985), 488–89.
119. Naomi Janowitz writes that the "equation of the term Torah with five books written by Moses, beginning with creation and ending with his final speech and death, is surprisingly late in the history of Judaism"; "The Rhetoric of Translation: Three Early Perspectives on Translating Torah," *HTR* 84 (1991): 129–40, at 131. On the various ways in which "Torah" could be perceived as authoritative, see S. Schorch, "Which Kind of Authority? The Authority of the Torah during the Hellenistic and the Roman Periods," in *Scriptural Authority in Early Judaism and Ancient Christianity* (ed. I. Kalimi, T. Nicklas, and G. G. Xeravits; Berlin: de Gruyter, 2013).
120. On the ambiguity of "torah" see H. Najman, "Torah of Moses: Pseudonymous Attribution in Second Temple Writings," in *The Interpretation of Scripture in Early Judaism and Christianity: Studies in Language and Tradition* (ed. C. A. Evans; JSPSup 33; Sheffield: Sheffield Academic Press, 2000), 202–16; Stone, *Ancient Judaism,* 123–50; Bowley and Reeves, "Rethinking the Concept of 'Bible,'" esp. 6–7; and J. C. VanderKam, "Questions of Canon Viewed through the Dead Sea Scrolls," *BBR* 11 (2001): 269–92.
121. See J. Pakkala, "The Quotations and References of the Pentateuchal Laws in Ezra-Nehemiah," in *Changes in Scripture: Rewriting and Interpreting Authoritative Traditions in the Second Temple Period* (Berlin: de Gruyter, 2011), 193–222; and M. LeFebvre, *Collections, Codes, and Torah: The Re-characterization of Israel's Written Law* (New York: T&T Clark, 2006), 101–31.
122. See M. LeFebvre and C. Houtman, "Ezra and the Law: Observations on the Supposed Relation between Ezra and the Pentateuch," in *Remembering All the Way: A Collection of Old Testament Studies Published on the Occasion of the 40th Anniversary of the Oudtestamentisch Werkgezelschap in Nederland* (ed. B. Albrektson; Leiden: Brill, 1981), 91–115; S. Japhet, "Law and 'the Law' in Ezra-Nehemiah," *Proceedings of the World Congress of Jewish Studies* 9 (1985): 99–115.
123. This sense of "Torah" is not attested till the second century BCE, in Aristobulus; see Janowitz, "Rhetoric of Translation"; and J. Blenkinsopp, *Wisdom and Law in the Old Testament and in Early Judaism* (Oxford: Oxford University Press, 1984), 11. Most recently, David Lambert has made a case that "*torat moshe* and its variants seem to denote some more limited body of law that came to be associated with the figure of Moses, not a mixture of law and narrative, such as that found in the Pentateuch," in "How the 'Torah of Moses' Became Revelation: An Early, Apocalyptic Theory of Pentateuchal Origins," *JSJ,* forthcoming. I thank the author for sharing a prepublication version of this essay with me.
124. See Reeves, "Problematizing the Bible," 145.
125. Emanuel Tov and Sidnie White Crawford have argued that 4QRP did preserve the whole Pentateuch, unlike other mss; see Crawford, "Reworked Pentateuch," in *Encyclopedia of the Dead Sea Scrolls* (ed. L. H. Schiffman and J. C. VanderKam; vol. 2; New York: Oxford University Press, 2000), 775–77, at 775, and Tov, "From 4QReworked Pentateuch to 4QPentateuch (?)," in *Authoritative Scriptures in Ancient Judaism* (ed. M. Popović; Leiden: Brill, 2010), 73–91.
126. On the Greek translation and its impact, see T. M. Law, *When God Spoke Greek: The Septuagint and the Making of the Christian Bible* (New York: Oxford University Press, 2013). For the *Letter of Aristeas,* see the new commentary from B. G. Wright III, *The Letter of Aristeas: 'Aristeas to Philocrates' or 'On the Translation of the Law of the Jews'* (Commentaries on Early Jewish Literature; Berlin: De Gruyter, 2015).
127. See, e.g., P. Davies, "The Authority of Deuteronomy," in *Deuteronomy-Kings as Emerging Authoritative Books: A Conversation* (ed. D. Edelman; Atlanta: SBL, 2014), 27–47, who assumes that the references to reading and interpreting *torat Moshe* in Ezra-Nehemiah must refer specifically either to Deuteronomy or to a Pentateuch. This identification leads him to conclude the narrative must reflect later concerns than the mid-fifth century, because Deuteronomy or the Pentateuch likely did not yet exist: "There must be doubts about the historical reliability of this narrative. Whether a scroll of Deuteronomy, let alone a proto-Pentateuch existed in the mid-fifth century B.C.E. is questionable. Like the anti-Samari(t)an tenor of the book, this seems to be an anachronism, reflecting conditions of a later period" (32 n.12). In the same volume, Thomas Römer argues that the reference in 2 Kgs 14:6 to Amaziah's conformity with "what is written in the Book of the Law of Moses" "contains a

quotation from Deut 24:16, [which] does not necessarily mean in the context of the late Persian period that the משה תורת [sic] was considered to be only the book of Deuteronomy; it already could allude to some kind of Pentateuch"; "The Case of the Book of Kings," 187–201, at 197. In a different context, Michael Satlow writes that the *Letter of Aristeas* presents the Pentateuch as a single divine book (*How the Bible Became Holy,* 165), but, as I argued above, there is no explicit identification of the law with the Pentateuch specifically, since Philo is the first to mention a fivefold collection of law. This ambiguity may in fact strengthen Satlow's broader argument about the late and gradual development of the normative authority of a specific collection of scriptural texts.

Chapter 2 The Sweetest Voice

1. J. G. Herder, *The Spirit of Hebrew Poetry* (trans. J. Marsh; Burlington, Vt.: Edward Smith, 1833), 2.223–29. The work first appeared in German in 1782 as *Vom Geiste der Ebräischen Poesie: Eine Anleitung für die Liebhaber derselben, und der ältesten Geschichte des menschlichen Geiste.*
2. *The Popular Cyclopaedia of Biblical Literature* (ed. J. Kitto; Boston: Gould and Lincoln, 1854), 686; repr. in the *Encyclopedia Britannica* entry on Psalms (1859), 678–79.
3. Michel Foucault presents the importance of the "author function" in our approach to texts as historically contingent—the question of who wrote a text, when, and under what circumstances has not always been central to the way texts are organized and studied, but presupposes modern ideas about intellectual property and intention. See Foucault, "What Is an Author?," in *Michel Foucault: Aesthetics, Method, and Epistemology* (ed. J. Faubion; trans. R. Hurley et al.; vol. 1 of *Essential Works of Foucault, 1954–84;* ed. P. Rainbow; New York: New Press, 1998). Hindy Najman has drawn on Foucault's historicization of the concept of authorship in *Seconding Sinai: The Development of Mosaic Discourse in Second Temple Judaism* (Leiden: Brill, 2003), where she reimagines Foucault's concept of a discourse tied to a founder in the context of literature attributed to ancient figures in early Judaism, and *Losing the Temple and Recovering the Future: An Analysis of* 4 Ezra (Cambridge: Cambridge University Press, 2014), especially chapter 2, "The Past and Future Ezra," 26–66, where she introduces the idea of a *genre* tied to a founder using the example of Homer—"all heroic epics were ascribed to Homer, and all didactic epics to Hesiod" (43–44), in a way not dissimilar to Herder's statement that "a beautiful song is synonymous with a song of David." I discuss Najman's work further below. On the historical contingency of the author's identity as an organizing principle for literature, see also R. Chartier, "Figures of the Author," in *The Order of Books: Readers, Authors, and Libraries in Europe between the Fourteenth and Eighteenth Centuries* (trans. L.G. Cochrane; Stanford, Calif.: Stanford University Press, 1994), 25–59.
4. A. Y. Reed, "Pseudepigraphy, Authorship, and the Reception of 'the Bible' in Late Antiquity," in *The Reception and Interpretation of the Bible in Late Antiquity: Proceedings of the Montréal Colloquium in Honour of Charles Kannengiesser, 11–13 October 2006* (ed. L. DiTommaso and L. Turcescu; Leiden: Brill, 2008), 467–490, at 477. On this idea in relation to Enoch as tradent of revelation see also Reed, "Heavenly Ascent, Angelic Descent, and the Transmission of Knowledge in 1 Enoch 6-16," in *Heavenly Realms and Earthly Realities in Late Antique Religions* (ed. R. Boustan and A. Y. Reed; New York: Cambridge University Press, 2004), 47–66.
5. "Pseudepigrapha" refers to a corpus of nonbiblical texts, many but not all of which are pseudonymously attributed, and "pseudepigraphy" is a literary phenomenon that appears in both biblical and nonbiblical texts. The terms have strongly negative connotations—they "imply that they are inherently and categorically 'false,' impressing them with modern judgments, predicated on anachronistic ideas of authorship and forgery alike," writes A. Y. Reed in "'The Modern Invention of 'Old Testament Pseudepigrapha,'" *Journal of Theological Studies* 60 (2009): 403–36, at 404. I discuss the modern publication history of these texts in chapter 4. On these problematic categories see Najman, *Seconding Sinai,* esp. 1–12; and elsewhere Reed, "Pseudepigraphy, Authorship and the Reception of 'the Bible' in Late Antiquity," which provides an excellent intellectual history of the practice with a specific focus on late

antique Christian conceptions of authorship and canon, and how this context has framed the earlier Jewish material. See the introduction by E. J. C. Tigchelaar, "Old Testament Pseudepigrapha and the Scriptures," in *Old Testament Pseudepigrapha and the Scriptures* (ed. E. J. C. Tigchelaar; BETL 270; Leuven: Peeters, 2014), 1–18. See also the earlier comments of J. H. Charlesworth in his "Introduction for the General Reader" to the *Old Testament Pseudepigrapha* (2 vols.; Garden City, N.Y.: Doubleday, 1983–85), 1:xxiv–xxv; and J. A. Sanders, "Introduction: Why the Pseudepigrapha?," in *Pseudepigrapha and Early Biblical Interpretation* (ed. J. H. Charlesworth and C. A. Evans; JSOPSS 14, SSEJC 2; Sheffield: JSOT, 1993), 13–19; and M. E. Stone, "The Dead Sea Scrolls and the Pseudepigrapha," *DSD* 3 (1996): 270–95. For an earlier account of pseudepigraphy as a phenomenon within the Bible, particularly Deuteronomy, see M. Smith, "Pseudepigraphy in the Israelite Tradition," in *Pseudepigrapha I* (ed. K. von Fritz; Geneva: Foundations Hardt, 1972), 189–215; writing before much of the material from the Scrolls was published, Smith dismisses later Hellenistic pseudepigraphy as narrowly sectarian. The literature on pseudepigraphy as a practice and its relationship with and distinction from forgery is copious. Among many others, see W. Speyer, *Die Literarische Falschung in Heidnischen und Christlichen Altertum: Ein Versuch Ihrer Deutung* (Munich: C. H. Beck'sche, 1971); B. Metzger, "Literary Forgeries and Canonical Pseudepigrapha," *JBL* 91 (1972): 3–24; D. G. Meade, *Pseudonymity and Canon: An Investigation into the Relationship of Authorship and Authority in Jewish and Earliest Christian Tradition* (Tübingen: J. C. B. Mohr, 1986); E. G. Chazon and M. E. Stone, eds., *Pseudepigraphic Perspectives: The Apocrypha and Pseudepigrapha in Light of the Dead Sea Scrolls* (Leiden: Brill, 1999), esp. the introductory essay by M. J. Bernstein, "Pseudepigraphy in the Qumran Scrolls: Categories and Functions," 1–26, and G. W. E. Nickelsburg, "The Nature and Function of Revelation in 1 Enoch, Jubilees, and Some Qumranic Documents," 91–119; J. Van Seters, "Creative Imitation in the Hebrew Bible," *SR* 29 (2000): 395–409; T. H. Lim, H. L. MacQueen, and C. M. Carmichael, eds., *On Scrolls, Artefacts and Intellectual Property* (JSPSup 38; Sheffield: Sheffield Academic Press, 2001); E. J. C. Tigchelaar, "Forms of Pseudepigraphy in the Dead Sea Scrolls," in *Pseudepigraphie und Verfasserfiktion in früh-christlichen Briefen* (ed. J. Frey et al.; WUNT 246; Tübingen: Mohr Siebeck, 2009), 85–101; H. Najman, "How Should We Contextualize Pseudepigrapha? Imitation and Emulation in 4 Ezra," in *Flores Florentino: Dead Sea Scrolls and Other Early Jewish Studies in Honour of Florentino García Martínez* (ed. A. Hilhorst, É. Puech, and E. J. C. Tigchelaar; JSJSup 122; Leiden: Brill, 2007), 529–36; L. T. Stuckenbruck, "The Epistle of Enoch: Genre and Authorial Presentation," *DSD* 17.3 (2010): 387–417.

6. H. Najman, "Reconsidering Jubilees: Prophecy and Exemplarity," in *Enoch and the Mosaic Torah: The Evidence of Jubilees* (ed. G. Boccaccini and G. Ibba; Grand Rapids, Mich.: Eerdmans, 2009), 229–43, at 238; repr. in Najman, *Past Renewals: Interpretative Authority, Renewed Revelation, and the Quest for Perfection in Jewish Antiquity* (Leiden: Brill, 2010), 189–204.

7. Trans. J. M. G. Barclay, *Flavius Josephus: Translation and Commentary*, vol. 10: *Against Apion* (ed. S. Mason; Leiden: Brill, 2007), 29–31. On this text and its significance for emerging concepts of canon, see chapter 5.

8. See J. Wyrick, *The Ascension of Authorship: Attribution and Canon Formation in Jewish, Hellenistic, and Christian Traditions* (Cambridge, Mass.: Harvard University Press, 2004). Wyrick writes that the drive to attribute texts to ancient figures emerges from a *horror vacui*, a discomfort with anonymous texts. Mark Griffith discerns such a move in the false attribution of classical literature in the context of Alexandrian scholarship, which reflects a preference for "giving works to well-known authors…rather than leaving them unassigned and anonymous—a sort of librarian's *horror vacui* for each work's official entry in the catalogue," in *The Authenticity of* Prometheus Bound (Cambridge: Cambridge University Press, 1977), 242.

9. J. G. Campbell, "Josephus' Twenty-Two Book Canon and the Qumran Scrolls," in *The Scrolls and the Scriptures: Proceedings of the Seventh Meeting of the IOQS in Helsinki* (ed. G. J. Brooke et al.; Leiden: Brill, 2012), 19–45, at 25.

10. As Foucault observed, the author function does not operate the same way for every kind of discourse. He describes, for example, the way in which the significance of the author function for literary and scientific texts was reversed in the seventeenth and eighteenth centu-

ries. Previously, literary texts "were accepted, put into circulation, and valorized without any question about the identity of their author," but their status was safeguarded by their antiquity, real or imagined, while scientific texts were "accepted as 'true,' only when marked with the name of their author." Later, the opposite was the case: scientific texts came to be accepted because of their membership in a genre, while literary texts came to require an authorial source. See Foucault, "What Is an Author?," 212–13.

11. See the landmark study *Seconding Sinai* on Mosaic discourse, as well as essays collected in *Past Renewals*. On Najman's interaction with Foucault's notion of the author function, see n. 3.

12. In this way, for example, the book of *Jubilees* does not set itself against earlier Torah traditions ("the first Torah"), but both draws on and extends their authority, claiming it also for itself through Mosaic revelation and dictation—even as it also claims authority from other sources, like the heavenly tablets and angelic speech.

13. The biblical Ezra of Ezra-Nehemiah, leader of the community who returned from the Babylonian Exile in the sixth century BCE, is recast in *4 Ezra* (ca. 100 CE) as an exemplary character who models mourning and recovery after the destruction of the Second Temple in 70 CE; see Najman, *Losing the Temple*, and earlier, "How Should We Contextualize Pseudepigrapha?"

14. K. Davis, *The Cave 4 Apocryphon of Jeremiah and the Qumran Jeremianic Traditions: Prophetic Persona and the Construction of Community Identity* (STDJ 111; Leiden: Brill, 2014), 15. See also the discussion of Jeremiah traditions in the previous chapter.

15. Davis, *The Cave 4 Apocryphon*, 303.

16. Davis, *The Cave 4 Apocryphon*, 304.

17. See G. Genette, *Seuils* (Paris: Éditions du Seuil, 1987), trans. J. E. Lewin as *Paratexts: Thresholds of Interpretation* (Cambridge: Cambridge University Press, 1997), 52–53.

18. *Leontion* fr. 7.27–34, in M. Payne, "Aristotle on Poets as Parents and the Hellenistic Poet as Mother," in *Classical Myth and Psychoanalysis: Ancient and Modern Stories of the Self* (ed. E. O'Gorman and V. Zajko; Oxford: Oxford University Press, 2013), 299–313, at 302.

19. Payne, "Aristotle on Poets as Parents," 302.

20. Aristotle, *Nicomachean Ethics*, 9.7.

21. H. Arendt, *The Human Condition* (Chicago: University of Chicago Press, 1958), 211–12.

22. H. Bloom, *The Anxiety of Influence: A Theory of Poetry* (Oxford: Oxford University Press, 1997), 10.

23. L. Pirandello, *Six Characters in Search of an Author: A Play in the Making* (trans. E. Storer; New York: E. P. Dutton, 1922), 10.

24. L. Pirandello, "Pirandello Confesses…Why and How He Wrote *Six Characters in Search of an Author*," *Virginia Quarterly Review* 1 (1925): 36–52.

25. Some scholars have recently compared this mode of text production to fan fiction. See e.g. the session at the European Association of Biblical Studies Annual Meeting in 2015 entitled "Fan Fiction and the Study of Biblical Commentary and Scribal Culture," organized by Sonja Ammann, Mette Bundvad, Solveig Grebe, and Frauke Uhlenbruch.

26. See K.-H. Bernhardt, *Das Problem der altorientalischen Konigsideologie im Alten Testament: Unter besonderer Berucksichtigung der Geschichte der Psalmenexegese dargestellt und kritisch gewurdigt* (VTS 8; Leiden: Brill, 1961).

27. See, e.g., R. Rentdorff, "The Psalms of David: David in the Psalms," in *The Book of Psalms: Composition and Reception* (ed. P. W. Flint and P. D. Miller; Leiden: Brill, 2005), 53–64; J. L. Mays, "The David of the Psalms," *Interpretation* 40 (1986): 143–55; M. Millard, *Die Komposition des Psalters* (FAT 9; Tübingen: Mohr Siebeck, 1994).

28. J. L. Kugel, "David the Prophet," in *Poetry and Prophecy: The Beginnings of a Literary Tradition* (ed. J. L. Kugel; Ithaca, N.Y.: Cornell University Press, 1990), 45–55, at 49. Scholars have long noted that the *lamed* does not necessarily denote authorial attribution; see already the note on the "lamed auctoris" under "Psalms" in the *Jewish Encyclopedia*, 1906; and, e.g., B. D. Eerdmans, *The Hebrew Book of Psalms* (Leiden: Brill, 1947), 36, 70.

29. See S. Mowinckel, *The Psalms in Israel's Worship* (trans. D. R. Ap-Thomas; 2 vols.; Oxford: Blackwell, 1962), 2:210–17; see also A. Weiser, *The Psalms: A Commentary* (trans. H. Hartwell; OTL; Philadelphia: Westminster, 1962), 96–97.

30. Mowinckel, *The Psalms in Israel's Worship*, 2:98.
31. Eerdmans writes that "nobody could suppose that Solomon made this psalm, speaking of himself in the third person as the king, reviewing his own reign. The term *liShelomo* must have been used by a scribe to express that the blessings, mentioned here, were the blessings Solomon received"; *Hebrew Book of Psalms*, 36.
32. N. M. Sarna, "The Psalm Superscriptions and the Guilds," in *Studies in Jewish Religious and Intellectual History* (ed. S. Stein and R. Loewe; Tuscaloosa: University of Alabama Press, 1979), 281–300.
33. Cf. the position of Gerald Wilson, who argues that the psalm headings in general mark subcollections in the editorial shaping of the Psalter, e.g. in *The Editing of the Hebrew Psalter* (SBLDS 76; Chico, Calif.: Scholars Press, 1985), and "The Shape of the Book of Psalms," *Interpretation* 46 (1992): 129–42, and "King, Messiah, and Reign of God: Revisiting the Royal Psalms and the Shape of the Psalter," in *The Book of Psalms: Composition and Reception*, 392–406.
34. See the analysis, including criteria for distinguishing translation from Greek original, in A. Pietersma, "David in the Greek Psalms," *VT* 30 (1980): 213–26.
35. Pietersma, "David in the Greek Psalms," and "Exegesis and Liturgy in the Superscriptions of the Greek Psalter," in *Proceedings of the Xth Congress of the International Organization for Septuagint and Cognate Studies, Oslo, July-August, 1998* (ed. B. A. Taylor; Atlanta: SBL, 2001), 99–138.
36. Pietersma, "Exegesis and Liturgy," 103.
37. See A. Pietersma and B. G. Wright, "To the Reader of NETS," in *A New English Translation of the Septuagint* (Oxford: Oxford University Press, 2007), xiii–xx; and Wright, "Moving beyond Translating a Translation: Reflections on A New English Translation of the Septuagint (NETS)," in *"Translation Is Required": The Septuagint in Retrospect and Prospect* (ed. R. Hiebert; SBLSCS 30; Atlanta: SBL, 2010), 23–39.
38. A. Pietersma, "To the Reader of Psalms," in *A New English Translation of the Septuagint*, 542–47, at 546.
39. The Greek is τῷ Δαυὶδ Ἰερεμίου or τῷ Δαυὶδ διὰ Ἰερεμίου.
40. The precise meaning of this term—presumably a hymn of some kind—is unknown.
41. See Rentdorff, "The Psalms of David," 59.
42. The Septuagint—beyond the thirteen additional *ledavid* notations—also adds expanded references to David's biography. For Ps 27 (LXX 26) the MT and 4QPs[r] have *ledavid*, and LXX adds "before he was anointed," which may be a Greek addition; Ps 97 (LXX 96) has "Pertaining to David, when his land is established," also likely secondary in Greek; Ps 143 (LXX 142) has "A psalm, pertaining to David, when [his] son pursued him," where MT and 11QPs[a] have only "a psalm of David"; finally, Ps 144 (LXX 143), which has *ledavid* in the MT and no heading in 11QPsalms[a], has "Pertaining to David, concerning Goliath," possibly a Greek development.
43. Rentdorff, "The Psalms of David," 63. On the patterns in these headings and another theory of how they begin with and reflect an interest in selected elements of David's biography, see T. Bolin, "1–2 Samuel and Jewish Paideia in the Persian and Hellenistic Periods," in *Deuteronomy-Kings as Emerging Authoritative Books: A Conversation* (ed. D. Edelman; Atlanta: SBL, 2014), 133–58, at 150–54. Bolin suggests, against the common view that the headings were appended to the psalms after the fact, that perhaps some of the psalms may have been pedagogical exercises composed specifically to match selected episodes in 1–2 Samuel.
44. This is also the case for the "Song of David" and "David's Last Words," 2 Sam 22 and 23, which are presented as sung by David. The hymns are placed in David's mouth in the context of the Samuel narrative, but their contents themselves do not present Davidic autobiography in any specific way.
45. See P. K. McCarter, *II Samuel* (AB 9; New York: Doubleday, 1984), 78–79. On the role of the lament in the narrative and its construction of David's character, see S. P. Weitzman, "David's Lament and the Poetics of Grief in 2 Samuel," *JQR* 85 (1995): 343–60, and *Song and Story in Biblical Narrative: The History of a Literary Convention in Ancient Israel* (Bloomington: Indiana University Press, 1997), 133–40.
46. I discuss this text and the idea of numbering psalms in depth in chapter 5.

47. As translated in F. García Martínez and E. J. C. Tigchelaar, *The Dead Sea Scrolls Study Edition* (2 vols.; Leiden: Brill, 1997–98), 2:1179.

48. B. S. Childs, "Psalm Titles and Midrashic Exegesis," *JSS* 16 (1971): 137–50, at 143; see also F. F. Bruce, "The Earliest Old Testament Interpretation," in *The Witness of Tradition; Papers Read at the Joint British-Dutch Old Testament Conference Held at Woudschoten, 1970* (ed. M.A. Beek et al.; *OTS* 17; Leiden: Brill, 1972), 40–52. See also M. Kleer, *Der liebliche Sänger der Psalmen Israels: Untersuchungen zu David als Dichter und Beter der Psalmen* (BBB 108; Bodenheim: Philo, 1996), 78–85.

49. E. Slomovic, "Toward an Understanding of the Formation of Historical Titles in the Book of Psalms," *ZAW* 91 (1979): 352–80.

50. M. Fishbane, *Biblical Interpretation in Ancient Israel* (Oxford: Clarendon, 1985).

51. For a rich analysis of the differences between exegesis, influence, and allusion as modes of intertextuality, see B. D. Sommer, *A Prophet Reads Scripture: Allusion in Isaiah 40–66* (Stanford, Calif.: Stanford University Press, 1998). See also the recent dissertation on inner-biblical allusion and intertextuality by J. R. Kelly, "Intertextuality and Allusion in the Study of the Hebrew Bible" (Ph.D. diss., Southern Baptist Theological Seminary, 2014).

52. See S. D. Fraade, "Midrash and Ancient Jewish Biblical Interpretation," in *The Cambridge Companion to the Talmud and Rabbinic Literature* (ed. C. E. Fonrobert and M. S. Jaffee; Cambridge: Cambridge University Press, 2007), 99–120, "'Comparative Midrash' Revisited: The Case of the Dead Sea Scrolls and Rabbinic Midrash," in *Agendas for the Study of Midrash in the Twenty-First Century* (ed. M. L. Raphael; Williamsburg, Va.: College of William and Mary Press, 1999), 4–17, "Looking for Legal Midrash at Qumran," in *Biblical Perspectives: Early Use and Interpretation of the Bible in Light of the Dead Sea Scrolls: Proceedings of the First International Symposium of the Orion Center for the Study of the Dead Sea Scrolls and Associated Literature, 12–14 May, 1996* (ed. M. E. Stone and E. G. Chazon; STDJ 28; Leiden: Brill, 1998), 59–79, and the companion piece, "Looking for Narrative Midrash at Qumran," in *Rabbinic Perspectives: Rabbinic Literature and the Dead Sea Scrolls: Proceedings of the Eighth International Symposium of the Orion Center for the Study of the Dead Sea Scrolls and Associated Literature, 7–9 January, 2003* (ed. S. D. Fraade, A. Shemesh, and R. A. Clements; STDJ 62; Leiden: Brill, 2006), 43–66. On the problematic use of the term "midrash" outside rabbinic literature, see L. Teugels, "Midrash in the Bible or Midrash on the Bible? Critical Remarks about the Uncritical Use of a Term," in *Bibel und Midrasch* (ed. G. Bodendorfer and M. Millard; FAT 22; Tübingen: Mohr Siebeck, 1998), 43–63.

53. See Rentdorff, "The Psalms of David," 54–55.

54. As Slomovic acknowledges in "Toward an Understanding," 356.

55. Slomovic, "Toward an Understanding," 371; and Childs, "Psalm Titles," 146.

56. S. Buber, ed., *Midrash Tehillim* (Vilna, 1891). This collection is not uniform; the manuscripts and earliest printed editions end at Ps 118, while other editions include commentary on the rest of the Psalter. Dating is uncertain, as the collection likely took shape over several centuries. English translation in W. G. Braude, *The Midrash on Psalms* (New Haven, Conn.: Yale University Press, 1959).

57. To be sure, this could refer to several different moments when David escapes Saul.

58. As translated in García Martínez and Tigchelaar, *The Dead Sea Scrolls Study Edition*, 2:1207.

59. On David as a prophet in the New Testament see, e.g., Y. Miura, *David in Luke-Acts: His Portrayal in the Light of Early Judaism* (Tübingen: Mohr Siebeck, 2007); and Kugel, "David the Prophet."

60. C. D. Yonge translation.

61. Greek text from P. Wendland, ed., *Philonis Alexandrini opera quae supersunt*, vol. 2 (Berlin: Reimer, 1897; repr. Berlin: De Gruyter, 1962).

62. On Philo's use of Psalms see J. Leonhardt, *Jewish Worship in Philo of Alexandria* (TSAJ 84; Tübingen: Mohr Siebeck, 2001), 142–72. Leonhardt, however, writes that the reference in *Confusion of Tongues* to the "sons of David, who wrote hymns to God" indicates that "David's authorship of the Davidic Psalter was an important fact for Philo, even if in his psalm quotations he does not mention David's name" (147). It is not clear why this would be so, since the *Confusion* passage is a brief aside about David as exemplar or founder, and Philo never chose to link David with any of the actual psalms he cites.

63. Pietersma, "David in the Greek Psalms," 225.
64. Text published in M. Gronewald, *Didymos der Blinde: Psalmenkommentar (Tura-Papyrus)*, book 2, *Kommentar zu Psalm 22–26,10* (Bonn: Rudolf Habelt, 1968). For discussion see Pietersma, "David in the Greek Psalms," 217.
65. Trans. M. Simon (London: Soncino Press, 1961).
66. On David's role as textualizer of the work of others, see Wyrick, *Ascension of Authorship*, chapter 2.
67. For an analysis of the language of "hanging" and the self-consciousness of attribution and merit in this text, see E. Mroczek, "A Peg to Hang On: Metaphor, Ancestral Merit, and the Midrashic Relationship of David and Solomon," in *Vixens Disturbing Vineyards: Embarrassment and Embracement of Scriptures: Festschrift in Honor of Harry Fox* (ed. A. Glazer et al.; Boston: Academic Studies Press, 2010), 219–40.
68. There is a large body of literature on this passage, also discussed in the previous chapter. See my 2012 University of Toronto dissertation, "Psalms Unbound: Ancient Concepts of Textual Tradition in 11QPsalms[a] and Related Texts," and my articles "'David Did Not Ascend into the Heavens' (Acts 2:34): Early Jewish Ascent Traditions and the Myth of Exegesis in the New Testament," *Judaïsme ancien—Ancient Judaism* 3 (2015): 261–94, and earlier, "Moses, David, and Scribal Revelation: Preservation and Renewal in Second Temple Jewish Textual Traditions," in *The Significance of Sinai: Traditions about Sinai and Divine Revelation in Judaism and Christianity* (ed. G. J. Brooke, H. Najman, and L. T. Stuckenbruck; Themes in Biblical Narrative 12; Leiden: Brill, 2008), 91–115. Recently see D. A. Teeter, "Torah, Wisdom, and the Composition of Rewritten Scripture: Jubilees and 11QPs[a] in Comparative Perspective," in *Wisdom and Torah: The Reception of "Torah" in the Wisdom Literature of the Second Temple Period* (ed. B. U. Schipper and D. A. Teeter; JSJSup 163; Leiden: Brill, 2013), 233–72, for a rich discussion of the biblical allusions in this passage.
69. On the nature of paratext and its role in framing and presenting a work, see Genette, *Paratexts: Thresholds of Interpretation*, and "Introduction to the Paratext," *New Literary History* 22 (1991): 261–72.
70. Genette, *Paratexts*, 12.
71. J. A. Sanders, *The Dead Sea Psalms Scroll* (Ithaca, N.Y.: Cornell University Press, 1967), 133–35 ("prose insert," a term that has been widely repeated in the scholarship); E. Ulrich, "The Text of the Hebrew Scriptures at the Time of Hillel and Jesus," in *Congress Volume: Basel 2001* (ed. A. Lemaire, VTSup 92; Leiden: Brill, 2002), 85–108, at 104 ("colophon," another popular designation); P. W. Flint, *The Dead Sea Psalms Scrolls and the Book of Psalms* (STDJ 17; Leiden: Brill, 1997), 224 ("a prose piece with the function of an extended superscription"); J. C. VanderKam, "Studies on 'David's Compositions,'" *Eretz Israel* 26 (1999): 212–20; U. Dahmen, *Psalmen- und Psalter-Rezeption im Frühjudentum: Rekonstruktion, Textbestand, Struktur und Pragmatik der Psalmenrolle 11QPs[a] aus Qumran* (STDJ 49; Leiden: Brill, 2003), 251–57, 278–80; Teeter, "Torah, Wisdom, and the Composition of Rewritten Scripture," calls it a "colophon-like prose metatext positioned as part of a concluding epilogue" (263), but perceptively acknowledges in a footnote that "it is clearly not a 'colophon' in the sense of standing outside the composition" (n. 95).
72. For example: "The prose 'epilogue' 'David's Compositions' must...be considered as functionally oriented. Its purpose is clearly to exalt David as the author of a myriad of pss for a variety of occasions. It may well intend to extend Davidic authorship and authority to all the works of the scroll" (Wilson, *Editing of the Hebrew Psalter*, 137); "the clear implication is that David, whose 4,050 compositions even surpassed Solomon's 4,005, was responsible for all those in this collection (11QPs[a])" (Flint, *Dead Sea Psalms Scrolls*, 208); "the real intent of this list is to validate a body of liturgical and poetic works in as many ways as possible" (Wyrick, *Ascension of Authorship*, 93). Among many others, see J. A. Sanders, *The Psalms Scroll of Qumrân Cave 11 (11QPs[a])* (DJD 4; Oxford: Clarendon, 1965), 63–64, 92; A. M. Cooper, "The Life and Times of King David according to the Book of Psalms," in *The Poet and the Historian: Essays in Literary and Historical Biblical Criticism*, ed. R. E. Friedman (HSS 26; Chico, Calif.: Scholars Press, 1983), 117–31; Kugel, "David the Prophet," esp. 46, 55.

73. There is a large indent in the first three lines of the composition, which might suggest a deliberate choice to lay out the text in a physically distinctive way, but the interpretation that indentation marks a distinct genre has no support from other scrolls. Instead, the scribe likely avoided inscribing that space because of scar tissue on the parchment surface: see J. Sanders, *Psalms Scroll*, 4, 93; and E. Tov, *Scribal Practices and Approaches Reflected in the Texts Found in the Judean Desert* (Leiden: Brill, 2004), 137. This was also the case in several other places on the same scroll (see J. Sanders, *Psalms Scroll*, 14). For instance, there is a clearly visible surface defect and indentation in col. 15 2–3. Tov in *Scribal Practices*, 115, lists other examples of Qumran manuscripts where scribes avoided inscribing a poor surface, for example, the multiple indented lines in 4QRP^b (4Q364) 9a–b 5–7 and 4QInstr^b (4Q416) 2 ii 19–21.

74. On psalms without a Davidic heading and the Solomonic Ps 127, Flint writes that "their presence in this Davidic collection indicates that the compilers regarded them as Davidic Psalms, however illogical this may seem"; *Dead Sea Psalms Scrolls*, 194. But this logical quandary disappears when we no longer understand "David's Compositions" to be a colophon for 11QPs^a. B. Ejrnæs, "David and His Two Women: An Analysis of Two Poems in the Psalms Scroll from Qumran (11Q5)," in *Scripture in Transition: Essays on Septuagint, Hebrew Bible, and Dead Sea Scrolls in Honour of Raija Sollamo* (ed. A. Voitila and J. Jokiranta; Leiden: Brill, 2008), 575–90, presents the anonymous hymn also known from Sir 51 as Davidic autobiography, which contributes to emphasizing "the authority of the Psalms Scroll, the book written by him" (588–89). But this view homogenizes a diverse collection, and extends Davidic attribution farther than the ancient scribes.

75. See the discussion of Davidic exemplarity in M. Leuenberger, "Aufbau und Pragmatik des 11QPs^a-Psalters: Der historisierte Dichter und Beter David als Vorbild und Identifikationsfigur: 11QPs^a als eschatologisches Lese- und Meditationsbuch des qumranischen," *RQ* 22 (2005): 1–44; my "Moses, David, and Scribal Revelation," and "Psalms Unbound," chapter 3; and Teeter, "Torah, Wisdom, and the Composition of Rewritten Scripture."

76. On the developing tradition of a prophetic David, see Kugel, "David the Prophet"; and P. W. Flint, "The Prophet David at Qumran," in *Biblical Interpretation at Qumran* (ed. M. Henze; Grand Rapids, Mich.: Eerdmans, 2005), 158–67.

77. W. H. Brownlee, "The Significance of David's Compositions," *RevQ* 5 (1964–66): 569–74. Likewise, B. Z. Wacholder called the text a "commentary" on 2 Sam 23; "David's Eschatological Psalter: 11QPsalms^a," *Hebrew Union College Annual* 59 (1988): 23–72, at 56.

78. See e.g. *Jubilees*, which says that Enoch was the first scribe; he "learned (the art of) writing, instruction, and wisdom and...wrote down in a book the signs of the sky in accord with the fixed pattern of their months so that mankind would know the seasons of the years according to the fixed patterns of each of their months.... The weeks of the jubilees he related, and made known the days of the years; the months he arranged, and related the sabbaths of the years, as we [the angels] had told him" (*Jubilees* 4:17–19; trans. J. C. VanderKam, *The Book of Jubilees: Translation* [CSCO 511; Scriptores Aethiopici 88; Louvain: Peeters, 1989]). Interestingly in light of its resonance with the "prose insert" in 11QPs^a, VanderKam notes that this *Jubilees* passage about Enoch may be poetic (26); while it is set in prose in his translation from the Ethiopic, he has reconstructed the Hebrew as poetry in an earlier publication, "Enoch Traditions in Jubilees and Other Second-Century Sources," *SBL Seminar Papers, 1978* (2 vols.; SBLSP 13; Missoula, Mont.: Scholars Press, 1978), 1:229–51, at 232–34.

79. For a study of the motif of the shining face in descriptions of angels or divinely transfigured human beings, including Moses, Enoch, David, and Jesus, see Mroczek, "David Did Not Ascend into the Heavens."

80. On this language of perfection see B. Strawn, "David as One of the 'Perfect of (the) Way': On the Provenience of David's Compositions (and 11QPs^a as a Whole?)," *RevQ* 24 (2010): 607–27; while Strawn posits a sectarian origin for the passage based on this language, I would argue that regardless of its specific provenance, the text reflects ideas about David's character that have currency in early Jewish traditions beyond the sect.

81. Trans. in García Martínez and Tigchelaar, *The Dead Sea Scrolls Study Edition*, 1:557.

82. I thank the anonymous reviewer of my article in *JAJ* for reminding me of this text and for the point about its presentation in medias res in the *Damascus Document*.

83. Trans. García Martínez and Tigchelaar, *The Dead Sea Scrolls Study Edition*, 2:803.
84. Here I allude to Najman's concept of "discourse tied to a founder" in *Seconding Sinai*, in which "Mosaic discourse" is a set of traditions associated with the figure of Moses. Discourses tied to David are also multivalent, including both extant and identifiable texts linked with David (such as many psalms) and imagined traditions that are not extant, but invoked in his name within other texts (such as the thousands of compositions in 11QPsalms[a] and the temple *tabnit* and liturgical ordinances of Chronicles, discussed below).
85. The translation is by D. J. Harrington, "Pseudo-Philo," in J. A. Charlesworth, *Old Testament Pseudepigrapha* (2 vols.; Garden City, N.Y.: Doubleday, 1983-85), 2:373, henceforth *OTP*.
86. See G. Bohak, "Exorcistic Psalms of David and Solomon," in *Old Testament Pseudepigrapha: More Noncanonical Scriptures* (ed. R. Bauckham, J. R. Davila, and A. Panayatov; Grand Rapids, Mich.: Eerdmans, 2013), 290, 296, and *Ancient Jewish Magic: A History* (Cambridge: Cambridge University Press, 2008), 232-34, 301-2.
87. Bohak, "Exorcistic Psalms"; and D. Levene, *A Corpus of Magic Bowls: Incantation Texts in Jewish Aramaic from Late Antiquity* (London: Kegan Paul, 2002), 77-82.
88. JPS translation. NRSV has "All this, in writing at the Lord's direction, he made clear to me—the plan of all the works."
89. See arguments for early dating in D. R. A. Hare, "The Lives of the Prophets," in *OTP*, 2:379-400. David Satran argues a fourth-century date based on early Byzantine interest in prophets' lives and the location of their tombs; see his *Biblical Prophets in Byzantine Palestine: Reassessing the Lives of the Prophets* (SVTP 11; Leiden: Brill, 1995).
90. Hare, "Lives of the Prophets," 2:386.
91. See the discussion of these two areas of Davidic authority in S. Japhet, *The Ideology of the Book of Chronicles and Its Place in Biblical Thought* (trans. A. Barber; BEATAJ 9; Frankfurt am Main: Lang, 1989), 236. On these references to texts and their possible oral context, see R. F. Person, *The Deuteronomic History and the Book of Chronicles: Scribal Works in an Oral World* (SBLAIL 6; Atlanta: Society of Biblical Literature, 2010), 58-61.
92. See, e.g., 2 Chr 35. For a discussion of Mosaic and Davidic authority, see S. J. DeVries, "Moses and David as Cult Founders in Chronicles," *JBL* 107 (1988): 619-39.
93. See discussion in chapter 1.
94. Cooper, for instance, writes that "we arrive at the positivistic claim that all of the psalms are Davidic (perhaps as early as Ben Sira)" ("Life and Times," 130). Kugel writes that "though this does seem to be an allusion to the Davidic authorship of some psalms, it is still far from an assertion that he wrote all of them, or even many; nor yet is there evidence of the association of psalm writing with prophecy or divine inspiration" ("David the Prophet," 53).
95. C. D. G. Müller, "The Ascension of Isaiah," in *New Testament Apocrypha*, vol. 2: *Writings Relating to the Apostles Apocalypses and Related Subjects* (ed. W. Schneemelcher; rev. ed.; trans. R. M. Wilson; Louisville: Westminster John Knox, 1992), 603-19, at 604-5; M. A. Knibb, "Martyrdom and Ascension of Isaiah," in *OTP* 2:143-76, at 149-50.
96. Knibb, "Martyrdom," 2:149.
97. Knibb, "Martyrdom," 2:162-63.
98. The texts were first published by A. E. Harkavy, "A Prayer by an Anonymous Writer in the Style of the Psalms," *HaGoren* 3 (1902): 82-85 (Hebrew). David Flusser and Shmuel Safrai's 1982 publication was a more detailed study with an emphasis on Davidic attribution; "A Fragment of the Songs of David and Qumran" (Hebrew), in *Bible Studies: Y. M. Grintz in Memoriam* (ed. B. Uffenheimer; Te'uda 2; Tel Aviv: Tel Aviv University, 1982), 83-105; English translation in Flusser, *Judaism of the Second Temple Period*, vol. 1: *Qumran and Apocalypticism* (trans. A. Yadin; Grand Rapids, Mich.: Eerdmans, 2007), 258-82. Ezra Fleischer disputed both Flusser and Safrai's claim for Davidic attribution and their claim that the text originated from Qumran, arguing instead for a medieval origin; "Medieval Hebrew Poems in Biblical Style" (Hebrew), in *Studies in Judaica* (ed. M. A. Friedman; Te'uda 7; Tel Aviv: Tel Aviv University, 1991), 201-248. More recently see the incisive discussion by M. Bar-Ilan, "Non-Canonical Psalms from the Genizah," in *The Dead Sea Scrolls in Context: Integrating the Dead Sea Scrolls in the Study of Ancient Texts, Languages, and Cultures* (ed. A. Lange et al.; 2 vols.; VTSup 140; Leiden: Brill,

2011), 2:693–718, who writes that there is little ground for claiming Qumran origins specifically, but that the text reflects the diversity of Judaism in Palestine shortly after the destruction of the Second Temple. See now the text and in-depth commentary in D. M. Stec, *The Genizah Psalms* (Cambridge Genizah Studies Series 5; Leiden: Brill, 2013); and my review of this publication in *JSJ* 46 (2015): 152–54. See also G. W. Lorein and E. van Staalduine-Sulman, "A Song of David for Each Day: The Provenance of the Songs of David," *RevQ* 85 (2005): 33–59, and now "Songs of David," their contribution to *Old Testament Pseudepigrapha: More Noncanonical Scriptures* (ed. R. Bauckham, J. R. Davila, and A. Panayatov; Grand Rapids, Mich.: Eerdmans, 2013), 257–71.

99. Stec argues that David is both the subject and the intended speaker of the compositions, based on, e.g., several uses of the term עֶבֶד, which he interprets as an allusion to David. He observes that David is considered a prophet in Second Temple sources and that the prophetic, visionary claims of these compositions would fit such a characterization (although it is not David, but strangely God who is said to prophesy in *Genizah Psalms*); Stec, introduction to *Genizah Psalms*. Lorein and Staalduine-Sulman also present the text as Davidic, as do M. Philonenko and A. Marx, "Quatre 'chants' pseudo-davidiques trouvés dans la Gueniza du Caire et d'origine esséno-qoumrânienne," *RHPR* 77 (1997): 385–406.

100. Bar-Ilan, "Non-Canonical Psalms from the Genizah," 701, 704.

101. Lorein and Staalduine-Sulman, "Songs of David."

102. On the connection between scribal figures and immortality, see the important essay by S. I. Thomas, "Eternal Writing and Immortal Writers: On the Non-Death of the Scribe in Early Judaism," in *A Teacher for All Generations: Essays in Honor of James C. VanderKam* (2 vols.; ed. E. F. Mason et al.; Leiden: Brill, 2011), 1:573–88. Thomas also discusses Moses, Ezra, and Baruch traditions as participating in this trope, concluding that in some Second Temple traditions "being a scribe makes one immortal at least insofar as death may be overcome in the transmission, elaboration, and new life of sacred tradition, which itself is understood to come from an eternal and often esoteric source" (588).

103. Stec, *Genizah Psalms*, 35–37.

104. For this text see P. Schäfer, *Synopse zur Hekhalot-Literatur* (Texte und Studien zum Antiken Judentum 2; Tübingen: Mohr Siebeck, 1981), 122–26; and A. Jellinek, *Beit ha-Midrash* (6 vols.; 3rd ed.; Jerusalem: Wahrmann, 1938), 5:168; translation and discussion in the context of heavenly coronation traditions are in A. Green, *Keter: The Crown of God in Early Jewish Mysticism* (Princeton, N.J.: Princeton University Press, 1997), 66–68. See now also R. Bauckham, , J. R. Davila, and A. Panayatov, eds., *Old Testament Pseudepigrapha: More Noncanonical Scriptures* (Grand Rapids, Mich.: Eerdmans, 2013), where it is now published as the "David Apocalypse," 751–53.

105. A smaller midrash found in Jellinek, *Beit ha-Midrash*, 5:46.

106. For the *Apocalypse of Paul* see M. R. James, *The Apocryphal New Testament* (Oxford: Oxford University Press, 1924), 526–55; J. K. Elliott, *The Apocryphal New Testament: A Collection of Apocryphal Christian Literature in an English Translation* (Oxford: Oxford University Press, 1993), 616–44; E. Hennecke et al., *New Testament Apocrypha* (2 vols.; Philadelphia: Westminster Press, 1963), 2:755–803; for the Latin text, see T. Silverstein and A. Hilhorst, eds., *Apocalypse of Paul: A New Critical Edition of Three Long Latin Versions* (Geneva: P. Cramer, 1997). A third-century origin had been proposed for the text, but see now the strong case for a ca. 400 dating in P. Piovanelli, "Les origines de l'*Apocalypse de Paul* reconsidérées," *Apocrypha* 4 (1993): 25–64. This *Apocalypse of Paul*, also called the *Visio Pauli*, is a different text from the Nag Hammadi *Apocalypse of Paul*. Both are discussed in the collection edited by J. N. Bremmer and I. Czachesz, *The Visio Pauli and the Gnostic Apocalypse of Paul* (Studies on Early Christian Apocrypha 9; Leuven: Peeters, 2007).

107. Thomas, "Eternal Writing," 588.

108. Thomas, "Eternal Writing," 588.

109. *Jubilees* 10:17; on Enoch's eternal scribal role, see further chapter 4.

110. R. Barthes, "The Death of the Author," in *Image-Music-Text* (trans. S. Heath; New York: Hill and Wang, 1977), 142–48. Barthes argued that the identity, psychology, and putative intentions of an author should be disentangled from the process of interpreting a text.

Chapter 3 Like a Canal from a River

1. Translation adapted from J. A. Sanders, *The Psalms Scroll of Qumrân Cave 11 (11QPsᵃ)* (DJD 4; Oxford: Clarendon, 1965), 79–85.

2. See P. C. Beentjes, *The Book of Ben Sira in Hebrew* (Leiden: Brill, 1997); É. Puech, "Le livre de Ben Sira et les manuscrits de la Mer Morte," in *Treasures of Wisdom: Studies in Ben Sira and the Book of Wisdom: Festschrift M. Gilbert* (ed. N. Calduch-Benages and J. Vermeylen; Leuven: Peeters, 1999), 411–26, and "Ben Sira and Qumran," in *The Wisdom of Ben Sira: Studies on Tradition, Redaction, and Theology* (ed. A. Passaro and G. Bellia; Berlin: de Gruyter, 2008), 79–118. M. Delcor, "Le texte hébreu du Cantique de Siracide LI,13 et ss. et les anciennes versions," *Textus* 6 (1968): 27–47; T. Muraoka, "Sir. 51, 13–30: An Erotic Hymn to Wisdom?" *JSJ* 10 (1979): 166–78; J. A. Sanders, "The Sirach 51 Acrostic," in *Hommages à André Dupont-Sommer* (ed. A. Caquot and M. Philonenko; Cerf: Paris, 1971), 429–38; P. W. Skehan, "The Acrostic Poem in Sirach 51:13–30," *HTR* 64 (1971): 387–400; I. Rabinowitz, "The Qumran Hebrew Original of Ben Sira's Concluding Acrostic on Wisdom," *HUCA* 42 (1971): 173–84; E. D. Reymond, "Sirach 51:13–30 and 11Q5 (=11QPsᵃ) 21.11–22.1," *RevQ* 23 (2007): 207–23, *Innovations in Hebrew Poetry: Parallelism and the Poems of Sirach* (Leiden: Brill, 2004), and *New Idioms within Old: Poetry and Parallelism in the Non-Masoretic Poems of 11Q5 (=11QPsᵃ)* (EJL 31; Atlanta: SBL, 2011), 21–50.

3. P. W. Flint, *The Dead Sea Psalms Scrolls and the Book of Psalms* (STDJ 17; Leiden: Brill, 1997), 193–94; and B. Ejrnæs, "David and His Two Women: An Analysis of Two Poems in the Psalms Scroll from Qumran (11Q5)," in *Scripture in Transition: Essays on Septuagint, Hebrew Bible, and Dead Sea Scrolls in Honour of Raija Sollamo* (ed. A. Voitila and J. Jokiranta; Leiden: Brill, 2008), 575–90, at 588–89.

4. I have relied on the edition of all extant Hebrew manuscripts (Cairo Genizah, Qumran, and Masada) by Beentjes, *The Book of Ben Sira in Hebrew*. The earlier Hebrew edition of M. H. Segal, *Sefer ben Sira ha-Shalem* (2nd ed.; Jerusalem: Mosad Byalik, 1958) included MSS A–E and provided retranslations of nonextant portions from Greek or Syriac into Hebrew. On the Hebrew texts, see A. A. Di Lella, *The Hebrew Text of Sirach: A Text-Critical and Historical Study* (The Hague: De Gruyter Mouton, 1966); M. H. Segal, "The Evolution of the Hebrew Text of Ben Sira," *JQR* 25 (1934–35): 91–149; and H. P. Rüger, *Text und Textform im hebräischen Sirach I* (BZAW 112; Berlin: De Gruyter, 1970). Each of these scholars confirmed the reliability of the medieval Cairo Genizah manuscripts as witnesses to an ancient Hebrew text of Ben Sira.

5. M. Baillet, J. T. Milik, and R. de Vaux, *Les "Petites Grottes"* (DJD 3; Oxford: Clarendon, 1962), 75–77. See also Puech, "Le livre de Ben Sira."

6. The Masada text covers Ben Sira 39:27–44:17. See Y. Yadin, *The Ben Sira Scroll from Masada* (Jerusalem: Israel Exploration Society, 1965). The Masada scroll gave further evidence for the reliability of the medieval Hebrew MSS from the Geniza.

7. On the expanded form see C. Kearns, "Ecclesiasticus or the Wisdom of Jesus the Son of Sirach," in *A New Catholic Commentary on Holy Scripture* (ed. R. C. Fuller; London: Nelson, 1969), 541–62, and Kearns's newly published 1951 doctoral thesis, *The Expanded Text of Ecclesiasticus: Its Teaching on the Future Life as a Clue to Its Origin* (ed. P. C. Beentjes; Berlin: De Gruyter, 2011); P. W. Skehan and A. A. Di Lella, *The Wisdom of Ben Sira* (AB 39; New York: Doubleday, 1987), 55–62; M. Gilbert, "L' ecclesiastique: Quel texte? Quelle autorité?," *RB* 94 (1987): 233–50, and "Methodological and Hermeneutical Trends in Modern Exegesis on the Book of Ben Sira," in *The Wisdom of Ben Sira: Studies on Tradition, Redaction, and Theology* (ed. A. Passaro and G. Bellia; Berlin: de Gruyter, 2008), 1–20.

8. See most recently J. Giles, "The Additions to Ben Sira and the Book's Multiform Textual Witness," in *The Texts and Versions of the Book of Ben Sira: Transmission and Interpretations* (ed. J.-S. Rey and J. Joosten; JSJSupp; Leiden: Brill, 2011), 237–56, and the other essays in this volume.

9. This is mainly said of the messianic-eschatological passages. See most notably Kearns, *Expanded Text of Ecclesiasticus*. See also M. Philonenko, "Sur une proposition essénisante dans le Siracide (16:15–16)," *Orientalia Suecana* 33–35 (1984–86): 317–21. The psalm in 52:12 that is extant only in MS B has also been called "Essene" based on its expression of

messianic hopes; Puech, "Ben Sira and Qumran,"108 n.89; and Di Lella, *The Hebrew Text of Sirach*, 101–5. It is my sense that such assessments may betray an impulse to marginalize practices of rewriting and expanding Scripture by associating them with a supposedly marginal group or movement.

10. This parallel is evident within Ben Sira itself, where both the praise of David and the praise of the scribe include references to forgiveness (47:11 and 39:5). David's calendrical arrangement of songs reflects his inauguration of liturgical music and "setting the festivals in order" in Ben Sira (47:10). See chapter 2.

11. Note the use of the word עליון here, a feature that several passages in 11QPs[a] and Ben Sira share.

12. This exceptional feature is mentioned in virtually all scholarship on Ben Sira, with some scholars linking the self-attribution to Hellenistic influence. See J. J. Collins, *Jewish Wisdom in the Hellenistic Age* (Louisville: Westminster John Knox, 1997), 23, 37–38; M. Hengel, *Judaism and Hellenism: Studies in Their Encounter in Palestine during the Early Hellenistic Period* (2 vols.; trans. J. Bowden; Philadelphia: Fortress Press, 1974); T. Middendorp, *Die Stellung Jesu Ben Siras zwischen Judentum und Hellenismus* (Leiden: Brill, 1973); Skehan and Di Lella, *The Wisdom of Ben Sira*; R. Smend, *Die Weisheit des Jesus Sirach erklärt* (Berlin: Reimer, 1906); and O. Mulder, *Simon the High Priest in Sirach 50: An Exegetical Study of the Significance of Simon the High Priest as Climax to the Praise of the Fathers in Ben Sira's Concept of the History of Israel* (Leiden: Brill, 2003), 2. See also R. A. Horsley and P. Tiller, "Ben Sira and the Sociology of the Second Temple," in *Second Temple Studies III: Studies in Politics, Class and Material Culture* (ed. P. R. Davies and J. M. Halligan; JSOTSup 340; Sheffield: Sheffield Academic Press, 2002), 74–107, at 99–103; see now C. V. Camp, *Ben Sira and the Men Who Handle Books: Gender and the Rise of Canon-Consciousness* (Sheffield: Sheffield Phoenix, 2013), esp. chapter 8, "Men Who Handle Books II: Textuality and the Birth of Authorial Self-Consciousness."

13. Hengel, *Judaism and Hellenism*, 1:79. See also T. Middendorp, *Die Stellung Jesu Ben Siras zwischen Judentum und Hellenismus*.

14. Translation adapted from NRSV.

15. MS B is the only source that names the author "Simon"; this may be a mistake influenced by the praise of the high priest Simon in chapter 50. See Collins, *Jewish Wisdom*, 23 n.1; and Skehan and Di Lella, *The Wisdom of Ben Sira*, 3–4.

16. C. Mopsik in *La Sagesse de ben Sira* (Lagrasse: Verdier, 2004) translates from Hebrew into French thus: "Discipline d'intelligence et directive d'equilibre, de Simon fils de Josue, fils d'Eleazar, fils de Sira, que son coeur a fait jaillir comme une pluise, et qu'il a repandues avec intelligence"; Mopsik takes אופנים as a dual, an image that illustrates the dual, i.e., bicolon, structure of Ben Sira's proverbs. See his clarification, 321 n.4.

17. Mulder, *Simon the High Priest in Sirach 50*, 2. Mulder adds that the Syriac has yet a different text here: "The height of the fear of the Lord is exalted above everything; hold on to it my son and do not let it go." On the Syriac Ben Sira see M. D. Nelson, *The Syriac Version of the Wisdom of Ben Sira Compared to the Greek and Hebrew Materials* (SBLDS 107; Atlanta: SBL, 1988); W. T. van Peursen, *Language and Interpretation in the Syriac Text of Ben Sira: A Comparative Linguistic and Literary Study* (Leiden: Brill, 2007); R. J. Owens, "The Early Syriac Text of Ben Sira in the Demonstrations of Aphrahat," *JSSt* 34 (1989): 39–75; G. Rizzi, "Christian Interpretations in the Syriac Version of Sirach," in *The Wisdom of Ben Sira: Studies on Tradition, Redaction, and Theology* (ed. A. Passaro and G. Bellia; Berlin: de Gruyter, 2008), 278–308; M. M. Winter, "The Origins of Ben Sira in Syriac," *VT* 27 (1977): 237–53, 494–507.

18. We do have a Hebrew reference to writing in MS B in 39:32:

על כן מראש התי[.].בתי והתבוננתי ובכתב הנחתי –

Therefore from the beginning I have been convinced[?] and thought it out and left [it] in writing.

There is no mention of *sefer* here, but only the looser and more general sense that Ben Sira has handed on the wisdom he has learned in written form.

19. See Beentjes, *The Book of Ben Sira in Hebrew*, 7; Yadin, *The Ben Sira Scroll from Masada*, 7 (Hebrew section) and 9 (English section).

20. See Camp, *Ben Sira and the Men Who Handle Books*, esp. chapter 6, "Becoming Canon: Women, Texts, and Scribes from Proverbs to Sirach."
21. On Ben Sira's metaphors of flowing, gushing water and their counterparts in some strands of midrashic literature, and their connection to the idea of Torah as continuously speaking, see A. Yadin, *Scripture as Logos: Rabbi Ishmael and the Origins of Midrash* (Philadelphia: University of Pennsylvania Press, 2004), 162–63. For another view on the metaphor of water and anxiety about the possession of Wisdom, see Camp, *Ben Sira and the Men Who Handle Books*, chapter 7, "Men Who Handle Books I: Textuality and the Problem of Theodicy."
22. Verse 24:34 is lacking in the Syriac, and there are other differences between the Greek and Syriac versions of this passage, although the basic metaphor remains the same.
23. B. G. Wright III, "Ben Sira on the Sage as Exemplar," in *Praise Israel for Wisdom and Instruction: Essays on Ben Sira and Wisdom, the Letter of Aristeas and the Septuagint* (Leiden: Brill, 2008), 165–82, at 172.
24. See Wright, "Ben Sira on the Sage as Exemplar"; and J. Corley, "Searching for Structure and Redaction in Ben Sira," in *The Wisdom of Ben Sira: Studies on Tradition, Redaction, and Theology* (ed. A. Passaro and G. Bellia; Berlin: de Gruyter, 2008), 21–47, at 31.
25. J. L. Kugel, "Wisdom and the Anthological Temper," in *The Anthology in Jewish Literature* (ed. D. Stern; New York: Oxford University Press, 2004), 32–52, esp. 9, 18, 30. See also the introduction to this volume by David Stern, who emphasizes the creative and influential role of the scribe, editor, and anthologist in preserving, transmitting and creating tradition. Most recently, see J. Vayntrub, "Proverbs and the Limits of Poetry" (Ph.D. diss., University of Chicago, 2015), on the shaping of the book of Proverbs and the role of the ideal sage in the framing and transmission of the collection.
26. Hengel, *Judaism and Hellenism*, 1:79.
27. See S. Schorch, "The Pre-eminence of the Hebrew Language and the Emerging Concept of the 'Ideal Text' in Late Second Temple Judaism," in *The Book of Ben Sira: Papers of the Third International Conference on the Deuterocanonical Books, Pápa, Hungary 2006* (ed. G. G. Xeravits and J. Zsengellér; JSJS 127; Leiden: Brill, 2008), 43–54; Schorch argues that it is the Greek translator's prologue that shows a move toward the idea of a privileged original (Hebrew) text.
28. For a discussion of the prologue's rhetoric as it relates to sacred books and canon, see F. Borchardt, "The Prologue of Sirach (Ben Sira) and the Question of Canon," in *Sacra Scriptura: How "Non-Canonical" Texts Functioned in Early Judaism and Early Christianity* (ed. J. H. Charlesworth and L. M. McDonald with B. A. Jurgens; T&T Clark Jewish and Christian Text Series; London: Bloomsbury T&T Clark, 2014), 64–71. Borchardt writes that the author of the prologue rhetorically communicates

> the idea that his ancestor's work belongs among the praiseworthy books. This is not to say that there is a set number of books that are counted as inspired and of divine origin for the translator. Rather, there is/are (a) collection(s) of books, very likely open-ended, that he sees as having a special value because of the nature of the wisdom they contain. Whether this value was limited to the ancestral books of Israel, and whether it was shared by other Judeans is unclear. What is clear is that Ben Sira's descendant is making a strong argument for this value to be recognized in his ancestor's work (69).

29. NETS translation.
30. B. G. Wright, "Ben Sira on the Sage as Exemplar," 169. For earlier studies on the "autobiographical" passages and Ben Sira's self-presentation, see esp. J. Liesen, "Strategical Self-References in Ben Sira," in *Treasures of Wisdom: Studies in Ben Sira and the Book of Wisdom: Festschrift M. Gilbert* (ed. N. Calduch-Benages and J. Vermeylen; BEThL 143; Leuven: Peeters, 1999), 64–74; and Gilbert, "Methodological and Hermeneutical Trends," 7–10. See also J. H. Newman's account of Ben Sira's self-presentation as an exemplary prophetic sage in "Liturgical Imagination in the Composition of Ben Sira," in *Prayer and Poetry in the Dead Sea Scrolls and Related Literature: Essays in Honor of Eileen Schuller on the Occasion of Her 65th Birthday* (ed. J. Penner, K. M. Penner, and C. Wassen; STDJ 98; Leiden: Brill, 2011), 323–38.

31. B. G. Wright, "From Generation to Generation: The Sage as Father in Early Jewish Literature," in *Praise Israel for Wisdom and Instruction: Essays on Ben Sira and Wisdom, the Letter of Aristeas and the Septuagint* (Leiden: Brill, 2008), 25–47, and "Ben Sira on the Sage as Exemplar," 169–71. See also an earlier study of familial metaphors in Proverbs, C. Newsom, "Women and the Discourse of Patriarchal Wisdom: A Study of Proverbs 1–9," in *Gender and Difference in Ancient Israel* (ed. P. L. Day; Minneapolis: Fortress, 1989), 142–60. This convention may have roots in Egyptian instructional texts; see Collins, *Jewish Wisdom in the Hellenistic Age*, 37–38.

32. Most notably Gert Jeremias, Jurgen Becker, and H.-W. Kuhn.

33. Wise believes the Teacher's name was Judah; M. O. Wise, *The First Messiah: Investigating the Savior before Jesus* (San Francisco: HarperCollins, 1999).

34. See M. Grossman, "Roland Barthes and the Teacher of Righteousness: The Death of the Author of the Dead Sea Scrolls," in *The Oxford Handbook of the Dead Sea Scrolls* (ed. T. H. Lim and J. J. Collins; Oxford: Oxford University Press, 2010), 709–22.

35. See A. K. Harkins, "Who Is the Teacher of the Teacher Hymns? Re-examining the Teacher Hymns Hypothesis Fifty Years Later," in *A Teacher for All Generations: Essays in Honor of James C. VanderKam* (2 vols.; ed. E. Mason et al; Leiden: Brill, 2012), 1:449–67, and *Reading with an "I" to the Heavens: Looking at the Qumran Hodayot through the Lens of Visionary Traditions* (Boston: de Gruyter, 2012), 69–75. See also Grossman, "Roland Barthes and the Teacher of Righteousness."

36. Harkins, *Reading*, 70.

37. See C. Newsom, *The Self as Symbolic Space: Constructing Identity and Community at Qumran* (Leiden: Brill, 2004), 288–300, and F. García Martínez, "Beyond the Sectarian Divide: The 'Voice of the Teacher' as an Authority-Conferring Strategy in Some Qumran Texts," in *The Dead Sea Scrolls: Transmission of Traditions and Production of Texts* (ed. S. Metso, H. Najman, and E. Schuller; Leiden: Brill, 2010), 227–44.

38. Harkins, *Reading*, 72, 69.

39. E. J. Bickerman, *The Jews in the Greek Age* (Cambridge, Mass.: Harvard University Press, 1988), 204.

40. P. McKechnie, "The Career of Joshua Ben Sira," *JTS* 51 (2000): 1–26.

41. The Syriac goes so far as to avoid any mention of slander, making the passage into a rather generic prayer.

42. For similar sentiments about liars and persecutors, see e.g. Job 13:4, 7, Ps 119:69, Ps 52, Ps 64, Ps 86, Ps 88, and Jer 9.

43. Puech, "Ben Sira and Qumran," 84; Gilbert, "Methodological and Hermeneutical Trends," 9, and "Venez à mon école (Si 51,13–30)," in *Auf der Spuren der Schriftgelehrten Weisen: Festschrift für Johannes Marbock* (ed. I. Fischer et al.; Berlin: de Gruyter, 2003), 283–90. *Beit midrash* is the text found in MS B, which is not considered a reliable witness to the early Hebrew text for this passage; the "original" reading may also be *beit musar*, as argued by Skehan and Di Lella in *The Wisdom of Ben Sira*, 575. See J. Crenshaw, *Education in Ancient Israel: Across the Deadening Silence* (New York: Doubleday, 1998), 271; Collins, *Jewish Wisdom in the Hellenistic Age*, 36–37; see also C. Rollston, "Ben Sira 38:24–39:11 and the Egyptian Satire of the Trades: A Reconsideration," *JBL* 120 (2001): 131–39, who writes that 51:23–30 contains "exhortations to pursue the scribal vocation," similarly to chapter 39, 139.

44. Gilbert, "Methodological and Hermeneutical Trends," 8. Skehan and DiLella, *Wisdom of Ben Sira*, 576–80, defend its autobiographical character; see also H. Stadelman, *Ben Sira als Schriftgelehrter* (Tübingen: Mohr Siebeck, 1980), 30–33, as cited in Gilbert's essay.

45. M. Gilbert, "The Book of Ben Sira: Implications for Jewish and Christian Traditions," in *Jewish Civilization in the Hellenistic-Roman Period* (ed. S. Talmon; Philadelphia: Trinity Press International, 1991), 81–91, at 83, and "Venez à mon école."

46. Corley, "Searching for Structure," 45.

47. J. Vayntrub, "The Book of Proverbs and the Idea of Ancient Israelite Education," *ZAW* (forthcoming).

48. It is, however, from the same root as *musar*, discipline, which may be significant if *beit musar* is the correct reconstruction over *beit midrash*; see n. 43 above.

49. See, for example, the shift between the voice of the narrator and another personified female figure, Zion, in another acrostic poem, Lam 1.

50. This is in contrast to the rabbinic use of Ben Sira as a character and body of wisdom, which I will discuss below.

51. On the authorial persona of Qohelet, see Thomas Bolin's forthcoming monograph, *Ecclesiastes and the Riddle of Authorship.*

52. By this I mean that the traditional attribution to Solomon is never made explicit with his name, although the description of Qohelet as wealthy king and son of David implicitly makes this identification.

53. On the importance of a text's literary self-presentation and implicit theory of itself for understanding its production and transmission in antiquity, see Vayntrub, "Proverbs and the Limits of Poetry," especially the introduction, and "The Book of Proverbs and the Idea of Ancient Israelite Education."

54. Beentjes, *The Book of Ben Sira in Hebrew,* 4.

55. S. Schechter, "A Further Fragment of Ben Sira," *JQR* 12 o.s. (1900): 456–65, at 458.

56. P. C. Beentjes, "Hermeneutics in the Book of Ben Sira: Some Observations on the Hebrew Ms. C," *EstBib* 45 (1988): 45–60, at 54.

57. Beentjes, "Hermeneutics," 57.

58. Beentjes, *The Book of Ben Sira in Hebrew,* 3.

59. B. G. Wright, "Preliminary Thoughts about Preparing the Text of Ben Sira for a Commentary," in *Die Septuaginta: Text—Wirkung—Rezeption* (ed. W. Kraus and M. Karrer; Tübingen: Mohr Siebeck. 2014), 89–109, at 107.

60. Wright, "Preliminary Thoughts," 107. On this issue see also Newman, "Liturgical Imagination."

61. This school of scholarly editing, standing staunchly against the tendencies of New Criticism, is associated with W. W. Greg, F. Bowers, and G. T. Tanselle, who are responsible for some of the most influential statements on editorial practice in the twentieth century. See the early programmatic article of W. W. Greg, "The Rationale of Copy-Text," *Studies in Bibliography* 3 (1950): 19–36; F. Bowers, "Multiple Authority: New Problems and Concepts of Copy-Text," *Library,* 5th ser. 27 (1975): 81–115, "Established Texts and Definitive Editions," *Philological Quarterly* 41 (1962):1–117, and "Notes on Theory and Practice in Editing Texts," in *The Book Encompassed* (ed. P. Davison; Cambridge: Cambridge University Press, 1992), 244–57; G. T. Tanselle, "The Editorial Problem of Final Authorial Intention," *Studies in Bibliography* 29 (1976): 167–211, "Recent Editorial Discussion and the Central Questions of Editing," *Studies in Bibliography* 34 (1981): 23–65, "Historicism and Critical Editing," *Studies in Bibliography* 39 (1986): 1–46, and "The Varieties of Scholarly Editing," in *Scholarly Editing: A Guide to Research* (ed. D. C. Greetham; New York: MLA, 1995), 9–32. See more theoretical discussions of such editorial issues with an engagement of Barthes's and Foucault's work on concepts of authorship in H. L. Hix, *Morte d'Author: An Autopsy* (Philadelphia: Temple University Press), 1990; and M. North, "Authorship and Autography," *PMLA* 116 (2001): 1377–85. A methodological and historical discussion of changing approaches to editing can be found in D. C. Greetham, *Theories of the Text* (Oxford: Oxford University Press, 1999). The Oxford Hebrew Bible project, which aims at producing a critical edition of each book of the Hebrew Bible, has recently placed concepts of definitive texts and editorial methodology in sharp relief for biblical scholars; see the project's rationale and methodology as described by its editor-in-chief, R. S. Hendel, in "The Oxford Hebrew Bible: Prologue to a New Critical Edition," *VT* (2008): 324–51.

62. P. Schäfer, *The Hidden and Manifest God: Some Major Themes in Early Jewish Mysticism* (trans. A. Pomerance; Albany: State University of New York Press, 1992), 6 n. 14.

63. R. Boustan, "The Study of Heikhalot Literature: Between Mystical Experience and Textual Artifact," *Currents in Biblical Research* 6 (2007): 130–60, at 150. For a study of this phenomenon in medieval Jewish mysticism, see D. Abrams's monumental *Kabbalistic Manuscripts and Textual Theory: Methodologies of Textual Scholarship and Editorial Practice in the Study of Jewish Mysticism* (2nd rev. ed.; Jerusalem: Magnes Press, 2013), especially chapter 4, "The Invention of the Zohar as a Book."

64. Kearns, "Ecclesiasticus, or Wisdom," 547–50; Segal, "Evolution of the Hebrew Text."

65. B. W. Breed, *Nomadic Text: A Theory of Biblical Reception History* (Indiana Studies in Biblical Literature; Bloomington: Indiana University Press, 2014), 203.

66. I. M. Ta-Shma, "The 'Open' Book in Medieval Hebrew Literature: The Problem of Authorized Editions," *BJRL* 75 (1993): 17–24, at 17.

67. See Abrams, *Kabbalistic Manuscripts and Textual Theory.*

68. Newman, "Liturgical Imagination," 337.

69. Corley, "Searching for Structure," 45.

70. L. Schrader, *Leiden und Gerechtigkeit: Studien zu Theologie und Textgeschichte des Sirachbuches* (BBET 27; Frankfurt a.M.: Peter Lang, 1994), 67.

71. See discussion and notes on Ben Sira's textual history earlier in this chapter.

72. This is related to the fraught boundary between the "text" and its "reception" or the difference between "composition" and "redaction," which, if texts are processes or projects, rather than contained and finished entities, cannot be meaningfully separated from each other; see the discussion in Breed, *Nomadic Text*, esp. "Introduction: The Constitutive Divide of Reception History," 1–14.

73. Newsom, "Women and the Discourse of Patriarchal Wisdom," 143–44.

74. Wright, "From Generation to Generation." For the continuity between the personal and the textual in pedagogy in the later rabbinic context, see M. Jaffee, *Torah in the Mouth* (New York: Oxford University Press, 2001).

75. I am thinking here of such comments as Flint's statement that a psalm with a Solomonic superscription must have been considered to have been authored by David, "no matter how illogical this may seem" (*Dead Sea Psalms Scrolls*, 194); or Sanders's sense that the sapiential hymn that is also in Ben Sira 51 must have been imagined to be Davidic autobiography if it was present in the Psalms Scroll (*The Psalms Scroll of Qumrân Cave 11 (11QPsᵃ)*, 85). For the same tendency, see Ejrnæs, "David and His Two Women"; see my comments in chapter 2.

76. F. Mies, "Le Psaume de Ben Sira 51,12a–o hébreu: L'hymne aux noms divins," *RB* 116.3 (2009): 336–67 (part 1) and 116.4 (2009): 481–504 (part 2).

77. The Syriac, coming from the third or fourth century, was far removed from these political concerns, and likely indifferent to them; Mies, "Le Psaume de Ben Sira 51,12a–o hébreu," 501.

78. On this subject see S. Schechter, "The Quotations from Ecclesiasticus in Rabbinic Literature," *JQR* 3 (1891): 682–706; Segal, "Evolution of the Hebrew Text of Ben Sira"; M. R. Lehmann, "11QPsᵃ and Ben Sira," *RevQ* 11 (1983): 239–51; S. Z. Leiman, *The Canonization of Hebrew Scripture: The Talmudic and Midrashic Evidence* (Hamden, Conn.: Archon Books, 1976), 92–102; Gilbert, "The Book of Ben Sira"; J. R. Labendz, who differentiates between Palestinian and Babylonian references to Ben Sira, "The Book of Ben Sira in Rabbinic Literature," *AJS Review* 30 (2006): 347–92; B. G. Wright, "B. Sanhedrin 100b and Rabbinic Knowledge of Ben Sira," in *Praise Israel for Wisdom and Instruction: Essays on Ben Sira and Wisdom, the Letter of Aristeas and the Septuagint* (Leiden: Brill, 2008), 183–93; and T. A. Ellis, "Negotiating the Boundaries of Tradition: The Rehabilitation of the Book of Ben Sira (Sirach) in B. Sanhedrin 100B," in *Sacra Scriptura: How "Non-Canonical" Texts Functioned in Early Judaism and Early Christianity* (ed. J. H. Charlesworth and L. M. McDonald with B. A. Jurgens; T&T Clark Jewish and Christian Text Series; London: Bloomsbury T&T Clark, 2014), 46–63.

79. Micah 7:5 and Prov 27:1b appear to be cited as part of Ben Sira in B. Sanh. 100b; Wright, "Rabbinic Knowledge," 186, 187.

80. See, e.g. the earliest citation, m. *Avot* 4:4: "R. Levitas of Yavneh says: Be very humble of spirit, as the hope of humanity is a worm" (cf. Ben Sira 7:17). A conflated version of Sir 13:7b and 26:9a is cited as part of the Ketuvim in B. Baba Kama 92b. See Labendz's discussion of the unattributed citations, "The Book of Ben Sira," 348–51.

81. Segal, "Evolution of the Hebrew Text of Ben Sira," 135.

82. Lehmann, "11QPsᵃ and Ben Sira," 241.

83. Wright, "Rabbinic Knowledge," 192.

84. Labendz, "The Book of Ben Sira," 347.

85. Labendz, "The Book of Ben Sira," 354.
86. Labendz, "The Book of Ben Sira," 348.
87. Labendz, "The Book of Ben Sira," 367.
88. See detailed discussion of each citation in Wright, "Rabbinic Knowledge," 184–87; Labendz, "The Book of Ben Sira," 383–92; and Ellis, "Negotiating the Boundaries." See also J. C. Greenfield, who argues that Sanh 100b reflects a "remade text" and "a different compositional principle": "Ben Sira 42:9–10 and Its Talmudic Paraphrase," in *A Tribute to Geza Vermes: Essays on Jewish and Christian Literature and History* (ed. P. R. Davis and R. T. White; Sheffield: JSOT Press, 1990), 167–73, at 170.
89. Gilbert, "The Book of Ben Sira," 88.
90. According to Gilbert and Wright, this type of rearranged collection or "florilegium" may also lie behind the citations of Sanhedrin 100b; Gilbert, "The Book of Ben Sira," 85; Wright, "Rabbinic Knowledge," 191.
91. Segal, "Evolution of the Hebrew Text," 123.
92. Segal, "Evolution of the Hebrew Text," 123.
93. Wright, "Rabbinic Knowledge," 192; and Labendz, "The Book of Ben Sira," 350.
94. Wright, "Rabbinic Knowledge," 192.
95. Labendz, "The Book of Ben Sira," 350.
96. Labendz, "The Book of Ben Sira," 366–67.
97. D. F. McKenzie, *Bibliography and the Sociology of Texts* (Panizzi Lectures; London: British Library, 1986; Cambridge: Cambridge University Press, 1999), 23.

Chapter 4 Shapes of Scriptures

1. R. Chartier, "Libraries without Walls," chapter 3 of *The Order of Books: Readers, Authors, and Libraries in Europe between the Fourteenth and Eighteenth Centuries* (trans. L. G. Cochrane; Stanford, Calif.: Stanford University Press, 1992), 61–88, at 62. On the idea of the universal library in the history of book media, see also A. Grafton, *Codex in Crisis* (New York: Crumpled Press, 2008).
2. M. Hadas, trans., *Aristeas to Philocrates (Letter of Aristeas)* (New York: Harper & Brothers, 1951; Eugene, Ore.: Wipf & Stock, 2007), 97.
3. Chartier, *The Order of Books*, 3.
4. On information overload in the age of print but also earlier, see A. M. Blair, *Too Much to Know: Managing Scholarly Information before the Modern Age* (New Haven, Conn.: Yale University Press, 2010); see also Grafton, *Codex in Crisis*.
5. Chartier, *The Order of Books*, 65–71.
6. On this text and its theory of biblical hermeutics, see S. Handelman, "Everything Is in It: Rabbinic Interpretation and Modern Literary Theory," *Judaism* 35 (1986): 429–40, and further discussion in chapter 5.
7. J. L. Borges, "The Library of Babel," in *Labyrinths: Selected Stories and Other Writings* (ed. D. A. Yates and J. E. Irby; New York: New Directions, 1964), 51–58, at 54–55, cited in Chartier, *The Order of Books*, 63.
8. For the most fully articulated critique of such an assumption about rabbinic scriptural ideology, see R. S. Wollenberg, "The People of the Book without the Book: Jewish Ambivalence toward Biblical Text after the Rise of Christianity" (PhD diss., University of Chicago, 2015).
9. M. Haran, "Archives, Libraries, and the Order of the Biblical Books," *JANES* 22 (1993): 52–61, at 57.
10. M. Fishbane, "Use, Authority and Interpretation of Mikra at Qumran," in *Mikra: Text, Translation, Reading and Interpretation of the Hebrew Bible in Ancient Judaism and Early Christianity* (ed. M. J. Mulder and H. Sysling; Assen: Van Gorcum; Philadelphia: Fortress, 1988), 339–77, at 377.
11. On books in heaven see the comprehensive study by L. Baynes, *The Heavenly Book Motif in Judeo-Christian Apocalypses 200 B.C.E.–200 C.E.* (JSJSup 152; Leiden: Brill, 2012). On mythical books see, e.g., L. S. Schiffman, "Pseudepigrapha in the Pseudepigrapha: Mythical Books in Second Temple Literature," *RevQ* 21 (2004): 429–38.

12. In a sense, then, this chapter is a kind of prequel to the works collected in the volume *Jewish Concepts of Scripture* (ed. B. D. Sommer; New York: New York University Press, 2012). The contributors explore how Jews have conceived of Scripture, at various points in history from the rabbinic period to the present, asking some of the same questions I have raised here.

13. In a 2015 University of Chicago dissertation, Jacqueline Vayntrub discusses the scholarly perception that ancient texts do not have a "native theory" of their own production, but argues, on the basis of Proverbs, that we can discern there its own theory of literary expression, even though "this native theory may not present itself in the texts in the manner to which we are accustomed"; "Proverbs and the Limits of Poetry," 370.

14. I owe the phrase "mental architecture" to Sonja Anderson.

15. G. Vermes, *Scripture and Tradition in Judaism: Haggadic Studies* (Leiden: Brill, 1961; 2nd ed., 1973). The literature on rewritten Bible since Vermes is too vast to cite fully here. Excellent recent analyses, each containing reviews of scholarship to date, include S. W. Crawford, *Rewriting Scripture in Second Temple Times* (Grand Rapids, Mich.: Eerdmans, 2008); M. M. Zahn, *Rethinking Rewritten Scripture: Composition and Exegesis in the 4QReworked Pentateuch Manuscripts* (STDJ 95; Leiden: Brill, 2011); and D. Falk, *The Parabiblical Texts: Strategies for Extending the Scriptures among the Dead Sea Scrolls* (Companion to the Qumran Scrolls 8; London: T&T Clark, 2007). See also specifically methodological studies in M. J. Bernstein, "'Rewritten Bible': A Generic Category Which Has Outlived Its Usefulness?," *Textus* 22 (2005): 169–96; A. K. Petersen, "Rewritten Bible as a Borderline Phenomenon—Genre, Textual Strategy, or Canonical Anachronism?," in *Flores Florentino: Dead Sea Scrolls and Other Early Jewish Studies in Honour of Florentino García Martínez* (ed. A. Hilhorst, É. Puech, and E. J. C. Tigchelaar; JSJSup 122; Leiden: Brill, 2007), 285–306; and G. J. Brooke's important discussion of the relationship between canon formation and rewritten Bible, "Between Authority and Canon: The Significance of Reworking the Bible for Understanding the Canonical Process," in *Reworking the Bible: Apocryphal and Related Texts at Qumran* (ed. E. G. Chazon, D. Dimant, and R. A. Clements; STDJ 58; Leiden: Brill, 2005), 85–104. Now see the essays in the collection *Rewritten Bible after Fifty Years: Texts, Terms, or Techniques? A Last Dialogue with Geza Vermes* (ed. J. Zsengellér; JSJSupp 166; Leiden: Brill, 2014).

16. See a complimentary view in J. G. Campbell, "'Rewritten Bible' and 'Parabiblical Texts': A Terminological and Ideological Critique," in *New Directions in Qumran Studies: Proceedings of the Bristol Colloquium on the Dead Sea Scrolls, 8–10 September, 2003* (ed. J. G. Campbell, W. J. Lyons, and L. K. Pietersen; LSTS 52; London: T & T Clark, 2005), 43–68; Campbell writes that the texts are "rewritten" only from the perspective of their authors, not their audiences.

17. Daniel Harrington sees "rewritten Bible" as "a kind of activity or process [rather than] as a distinctive literary genre"; "Palestinian Adaptations of Biblical Narratives and Prophecies," in *Early Judaism and Its Modern Interpreters* (ed. R. A. Kraft and G. W. E. Nickelsburg; Atlanta: Scholars Press, 1986), 239–58, at 243. More recently see Falk, *Parabiblical Texts*, 16. For a balanced discussion of competing views in the scholarship on the question of "rewritten Bible" as a literary genre, see J. J. Collins, "The Genre of the Book of *Jubilees*," in *A Teacher for All Generations: Essays in Honor of James C. VanderKam* (2 vols.; ed. E. F. Mason et al.; Leiden: Brill, 2012), 2:737–55. Anders Klostergaard Petersen articulates the importance of seeing "rewritten Bible" as an etic, not emic, category in "Rewritten Bible as a Borderline Phenomenon," and argues for retaining the term "rewritten Scripture" to describe a kind of intertextuality that need not come with canonical presuppositions but can have theoretical value for comparative work beyond biblical studies; see also his article "The Riverrun of Rewriting Scripture: From Textual Cannibalism to Scriptural Completion," *JSJ* 43 (2012): 475–96. It seems to me suggestive that here, Petersen has chosen to use a verb phrase, "rewriting Scripture," rather than the noun phrase, "rewritten Scripture," in his title.

18. The scholarship on Deuteronomy's relationship to its precursors is extensive. See the now-classic work by B. Levinson, *Deuteronomy and the Hermeneutics of Legal Innovation* (Oxford: Oxford University Press, 1997), in which the author argues that Deuteronomy disguises

itself as continuous with older law to hide its revolutionary agenda; see also Levinson, *Legal Revision and Religious Renewal in Ancient Israel* (Cambridge: Cambridge University Press, 2008); and J. Stackert, *Rewriting the Torah: Literary Revision in Deuteronomy and the Holiness Code* (Tübingen: Mohr Siebeck, 2007).

19. J. A. Charlesworth, "The Interpretation of the Tanak in the Jewish Apocrypha and Pseudepigrapha," in *A History of Biblical Interpretation*, vol. 1: *The Ancient Period* (ed. A. J. Hauser and D. F. Watson; Grand Rapids, Mich.: Eerdmans, 2003), 253–82, at 253.

20. See especially S. D. Fraade "'Comparative Midrash' Revisited: The Case of the Dead Sea Scrolls and Rabbinic Midrash," in *Agendas for the Study of Midrash in the Twenty-First Century* (ed. M. L. Raphael; Williamsburg, Va.: College of William and Mary Press, 1999), 4–17, "Midrash and Ancient Jewish Biblical Interpretation," in *The Cambridge Companion to the Talmud and Rabbinic Literature* (ed. C. E. Fonrobert and M. S. Jaffee; Cambridge: Cambridge University Press, 2007), 99–120, "Looking for Legal Midrash at Qumran," in *Biblical Perspectives: Early Use and Interpretation of the Bible in Light of the Dead Sea Scrolls: Proceedings of the First International Symposium of the Orion Center for the Study of the Dead Sea Scrolls and Associated Literature, 12–14 May, 1996* (ed. M. E. Stone and E. G. Chazon; STDJ 28; Leiden: Brill, 1998), 59–79, and "Looking for Narrative Midrash at Qumran," in *Rabbinic Perspectives: Rabbinic Literature and the Dead Sea Scrolls: Proceedings of the Eighth International Symposium of the Orion Center for the Study of the Dead Sea Scrolls and Associated Literature, 7–9 January, 2003* (ed. S. D. Fraade, A. Shemesh, and R. A. Clements; STDJ 62; Leiden: Brill, 2006), 43–66. Fraade, however, does show that some nonformal continuities with rabbinic exegetical methods can be found in early Jewish texts classified as "rewritten Bible," even as formal differences abound; see "Rewritten Bible and Rabbinic Midrash as Commentary," in *Current Trends in the Study of Midrash* (ed. C. Bakhos; Leiden: Brill, 2006), 59–78. See now the discussion by M. Satlow, *How the Bible Became Holy* (New Haven, Conn.: Yale University Press, 2014), 186–88, who writes that the lemma and commentary in *pesharim* are formally differentiated because the base text had oracular authority, secret meanings to be decoded.

21. On the relationship of *pesher* to biblical genres, see S. L. Sanders, "Daniel and the Origins of Biblical Interpretation," *Prooftexts*, forthcoming. Sanders shows that in Daniel, the idea of *pesher* or interpretation is applied to moments of new revelation, but not to Scripture.

22. J. C. Reeves, "Problematizing the Bible . . . Then and Now," *JQR* 100 (2010): 139–52, at 147.

23. J. E. Bowley, "Missing Books and Their Ancient Libraries," paper presented at the Society of Biblical Literature Annual Meeting, November 24, 2014.

24. F. García Martínez, "Parabiblical Literature from Qumran and the Canonical Process," *RevQ* 25 (2012): 525–56.

25. See, e.g., M. A. Knibb, "The Use of Scripture in 1 Enoch 17-19," in *Alexandria, Rome: Studies in Ancient Cultural Interaction in Honour of A. Hilhorst* (ed. F. García Martínez and G. Luttikhuizen; JSJS 82; Leiden: Brill, 2003), 165–78; and G. W. E. Nickelsburg's Hermeneia commentary, *1 Enoch 1: A Commentary on the Book of 1 Enoch, Chapters 1–36; 81–108* (Hermeneia; Minneapolis: Fortress Press, 2001), esp. 57–58.

26. García Martínez, "Parabiblical Literature," 542.

27. Trans. J. C. VanderKam in G. W. E. Nickelsburg and J. C. VanderKam. *1 Enoch: The Hermeneia Translation* (Minneapolis: Fortress Press, 2012). This passage, writes Robert Kraft, "seems to be as clear a claim of authority as possible, although exactly which Enochic 'book' (or 'books') is referred to, if distinct from the one he is 'writing down' at the time, is unclear. Perhaps anything believed to be from 'Enoch' could fit into this category"; "'Enoch' Texts and Parabiblical Literature: Language about Authoritative Writing," n.p., online: http://ccat.sas.upenn.edu/rak/courses/525/Enoch.html.

28. See the commentary by L. T. Stuckenbruck, *1 Enoch 91–108* (Commentaries on Early Jewish Literature; Berlin: de Gruyter, 2007), and specifically on this issue, "Reflections on Sources behind the Epistle of Enoch and the Significance of 1 Enoch 104:9–13 for the Reception of Enochic Tradition," in *A Teacher for All Generations: Essays in Honor of James C. VanderKam* (2 vols; E. F. Mason et al; Leiden: Brill, 2011), 1:704–14. Stuckenbruck writes that here the text "presents itself as the reception of Enochic tradition by a claimant to Enoch's name who, in his very interpretation and transmission of the tradition, regards himself as divinely inspired" (713).

29. See the work of Andrei Orlov on *2 Enoch*, esp. *The Enoch-Metatron Tradition* (Tübingen: Mohr Siebeck, 2005); and the essays in *New Perspectives on 2 Enoch: No Longer Slavonic Only* (ed. A. A. Orlov and G. Boccaccini; Leiden: Brill, 2012).

30. See A. Y. Reed, "Textuality between Death and Memory: The Prehistory and Formation of the Parabiblical Testament," *JQR* 104 (2014): 381–412, on the narrative roles of writing in ensuring the continuity of ancestral tradition in testamentary texts.

31. See É. Puech, "Testament de Qahat," in *Qumrân Grotte 4. XXII : Textes Araméens : Première partie* (DJD 31; Oxford: Clarendon, 2001), 257–82; and H. Drawnel, "The Literary Form and Didactic Content of the Admonitions (Testament) of Qahat," in *From 4QMMT to Resurrection: Mélanges qumraniens en hommage À Émile Puech* (ed. F. García Martínez, A. Steudel, and E. J.C. Tigchelaar; STDJ 61; Leiden: Brill, 2006), 55–73.

32. Translation from F. García Martínez and E. J. C. Tigchelaar, *The Dead Sea Scrolls Study Edition* (2 vols,; Leiden: Brill, 1997–98). Puech's reconstruction, "Testament de Qahat" (DJD 31), adds several more references to writing, but even unreconstructed, it is clear that the heritage of the ancestors is a written one.

33. On this text see D. A. Machiela, *The Dead Sea Genesis Apocryphon: A New Text Edition and Translation with Introduction and Special Treatment of Columns 13–17* (STDJ 79; Leiden: Brill, 2009); and the commentary of J. A. Fitzmyer, *The Genesis Apocryphon of Qumran Cave 1 (1Q20)* (3d ed.; Rome: Pontifical Biblical Institute, 2004).

34. M. Bernstein, "Is the Genesis Apocryphon a Unity? What Sort of Unity Were You Looking For?," *Aramaic Studies* 8 (2010): 107–34, at 112–13. Bernstein sees the text as a two-part composition, while Esther Eshel divides it into a cycle of three parts; see "The Genesis Apocryphon: A Chain of Traditions," in *The Dead Sea Scrolls and Contemporary Culture: Proceedings of the International Conference Held at the Israel Museum, Jerusalem (July 6–8, 2008)* (ed. A. D. Roitman, L. H. Schiffman, and S. Tzoref; STDJ 93; Leiden: Brill, 2010), 181–93. See also Bernstein, "The Genesis Apocryphon: Compositional and Interpretive Perspectives," in *A Companion to Biblical Interpretation in Early Judaism* (ed. M. Henze; Grand Rapids, Mich.: Eerdmans, 2012), 157–79.

35. Transcription and translation from Machiela, *The Dead Sea Genesis Apocryphon*, 73. Machiela, with Bernstein, reads ספרא, although the *peh* is not clear and could possibly be read as a *bet*, which would make the reading סברא, "brilliance, understanding," also plausible in this context; Machiela, however, renders ספרא, which he reads as a reference to "'book learning, scribal wisdom, erudition' (*safrah* or *saparah*), rather than an actual book (*sifra*)"; he cites a similar usage in the *Aramaic Levi Document* 13:4.

36. See James Kugel's explanation of this passage as exegesis in *The Bible as It Was* (Cambridge, Mass.: Harvard University Press, 1997), 146–48; Kugel sees its origin in Abraham's words in Gen 12:11, "Behold, now I know (ידעתי) that you are a beautiful woman; and when the Egyptians see you, they will say, 'this is his wife,' and they will kill me and let you live." The writer of the *Genesis Apocryphon* interpreted this phrase to mean that Abraham *came to know* not that Sarah was beautiful, but what would happen as a consequence of her beauty: the Egyptians would try to kill him. The writer then embellished the story to add that the way Abraham *came to know* this was through a prophetic dream.

37. See J. M. Allegro, "4Q175, 4QTestimonia," in *Qumrân Cave 4*, vol. 1: *4Q158–4Q186* (DJD 5; Oxford: Clarendon, 1968), 57–60. See also my entry "4QTestimonia," in *The T&T Clark Companion to the Dead Sea Scrolls* (ed. G. J. Brooke and C. Hempel; London: T&T Clark, forthcoming.

38. These include 4Q378, 4Q379, 4Q522, perhaps 5Q9, 4QpaleoParaJosh, and MasParaJosh. On these texts see E. Tov, "The Rewritten Book of Joshua as Found at Qumran and Masada," in *Biblical Perspectives: Early Use and Interpretation of the Bible in the Light of the Dead Sea Scrolls: Proceedings of the First International Symposium of the Orion Center, 12–14 May 1996* (ed. M. E. Stone and E. G. Chazon; STDJ 28; Leiden: Brill, 1998), 233–56, repr. in Tov, *Hebrew Bible, Greek Bible, and Qumran: Collected Essays* (TSAJ 121; Tübingen: Mohr Siebeck, 2008), 71–91.

39. García Martínez, "Parabiblical Literature," 530.

40. J. A. Fabricius, *Codex Pseudepigraphus Veteris Testamenti* (Hamburg, 1713). See the thorough study of this edition by A. Y. Reed, "The Modern Invention of 'Old Testament Pseudepigrapha,'" *JTS* 60 (2009): 403–36.

41. Reed, "Modern Invention," 427.
42. R. H. Charles, *The Apocrypha and Pseudepigrapha of the Old Testament in English* (2 vols.; Oxford: Clarendon, 1913), henceforth *APOT*.
43. Charles, *APOT*, 2:x.
44. The idea that prophecy had come to an end in Second Temple Judaism—and that this was a belief that Jews themselves held at the time—has a long history in scholarship, and has been intertwined with supersessionist theologies. For a history and critique of this trope, see J. R. Levison, "Did the Spirit Withdraw from Israel? An Evaluation of the Earliest Jewish Data," *NTS* 43 (1997): 35–57.
45. Charles, *APOT*, 2:ix.
46. Charles, *APOT*, 1:x.
47. Charles, *APOT*, 2:xi.
48. Charles, *APOT*, 2:xi.
49. J. A. Charlesworth, *The Old Testament Pseudepigrapha*, vol. 1: *Apocalyptic Literature and Testaments*; vol. 2: *Expansions of the "Old Testament" and Legends, Wisdom and Philosophical Literature, Prayers, Psalms, and Odes, Fragments of Lost Judeo-Hellenistic Works* (Garden City, N.Y.: Doubleday, 1983–85), henceforth *OTP*; H. F. D. Sparks, *The Apocryphal Old Testament* (Oxford: Clarendon, 1984). For an analysis of both collections see R. A. Kraft, "Combined Review," in *Exploring the Scripturesque: Jewish Texts and Their Christian Contexts* (JSJSup 137; Leiden: Brill, 2009), 94–106; the review essay was first published in *RelSRev* 14.2 (1988): 113–17, along with M. E. Stone's companion review in the same issue (111–13).
50. He has also retained a confessional Christian tone in the introductory material. See the characterization of Sparks's collection in Kraft, "Combined Review," esp. 95–96, 102–3.
51. Kraft, "Combined Review," 96.
52. Charlesworth, *OTP*, 1:xii. The "Foreword for Christians" by J. T. Cleland is more effusive, and retains the general structure of Charles's scheme of "intertestamental" texts as a bridge between the Old and New Testaments, but with a different affective resonance: "may it come to pass that what unites us as brethren will far surpass what seems to separate us.…We are both children of the Kingdom, and the Pseudepigrapha may become a bridge between the Old and New testaments [*sic*], helping us cross to and fro, back and forth, until we are equally at home in both, to our mental satisfaction, and our spiritual growth in grace" (xi).
53. Charlesworth, *OTP*, 1:xv.
54. Charlesworth, *OTP*, 1:xi.
55. Charlesworth, *OTP*, 1:xxiv.
56. Kraft, "Combined Review," 102.
57. Kraft, "Combined Review," 102–3.
58. Kraft, "Combined Review," 105.
59. L. H. Feldman, J. L. Kugel, and L. H. Schiffman, eds., *Outside the Bible: Ancient Jewish Writings Related to Scripture* (3 vols.; Lincoln: University of Nebraska Press, 2013). Originally the name of the collection was to be "The Lost Bible." A precursor to the title was a shorter collection of excerpts entitled *Outside the Old Testament* (ed. M. de Jonge; Cambridge: Cambridge University Press, 1985).
60. Kugel, *The Bible as It Was, Traditions of the Bible: A Guide to the Bible as It Was at the Start of the Common Era* (Cambridge, Mass.: Harvard University Press, 1999), and *How to Read the Bible: A Guide to Scripture, Then and Now* (New York: Free Press, 2007).
61. Kugel, *How to Read the Bible*, 679.
62. Kugel, *How to Read the Bible*, 668.
63. Kugel, *The Bible as It Was*, 3.
64. Kugel has also, implicitly, done something important for scholars who want to historicize reading practices, especially when it comes to practices of "linear" and "nonlinear" or discontinuous reading. In a classic narrative of book history, the scroll was a linear medium, while the codex then later allowed for nonlinear, fragmented reading. This evolutionary, materially determinist scheme does not account for the complex reading practices of early Judaism. Kugel's work in building a database of fragments that he sees reflected in diverse

sources gives us a way to complicate that kind of evolutionary media narrative. On linear
and fragmented reading and its material contexts see D. Stern, "The First Jewish Books and
the Early History of Jewish Reading." *JQR* 98 (2008): 163–202; and my article "Thinking
Digitally about the Dead Sea Scrolls: 'Book History' before and beyond the Book," *Book
History* 13 (2011): 235–63.

65. Reeves, "Problematizing the Bible," 149.
66. Feldman has published his work on Josephus's biblical exegesis in two volumes: *Josephus's
    Interpretation of the Bible* (Hellenistic Culture and Society 27; Berkeley: University of
    California Press, 1999) and a collection of thirty-five essays entitled *Studies in Josephus'
    Rewritten Bible* (JSJSupp 58; Leiden: Brill, 2005).
67. See Schiffman's popular works, such as *Reclaiming the Dead Sea Scrolls: The History of
    Judaism, the Background of Christianity, the Lost Library of Qumran* (Philadelphia: Jewish
    Publication Society, 1994), and *Understanding Second Temple and Rabbinic Judaism* (ed.
    J. Bloomberg and S. Kapustin; Jersey City, N.J.: Ktav, 2003).
68. Feldman, Kugel, and Schiffman, "Introduction," in *Outside the Bible*, xv–xviii, at xvi–xvii.
69. The bibliography on *Jubilees* is vast. For a clear and insightful overview of the text and its
    place in Second Temple Jewish history, literature, and traditions, as well as its relationship
    to its scriptural precursors, see Crawford, *Rewriting Scripture in Second Temple Times*, chap-
    ter 4, "The Book of Jubilees," 60–82. For the Ethiopic text and the translation used in this
    chapter, see J. C. VanderKam, *The Book of Jubilees: A Critical Text* (CSCO 510 Scriptores
    Aethiopici 87; Louvain: E. Peeters, 1989), and *The Book of Jubilees: Translation* (CSCO 511
    Scriptores Aethiopici 88; Louvain: E. Peeters, 1989). For the Qumran fragments, see J. C.
    VanderKam, *Qumran Cave 4.VIII: Parabiblical Texts*, Part 1 (DJD 13; Oxford: Clarendon,
    1994), 1–185. Important recent studies of *Jubilees* as rewritten and interpreted Scripture
    include J. T. A. G. M. van Ruiten, *Primeval History Interpreted: The Rewriting of Genesis 1–11
    in the Book of Jubilees* (JSJS 66; Leiden: Brill, 2000); M. Segal, *The Book of Jubilees: Rewritten
    Bible, Redaction, Ideology and Theology* (Leiden: Brill, 2007); and J. L. Kugel, *A Walk
    through Jubilees* (Leiden: Brill, 2012). See the references compiled by V. Bachmann and
    I. W. Oliver in "The Book of Jubilees: A Bibliography, 1850–Present," in *Enoch and the
    Mosaic Torah: The Evidence of Jubilees* (ed. G. Boccaccini and G. Ibba; Grand Rapids, Mich.:
    Eerdmans, 2009), 441–68. Most recently, see the essays collected in H. Najman and E. J. C.
    Tigchelaar, eds., *Composition, Rewriting and Reception of the Book of Jubilees*, a special issue
    of *RevQ* 104 (2014). Quotation from Kugel, "Jubilees," in *Outside the Bible*, 272–465, at 272.
70. See, e.g., Epiphanius, Syncellus, Didymus of Alexandria, and Jerome; on this title see
    O. Wintermute's introduction to *Jubilees* in Charlesworth, *OTP*, 41. *Jubilees* is longer than
    Genesis, so the name cannot refer to its length but to something else, perhaps its minor
    status, although Charles, *APOT* 2:2, and A. Dillmann and H. Rönsch, *Das Buch der Jubiläen
    oder die kleine Genesis* (Leipzig: Fues, 1874), 467–68, think the title reflects *Jubilees'* atten-
    tion to minutiae.
71. Kugel, "*Jubilees*," in *Outside the Bible*, 272–465, at 272. Kugel gives examples of the kinds of
    interpretive questions that are answered in *Jubilees*: "How did humanity continue to de-
    velop if Adam and Eve had only sons? When did God decide that Israel was to be His spe-
    cial people? Where was Abraham when God first spoke to him? When and why was the
    tribe of Levi chosen for the priesthood in Israel?"
72. Besides Kugel's important work on this issue, see also, for example, the work of D. A. Teeter, e.g.
    "On 'Exegetical Function' in Rewritten Scripture: Inner-Biblical Exegesis and the Abram/
    Ravens Narrative in Jubilees," *HTR* 106 (2013): 373–402, and "Torah, Wisdom, and the
    Composition of Rewritten Scripture: Jubilees and 11QPs^a in Comparative Perspective," in
    *Wisdom and Torah: The Reception of "Torah" in the Wisdom Literature of the Second Temple
    Period* (ed. B. U. Schipper and D. A. Teeter; JSJSup 163; Leiden: Brill, 2013), 233–72. See also
    J. van Ruiten, "Between Jacob's Death and Moses' Birth: The Intertextual Relationship be-
    tween Genesis 50:15—Exodus 1:14 and Jubilees 46:1–16," in *Flores Florentino: Dead Sea
    Scrolls and Other Early Jewish Studies in Honour of Florentino García Martínez* (ed. A. Hilhorst,
    É. Puech, and E. J. C. Tigchelaar; JSJSup 122; Leiden: Brill, 2007), 467–89, and his mono-
    graph *Abraham in the Book of Jubilees: The Rewriting of Genesis 11:26–25:10 in the Book of
    Jubilees* (JSJSup 161; Leiden: Brill, 2012). Hans Debel, like Teeter, compares *Jubilees'* rewriting

of texts now called biblical to the rewriting of texts within the biblical corpus; see "Anchoring Revelations in the Authority of Sinai: A Comparison of the Rewritings of 'Scripture' in *Jubilees* and in the P Stratum of Exodus," *JSJ* 45 (2014): 1–22.

73. On *Jubilees'* reception as authoritative text see J. C. VanderKam, "Moses Trumping Moses," in *The Dead Sea Scrolls: Transmission of Traditions and Production of Texts* (ed. S. Metso, H. Najman, and E. Schuller; STDJ 92; Leiden: Brill, 2010), 25–44, at 43–44, and "Authoritative Literature in the Dead Sea Scrolls," *DSD* 5 (1998): 396–401; E. C. Ulrich, "The Bible in the Making: The Scriptures Found at Qumran," in *The Bible at Qumran: Text, Shape and Interpretation* (ed. P. W. Flint; Grand Rapids, Mich.: Eerdmans, 2001), 51–66; C. Hempel, "The Place of the *Book of Jubilees* at Qumran and Beyond," in *The Dead Sea Scrolls in Their Historical Context* (ed. T. H. Lim; Edinburgh: T&T Clark, 2000), 187–96; A. Shemesh, "4Q265 and the Authoritative Status of Jubilees at Qumran," in *Enoch and the Mosaic Torah: The Evidence of Jubilees* (ed. G. Boccaccini and G. Ibba; Grand Rapids, Mich.: Eerdmans, 2009), 247–60; T. R. Hanneken, "The Status and Interpretation of Jubilees in 4Q390," in *A Teacher for All Generations: Essays in Honor of James C. VanderKam* (ed. E. F. Mason et al.; Leiden: Brill, 2011), 1:407–428; and M. Himmelfarb, *A Kingdom of Priests: Ancestry and Merit in Ancient Judaism* (Philadelphia: University of Pennsylvania Press, 2006), 53–55.

74. García Martínez, "Parabiblical Literature," 538.

75. Trans. García Martínez and Tigchelaar, *The Dead Sea Scrolls Study Edition*, 1:565.

76. For the *Pseudo-Jubilees* texts see J. C. VanderKam and J. T. Milik in H. Attridge et al., eds., *Qumran Cave 4.VIII: Parabiblical Texts, Part 1* (DJD 13; Oxford: Clarendon Press, 1994), 141–75. See also J. L. Kugel, "Exegetical Notes on 4Q225 'Pseudo-Jubilees,'" *DSD* 13 (2006): 73–98.

77. Collins, "The Genre of the Book of Jubilees," 747. See also D. Lambert, "How the 'Torah of Moses' Became Revelation: An Early, Apocalyptic Theory of Pentateuchal Origins," *JSJ* (forthcoming), who emphasizes that the fact Second Temple texts "include interpretive material is hardly sufficient reason to assume that, in their own conceptualization, they are forms of interpretation." I thank the author for sharing a prepublication version of this essay.

78. H. Najman, "Reconsidering Jubilees: Prophecy and Exemplarity," in her collected essays, *Past Renewals: Interpretive Authority, Renewed Revelation, and the Quest for Perfection in Jewish Antiquity* (JSJSup 53; Leiden: Brill, 2010), 190–204, at 192; first published in *Enoch and Mosaic Torah: The Evidence of Jubilees* (ed. G. Boccaccini and G. Ibba; Grand Rapids, Mich.: Eerdmans, 2009), 229–43.

79. For a documentary analysis and review of scholarship see J. Baden, *The Composition of the Pentateuch: Renewing the Documentary Hypothesis* (New Haven, Conn.: Yale University Press, 2012), who himself argues Deuteronomy had E and J in separate forms. For an alternative point of view, see E. Blum, *Studien zur Komposition des Pentateuch* (BZAW 189; Berlin: de Gruyter, 1990).

80. Although there is disagreement among scholars about whether Deuteronomy intends to solve problems in the earlier tradition or replace it outright; see n. 17.

81. Lambert, "How the 'Torah of Moses' Became Revelation."

82. As Collins writes, "there is no admission that its authority is derivative from that of the first law"; "The Genre of the Book of Jubilees," 747. David Lambert takes this further, writing that "in the pseudepigraphic imagination, such works [as *Jubilees*] are configured as sources for the canonical works, not the other way around"; see "How the 'Torah of Moses' Became Revelation." On *Jubilees'* claims to authority, see H. Najman, "Interpretation as Primordial Writing: *Jubilees* and Its Authority Conferring Strategies," *JSJ* 30 (1999): 379–410; and M. Himmelfarb, "Torah, Testimony, and Heavenly Tablets: The Claim to Authority in the Book of Jubilees," in *A Multiform Heritage: Studies on Early Judaism and Christianity in Honor of Robert A. Kraft* (ed. B. G. Wright III, Homage Series 24; Atlanta: Scholars Press, 1999), 19–29. R. A. Kraft, in "Scripture and Canon in the Commonly Called Apocrypha and Pseudepigrapha and in the Writings of Josephus," in *Hebrew Bible/Old Testament: The History of its Interpretation*, vol. 1: *From the Beginnings to the Middle Ages (until 1300); Part 1: Antiquity* (ed. M. Saebø; Göttingen: Vandenhoeck & Ruprecht, 1996), 199–216, esp. 205–9, also sees *Jubilees'* authoritative "source" as the heavenly tablets. The heavenly tablets

themselves seem to be multiform in nature, containing laws that are part of the Torah of Moses, other laws that claim to be rooted in primeval narratives, calendrical and chronological lore that legitimizes *Jubilees'* organization of time, records of human deeds, and accounts of the future. On the tablets see F. García Martínez, "The Heavenly Tablets in the Book of Jubilees," in *Studies in the Book of Jubilees* (ed. M. Albani et al.; Tübingen: Mohr Siebeck, 1997), 243–60. See also L. Ravid, "The Special Terminology of the Heavenly Tablets" [Hebrew], *Tarbiz* 68.4 (1999): 463–71; and S. Tzoref (Berrin), "'Heavenly Tablets' in the Book of Jubilees," in *Anafim: Proceedings of the Australian Jewish Studies Forum, University of Sydney, 8–9 February 2004* (ed. S. Faigan; Sydney: Mandelbaum, 2006), 29–47, and "Covenantal Election in 4Q252 and Jubilees' Heavenly Tablets," *DSD* 18 (2011): 74–89.

83. A. Y. Reed, "Enochic and Mosaic Traditions in Jubilees: The Evidence of Angelology and Demonology," in *Enoch and the Mosaic Torah: The Evidence of Jubilees* (ed. G. Boccaccini and G. Ibba; Grand Rapids, Mich.: Eerdmans, 2009), 353–68, at 363.

84. Translations from VanderKam, *The Book of Jubilees: Translation.*

85. On the contents of the heavenly tablets, see n. 82 above. For an account and review of scholarship on what the different kinds of "torah" might mean in *Jubilees*, see D. Lambert, "How the 'Torah of Moses' Became Revelation." On the testimony, VanderKam writes that given "everything *Jubilees* says about the testimony, it is to be roughly identified with *Jubilees* itself, though the book may not exhaust all that is present in the written testimony on the heavenly tablets"; "Moses Trumping Moses," 42. A. Caquot sees the "testimony" as a complement to the "law" in "'Loi' et 'témoignage' dans le Livre des Jubilés," in *Mélanges linguistiques offerts à Maxime Rodinson par ses élèves, ses collègues et ses amis* (ed. C. Robin; Comptes Rendus du groupe linguistique d'études chamito-sémitiques Supplement 12; Paris: Geuthner, 1985), 137–45. For a different view see C. Werman, "The 'tôrâ and the tě'ûdâ' Engraved on the Tablets," *DSD* 9 (2002): 75–103; Werman sees the "testimony" as preordained history. Kugel understands "*Torah* and Te'udah" as a reference to two authoritative books on which *Jubilees* claims to be based, their titles drawn from Isa 8:16, "Bind up the testimony [te'udah], seal up the instruction [torah] with My disciples"; "*Jubilees*," in Feldman, Kugel, and Schiffman, *Outside the Bible*, 273–74.

86. A proponent of the theory that *Jubilees did* intend to replace Genesis and Exodus is B. Z. Wacholder, "Jubilees as the Super Canon: Torah-Admonition versus Torah-Commandment," in *Legal Texts and Legal Issues: Proceedings of the Second Meeting of the International Organization for Qumran Studies, Cambridge 1995* (ed. M. J. Bernstein, F. García Martínez, and J. Kampen, STDJ 23; Leiden: Brill, 1997), 195–211; but see the full review of scholarship and critique of such a position in H. Najman, *Seconding Sinai: The Development of Mosaic Discourse in Second Temple Judaism* (Leiden: Brill, 2003), esp. 43–50; as well as Himmelfarb, "Torah, Testimony, and Heavenly Tablets."

87. See Petersen, "The Riverrun of Rewriting Scripture," 492.

88. See a different but complementary articulation of this idea of narrated textual tradition by H. S. Kvanvig, "Jubilees—Read as a Narrative," in *Enoch and Qumran Origins: New Light on a Forgotten Connection* (ed. G. Boccaccini; Grand Rapids, Mich.: Eerdmans, 2005), 75–83.

89. Najman, "Interpretation as Primordial Writing," 388.

90. D. F. McKenzie, *Bibliography and the Sociology of Texts* (Panizzi Lectures; Cambridge: Cambridge University Press, 1999), 12.

91. On such catalogs see chapter 1 of S. L. Sanders, *From Adapa to Enoch: Scribal Culture and Religious Vision in Judea and Babylon* (Tübingen: Mohr Siebeck, 2016); sources appear in publications by W. G. Lambert, e.g. "Ancestors, Authors, and Canonicity," *Journal of Cuneiform Studies* 11 (1957): 1–14, and "A Catalogue of Texts and Authors," *Journal of Cuneiform Studies* 16 (1962): 59–77.

92. See Kraft's discussion of "scripture before Moses' scriptures" in "Scripture and Canon," 205. On imaginary books see Schiffman, "Pseudepigrapha in the Pseudepigrapha"; and Baynes, *Heavenly Book Motif*. Steven P. Weitzman discusses a fascinating related cultural phenomenon: indexing lost, missing, and mythical treasures, such as the inventory of long-lost gifts to the temple of Athena in the first-century BCE Lindian Chronicle. Weitzman suggests the Copper Scroll from Qumran, with its list of treasures, may reflect a similar

practice of accounting for what is not available; "Absent but Accounted For: A New Approach to the Copper Scroll," *HTR* 108 (2015): 423–47. Just as Michael Satlow points out for writing in *1 Enoch,* many of the references in *Jubilees* are not about specific, exact knowledge of a textual source, but "more abstract and conceptual" references to divine writing that is "indelibly written but accessible only by means of special revelation" (*How the Bible Became Holy,* 121).

93. In *1 Enoch* 72:1: "The book about the motion of the heavenly luminaries all as they are in their kinds, their jurisdiction, their time, their name, their origins, and their months which Uriel, the holy angel who was with me (and) who is their leader, showed me. The entire book about them, as it is, he showed me and how every year of the world will be forever, until a new creation lasting forever is made." Trans. VanderKam, in Nickelsburg and VanderKam, *1 Enoch.*

94. Samuel Thomas writes that Enoch "takes the place of Adam in the garden, gaining what Adam is said to have forsaken (life without death) while retaining that which Adam gained by transgression (knowledge), which Enoch then passes along to his progeny." S. I. Thomas, "Eternal Writing and Immortal Writers: On the Non-Death of the Scribe in Early Judaism," in *A Teacher for All Generations: Essays in Honor of James C. VanderKam* (ed. E. F. Mason et al; Leiden: Brill, 2011), 1:573–88, at 577.

95. See G. Boccaccini, *Beyond the Essene Hypothesis: The Parting of the Ways between Qumran and Enochic Judaism* (Grand Rapids, Mich.: Eerdmans, 1998); influenced by P. Sacchi, *Jewish Apocalyptic and Its History* (JSPSup 20; Sheffield: Sheffield Academic Press, 1997). But many scholars have critiqued this model; see in particular the essays collected in G. Boccaccini and J. J. Collins, eds., *The Early Enoch Literature* (JSJSup, 121; Leiden: Brill, 2007), esp. J. C. VanderKam, "Mapping Second Temple Judaism," 1–20; and F. García Martínez, "Conclusion: Mapping the Threads," 329–35. For an overview of this debate and an analysis of the *Book of the Watchers* in light of it, see V. Bachmann, "The Book of the Watchers (*1 Enoch* 1–36): An Anti-Mosaic, Non-Mosaic, or Even Pro-Mosaic Writing?" *Journal of Hebrew Scriptures* 11 (2011); Bachmann shows that the *Book of the Watchers* does not allow for the conclusion that the Enoch literature reflects a distinctive "Enochic" form of Judaism. See also H. Najman, review of *Beyond the Essene Hypothesis,* *AJSR* 26 (2002): 352–53.

96. On Enochic literature as polemicizing against other mediatory figures, see e.g. Orlov, *The Enoch-Metatron Tradition*; and my review of Orlov in the *Journal of Hebrew Scriptures* 6 (2006).

97. This is reminiscent of older models of textual criticism, which posited original, stable, unitary texts, which were subsequently disrupted by variation and blending.

98. As Reed observes, *Jubilees* is not interested in adjudicating the relative worth of different constitutive traditions, but emphasizes that Jewish literary heritage stretches back to a time that long predates Moses; Reed, "Enochic and Mosaic Traditions in Jubilees."

99. On the idea of revelation over time in *Jubilees* see S. Tzoref (Berrin), "The 'Hidden' and the 'Revealed': Progressive Revelation of Law and Esoterica" (Hebrew), in *Meghillot: Studies in the Dead Sea Scrolls* 7 (ed. M. Bar-Asher and D. Dimant; Jerusalem: Haifa University and Bialik Institute, 2009), 157–90.

100. J. M. Scott, "Geographic Aspects of Noachic Materials in the Scrolls at Qumran," in *The Scrolls and the Scriptures* (ed. S. E. Porter and C. A. Evans; Sheffield: Sheffield Academic Press, 1997) 368–81; C. Sulzbach, "The Function of the Sacred Geography in the Book of Jubilees," *Journal for Semitics* 14 (2005): 283–305; and the discussion in M. E. Stone, "The Book(s) Attributed to Noah," *DSD* 13 (2006): 2–23, at 14–15.

101. Najman, "Interpretation as Primordial Writing," 383.

102. *Jubilees* here presents a different mode of transmission from Enoch's written testimony, which was "placed upon the earth" (4:19), not handed down to the next generation.

103. See the collected essays in M. E. Stone, V. Hillel, and A. Amihay, eds., *Noah and His Book(s)* (Atlanta: Society of Biblical Literature, 2010), esp. in part 1 dealing with the "book of Noah," including a reprint of Stone's "The Book(s) Attributed to Noah," 7–25.

104. This is separate from the story of Noah's birth, which appears earlier in *Genesis Apocryphon* and is related in the third person, similarly to *1 Enoch* 106–7; on traditions about Noah's

birth, see E. Eshel, "The Genesis Apocryphon and Other Related Aramaic Texts from Qumran: The Birth of Noah," in *Aramaica Qumranica: Proceedings of the Conference on the Aramaic Texts from Qumran in Aix-en-Provence, 30 June–2 July 2008* (ed. K. Berthelot and D. Stökl Ben Ezra; STDJ 94; Leiden: Brill, 2010), 277–94; and A. Amihay and D. Machiela, "Traditions of the Birth of Noah," in Stone, Hillel, and Amihay, *Noah and His Book(s)*, 53–69.

105. Stone, "The Book(s) Attributed to Noah," 10. The phrase "the book of Noah concerning the blood" has not survived in Aramaic, but only in a Greek excerpt, but, Stone writes, "there is no reason to doubt its originality." See also J. C. Greenfield, M. E. Stone, and E. Eshel, eds., *The Aramaic Levi Document: Edition, Translation, Commentary* (SVTP 19; Leiden: Brill, 2004), 180.

106. Enoch and Noah are further linked as writers in a brief subscription to the *Book of Parables* or *Similitudes of Enoch*, the one part of *1 Enoch* that was not found in any Qumran manuscripts. Noah claims he has received a book from Enoch: "my great-grandfather gave me the explanation of all the secrets in a book, and the parables that were given to him, and gathered them for me in the words of the Book of Parables" (*1 Enoch* 68:1).

107. See the introduction and translation of the relevant passage by M. Himmelfarb, in "The Book of Noah," in *Old Testament Pseudepigrapha: More Noncanonical Scriptures* (vol. 1; ed. R. Bauckham, J. Davila, and A. Panayotov; Grand Rapids, Mich.: Eerdmans, 2013), 40–46. On this text see R. Scharbach (Wollenberg), "The Rebirth of a Book: Noachic Writing in Medieval and Renaissance Europe," in Stone, Hillel, and Amihay, *Noah and his Book(s)*, 113–33.

108. Himmelfarb, "Book of Noah," 46.

109. This is the view of Himmelfarb, "Some Echoes of Jubilees in Medieval Hebrew Literature," in *Tracing the Threads: Studies in the Vitality of Jewish Pseudepigrapha* (ed. J. C. Reeves; Atlanta: Scholars Press, 1994), 127–36, and "Book of Noah."

110. One fragmentary text from Qumran, 1Q19, has been called the "book of Noah" by its editor, J. T. Milik, but this is a modern designation; see "Livre de Noë," in *Qumran Cave 1* (ed. D. Barthélemy and J. T. Milik; DJD 1; Oxford: Clarendon, 1955), 84–86. The text mentions Lamech and Methuselah and shares some features with *1 Enoch* 106–7 and the story of Noah's birth in the *Genesis Apocryphon*. On this text see A. Feldman, "1Q19 (The Book of Noah) Reconsidered," *Henoch* 31.2 (2009): 284–306; and C. Pfann, "A Note on 1Q19: The 'Book of Noah,'" in Stone, Hillel, and Amihay, *Noah and His Book(s)*, 71–76.

111. See especially the work of Devorah Dimant and Cana Werman, who are skeptical about such a book's existence: D. Dimant, "Noah in Early Jewish Literature," in *Biblical Figures outside the Bible* (ed. M. E. Stone and T. A. Bergren; Harrisburg, PA: Trinity Press, 1998), 123–50, and "Two 'Scientific' Fictions: The So-called Book of Noah and the Alleged Quotation of Jubilees in CD 16:3-4," in *Studies in the Hebrew Bible, Qumran, and the Septuagint Presented to Eugene Ulrich* (ed. P. W. Flint et al.; SVT 101; Leiden: Brill, 2006), 230–49; and C. Werman, "Qumran and the Book of Noah," in *Pseudepigraphic Perspectives: The Apocrypha and Pseudepigrapha in Light of the Dead Sea Scrolls* (ed. E. G. Chazon and M. E. Stone; STDJ 31; Leiden: Brill, 1999), 171–81. Werman writes that *Jubilees* "knows of a Book of Noah only by hearsay, from three secondary sources that contradict one another as to the nature of this putative work" (181).

112. Stone, "The Book(s) Attributed to Noah," 17.

113. Najman, "Interpretation as Primordial Writing," 383–84.

114. Stone, "The Book(s) Attributed to Noah," highlights the likely connection with the tradition of Noachic priestly writing in the *Aramaic Levi Document* 10:10, which mentions the "book of Noah concerning the blood"; the reference to Enoch, he writes, "is either an expansion of the information in ALD or else Jubilees knew a tradition that the words of Enoch were transmitted through Noah" (10–11), as we read in the *Book of Parables* (*1 Enoch* 68:1).

115. On this prohibition and the subsequent elevation of Jacob to visionary status, see my article "How Not to Build a Temple: Jacob, David, and the Unbuilt Ideal in Ancient Judaism," *JSJ* 46 (2015): 512–46.

116. On this episode, see Najman, "Interpretation as Primordial Writing," 386–87. The angel's seven tablets seem to be a different form of celestial writing from the heavenly tablets mentioned elsewhere in *Jubilees*. This, and the fact that *Jubilees* describes *two* dream visions in

one night, may suggest that the reference to Jacob's angelic tablets is a later addition by a different writer; on this source-critical issue see Kugel, "*Jubilees*," in Feldman, Kugel, and Schiffman, *Outside the Bible*, 406, and 462 n.210 and 213; Kugel writes that a later writer added this episode in order to lend an air of authority to some other text that claims to contain a revelation to Jacob—perhaps 4Q537.

117. See an exemplary discussion of these sources for Jacob's identity as a visionary in E. J. C. Tigchelaar, "The Imaginal Context and the Visionary of the Aramaic *New Jerusalem*," in *Flores Florentino: Dead Sea Scrolls and Other Early Jewish Studies in Honour of Florentino García Martínez* (ed. A. Hilhorst, É. Puech, and E. J. C. Tigchelaar; JSJSup 122; Leiden: Brill, 2007), 257–70.
118. J. Z. Smith, "Prayer of Joseph," in Charlesworth, *OTP*, 2:699–714.
119. On this theme see Tigchelaar, "The Imaginal Context"; and Mroczek, "How Not to Build a Temple."

Chapter 5   Outside the Number

1. Habte-Mariam Workineh, *yeEthiopia Orthodox Tewahedo Bete Kristian Emnetna Timihirt (The Ethiopian Orthodox Tewahedo Church Faith and Doctrine)* [Amharic] (Addis Ababa: Berhanena Selam Printing Press, 1969–70), 47; cited in Bruk A. A., "Mapping the Reception, Transmission, and Translation of Scriptural Writings in the EOTC: How and Why Some 'Pseudepigraphical' Works Receive 'Canonical' Status in the Ethiopian Bible," *Journal of Semitics* 22.2 (2013): 358–75, at 371–72.
2. R. W. Cowley, "The Biblical Canon of the Ethiopian Orthodox Church Today," *Ostkirchliche Studien* 23 (1974): 318–23.
3. This was the claim of Cowley (1974), and seems to still hold true as of my more recent sources, Bruk (2013) and Baynes (2012). See L. Baynes, "*Enoch* and *Jubilees* in the Canon of the Ethiopian Orthodox Church," in *A Teacher for All Generations: Essays in Honor of James C. VanderKam* (ed. E. F. Mason et al.; Leiden: Brill, 2012), 799–820; and Bruk, "Mapping the Reception."
4. English translation from Ge'ez is found in *Fetha Nagast: The Law of the Kings* (2nd ed; ed. P. L. Strauss; trans. P. Tzadua; Durham, N.C.: Carolina Academic Press, 2009; first published Addis Ababa: Faculty of Law, Haile Selassie I University, 1968). This code was compiled by an Egyptian Christian writer in Arabic around 1240, and translated into Ge'ez and supplemented in Ethiopia.
5. R. W. Cowley, "Old Testament Introduction in the Andemta Commentary Tradition," *Journal of Ethiopian Studies* 12.1 (1974): 38–139; and Baynes, "*Enoch* and *Jubilees* in the Canon," 805–6.
6. Bruk, "Mapping the Reception,," 359 n.3.
7. M.-S. Gebre-Ammanuel, "The Bible and Its Canon in the Ethiopian Orthodox Church," *Bible Translator* 44.1 (1993): 111–23; P. Brandt, "Geflecht aus 81 Büchern zur variantenreichen Gestalt des äthiopischen Bibelkanons," *Aethiopica* 3 (2000): 79–115.
8. Cowley, "The Biblical Canon."
9. Baynes, "*Enoch* and *Jubilees* in the Canon."
10. Bruk, "Mapping the Reception"; see also Bruk A. A. and P. B. Decock, "The Ethiopian Orthodox *Tewahido* Church (EOTC) Canon of Scripture: Neither Open nor Closed nor In-between," in *Surveying Student Research in the Humanities: Proceedings of the 2012 Postgraduate Conference of the University of KwaZulu Natal College of the Humanities, Howard College, Durban, 3–4 October 2012* (ed. J. Wassermann and S. Reddy; Durban, South Africa: Prontaprint, 2012), 178–88.
11. Baynes, "*Enoch* and *Jubilees* in the Canon," 801–2.
12. Baynes, "*Enoch* and *Jubilees* in the Canon," 802.
13. Baynes, "*Enoch* and *Jubilees* in the Canon," 802.
14. Bruk, "Mapping the Reception," 372.
15. Bruk, "Mapping the Reception," 373.

16. Bruk, "Mapping the Reception," 371.
17. T. H. Lim, *The Formation of the Jewish Canon* (New Haven, Conn.: Yale University Press, 2013).
18. See M. Poovey, *A History of the Modern Fact: Problems of Knowledge in the Sciences of Wealth and Society* (Chicago: University of Chicago Press, 1998), 54.
19. M. E. Stone, *Ancient Judaism: New Visions and Views* (Grand Rapids, Mich.: Eerdmans, 2011), x.
20. Trans. J. M. G. Barclay, *Flavius Josephus: Translation and Commentary*, vol. 10: *Against Apion* (ed. S. Mason; Leiden: Brill, 2007), 28–31.
21. On the complexities of identifying "Torah" with the "Pentateuch," see chapter 1.
22. S. Mason, "Josephus and His Twenty-Two Book Canon," in *The Canon Debate: On the Origins and Formations of the Bible* (ed. L. M. McDonald and J. A. Sanders; Peabody, Mass.: Hendrickson, 2002), 110–27, at 126.
23. S. Mason, "Josephus on Canon and Scriptures," in *The Hebrew Bible/Old Testament: The History of Its Interpretation*, vol. 1: *From the Beginnings to the Middle Ages (until 1300): Part 1: Antiquity* (ed. M. Sæbø; Göttingen: Vandenhoeck & Ruprecht, 1996), 217–235, at 234.
24. M. Haran, "Archives, Libraries, and the Order of the Biblical Books," *JANES* 22 (1993): 52–61, at 58.
25. Haran, "Archives, Libraries, and the Order of the Biblical Books," 57.
26. Mason, "Josephus and His Twenty-Two Book Canon," 126.
27. J. G. Campbell, "Josephus' Twenty-Two Book Canon and the Qumran Scrolls," in *The Scrolls and the Scriptures: Proceedings of the Seventh Meeting of the IOQS in Helsinki* (ed. G. J. Brooke et al.; Leiden: Brill, 2012), 19–45, at 37.
28. I am grateful to Azzan Yadin-Israel for helping me refine this argument.
29. See Epiphanius's *Weights and Measures*, chapter 22, and the parallels collected in R. H. Charles, *The Book of Jubilees or The Little Genesis* (London: Adam and Charles Black, 1902).
30. Armin Lange, "'Nobody Dared to Add to Them, to Take from Them, or to Make Changes' (Josephus, *Ag. Ap.* 1.42): The Textual Standardization of Jewish Scriptures in Light of the Dead Sea Scrolls," in *Flores Florentino: Dead Sea Scrolls and Other Early Jewish Studies in Honour of Florentino García Martínez* (ed. A. Hilhorst, É. Puech, and E. J. C. Tigchelaar; JSJSup 122; Leiden: Brill, 2007), 105–26, at 126.
31. G. Darshan, "Twenty-Four or Twenty-Two Books of the Bible and the Homeric Corpus" [Hebrew], *Tarbiz* 77 (2007): 1–22.
32. Mason, "Josephus and His Twenty-Two Book Canon."
33. Campbell, "Josephus' Twenty-Two Book Canon and the Qumran Scrolls," 39.
34. R. Chartier, *The Order of Books: Readers, Authors, and Libraries in Europe between the Fourteenth and Eighteenth Centuries* (trans. L. G. Cochrane; Stanford, Calif.: Stanford University Press, 1994), 68–69.
35. J. Z. Smith, "Sacred Persistence: Toward a Redescription of Canon," in *Imagining Religion: From Babylon to Jonestown* (Chicago: University of Chicago Press, 1982), 36–52.; C.-L. Seow, *Ecclesiastes: A New Translation with Introduction and Commentary* (Anchor Yale Bible Series; New Haven, Conn.: Yale University Press, 1997), 388 and 394; Seow writes that the original intent of "canon formulas" was not to delimit a corpus of texts as canonical but to emphasize the "sufficiency of the text." Also, see B. M. Levinson, "You Must Not Add Anything to What I Command You: Paradoxes of Canon and Authorship in Ancient Israel," *Numen* 50.1 (2003): 1–51, at 6–7. Levinson writes: "The essence of a canon is that it be stable, self-sufficient, and delimited" (6). See also "Rethinking the Relation between 'Canon' and 'Exegesis,'" in Levinson, *Legal Revision and Religious Renewal in Ancient Israel* (Cambridge: Cambridge University Press, 2008), 12–21. See my discussion of Levinson's challenge to Smith's model below.
36. This is the other way of counting the Old Testament canon according to patristic sources. See above on Josephus's 22.
37. Translations of *4 Ezra* are by M. E. Stone, found in *4 Ezra and 2 Baruch: Translations, Introductions, and Notes* (ed. M. Henze and M. E. Stone; Minneapolis: Fortress Press, 2013).
38. See H. Najman, *Losing the Temple and Recovering the Future: An Analysis of 4 Ezra* (Cambridge: Cambridge University Press, 2014), and "The Exemplary Protagonist: The

Case of 4Ezra," in *Old Testament Pseudepigrapha and the Scriptures* (ed. E. Tigchelaar; BETL; Leuven: Peeters, 2014), 261–87.

39. The reference to "characters they did not know" may refer to the tradition that it was Ezra who inaugurated the use of the Aramaic ("square") script for the Hebrew Scriptures in lieu of the ancient Hebrew alphabet; see: b. Sanh. 21b; see M. E. Stone, *Fourth Ezra: A Commentary on the Book of Fourth Ezra* (Minneapolis: Fortress Press, 1990), 411.

40. G. Darshan, "The Twenty-Four Books of the Hebrew Bible and Alexandrian Scribal Methods," in *Homer and the Bible in the Eyes of Ancient Interpreters: Between Literary and Religious Concerns* (ed. M. R. Niehoff; JSRC 16; Leiden: Brill, 2012), 221–44, at 227.

41. B. W. Longenecker, *2 Esdras* (Sheffield: Sheffield Academic Press, 1995), 91; see also Campbell, "Josephus' Twenty-Two Book Canon and the Qumran Scrolls."

42. Najman, *Losing the Temple*, 152.

43. On these traditions see L. S. Fried, *Ezra and the Law in History and Tradition* (Columbia: University of South Carolina Press, 2014).

44. Levinson, "You Must Not Add Anything to What I Command You," 6.

45. Part of this research is published in a different form, with more detail, in my essay, "The End of the Psalms in the Dead Sea Scrolls, Greek Codices, and Syriac Manuscripts," in *Snapshots of Evolving Traditions: Textual Fluidity, Manuscript Culture and New Philology* (ed. L. I. Lied and H. Lundhaug; Berlin: de Gruyter, forthcoming).

46. English translation in P. Schaff and H. Wace, eds., *Nicene and Post-Nicene Fathers*, Second Series (14 vols.; Buffalo, N.Y.: Christian Literature, 1900), 14:159–60. For the Latin and Greek see P.-P. Joannou, *Discipline générale antique* (3 vols. in 4; Grottaferrata [Rome]: Tipografia Italo-Orientale "S. Nilo," 1962–64), vol. 1, pt. 2, 154.

47. While the Leningradensis is the basis for the BHS, it is not completely followed here; the psalms are numbered up to 150, with the codex's original Hebrew enumeration in small print under the large Arabic numerals. See the BHS apparatus for other manuscripts that count 114 and 115 as one composition.

48. W. Yarchin, "Was 11Q5 a True Psalter?," paper presented at the Society of Biblical Literature Annual Meeting, November 23, 2013, now published as "Were the Psalms Collections at Qumran True Psalters?" *JBL* 134 (2015): 775–89; and N. L. deClaissé-Walford et al., *The Book of Psalms* (New International Commentary on the Old Testament; Grand Rapids, Mich.: Eerdmans, 2014), 3–4.

49. For the translations of Ps 151, see J. C. Reeves, "Exploring the Afterlife of Jewish Pseudepigrapha in Medieval Near Eastern Religious Traditions: Some Initial Soundings," *Journal for the Study of Judaism* 30 (1999): 148–77, at 166–70, 175–77.

50. The precise meaning of the superscription is enigmatic. What, in this context, is an "idiograph"? A handful of other ancient witnesses use the word to mean an autograph, a text written in somebody's own hand. For ἰδιόγραφος see Liddell and Scott, p. 818, e.g. Aulus Gellus, Attic Nights, 19.14.7, on a manuscript written in Virgil's own hand, and in POxy 250.13, a registration of property, in a reference to a written agreement. Liddell and Scott also list a vague definition of something "specially or separately written"—but provide only Ps 151 as an example.

51. NETS translation, 2007.

52. The εἰς Δαυιδ is analogous to the לדוד in Hebrew psalms superscriptions, which the Old Greek translates also with the dative, τῷ; later recensions change τῷ to τοῦ to clarify the authorial relationship. On this move see A. Pietersma, "Exegesis and Liturgy in the Superscriptions of the Greek Psalter," in *Proceedings of the Xth Congress of the International Organization for Septuagint and Cognate Studies, Oslo, July–August, 1998* (ed. B. A. Taylor; SBLSCS 51; Atlanta: Society of Biblical Literature, 2001), 99–138, at 103. The variant in Alexandrinus—τοῦ Δαυιδ for εἰς Δαυιδ—seems to reflect a similar impulse to move from an ambiguous relationship of association to one of authorship; see chapter 2 for full discussion.

53. This "supernumerary" role for Ps 151 and the established count of 150 represents a different situation from what we find in the Qumran Psalms Scroll. In the Qumran collection, it is the final composition; but unlike in the Septuagint, it bears no marker of otherness: its heading is only הללויה לדויד בן ישי, "Hallelujah of David, son of Jesse." James A. Sanders calls the Qumran composition "in no wise supernumerary"; see DJD 4, 58.

54. H. F. van Rooy, *Studies on the Syriac Apocryphal Psalms* (JSSSup 7; Oxford: Oxford University Press, 1999), 28.

55. Willem Baars uses this term in the introduction to "Apocryphal Psalms," in *Vetus Testamentum Syriace iuxta simplicem Syrorum Versionem*, part 4, fasc. 6 (Leiden: Brill, 1972).

56. Translations of the Syriac adapted from van Rooy, *Studies on the Syriac Apocryphal Psalms*.

57. John of Damascus, writing in the eighth century on the canon of the Old Testament, had a similar sense of the relationship between canonicity and serialization. Of two texts among the Apocrypha, the Wisdom of Solomon and Ben Sira, he wrote that they are "virtuous (ἐνάρετοι) and noble (καλαί), but they are not counted, nor were they placed in the ark" (*De Fide Orthodoxa*, iv.17).

58. For this text see M. Beit-Arié, "Perek Shirah: Introduction and Critical Edition" (2 vols.; Ph.D. diss., Hebrew University of Jerusalem, 1966). Manuscript witnesses to the text date as early as the tenth century, but Beit-Arié argues for a much earlier origin. J. M. Baumgarten argues that the author of this text knew Ps 151, which, as we have seen, was not known to scholars in Hebrew until the discovery of the Dead Sea Scrolls; see "Perek Shira, an Early Response to Psalm 151," *RevQ* 9 (1978): 575–78.

59. Smith, "Sacred Persistence," 48.

60. Smith, "Sacred Persistence," 52.

61. Smith, "Sacred Persistence," 48.

62. Smith, "Sacred Persistence," 50.

63. Smith, "Sacred Persistence," 43.

64. Levinson, "You Must Not Add Anything to What I Command You," and *Legal Revision*.

65. Levinson, "You Must Not Add Anything to What I Command You," 47, and *Legal Revision*.

66. S. Handelman, "Everything Is in It: Rabbinic Interpretation and Modern Literary Theory," *Judaism: A Quarterly Journal of Jewish Life and Thought* 35 (1986): 429–40, at 435; on the significance of the sealed canon for hermeneutics see M. Halbertal, *People of the Book: Canon, Meaning, Authority* (Cambridge, Mass.: Harvard University Press, 1997).

67. See esp. R. S. Wollenberg, "The People of the Book without the Book: Jewish Ambivalence toward Biblical Text after the Rise of Christianity" (PhD diss., University of Chicago, 2015); A. Yadin-Israel, *Scripture as Logos: Rabbi Ishmael and the Origins of Midrash* (Philadelphia: University of Pennsylvania Press, 2004), and *Scripture and Tradition: Rabbi Akiva and the Triumph of Midrash* (Philadelphia: University of Pennsylvania Press, 2014); B. D. Sommer, "Introduction: Scriptures in Jewish Tradition and Tradition in Jewish Scriptures," in *Jewish Concepts of Scripture: A Comparative Introduction* (ed. B. D. Sommer; New York: New York University Press, 2012), 1-14; and the essays by S. D. Fraade and A. Yadin-Israel in the same volume.

68. Note that the MT has "a burning fire shut up (עָצֻר) in my bones," but both the LXX and the Syriac Peshitta, which is cited in Timothy's letter, reflect a different reading, with two words for burning.

Conclusion

1. See D. Boyarin, *Border Lines: The Partition of Judaeo-Christianity* (Philadelphia: University of Pennsylvania Press, 2004), esp. 112–27, and *The Jewish Gospels: The Story of the Jewish Christ* (New York: New Press, 2012).

2. S. Magid, *Hasidism Incarnate: Hasidism, Christianity, and the Construction of Modern Judaism* (Stanford, Calif.: Stanford University Press, 2015). I thank my friend and colleague Shaul Magid, whose colloquium on this book sparked a conversation that inspired the ending of mine.

3. R. S. Wollenberg, "The People of the Book without the Book: Jewish Ambivalence toward Biblical Text after the Rise of Christianity" (PhD diss., University of Chicago, 2015); A. Yadin-Israel, *Scripture as Logos: Rabbi Ishmael and the Origins of Midrash* (Philadelphia:

University of Pennsylvania Press, 2004), and *Scripture and Tradition: Rabbi Akiva and the Triumph of Midrash* (Philadelphia: University of Pennsylvania Press, 2015).

4. R. A. Kraft, "Scripture and Canon in the Commonly Called Apocrypha and Pseudepigrapha and in the Writings of Josephus," in *The Hebrew Bible/Old Testament: The History of Its Interpretation*, vol. 1: *From the Beginnings to the Middle Ages (until 1300): Part 1: Antiquity* (ed. M. Saebø; Göttingen: Vandenhoeck & Ruprecht, 1996), 199–216, at 207.

5. See J. Priest, "Testament of Moses," in *The Old Testament Pseudepigrapha*, vol. 1: *Apocalyptic Literature and Testaments* (ed. J. A. Charlesworth; Garden City, N.Y.: Doubleday, 1983) 919–34.

BIBLIOGRAPHY

Abrams, Daniel. *Kabbalistic Manuscripts and Textual Theory: Methodologies of Textual Scholarship and Editorial Practice in the Study of Jewish Mysticism*. 2nd rev. ed. Jerusalem: Magnes Press, 2013.

Allegro, John M. *Qumrân Cave 4*. Vol. 1, *4Q158–4Q186*. DJD 5. Oxford: Clarendon Press, 1968.

Amihay, Aryeh, and Daniel Machiela. "Traditions of the Birth of Noah." In *Noah and His Book(s)*, ed. Michael E. Stone, Aryeh Amihay, and Vered Hillel, 53–69. Atlanta: Society of Biblical Literature, 2010.

Arendt, Hannah. *The Human Condition*. Chicago: University of Chicago Press, 1958.

Attridge, Harold, et al., eds. *Qumran Cave 4.VIII: Parabiblical Texts, Part 1*. DJD 13. Oxford: Clarendon Press, 1994.

Baars, Willem. "Apocryphal Psalms." In *Vetus Testamentum Syriace iuxta simplicem Syrorum Versionem*, part 4, fasc. 6. Leiden: Brill, 1972.

Bachmann, Veronika. "The Book of the Watchers (*1 Enoch* 1-36): An Anti-Mosaic, Non-Mosaic, or Even Pro-Mosaic Writing?" *Journal of Hebrew Scriptures* 11 (2011).

Bachmann, Veronika, and Isaac W. Oliver. "The Book of Jubilees: A Bibliography, 1850–Present." In *Enoch and the Mosaic Torah: The Evidence of Jubilees*, ed. Gabriele Boccaccini and Giovanni Ibba, 441–68. Grand Rapids, Mich.: Eerdmans, 2009.

Baden, Joel. *The Composition of the Pentateuch: Renewing the Documentary Hypothesis*. New Haven, Conn.: Yale University Press, 2012.

Baillet, Maurice. *Qumrân Grotte 4 III (4Q482–4Q520)*. DJD 7. Oxford: Clarendon Press, 1982.

Baillet, Maurice, Józef T. Milik, and Roland de Vaux. *Les "Petites Grottes."* DJD 3. Oxford: Clarendon Press, 1962.

Barclay, John M. G., trans. *Flavius Josephus: Translation and Commentary*. Vol. 10: *Against Apion*, ed. S. Mason. Leiden: Brill, 2007.

Bar-Ilan, Meir. "Non-Canonical Psalms from the Genizah." In *The Dead Sea Scrolls in Context: Integrating the Dead Sea Scrolls in the Study of Ancient Texts, Languages, and Cultures*. 2 vols. Ed. Armin Lange, Emanuel Tov, Matthias Weigold, and Bennie H. Reynolds III, 2: 693–718. VTSup 140. Leiden: Brill, 2011.

Barthélemy, Dominique, and Józef T. Milik, eds. *Qumran Cave 1*. DJD 1. Oxford: Clarendon Press, 1955.

Barthes, Roland. "The Death of the Author." In *Image-Music-Text*. Trans. Stephen Heath, 142–48. New York: Hill and Wang, 1977.

Barton, John. *Oracles of God: Perceptions of Ancient Prophecy in Israel after the Exile*. New York: Oxford University Press, 1986.

Bauckham, Richard, James Davila, and Alexander Panayotov, eds. *Old Testament Pseudepigrapha: More Noncanonical Scriptures*. Vol. 1. Grand Rapids, Mich.: Eerdmans, 2013.

Baumgarten, Joseph M. "Perek Shira, an Early Response to Psalm 151," *Revue de Qumran* 9 (1978): 575–78.

Baynes, Leslie. "*Enoch* and *Jubilees* in the Canon of the Ethiopian Orthodox Church." In *A Teacher for All Generations: Essays in Honor of James C. VanderKam*, 2 vols. Ed. Eric F. Mason et al., 2: 799–820. Leiden: Brill, 2012.

Baynes, Leslie. *The Heavenly Book Motif in Judeo-Christian Apocalypses, 200 B.C.E.–200 C.E.* JSJSup 152. Leiden: Brill, 2012.

Beentjes, Pancratius C. *The Book of Ben Sira in Hebrew.* Leiden: Brill, 1997.

Beentjes, Pancratius C. "Hermeneutics in the Book of Ben Sira: Some Observations on the Hebrew Ms. C," *Estudios Biblicos* 45 (1988): 45–60.

Begg, Christopher. *Flavius Josephus: Translation and Commentary.* Vol. 4: *Judean Antiquities Books 5–7.* Ed. Steve Mason. Leiden: Brill, 2005.

Beit-Arié, Malachi. *Hebrew Manuscripts of East and West: Towards a Comparative Codicology* (Panizzi Lectures). London: British Library, 1993.

Beit-Arié, Malachi. "Perek Shirah: Introduction and Critical Edition." 2 vols. Ph.D. thesis, Hebrew University of Jerusalem, 1966.

Bernhardt, K.-H. *Das Problem der altorientalischen Konigsideologie im Alten Testament: Unter besonderer Berucksichtigung der Geschichte der Psalmenexegese dargestellt und kritisch gewurdigt.* VTS 8. Leiden: Brill, 1961.

Bernstein, Moshe J. "The Employment and Interpretation of Scripture in 4QMMT: Preliminary Observations." In *Reading 4QMMT: New Perspectives on Qumran Law and History*, ed. John Kampen and Moshe J. Bernstein, 29–51. SBLSymS 2. Atlanta: Scholars Press, 1996.

Bernstein, Moshe J. "The Genesis Apocryphon: Compositional and Interpretive Perspectives." In *A Companion to Biblical Interpretation in Early Judaism*, ed. Matthias Henze, 157–79. Grand Rapids, Mich.: Eerdmans, 2012.

Bernstein, Moshe J. "Is the Genesis Apocryphon a Unity? What Sort of Unity Were You Looking For?" *Aramaic Studies* 8 (2010): 107–34.

Bernstein, Moshe J. "Pseudepigraphy in the Qumran Scrolls: Categories and Functions." In *Pseudepigraphic Perspectives: The Apocrypha and Pseudepigrapha in Light of the Dead Sea Scrolls*, ed. Esther G. Chazon and Michael E. Stone, 1–26. Leiden: Brill, 1999.

Bernstein, Moshe J. *Reading and Re-reading Scripture at Qumran.* 2 vols. STDJ 107. Leiden: Brill, 2013.

Bernstein, Moshe J. "'Rewritten Bible': A Generic Category Which Has Outlived Its Usefulness?" *Textus* 22 (2005): 169–96.

Berthelot, Katell. "4QMMT et la question du canon de la Bible hébraïque." In *From 4QMMT to Resurrection: Mélanges qumraniens en hommage à Émile Puech*, ed. Florentino García Martínez et al., 1–14. STDJ 61. Leiden: Brill, 2006.

Bickerman, Elias J. *The Jews in the Greek Age.* Cambridge, Mass.: Harvard University Press, 1988.

Bidawid, Raphael J. *Les lettres du patriarche nestorien Timothée I.* Vatican City: Biblioteca Apostolica Vaticana, 1956.

Blair, Ann M. *Too Much to Know: Managing Scholarly Information before the Modern Age.* New Haven, Conn.: Yale University Press, 2010.

Blenkinsopp, J. *Wisdom and Law in the Old Testament and in Early Judaism.* Oxford: Oxford University Press, 1984.

Bloom, Harold. *The Anxiety of Influence: A Theory of Poetry.* 2nd ed. Oxford: Oxford University Press, 1997.

Blum, Erhard. *Studien zur Komposition des Pentateuch.* BZAW 189. Berlin: de Gruyter, 1990.

Boccaccini, Gabriele. *Beyond the Essene Hypothesis: The Parting of the Ways between Qumran and Enochic Judaism.* Grand Rapids, Mich.: Eerdmans, 1998.

Boccaccini, Gabriele. "Is Biblical Literature Still a Useful Term in Scholarship?" In *What Is Bible?*, ed. Karin Finsterbusch and Armin Lange, 41–51. Leuven: Peeters, 2012.

Boccaccini, Gabriele, and John J. Collins, eds. *The Early Enoch Literature.* JSJSup 121. Leiden: Brill, 2007.

Bohak, Gideon. *Ancient Jewish Magic: A History.* Cambridge: Cambridge University Press, 2008.

Bohak, Gideon. "Exorcistic Psalms of David and Solomon." In *Old Testament Pseudepigrapha: More Noncanonical Scriptures,* ed. Richard Bauckham, James Davila, and Alexander Panayotov, 1: 287–97. Grand Rapids, Mich.: Eerdmans, 2013.

Bolin, Thomas. "1–2 Samuel and Jewish Paideia in the Persian and Hellenistic Periods." In *Deuteronomy-Kings as Emerging Authoritative Books: A Conversation,* ed. Diana Edelman, 133–58. Atlanta: Society of Biblical Literature, 2014.

Bolin, Thomas. *Ecclesiastes and the Riddle of Authorship.* Forthcoming.

Borchardt, Francis. "The Prologue of Sirach (Ben Sira) and the Question of Canon." In *Sacra Scriptura: How "Non-Canonical" Texts Functioned in Early Judaism and Early Christianity,* ed. James H. Charlesworth and Lee Martin McDonald with Blake A. Jurgens, 64–71. T&T Clark Jewish and Christian Text Series. London: Bloomsbury T&T Clark, 2014.

Borges, Jorge Luis. "The Library of Babel." In *Labyrinths: Selected Stories and Other Writings,* ed. Donald A. Yates and James E. Irby, 51–58. New York: New Directions, 1964.

Boustan, Ra'anan. "The Study of Heikhalot Literature: Between Mystical Experience and Textual Artifact," *Currents in Biblical Research* 6 (2007): 130–60.

Bowers, Fredson. "Established Texts and Definitive Editions," *Philological Quarterly* 41 (1962): 1–117.

Bowers, Fredson. "Multiple Authority: New Problems and Concepts of Copy-Text," *Library,* 5th ser. 27 (1975): 81–115.

Bowers, Fredson. "Notes on Theory and Practice in Editing Texts." In *The Book Encompassed,* ed. P. Davison, 244–57. Cambridge: Cambridge University Press, 1992.

Bowley, James E. "Missing Books and Their Ancient Libraries." Paper presented at the Society of Biblical Literature Annual Meeting, November 24, 2014.

Bowley, James E., and John C. Reeves. "Rethinking the Concept of 'Bible': Some Theses and Proposals," *Henoch* 25 (2003): 3–18.

Boyarin, Daniel. *Border Lines: The Partition of Judaeo-Christianity.* Philadelphia: University of Pennsylvania Press, 2004.

Boyarin, Daniel. *The Jewish Gospels: The Story of the Jewish Christ.* New York: New Press, 2012.

Brakke, David. "Scriptural Practices in Early Christianity: Towards a New History of the New Testament Canon." In *Invention, Rewriting, Usurpation: Discursive Fights over Religious Traditions in Antiquity,* ed. Jorg Ulrich, Anders-Christian Jacobsen, and David Brakke, 263–80. Early Christianity in the Context of Late Antiquity 11. New York: Peter Lang, 2012.

Brandt, Peter. "Geflecht aus 81 Büchern zur variantenreichen Gestalt des äthiopischen Bibelkanons," *Aethiopica* 3 (2000): 79–115.

Braude, William G. *The Midrash on Psalms.* New Haven, Conn.: Yale University Press, 1959.

Braun, Oskar. "Ein Brief des Katholikos Timotheos I über biblische Studien des 9 Jahrhunderts," *Oriens Christianus* 1 (1901): 299–313.

Breed, Brennan W. *Nomadic Text: A Theory of Biblical Reception History.* Indiana Studies in Biblical Literature. Bloomington: Indiana University Press, 2014.

Bremmer, Jan N., and István Czachesz, *The Visio Pauli and the Gnostic Apocalypse of Paul.* Studies on Early Christian Apocrypha 9. Leuven: Peeters, 2007.

Brooke, George J. "Between Authority and Canon: The Significance of Reworking the Bible for Understanding the Canonical Process." In *Reworking the Bible: Apocryphal and Related Texts at Qumran,* ed. Esther G. Chazon, Devorah Dimant, and Ruth A. Clements, 85–104. STDJ 58. Leiden: Brill, 2005.

Brooke, George J. "The Book of Jeremiah and Its Reception in the Qumran Scrolls." In *The Book of Jeremiah and Its Reception,* ed. A. H. W. Curtis and Thomas Römer, 183–205. BETL 128. Leuven: Peeters, 1997.

Brooke, George J. "The Explicit Presentation of Scripture in 4QMMT." In *Legal Texts and Legal Issues: Proceedings of the Second Meeting of the International Organization for Qumran Studies, Published in Honour of Joseph M. Baumgarten,* ed. Moshe J. Bernstein et al., 85–87. STDJ 23. Leiden: Brill, 1997.

Brooke, George J. "The Psalms in Early Jewish Literature in the Light of the Dead Sea Scrolls." In *The Psalms in the New Testament*, ed. Steve Moyise and Maarten J. J. Menken, 5–24. London: T&T Clark, 2004.

Brooke, George J. *Reading the Dead Sea Scrolls: Essays in Method.* Early Judaism and Its Literature 39. Atlanta: Society of Biblical Literature, 2013.

Brownlee, William H. "The Significance of David's Compositions," *Revue de Qumran* 5 (1964–66): 569–74.

Bruce, Frederick F. "The Earliest Old Testament Interpretation." In *The Witness of Tradition: Papers Read at the Joint British-Dutch Old Testament Conference Held at Woudschoten, 1970*, ed. Martinus A. Beek et al., 40–52. OTS 17. Leiden: Brill, 1972.

Bruk Ayele Asale. "Mapping the Reception, Transmission, and Translation of Scriptural Writings in the EOTC: How and Why Some 'Pseudepigraphical' Works Receive 'Canonical' Status in the Ethiopian Bible," *Journal of Semitics* 22 (2013): 358–75.

Bruk Ayele Asale, and P. B. Decock. "The Ethiopian Orthodox *Tewahido* Church (EOTC) Canon of Scripture: Neither Open nor Closed nor In-Between." In *Surveying Student Sesearch in the Humanities: Proceedings of the 2012 Postgraduate Conference of the University of KwaZulu Natal College of the Humanities, Howard College, Durban, 3–4 October 2012*, ed. J. Wassermann and S. Reddy, 178–88. Durban, South Africa: Prontaprint, 2012.

Buber, Salomon, ed. *Midrash Tehillim.* Vilna, 1891.

Camp, Claudia V. *Ben Sira and the Men Who Handle Books: Gender and the Rise of Canon-Consciousness.* Sheffield: Sheffield Phoenix, 2013.

Campbell, Jonathan G. "Josephus' Twenty-Two Book Canon and the Qumran Scrolls." In *The Scrolls and the Scriptures: Proceedings of the Seventh Meeting of the IOQS in Helsinki*, ed. George J. Brooke et al., 19–45. Leiden: Brill, 2012.

Campbell, Jonathan G. "'Rewritten Bible' and 'Parabiblical Texts': A Terminological and Ideological Critique." In *New Directions in Qumran Studies: Proceedings of the Bristol Colloquium on the Dead Sea Scrolls, 8–10 September, 2003*, ed. Jonathan G. Campbell, William J. Lyons, and Lloyd K. Pietersen, 43–68. LSTS 52. London: T & T Clark, 2005.

Caquot, André. "'Loi' et 'témoignage' dans le Livre des Jubilés." In *Mélanges linguistiques offerts à Maxime Rodinson par ses élèves, ses collègues et ses amis*, ed. C. Robin, 137–45. Comptes rendus du groupe linguistique d'études chamito-sémitiques Supplement 12. Paris: Geuthner, 1985.

Carr, David M. *Writing on the Tablet of the Heart: Origins of Scripture and Literature.* New York: Oxford University Press, 2008.

Charles, R. H. *The Apocrypha and Pseudepigrapha of the Old Testament in English.* 2 vols. Oxford: Clarendon Press, 1913.

Charles, R. H. *The Book of Jubilees or The Little Genesis.* London: Adam and Charles Black, 1902.

Charlesworth, James A. *Damascus Document, War Scroll and Related Documents.* Tübingen: Mohr Siebeck, 1995.

Charlesworth, James A. *The Dead Sea Scrolls: Hebrew, Aramaic, and Greek Texts with English Translations: Pseudepigraphic and Non-Masoretic Psalms and Prayers.* Tübingen: Mohr Siebeck, 1997.

Charlesworth, James A. "The Interpretation of the Tanak in the Jewish Apocrypha and Pseudepigrapha." In *A History of Biblical Interpretation*, vol. 1: *The Ancient Period*, ed. Alan J. Hauser and Duane F. Watson, 253–82. Grand Rapids, Mich.: Eerdmans, 2003.

Charlesworth, James A. *The Old Testament Pseudepigrapha*, vol. 1: *Apocalyptic Literature and Testaments*; vol. 2: *Expansions of the "Old Testament" and Legends, Wisdom and Philosophical Literature, Prayers, Psalms, and Odes, Fragments of Lost Judeo-Hellenistic Works.* Garden City, N.Y.: Doubleday, 1983–85.

Chartier, Roger. "Languages, Books, and Reading from the Printed Word to the Digital Text," trans. T. L. Fagan, *Critical Inquiry* 31 (2004): 133–51.

Chartier, Roger. *The Order of Books: Readers, Authors, and Libraries in Europe between the Fourteenth and Eighteenth Centuries.* Trans. L. G. Cochrane. Stanford, Calif.: Stanford University Press, 1994.

Chartier, Roger. "Representations of the Written Word." In *Forms and Meanings: Texts, Performances and Audiences from Codex to Computer*, 6–24. Philadelphia: University of Pennsylvania Press, 1995.

Chazon, Esther, and Michael Stone, eds. *Pseudepigraphic Perspectives: The Apocrypha and Pseudepigrapha in Light of the Dead Sea Scrolls*. Leiden: Brill, 1999.

Childs, Brevard S. "Psalm Titles and Midrashic Exegesis," *Journal of Semitic Studies* 16 (1971): 137–50.

Chyutin, Michael. "The Redaction of the Qumranic and the Traditional Book of Psalms as a Calendar," *Revue de Qumran* 16 (1994): 367–95.

Cohen, Shaye J. D. *From the Maccabees to the Mishnah*. 2nd ed. Louisville: Westminster John Knox, 2006.

Collins, John J. "The Genre of the Book of *Jubilees*." In *A Teacher for All Generations: Essays in Honor of James C. VanderKam*, 2 vols. Eds Eric F. Mason et al., 2: 737–55. Leiden: Brill, 2012.

Collins, John J. *Jewish Wisdom in the Hellenistic Age*. Louisville: Westminster John Knox, 1997.

Cooper, Alan M. "The Life and Times of King David according to the Book of Psalms." In *The Poet and the Historian: Essays in Literary and Historical Biblical Criticism*, ed. Richard E. Friedman, 117–31. HSS 26. Chico, Calif.: Scholars Press, 1983.

Corley, Jeremy. "Searching for Structure and Redaction in Ben Sira." In *The Wisdom of Ben Sira: Studies on Tradition, Redaction, and Theology*, ed. Angelo Passaro and Giuseppe Bellia, 21–47. Berlin: de Gruyter, 2008.

Cowley, R. W. "The Biblical Canon of the Ethiopian Orthodox Church Today," *Ostkirchliche Studien* 23 (1974): 318–23.

Cowley, R. W. "Old Testament Introduction in the Andemta Commentary Tradition," *Journal of Ethiopian Studies* 12.1 (1974): 38–139.

Crawford, Sidnie White. "Biblical Text: Yes or No?" In *What Is Bible?*, ed. Karin Finsterbusch and Armin Lange, 113–19. Leuven: Peeters, 2012.

Crawford, Sidnie White. "Has *Esther* Been Found at Qumran? 4QProto-Esther and the *Esther* Corpus," *Revue de Qumran* 17 (1996): 307–25.

Crawford, Sidnie White. "Reworked Pentateuch." In *Encyclopedia of the Dead Sea Scrolls*, ed. Lawrence H. Schiffman and James C. VanderKam, 2: 775–77. Oxford: Oxford University Press, 2000.

Crawford, Sidnie White. *Rewriting Scripture in Second Temple Times*. Grand Rapids, Mich.: Eerdmans, 2008.

Crawford, Sidnie White. " 'Rewritten Bible' in North American Scholarship." In *The Dead Sea Scrolls in Scholarly Perspective: A History of Research*, ed. Devorah Dimant, 75–78. Leiden: Brill, 2012.

Crenshaw, James L. *Education in Ancient Israel: Across the Deadening Silence*. New York: Doubleday, 1998.

Dahmen, Ulrich. *Psalmen- und Psalter-Rezeption im Frühjudentum: Rekonstruktion, Textbestand, Struktur und Pragmatik der Psalmenrolle 11QPs^a aus Qumran*. STDJ 49. Leiden: Brill, 2003.

Darshan, Guy. "The Twenty-Four Books of the Hebrew Bible and Alexandrian Scribal Methods." In *Homer and the Bible in the Eyes of Ancient Interpreters: Between Literary and Religious Concerns*, ed. Maren R. Niehoff, 221–44. JSRC 16; Leiden: Brill, 2012.

Darshan, Guy. "Twenty-Four or Twenty-Two Books of the Bible and the Homeric Corpus" [Hebrew], *Tarbiz* 77 (2007): 1–22.

Davies, Philip. "The Authority of Deuteronomy." In *Deuteronomy-Kings as Emerging Authoritative Books: A Conversation*, ed. Diana Edelman, 27–47. Atlanta: Society of Biblical Literature, 2014.

Davis, Kipp. *The Cave 4 Apocryphon of Jeremiah and the Qumran Jeremianic Traditions: Prophetic Persona and the Construction of Community Identity*. STDJ 111. Leiden: Brill, 2014.

Davis, Kipp. " 'Self-Glorification Hymn(s)' and the Usage of 'Scripture' in the Context of War: A Study of ספר התהלים in 4QM^a (4Q491) Frg. 17." Forthcoming in *Text and Interpretation of the Hebrew Bible* (provisional title), ed. Daniel K. Falk et al. Atlanta: SBL Press.

Debel, Hans. "Anchoring Revelations in the Authority of Sinai: A Comparison of the Rewritings of 'Scripture' in *Jubilees* and in the P Stratum of Exodus," *Journal for the Study of Judaism* 45 (2014): 1–22.

DeClaissé-Walford, Nancy L., et al. *The Book of Psalms.* New International Commentary on the Old Testament. Grand Rapids, Mich.: Eerdmans, 2014.

De Jonge, Marinus, ed. *Outside the Old Testament.* Cambridge: Cambridge University Press, 1985.

Delcor, Mathias. "Le texte hébreu du Cantique de Siracide LI,13 et ss. et les anciennes versions," *Textus* 6 (1968): 27–47.

De Troyer, Kristin. "Once More, the So-Called Esther Fragments of Cave 4," *Revue de Qumran* 19 (2000): 401–22.

DeVries, Simon J. "Moses and David as Cult Founders in Chronicles," *Journal of Biblical Literature* 107 (1988): 619–39.

Di Lella, Alexander A. *The Hebrew Text of Sirach: A Text-Critical and Historical Study.* The Hague: de Gruyter Mouton, 1966.

Dillman, A., and H. Rönsch. *Das Buch der Jubiläen oder die kleine Genesis.* Leipzig: Fues, 1874.

Dimant, Devorah. "Noah in Early Jewish Literature." In *Biblical Figures outside the Bible,* ed. Michael E. Stone and Theodore A. Bergren, 123–50. Harrisburg, Pa.: Trinity Press, 1998.

Dimant, Devorah."Two 'Scientific' Fictions: The So-called Book of Noah and the Alleged Quotation of Jubilees in CD 16:3-4." In *Studies in the Hebrew Bible, Qumran, and the Septuagint Presented to Eugene Ulrich,* ed. Peter W. Flint et al., 230–49. SVT 101. Leiden: Brill, 2006.

Drawnel, Henryk. "The Literary Form and Didactic Content of the Admonitions (Testament) of Qahat." In *From 4QMMT to Resurrection: Mélanges qumraniens en hommage à Émile Puech,* ed. Florentino García Martínez, Annette Steudel, and Eibert J. C. Tigchelaar, 55–73. STDJ 61. Leiden: Brill, 2006.

Eerdmans, B. D. *The Hebrew Book of Psalms.* Leiden: Brill, 1947.

Eisenman, Robert H., and Michael O. Wise, *The Dead Sea Scrolls Uncovered.* Shaftesbury: Element, 1992.

Ejrnæs, Bodil. "David and His Two Women: An Analysis of Two Poems in the Psalms Scroll from Qumran (11Q5)." In *Scripture in Transition: Essays on Septuagint, Hebrew Bible, and Dead Sea Scrolls in Honour of Raija Sollamo,* ed. Anssi Voitila and Jutta Jokiranta, 575–90. Leiden: Brill, 2008.

Elgvin, Torleif. *Gleanings from the Caves: Dead Sea Scrolls and Artifacts from the Schøyen Collection.* Library of Second Temple Studies 71. London: Bloomsbury T&T Clark, 2016.

Elliott, J. K. *The Apocryphal New Testament: A Collection of Apocryphal Christian Literature in an English Translation.* Oxford: Oxford University Press, 1993.

Ellis, Teresa A. "Negotiating the Boundaries of Tradition: The Rehabilitation of the Book of Ben Sira (Sirach) in B. Sanhedrin 100B." In *Sacra Scriptura: How "Non-Canonical" Texts Functioned in Early Judaism and Early Christianity,* ed. James H. Charlesworth and Lee Martin McDonald with Blake A. Jurgens, 46–63. T&T Clark Jewish and Christian Text Series; London: Bloomsbury T&T Clark, 2014.

Eshel, Esther. "The Genesis Apocryphon: A Chain of Traditions." In *The Dead Sea Scrolls and Contemporary Culture: Proceedings of the International Conference Held at the Israel Museum, Jerusalem,* ed. Adolfo D. Roitman, Lawrence H. Schiffman, and Shani Tzoref, 181–93. STDJ 93. Leiden: Brill, 2010.

Eshel, Esther. "The Genesis Apocryphon and Other Related Aramaic Texts from Qumran: The Birth of Noah." In *Aramaica Qumranica: Proceedings of the Conference on the Aramaic Texts from Qumran in Aix-en-Provence, 30 June-2 July 2008,* ed. Katell Berthelot and Daniel Stökl Ben Ezra, 277–94. STDJ 94. Leiden: Brill, 2010.

Eshel, Hanan. "4QMMT and the History of the Hasmonean Period." In *Reading 4QMMT: New Perspectives on Qumran Law and History,* ed. Moshe J. Bernstein and John Kampen, 53–65. SBLSymS 2. Atlanta: Scholars Press, 1996.

Fabricius, Johann A. *Codex Pseudepigraphus Veteris Testamenti.* Hamburg, 1713.

Falk, Daniel K. *The Parabiblical Texts: Strategies for Extending the Scriptures among the Dead Sea Scrolls.* Companion to the Qumran Scrolls 8. London: T&T Clark, 2007.

Feldman, Ariel. "1Q19 (The Book of Noah) Reconsidered," *Henoch* 31.2 (2009): 284–306.

Feldman, Louis H. *Josephus's Interpretation of the Bible.* Hellenistic Culture and Society 27. Berkeley: University of California Press, 1999.

Feldman, Louis H. *Studies in Josephus' Rewritten Bible.* JSJSupp 58. Leiden: Brill, 2005.

Feldman, Louis H., James L. Kugel, and Lawrence H. Schiffman, eds. *Outside the Bible: Ancient Jewish Writings Related to Scripture.* 3 vols. Lincoln: University of Nebraska Press, 2013.

Finkel, Joshua. "The Author of the Genesis Apocryphon Knew the Book of Esther." In *Essays on the Dead Sea Scrolls in Memory of E. L. Sukenik,* ed. Chaim Rabin and Yigael Yadin, 163–82. Jerusalem: Hekhal Ha-Sefer, 1961.

Finsterbusch, Karin, and Armin Lange, eds. *What Is Bible?* Leuven: Peeters, 2012.

Fishbane, Michael. *Biblical Interpretation in Ancient Israel.* Oxford: Clarendon Press, 1985.

Fishbane, Michael. "Use, Authority and Interpretation of Mikra at Qumran." In *Mikra: Text, Translation, Reading and Interpretation of the Hebrew Bible in Ancient Judaism and Early Christianity,* ed. Martin Jan Mulder and Harry Sysling, 339–77. Assen: Van Gorcum; Philadelphia: Fortress, 1988.

Fitzmyer, Joseph A. *The Genesis Apocryphon of Qumran Cave 1 (1Q20).* 3d ed. Rome: Pontifical Biblical Institute, 2004.

Fleischer, Ezra. "Medieval Hebrew Poems in Biblical Style," *Te'uda* 7 (1991): 200–248.

Flint, Peter W. *The Dead Sea Psalms Scrolls and the Book of Psalms.* STDJ 17. Leiden: Brill, 1997.

Flint, Peter W. "The Prophet David at Qumran." In *Biblical Interpretation at Qumran,* ed. Matthias Henze, 158–67. Grand Rapids, Mich.: Eerdmans, 2005.

Flint, Peter W. "Psalms, Book of: Biblical Texts." In *Encyclopedia of the Dead Sea Scrolls,* ed. Lawrence H. Schiffman and James C. VanderKam, 2: 702–7. Oxford: Oxford University Press, 2000.

Flint, Peter W. "Unrolling the Dead Sea Psalms Scrolls." In *The Oxford Handbook of the Psalms,* ed. William P. Brown, 229–50. New York: Oxford University Press, 2014.

Flint, Peter W. "Variant Readings of the Dead Sea Psalms Scrolls against the Massoretic Text and the Septuagint Psalter." In *Der Septuaginta-Psalter und seine Tochterübersetzungen,* ed. Anneli Aejmelaeus and Udo Quast, 337–65. Göttingen: Vandenhoeck & Ruprecht, 2000.

Flusser, David. *Judaism of the Second Temple Period,* vol. 1: *Qumran and Apocalypticism.* Trans. Azzan Yadin; Grand Rapids, Mich.: Eerdmans, 2007.

Flusser, David, and Shmuel Safrai. "A Fragment of the Songs of David and Qumran." In *Bible Studies: Y.M. Grintz in Memoriam,* ed. Benjamin Uffenheimer, 83–105. *Te'uda* 2. Tel Aviv: Hakibbutz Hameuchad, 1982.

Foucault, Michel. "What Is an Author?" In *Michel Foucault: Aesthetics, Method, and Epistemology,* ed. James Faubion, trans. Robert Hurley et al.; vol. 1 of *Essential Works of Foucault, 1954–84,* ed. Paul Rainbow, 205–22. New York: New Press, 1998.

Fraade, Steven D. "'Comparative Midrash' Revisited: The Case of the Dead Sea Scrolls and Rabbinic Midrash." In *Agendas for the Study of Midrash in the Twenty-First Century,* ed. M. L. Raphael, 4–17. Williamsburg, Va.: College of William and Mary Press, 1999.

Fraade, Steven D. "Looking for Legal Midrash at Qumran." In *Biblical Perspectives: Early Use and Interpretation of the Bible in Light of the Dead Sea Scrolls: Proceedings of the First International Symposium of the Orion Center for the Study of the Dead Sea Scrolls and Associated Literature, 12–14 May, 1996,* ed. Michael E. Stone and Esther G. Chazon, 59–79. STDJ 28. Leiden: Brill, 1998.

Fraade, Steven D. "Looking for Narrative Midrash at Qumran." In *Rabbinic Perspectives: Rabbinic Literature and the Dead Sea Scrolls: Proceedings of the Eighth International Symposium of the Orion Center for the Study of the Dead Sea Scrolls and Associated Literature, 7–9 January, 2003,* ed. Steven D. Fraade, Aharon Shemesh, and Ruth A. Clements, 43–66. STDJ 62. Leiden: Brill, 2006.

Fraade, Steven D. "Midrash and Ancient Jewish Biblical Interpretation." In *The Cambridge Companion to the Talmud and Rabbinic Literature,* ed. Charlotte E. Fonrobert and Martin S. Jaffee, 99–120. Cambridge: Cambridge University Press, 2007.

Fraade, Steven D. "Rewritten Bible and Rabbinic Midrash as Commentary." In *Current Trends in the Study of Midrash,* ed. Carol Bakhos, 59–78. Leiden: Brill, 2006.

Fried, Lisbeth S. *Ezra and the Law in History and Tradition.* Columbia: University of South Carolina Press, 2014.

García Martínez, Florentino. "Beyond the Sectarian Divide: The 'Voice of the Teacher' as an Authority-Conferring Strategy in Some Qumran Texts." In *The Dead Sea Scrolls: Transmission of Traditions and Production of Texts,* ed. Sarianna Metso, Hindy Najman, and Eileen Schuller, 227–44. Leiden: Brill, 2010.

García Martínez, Florentino. "The Heavenly Tablets in the Book of Jubilees." In *Studies in the Book of Jubilees,* ed. Matthias Albani et al., 243–60. Tübingen: Mohr Siebeck, 1997.

García Martínez, Florentino. "Les manuscrits du désert de Juda et le Deutéronome." In *Studies in Deuteronomy in Honour of C. J. Labuschagne on the Occasion of His 65th Birthday,* ed. Florentino García Martínez et al., 63–82. VTSup 53. Leiden: Brill, 1994.

García Martínez, Florentino. "Old Texts and Modern Mirages: The 'I' in Two Qumran Hymns." In *Qumranica Minora I: Qumran Origins and Apocalypticism,* ed. Florentino García Martínez, 105–28. STDJ 63. Leiden: Brill, 2007.

García Martínez, Florentino. "Parabiblical Literature from Qumran and the Canonical Process," *Revue de Qumran* 25 (2012): 525–56.

García Martínez, Florentino. "Rethinking the Bible: Sixty Years of Dead Sea Scrolls Research and Beyond." In *Authoritative Scriptures in Ancient Judaism,* ed. Mladen Popović, 19–36. Leiden: Brill, 2010.

García Martínez, Florentino, and Eibert J. C. Tigchelaar. *The Dead Sea Scrolls Study Edition.* 2 vols, Leiden: Brill, 1997–98.

Gebre-Ammanuel, Mikre-Selassie. "The Bible and Its Canon in the Ethiopian Orthodox Church," *Bible Translator* 44.1 (1993): 111–23.

Genette, Gérard. "Introduction to the Paratext," *New Literary History* 22 (1991): 261–72.

Genette, Gérard. *Seuils.* Paris: Éditions du Seuil, 1987. Trans. J. E. Lewin as *Paratexts. Thresholds of Interpretation.* Cambridge: Cambridge University Press, 1997.

Gilbert, Maurice. "The Book of Ben Sira: Implications for Jewish and Christian Traditions." In *Jewish Civilization in the Hellenistic-Roman Period,* ed. Shemaryahu Talmon, 81–91. Philadelphia: Trinity Press International, 1991.

Gilbert, Maurice. "L' écclesiastique: Quel texte? Quelle autorité?" *Revue Biblique* 94 (1987): 233–50.

Gilbert, Maurice. "Methodological and Hermeneutical Trends in Modern Exegesis on the Book of Ben Sira." In *The Wisdom of Ben Sira: Studies on Tradition, Redaction, and Theology,* ed. Angelo Passaro and Guiseppe Bellia, 1–20. Berlin: de Gruyter, 2008.

Gilbert, Maurice. "Venez à mon école (Si 51,13–30)." In *Auf der Spuren der Schriftgelehrten Weisen: Festschrift für Johannes Marbock,* ed. I. Fischer et al., 283–90. Berlin: de Gruyter, 2003.

Giles, Jason. "The Additions to Ben Sira and the Book's Multiform Textual Witness." In *The Texts and Versions of the Book of Ben Sira: Transmission and Interpretations,* ed. Jean-Sébastien Rey and Jan Joosten, 237–56. JSJSupp 150. Leiden: Brill, 2011.

Gillingham, Susan. *Psalms through the Centuries.* Vol. 1. Oxford: Blackwell, 2008.

Grafton, Anthony. *Codex in Crisis.* New York: Crumpled Press, 2008.

Green, Arthur. *Keter: The Crown of God in Early Jewish Mysticism.* Princeton, N.J.: Princeton University Press, 1997.

Greenfield, Jonas C. "Ben Sira 42: 9–10 and Its Talmudic Paraphrase." In *A Tribute to Geza Vermes: Essays on Jewish and Christian Literature and History,* ed. Philip R. Davis and Richard T. White, 167–73. Sheffield: JSOT Press, 1990.

Greenfield, Jonas C., Michael E. Stone, and Esther Eshel, eds. *The Aramaic Levi Document: Edition, Translation, Commentary.* SVTP 19. Leiden: Brill, 2004.

Greetham, David C. *Theories of the Text.* Oxford: Oxford University Press, 1999.

Greg, Walter W. "The Rationale of Copy-Text," *Studies in Bibliography* 3 (1950): 19–36.

Griffith, Mark. *The Authenticity of Prometheus Bound.* Cambridge: Cambridge University Press, 1977.

Gronewald, Michael. *Didymos der Blinde: Psalmenkommentar (Tura-Papyrus).* Book 2: *Kommentar zu Psalm 22–26,10.* Bonn: Rudolf Habelt, 1968.

Grossman, Maxine L. "Reading 4QMMT: Genre and History," *Revue de Qumran* 20 (2001): 3–22.

Grossman, Maxine L. "Roland Barthes and the Teacher of Righteousness: The Death of the Author of the Dead Sea Scrolls." In *The Oxford Handbook of the Dead Sea Scrolls*, ed. Timothy H. Lim and John J. Collins, 709–22. Oxford: Oxford University Press, 2010.

Hadas, Moses, trans. *Aristeas to Philocrates (Letter of Aristeas)*. New York: Harper & Brothers, 1951; Eugene, Ore.: Wipf & Stock, 2007.

Halbertal, Moshe. *People of the Book: Canon, Meaning, Authority*. Cambridge, Mass.: Harvard University Press, 1997.

Handelman, Susan. "Everything Is in It: Rabbinic Interpretation and Modern Literary Theory," *Judaism* 35 (1986): 429–40.

Hanneken, Todd R. "The Status and Interpretation of Jubilees in 4Q390." In *A Teacher for All Generations: Essays in Honor of James C. VanderKam*, 2 vols. Ed. Eric F. Mason et al., 1: 407–28. Leiden: Brill, 2011.

Haran, Menahem. "Archives, Libraries, and the Order of the Biblical Books," *Journal of the Ancient Near Eastern Society* 22 (1993): 52–61.

Hare, D. R. A. "The Lives of the Prophets." In *The Old Testament Pseudepigrapha*, vol. 2: *Expansions of the "Old Testament" and Legends, Wisdom and Philosophical Literature, Prayers, Psalms, and Odes, Fragments of Lost Judeo-Hellenistic Works*, ed. James A. Charlesworth, 379–400. Garden City, N.Y.: Doubleday, 1985.

Harkavy, A. E. "A Prayer by an Anonymous Writer in the Style of the Psalms," *HaGoren* 3 (1902): 82–85.

Harkins, Angela Kim. *Reading with an "I" to the Heavens: Looking at the Qumran Hodayot through the Lens of Visionary Traditions*. Boston: de Gruyter, 2012.

Harkins, Angela Kim. "Who Is the Teacher of the Teacher Hymns? Re-examining the Teacher Hymns Hypothesis Fifty Years Later." In *A Teacher for All Generations: Essays in Honor of James C. VanderKam*. 2 vols. Ed. Eric F. Mason et al., 2: 449–67. Leiden: Brill, 2012.

Harrington, Daniel J. "Palestinian Adaptations of Biblical Narratives and Prophecies." In *Early Judaism and Its Modern Interpreters*, ed. Robert A. Kraft and George W. E. Nickelsburg, 239–58. Atlanta: Scholars Press, 1986.

Harrington, Daniel J. "Pseudo-Philo." In Charlesworth, *The Old Testament Pseudepigrapha*, vol. 2: *Expansions of the "Old Testament" and Legends, Wisdom and Philosophical Literature, Prayers, Psalms, and Odes, Fragments of Lost Judeo-Hellenistic Works*, ed. James Charlesworth, 297–377. Garden City, N.Y.: Doubleday, 1985.

Hayles, N. Katherine. "Translating Media: Why We Should Rethink Textuality," *Yale Journal of Criticism* 16 (2003): 263–90.

Hempel, Charlotte. "The Place of the *Book of Jubilees* at Qumran and Beyond." In *The Dead Sea Scrolls in Their Historical Context*, ed. Timothy H. Lim, 187–96. Edinburgh: T&T Clark, 2000.

Hendel, Ronald S. "The Oxford Hebrew Bible: Prologue to a New Critical Edition," *Vetus Testamentum* 58 (2008): 324–51.

Hengel, Martin. *Judaism and Hellenism: Studies in Their Encounter in Palestine during the Early Hellenistic Period*. 2 vols. Trans. J. Bowden. Philadelphia: Fortress Press, 1974.

Hennecke, Edgar, et al., eds. *New Testament Apocrypha*. 2 vols. Philadelphia: Westminster Press, 1963.

Henze, Matthias, and Michael E. Stone, eds. *4 Ezra and 2 Baruch: Translations, Introductions, and Notes*. Minneapolis: Fortress Press, 2013.

Henze, Matthias. "The Use of Scripture in the Book of Daniel." In *A Companion to Biblical Interpretation in Early Judaism*, ed. Matthias Henze, 279–307. Grand Rapids, Mich.: Eerdmans, 2012.

Herder, Johann Gottfried. *The Spirit of Hebrew Poetry*, trans. J. Marsh. Burlington, Vt.: Edward Smith, 1833.

Hiebert, Robert J. V., Claude E. Cox, and Peter J. Gentry, eds. *The Old Greek Psalter: Studies in Honour of Albert Pietersma*. Sheffield: Sheffield Academic Press, 2001.

Himmelfarb, Martha. "The Book of Noah." In *Old Testament Pseudepigrapha: More Noncanonical Scriptures*, ed. Richard Bauckham, James Davila, and Alexander Panayotov, 1: 40–46. Grand Rapids, Mich.: Eerdmans, 2013.

Himmelfarb, Martha. *A Kingdom of Priests: Ancestry and Merit in Ancient Judaism.* Philadelphia: University of Pennsylvania Press, 2006.

Himmelfarb, Martha. "Some Echoes of Jubilees in Medieval Hebrew Literature." In *Tracing the Threads: Studies in the Vitality of Jewish Pseudepigrapha*, ed. John C. Reeves, 127–36. Atlanta: Scholars Press, 1994.

Himmelfarb, Martha. "Torah, Testimony, and Heavenly Tablets: The Claim to Authority in the Book of Jubilees." In *A Multiform Heritage: Studies on Early Judaism and Christianity in Honor of Robert A. Kraft*, ed. Benjamin G. Wright III, 19–29. Homage Series 24. Atlanta: Scholars Press, 1999.

Hix, Harvey L. *Morte d'Author: An Autopsy.* Philadelphia: Temple University Press, 1990.

Holladay, William. *The Psalms through Three Thousand Years: Prayerbook of a Cloud of Witnesses.* Minneapolis: Fortress, 1993.

Horsley, Richard A., and Patrick Tiller. "Ben Sira and the Sociology of the Second Temple." In *Second Temple Studies III: Studies in Politics, Class and Material Culture*, ed. Philip R. Davies and John M. Halligan, 74–107. JSOTSup 340. Sheffield: Sheffield Academic Press, 2002.

Howsam, Leslie. *Old Books and New Histories: An Orientation to Studies in Book and Print Culture.* Toronto: University of Toronto Press, 2006.

Jaffee, Martin S. *Torah in the Mouth.* New York: Oxford University Press, 2001.

Jain, Eva. *Psalmen oder Psalter? Materielle Rekonstruktion und inhaltliche Untersuchung der Psalmenhandschriften aus der Wüste Juda.* Leiden: Brill, 2014.

James, Montague R. *The Apocryphal New Testament.* Oxford: Oxford University Press, 1924.

Janowitz, Naomi. "The Rhetoric of Translation: Three Early Perspectives on Translating Torah," *Harvard Theological Review* 84 (1991): 129–40.

Japhet, Sara. *I and II Chronicles: A Commentary.* Louisville: Westminster John Knox, 1993.

Japhet, Sara. *The Ideology of the Book of Chronicles and Its Place in Biblical Thought.* Trans. A. Barber. BEATAJ 9. Frankfurt am Main: Lang, 1989.

Japhet, Sara. "Law and 'the Law' in Ezra-Nehemiah," *Proceedings of the World Congress of Jewish Studies* 9 (1985): 99–115.

Jellinek, Adolf. *Beit ha-Midrash.* 6 vols. 3rd ed. Jerusalem: Wahrmann, 1967.

Joannou, Périclès-Pierre. *Discipline générale antique.* 3 vols in 4. Grottaferrata (Rome): Tipografia Italo-Orientale "S. Nilo," 1962–64.

Jokiranta, Jutta. *Social Identity and Sectarianism in the Qumran Movement.* STDJ 105. Leiden: Brill, 2013.

Kearns, Conleth J. "Ecclesiasticus or the Wisdom of Jesus the Son of Sirach." In *A New Catholic Commentary on Holy Scripture*, ed. R. C. Fuller, 541–62. London: Nelson, 1969.

Kearns, Conleth J. *The Expanded Text of Ecclesiasticus: Its Teaching on the Future Life as a Clue to Its Origin.* Ed. Pancratius C. Beentjes. Berlin: de Gruyter, 2011.

Kelly, Joseph Ryan. "Intertextuality and Allusion in the Study of the Hebrew Bible." Ph.D. diss., Southern Baptist Theological Seminary, 2014.

Kitto, John, ed. *The Popular Cyclopaedia of Biblical Literature.* Boston: Gould and Lincoln, 1854.

Kleer, Martin. *Der liebliche Sänger der Psalmen Israels: Untersuchungen zu David als Dichter und Beter der Psalmen.* BBB 108. Bodenheim: Philo, 1996.

Knibb, Michael A. "Martyrdom and Ascension of Isaiah." In *The Old Testament Pseudepigrapha*, vol. 2: *Expansions of the "Old Testament" and Legends, Wisdom and Philosophical Literature, Prayers, Psalms, and Odes, Fragments of Lost Judeo-Hellenistic Works*, ed. James A. Charlesworth, 143–76. Garden City, N.Y.: Doubleday, 1985.

Knibb, Michael A. "The Use of Scripture in 1 Enoch 17-19." In *Alexandria, Rome: Studies in Ancient Cultural Interaction in Honour of A. Hilhorst*, ed. Florentino García Martínez and Gerard P. Luttikhuizen, 165–78. JSJS 82. Leiden: Brill, 2003.

Kraft, Robert A. "Combined Review." In Robert A. Kraft, *Exploring the Scripturesque: Jewish Texts and Their Christian Contexts*, 94–106. JSJSup 137. Leiden: Brill, 2009.

Kraft, Robert A. *Exploring the Scripturesque: Jewish Texts and Their Christian Contexts.* JSJSup 137. Leiden: Brill, 2009.

Kraft, Robert A. "Para-mania: Before, beside and beyond Biblical Studies," *Journal of Biblical Literature* 126 (2007): 5–27.

Kraft, Robert A. "Scripture and Canon in the Commonly Called Apocrypha and Pseudepigrapha and in the Writings of Josephus." In *Hebrew Bible/Old Testament: The History of Its Interpretation*, vol. 1: *From the Beginnings to the Middle Ages (until 1300): Part 1: Antiquity*, ed. Magne Sæbø, 199–216. Göttingen: Vandenhoeck & Ruprecht, 1996.

Kugel, James L. *The Bible as It Was*. Cambridge, Mass.: Harvard University Press, 1997.

Kugel, James L. "David the Prophet." In *Poetry and Prophecy: The Beginnings of a Literary Tradition*, ed. James L. Kugel, 45–55. Ithaca, N.Y.: Cornell University Press, 1990.

Kugel, James L. "Exegetical Notes on 4Q225 'Pseudo-Jubilees,'" *Dead Sea Discoveries* 13 (2006): 73–98.

Kugel, James L. *How to Read the Bible: A Guide to Scripture, Then and Now*. New York: Free Press, 2007.

Kugel, James L. *Traditions of the Bible: A Guide to the Bible as It Was at the Start of the Common Era*. Cambridge, Mass.: Harvard University Press, 1999.

Kugel, James L. *A Walk through Jubilees*. Leiden: Brill, 2012.

Kugel, James L. "Wisdom and the Anthological Temper." In *The Anthology in Jewish Literature*, ed. David Stern, 32–52. New York: Oxford University Press, 2004.

Kvanvig, Helge S. "Jubilees—Read as a Narrative." In *Enoch and Qumran Origins: New Light on a Forgotten Connection*, ed. G. Boccaccini, 75–83. Grand Rapids, Mich.: Eerdmans, 2005.

Labendz, Jenny R. "The Book of Ben Sira in Rabbinic Literature," *Association of Jewish Studies Review* 30 (2006): 347–92.

Lambert, David. "How the 'Torah of Moses' Became Revelation: An Early, Apocalyptic Theory of Pentateuchal Origins," *Journal for the Study of Judaism,* forthcoming.

Lambert, Wilfred G. "Ancestors, Authors, and Canonicity," *Journal of Cuneiform Studies* 11 (1957): 1–14.

Lambert, Wilfred G. "A Catalogue of Texts and Authors," *Journal of Cuneiform Studies* 16 (1962): 59–77.

Lange, Armin. "Collecting Psalms in Light of the Dead Sea Scrolls." In *A Teacher for All Generations: Essays in Honor of James C. VanderKam*, 2 vols. Ed. Eric F. Mason et al., 1:297–308. Leiden: Brill, 2011.

Lange, Armin. "'Nobody Dared to Add to Them, to Take from Them, or to Make Changes' (Josephus, *Ag. Ap.* 1.42): The Textual Standardization of Jewish Scriptures in Light of the Dead Sea Scrolls." In *Flores Florentino: Dead Sea Scrolls and Other Early Jewish Studies in Honour of Florentino García Martínez*, ed. Anthony Hilhorst, Émile Puech, and Eibert J. C. Tigchelaar, 105–26. JSJSup 122. Leiden: Brill, 2007.

Law, Timothy Michael. *When God Spoke Greek: The Septuagint and the Making of the Christian Bible*. New York: Oxford University Press, 2013.

LeFebvre, Michael. *Collections, Codes, and Torah: The Re-characterization of Israel's Written Law*. New York: T&T Clark, 2006.

LeFebvre, Michael, and Cornelis Houtman. "Ezra and the Law: Observations on the Supposed Relation between Ezra and the Pentateuch." In *Remembering All the Way: A Collection of Old Testament Studies Published on the Occasion of the 40th Anniversary of the Oudtestamentisch Werkgezelschap in Nederland*, ed. Bertil Albrektson, 91–115. Leiden: Brill, 1981.

Lehmann, Manfred R. "11QPsᵃ and Ben Sira," *Revue de Qumran* 11 (1983): 239–51.

Leiman, S. Z. *The Canonization of Hebrew Scripture: The Talmudic and Midrashic Evidence*. Hamden, Conn.: Archon Books, 1976.

Leonhardt, Jutta. *Jewish Worship in Philo of Alexandria*. TSAJ 84. Tübingen: Mohr Siebeck, 2001.

Leuenberger, Martin. "Aufbau und Pragmatik des 11QPsᵃ-Psalters: Der historisierte Dichter und Beter David als Vorbild und Identifikationsfigur: 11QPsᵃ als eschatologisches Lese- und Meditationsbuch des qumranischen," *Revue de Qumran* 22 (2005): 1–44.

Levene, Dan. *A Corpus of Magic Bowls: Incantation Texts in Jewish Aramaic from Late Antiquity*. London: Kegan Paul, 2002.

Levinson, Bernard M. *Deuteronomy and the Hermeneutics of Legal Innovation*. Oxford: Oxford University Press, 1997.

Levinson, Bernard M. *Legal Revision and Religious Renewal in Ancient Israel*. Cambridge: Cambridge University Press, 2008.

Levinson, Bernard M. "You Must Not Add Anything to What I Command You: Paradoxes of Canon and Authorship in Ancient Israel," *Numen* 50.1 (2003): 1–51.

Levison, John R. "Did the Spirit Withdraw from Israel? An Evaluation of the Earliest Jewish Data," *New Testament Studies* 43 (1997): 35–57.

Lied, Liv Ingeborg. "Manuscript Culture and the Myth of Golden Beginnings." In *Religion across Media: From Early Antiquity to Late Modernity*, ed. Knut Lundby, 54–70. New York: Peter Lang, 2013.

Lied, Liv Ingeborg. "*Nachleben* and Textual Identity: Variants and Variance in the Reception History of 2 Baruch." In *Fourth Ezra and Second Baruch: Reconstruction after the Fall*, ed. Matthias Henze and Gabriele Boccaccini, 403–28. JSJSup 164. Leiden: Brill, 2013.

Liesen, Jan. "Strategical Self-References in Ben Sira." In *Treasures of Wisdom: Studies in Ben Sira and the Book of Wisdom: Festschrift M. Gilbert*, ed. Núria Calduch-Benages and Jacques Vermeylen, 64–74. BEThL 143. Leuven: Peeters, 1999.

Lim, Timothy H. "The Alleged Reference to the Tripartite Division of the Hebrew Bible," *Revue de Qumran* 20 (2001): 23–37.

Lim, Timothy H. *The Formation of the Jewish Canon*. New Haven, Conn.: Yale University Press, 2013.

Lim, Timothy H., Hector L. MacQueen, and Calum M. Carmichael, eds. *On Scrolls, Artefacts and Intellectual Property*. JSPSup 38. Sheffield: Sheffield Academic Press, 2001.

Longenecker, Bruce W. *2 Esdras*. Sheffield: Sheffield Academic Press, 1995.

Lorein, G. W., and E. van Staalduine-Sulman. "A Song of David for Each Day: The Provenance of the Songs of David," *Revue de Qumran* 85 (2005): 33–59.

Lorein, G. W., and E. van Staalduine-Sulman. "Songs of David." In *Old Testament Pseudepigrapha: More Noncanonical Scriptures*, ed. Richard Bauckham, James R. Davila, and Alexander Panayatov, 257–71. Grand Rapids, Mich.: Eerdmans, 2013.

Machiela, Daniel A. *The Dead Sea Genesis Apocryphon: A New Text Edition and Translation with Introduction and Special Treatment of Columns 13–17*. STDJ 79. Leiden: Brill, 2009.

Magid, Shaul. *Hasidism Incarnate: Hasidism, Christianity, and the Construction of Modern Judaism*. Stanford, Calif.: Stanford University Press, 2015.

Mason, Steven. "Josephus and His Twenty-Two Book Canon." In *The Canon Debate: On the Origins and Formations of the Bible*, ed. Lee Martin McDonald and James A. Sanders, 110–27. Peabody, Mass.: Hendrickson, 2002.

Mason, Steven. "Josephus on Canon and Scriptures." In *Hebrew Bible/Old Testament: The History of Its Interpretation*, vol. 1: *From the Beginnings to the Middle Ages (until 1300): Part 1: Antiquity*, ed. Magne Sæbø, 217–35. Göttingen: Vandenhoeck & Ruprecht, 1996.

Mays, J. L. "The David of the Psalms," *Interpretation* 40 (1986): 143–55.

McCarter, P. Kyle. *II Samuel*. AB 9. New York: Doubleday, 1984.

McGann, Jerome J. *Radiant Textuality: Literature after the World Wide Web*. New York: Palgrave, 2001.

McKechnie, P. "The Career of Joshua Ben Sira," *Journal of Theological Studies* 51 (2000): 1–26.

McKenzie, D. F. *Bibliography and the Sociology of Texts* (Panizzi Lectures). London: British Library, 1986; Cambridge: Cambridge University Press, 1999.

Meade, David G. *Pseudonymity and Canon: An Investigation into the Relationship of Authorship and Authority in Jewish and Earliest Christian Tradition*. Tübingen: J. C. B. Mohr, 1986.

Metzger, Bruce. "Literary Forgeries and Canonical Pseudepigrapha," *Journal of Biblical Literature* 91 (1972): 3–24.

Middendorp, T. *Die Stellung Jesu Ben Siras zwischen Judentum und Hellenismus*. Leiden: Brill, 1973.

Mies, Françoise. "Le Psaume de Ben Sira 51,12a–o hébreu: L'hymne aux noms divins," *Revue biblique* 116.3 (2009): 336–67 (part 1) and 116.4 (2009): 481–504 (part 2).

Milik, Józef T. "Fragment d'une source du Psautier (4QPs89) et fragments des Jubilés, du Document de Damas, d'un phylactère dans la Grotte 4 de Qumran," *Revue Biblique* 73 (1966): 94–106.

Milik, Józef T. "Les modèles araméens du livre d'Esther dans la grotte 4 de Qumran," *Revue de Qumran* 15 (1992): 321–99.

Millard, Matthias. *Die Komposition des Psalters*. FAT 9. Tübingen: Mohr Siebeck, 1994.

Miura, Yuzuru. *David in Luke-Acts: His Portrayal in the Light of Early Judaism*. Tübingen: Mohr Siebeck, 2007.

Mopsik, Charles. *La Sagesse de ben Sira*. Lagrasse: Verdier, 2004.

Mowinckel, Sigmund. *The Psalms in Israel's Worship*. Trans. D. R. Ap-Thomas. 2 vols. Oxford: Blackwell, 1962.

Mroczek, Eva. "4QTestimonia." In *The T&T Clark Companion to the Dead Sea Scrolls*, ed. George J. Brooke and Charlotte Hempel. London: T&T Clark, forthcoming.

Mroczek, Eva. "'David Did Not Ascend into the Heavens' (Acts 2:34): Early Jewish Ascent Traditions and the Myth of Exegesis in the New Testament," *Judaïsme ancien—Ancient Judaism* 3 (2015): 261–94.

Mroczek, Eva. "The End of the Psalms in the Dead Sea Scrolls, Greek Codices, and Syriac Manuscripts." In *Snapshots of Evolving Traditions: Textual Fluidity, Manuscript Culture and New Philology*, ed. Liv Ingeborg Lied and Hugo Lundhaug. Berlin: de Gruyter, forthcoming.

Mroczek, Eva. "The Hegemony of the Biblical in the Study of Second Temple Literature." *Journal of Ancient Judaism* 6 (2015): 2–35.

Mroczek, Eva. "How Not to Build a Temple: Jacob, David, and the Unbuilt Ideal in Ancient Judaism." *Journal for the Study of Judaism* 46 (2015): 512–46.

Mroczek, Eva. "Moses, David, and Scribal Revelation: Preservation and Renewal in Second Temple Jewish Textual Traditions." In *The Significance of Sinai: Traditions about Sinai and Divine Revelation in Judaism and Christianity*, ed. George J. Brooke, Hindy Najman, and Loren T. Stuckenbruck, 91–115. Themes in Biblical Narrative 12. Leiden: Brill, 2008.

Mroczek, Eva. "A Peg to Hang On: Metaphor, Ancestral Merit, and the Midrashic Relationship of David and Solomon." In *Vixens Disturbing Vineyards: Embarrassment and Embracement of Scriptures: Festschrift in Honor of Harry Fox*, ed. Aubrey Glazer et al., 219–40. Boston: Academic Studies Press, 2010.

Mroczek, Eva. "Psalms Unbound: Ancient Concepts of Textual Tradition in 11QPsalms^a and Related Texts." Ph.D. diss., University of Toronto, 2012.

Mroczek, Eva. Review of A. Orlov, *The Enoch-Metatron Tradition*, *Journal of Hebrew Scriptures* 6 (2006).

Mroczek, Eva. Review of D. M. Stec, *The Genizah Psalms*, *Journal for the Study of Judaism* 46 (2015): 152–54.

Mroczek, Eva. "Thinking Digitally about the Dead Sea Scrolls: Book History before and beyond the Book," *Book History* 13 (2011): 235–63.

Mulder, Otto. *Simon the High Priest in Sirach 50: An Exegetical Study of the Significance of Simon the High Priest as Climax to the Praise of the Fathers in Ben Sira's Concept of the History of Israel*. Leiden: Brill, 2003.

Müller, C. D. G. "The Ascension of Isaiah." In *New Testament Apocrypha*, vol. 2: *Writings Relating to the Apostles, Apocalypses and Related Subjects*, rev. ed., ed. W. Schneemelcher, trans. R. M. Wilson; Louisville: Westminster John Knox, 1992.

Muraoka, Takamitsu. "Sir. 51, 13–30: An Erotic Hymn to Wisdom?" *Journal for the Study of Judaism* 10 (1979): 166–78.

Najman, Hindy. "The Exemplary Protagonist: The Case of 4Ezra." In *Old Testament Pseudepigrapha and the Scriptures*, ed. Eibert J. C. Tigchelaar, 261–87. BETL. Leuven: Peeters, 2014.

Najman, Hindy. "How Should We Contextualize Pseudepigrapha? Imitation and Emulation in 4 Ezra." In *Flores Florentino: Dead Sea Scrolls and Other Early Jewish Studies in Honour of Florentino García Martínez*, ed. Anthony Hilhorst, Émile Puech, and Eibert J. C. Tigchelaar, 529–36. JSJSup 122. Leiden: Brill, 2007.

Najman, Hindy. "Interpretation as Primordial Writing: *Jubilees* and Its Authority Conferring Strategies," *Journal for the Study of Judaism* 30 (1999): 379–410.

Najman, Hindy. *Losing the Temple and Recovering the Future: An Analysis of 4 Ezra.* Cambridge: Cambridge University Press, 2014.

Najman, Hindy. *Past Renewals: Interpretative Authority, Renewed Revelation, and the Quest for Perfection in Jewish Antiquity.* JSJSup 53. Leiden: Brill, 2010.

Najman, Hindy. "Reconsidering Jubilees: Prophecy and Exemplarity." In *Enoch and the Mosaic Torah: The Evidence of Jubilees,* ed. Gabriele Boccaccini and Giovanni Ibba, 229–43. Grand Rapids, Mich.: Eerdmans, 2009.

Najman, Hindy. Review of *Beyond the Essene Hypothesis, Association for Jewish Studies Review* 26 (2002): 352–53.

Najman, Hindy. *Seconding Sinai: The Development of Mosaic Discourse in Second Temple Judaism.* Leiden: Brill, 2003.

Najman, Hindy. "Torah of Moses: Pseudonymous Attribution in Second Temple Writings." In *The Interpretation of Scripture in Early Judaism and Christianity: Studies in Language and Tradition,* ed. Craig A. Evans, 202–16. JSPSup 33. Sheffield: Sheffield Academic Press, 2000.

Najman, Hindy. "The Vitality of Scripture within and beyond the 'Canon,'" *Journal for the Study of Judaism* 43 (2012): 497–518.

Najman, Hindy, and Eibert J. C. Tigchelaar, eds. *Composition, Rewriting and Reception of the Book of Jubilees.* Special issue of *Revue de Qumrân* 104 (2014).

Nelson, Milward D. *The Syriac Version of the Wisdom of Ben Sira Compared to the Greek and Hebrew Materials.* SBLDS 107. Atlanta: Society of Biblical Literature, 1988.

Neusner, Jacob. *Songs of Songs Rabbah: An Analytical Translation.* 2 vols. Atlanta: Scholars Press, 1989.

Newman, Judith H. "Liturgical Imagination in the Composition of Ben Sira." In *Prayer and Poetry in the Dead Sea Scrolls and Related Literature: Essays in Honor of Eileen Schuller on the Occasion of Her 65th Birthday,* ed. Jeremy Penner, Ken M. Penner, and Cecilia Wassen, 323–38. STDJ 98. Leiden: Brill, 2011.

Newsom, Carol. *The Self as Symbolic Space: Constructing Identity and Community at Qumran.* Leiden: Brill, 2004.

Newsom, Carol. "Women and the Discourse of Patriarchal Wisdom: A Study of Proverbs 1–9." In *Gender and Difference in Ancient Israel,* ed. Peggy L. Day, 142–60. Minneapolis: Fortress, 1989.

Nickelsburg, George W. E. *1 Enoch 1: A Commentary on the Book of 1 Enoch, Chapters 1–36; 81–108.* Hermeneia. Minneapolis: Fortress Press, 2001.

Nickelsburg, George W. E. "The Nature and Function of Revelation in 1 Enoch, Jubilees, and Some Qumranic Documents." In *Pseudepigraphic Perspectives: The Apocrypha and Pseudepigrapha in Light of the Dead Sea Scrolls,* ed. Esther G. Chazon and Michael E. Stone, 91–119. Leiden: Brill, 1999.

Nickelsburg, George W. E., and James C. VanderKam. *1 Enoch: The Hermeneia Translation.* Minneapolis: Fortress Press, 2012.

Nickelsburg, George W. E., and James C. VanderKam. *1 Enoch 2: A Commentary on the Book of 1 Enoch, Chapters 37–82.* Hermeneia. Minneapolis: Fortress Press, 2012.

Niditch, Susan. *Oral World and Written Word: Ancient Israelite Literature.* Library of Ancient Israel. Louisville, Ky.: Westminster John Knox Press, 1996.

North, Michael. "Authorship and Autography," *PMLA* 116 (2001): 1377–85.

Orlov, Andrei. *The Enoch-Metatron Tradition.* Tübingen: Mohr Siebeck, 2005.

Orlov, Andrei, and Gabriele Boccaccini, eds. *New Perspectives on 2 Enoch: No Longer Slavonic Only.* Leiden: Brill, 2012.

Owens, Robert J. "The Early Syriac Text of Ben Sira in the Demonstrations of Aphrahat," *Journal of Semitic Studies* 34 (1989): 39–75.

Pajunen, Mika S. *The Land to the Elect and Justice for All: Reading Psalms in the Dead Sea Scrolls in Light of 4Q381.* JAJSupp 14. Göttingen: Vandenhoeck & Ruprecht, 2013.

Pajunen, Mika S. "Perspectives on the Existence of a Particular Authoritative Book of Psalms in the Late Second Temple Period," *Journal for the Study of the Old Testament* 39 (2014): 139–63.

Pakkala, Juha. "The Quotations and References of the Pentateuchal Laws in Ezra-Nehemiah." In *Changes in Scripture: Rewriting and Interpreting Authoritative Traditions in the Second Temple Period*, 193–222. Berlin: de Gruyter, 2011.

Payne, Mark. "Aristotle on Poets as Parents and the Hellenistic Poet as Mother." In *Classical Myth and Psychoanalysis: Ancient and Modern Stories of the Self*, ed. Ellen O'Gorman and Vanda Zajko, 299–313. Oxford: Oxford University Press, 2013.

Person, Raymond F. *The Deuteronomic History and the Book of Chronicles: Scribal Works in an Oral World*. SBLAIL 6. Atlanta: Society of Biblical Literature, 2010.

Petersen, Anders Klostergaard. "Rewritten Bible as a Borderline Phenomenon—Genre, Textual Strategy, or Canonical Anachronism?" In *Flores Florentino: Dead Sea Scrolls and Other Early Jewish Studies in Honour of Florentino García Martínez*, ed. Anthony Hilhorst, Émile Puech, and Eibert J. C. Tigchelaar, 285–306. JSJSup 122. Leiden: Brill, 2007.

Petersen, Anders Klostergaard. "The Riverrun of Rewriting Scripture: From Textual Cannibalism to Scriptural Completion," *Journal for the Study of Judaism* 43 (2012): 475–96.

Philonenko, Marc. "Sur une proposition essénisante dans le Siracide (16:15–16)," *Orientalia Suecana* 33–35 (1984–86): 317–21.

Philonenko, Marc, and Alfred Marx. "Quatre 'chants' pseudo-davidiques trouvés dans la Gueniza du Caire et d'origine esséno-qoumrânienne," *Revue d'Histoire et de Philosophie Religieuses* 77 (1997): 385–406.

Pietersma, Albert. "David in the Greek Psalms," Vetus Testamentum 30 (1980): 213–26.

Pietersma, Albert. "Exegesis and Liturgy in the Superscriptions of the Greek Psalter." In *Proceedings of the Xth Congress of the International Organization for Septuagint and Cognate Studies, Oslo, July–August, 1998*, ed. B. A. Taylor, 99–138. JBLSCS 5. Atlanta: Society of Biblical Literature, 2001.

Pietersma, Albert. "Ra 2110 (P. Bodmer XXIV) and the Text of the Greek Psalter." In *Studien zur Septuaginta—Robert Hanhart zu Ehren*, ed. Detlef Fraenkel, Udo Quast, and John W. Wevers, 262–86. MSU 20. Göttingen, Vandenhoeck & Ruprecht, 1990.

Pietersma, Albert. "To the Reader of Psalms." In *A New English Translation of the Septuagint*, 542–547. Oxford: Oxford University Press, 2007.

Pietersma, Albert, and Benjamin G. Wright, "To the Reader of NETS." In *A New English Translation of the Septuagint*, xiii–xx. Oxford: Oxford University Press, 2007.

Piovanelli, Pierluigi. "Les origines de l'*Apocalypse de Paul* reconsidérées," *Apocrypha* 4 (1993): 25–64.

Pirandello, Luigi. "Pirandello Confesses…Why and How He Wrote *Six Characters in Search of an Author*," *Virginia Quarterly Review* 1 (1925): 36–52.

Pirandello, Luigi. *Six Characters in Search of an Author: A Play in the Making*. Trans. E. Storer. New York: E. P. Dutton, 1922.

Poovey, Mary. *A History of the Modern Fact: Problems of Knowledge in the Sciences of Wealth and Society*. Chicago: University of Chicago Press, 1998.

Priest, J. "Testament of Moses." In Charlesworth, *The Old Testament Pseudepigrapha*, vol. 1: *Apocalyptic Literature and Testaments*, ed. James A. Charlesworth, 919–34.

Puech, Émile. "Ben Sira and Qumran." In *The Wisdom of Ben Sira: Studies on Tradition, Redaction, and Theology*, ed. Angelo Passaro and Giuseppe Bellia, 79–118. Berlin: de Gruyter, 2008.

Puech, Émile. "Fragments du Psaume 122 dans un manuscrit hébreu de la grotte IV," *Revue de Qumran* 9 (1978): 547–54.

Puech, Émile. "La pierre de Sion et l'autel des holocaustes d'après un manuscrit hébreu de la grotte 4 (4Q522)," *Revue Biblique* 99 (1992): 676–96.

Puech, Émile. "Le livre de Ben Sira et les manuscrits de la Mer Morte." In *Treasures of Wisdom: Studies in Ben Sira and the Book of Wisdom: Festschrift M. Gilbert*, ed. Núria Calduch-Benages and Jacques Vermeylen, 411–26. Leuven: Peeters, 1999.

Puech, Émile. "Les Psaumes davidiques du rituel d'exorcisme (11Q11)." In *Sapiential, Liturgical and Poetical Texts from Qumran: Proceedings of the Third Meeting of the International Organization for Qumran Studies, Oslo, 1998: Published in Memory of Maurice Baillet*, ed. Daniel Falk et al., 160–81. STDJ 35. Leiden: Brill, 2000.

Puech, Émile. "Testament de Qahat." In *Qumrân Grotte 4. XXII: Textes Araméens. Première Partie.* DJD 31. Oxford: Clarendon Press, 2001.

Qimron, Elisha. "Concerning 'Joshua Cycles' from Qumran," *Tarbiẓ* 63 (1994): 503–8.

Qimron, Elisha, and John Strugnell. *Qumran Cave 4. 5, Miqsat Ma'ase Ha-Torah.* DJD 10. Oxford: Clarendon Press, 1994.

Rabinowitz, Isaac. "The Qumran Hebrew Original of Ben Sira's Concluding Acrostic on Wisdom," *Hebrew Union College Annual* 42 (1971): 173–84.

Ravid, Liora. "The Special Terminology of the Heavenly Tablets" [Hebrew], *Tarbiẓ* 68.4 (1999): 463–471.

Reed, Annette Yoshiko. *Demons, Angels, and Writing in Ancient Judaism.* New York: Cambridge University Press, forthcoming.

Reed, Annette Yoshiko. "Enochic and Mosaic Traditions in Jubilees: The Evidence of Angelology and Demonology." In *Enoch and the Mosaic Torah: The Evidence of Jubilees,* ed. Gabriele Boccaccini and Giovanni Ibba, 353–68. Grand Rapids, Mich.: Eerdmans, 2009.

Reed, Annette Yoshiko. "Heavenly Ascent, Angelic Descent, and the Transmission of Knowledge in 1 Enoch 6-16." In *Heavenly Realms and Earthly Realities in Late Antique Religions,* ed. Ra'anan Boustan and Annette Yoshiko Reed, 47–66. New York: Cambridge University Press, 2004.

Reed, Annette Yoshiko. "The Modern Invention of 'Old Testament Pseudepigrapha,'" *Journal of Theological Studies* 60 (2009): 403–36.

Reed, Annette Yoshiko. "Pseudepigraphy, Authorship and the Reception of 'the Bible' in Late Antiquity." In *The Reception and Interpretation of the Bible in Late Antiquity: Proceedings of the Montréal Colloquium in Honour of Charles Kannengiesser, 11–13 October 2006,* ed. Lorenzo DiTommaso and Lucian Turcescu, 467–90. Leiden: Brill, 2008.

Reed, Annette Yoshiko. "Textuality between Death and Memory: The Prehistory and Formation of the Parabiblical Testament," *Jewish Quarterly Review* 104 (2014): 381–412.

Reeves, John C. "Exploring the Afterlife of Jewish Pseudepigrapha in Medieval Near Eastern Religious Traditions: Some Initial Soundings," *Journal for the Study of Judaism* 30 (1999): 148–77.

Reeves, John C. "Problematizing the Bible...Then and Now," *Jewish Quarterly Review* 100 (2010): 139–52.

Rentdorff, Rolf. "The Psalms of David: David in the Psalms." In *The Book of Psalms: Composition and Reception,* ed. Peter W. Flint and Patrick D. Miller, 53–64. Leiden: Brill, 2005.

Reymond, Eric D. *Innovations in Hebrew Poetry: Parallelism and the Poems of Sirach.* Leiden: Brill, 2004.

Reymond, Eric D. *New Idioms within Old: Poetry and Parallelism in the Non-Masoretic Poems of 11Q5 (=11QPsᵃ).* EJL 31. Atlanta: Society of Biblical Literature, 2011.

Reymond, Eric D. "Sirach 51:13-30 and 11Q5 (=11QPsᵃ) 21.11-22.1," *Revue de Qumran* 23 (2007): 207–23.

Reynolds, Kent A. *Torah as Teacher: The Exemplary Torah Student in Psalm 119.* VTSup 137. Leiden: Brill, 2010.

Rizzi, Giovanni. "Christian Interpretations in the Syriac Version of Sirach." In *The Wisdom of Ben Sira: Studies on Tradition, Redaction, and Theology,* ed. Angelo Passaro and Guiseppe Bellia, 278–308. Berlin: de Gruyter, 2008.

Rollston, Christopher. "Ben Sira 38:24–39:11 and the Egyptian Satire of the Trades: A Reconsideration," *Journal of Biblical Literature* 120 (2001): 131–39.

Romeny, Bas ter Haar. "Biblical Studies in the Church of the East: The Case of Catholicos Timothy I," *Studia Patristica* 34 (2001): 503–10.

Römer, Thomas. "The Case of the Book of Kings." In *Deuteronomy-Kings as Emerging Authoritative Books: A Conversation,* ed. Diana V. Edelman, 187–201. Atlanta: Society of Biblical Literature, 2014.

Rüger, H. P. *Text und Textform im hebräischen Sirach I.* BZAW 112. Berlin: de Gruyter, 1970.

Sacchi, Paolo. *Jewish Apocalyptic and Its History.* JSPSup 20. Sheffield: Sheffield Academic Press, 1997.

Sanders, James A. "Cave 11 Surprises and the Question of Canon," *McCormick Quarterly* 21 (1968): 284–98.

Sanders, James A. *The Dead Sea Psalms Scroll*. Ithaca, N.Y.: Cornell University Press, 1967.

Sanders, James A. "Introduction: Why the Pseudepigrapha?" In *Pseudepigrapha and Early Biblical Interpretation*, ed. James H. Charlesworth and Craig A. Evans, 13–19. JSOPSS 14, SSEJC 2. Sheffield: Journal for the Study of the Old Testament, 1993.

Sanders, James A. *The Psalms Scroll of Qumrân Cave 11 (11QPsᵃ)*. DJD 4. Oxford: Clarendon Press, 1965.

Sanders, James A. "The Sirach 51 Acrostic." In *Hommages à André Dupont-Sommer*, ed. André Caquot and Marc Philonenko, 429–38. Paris: Cerf, 1971.

Sanders, Seth L. "Daniel and the Origins of Biblical Interpretation," *Prooftexts*, forthcoming.

Sanders, Seth L. *From Adapa to Enoch: Scribal Culture and Religious Vision in Judea and Babylon*. TSAJ. Tübingen: Mohr Siebeck, 2016.

Sarna, Nahum M. "The Psalm Superscriptions and the Guilds." In *Studies in Jewish Religious and Intellectual History*, ed. Siegfried Stein and Raphael Loewe, 281–300. Tuscaloosa: University of Alabama Press, 1979.

Satlow, Michael. *How the Bible Became Holy*. New Haven, Conn.: Yale University Press, 2014.

Satran, David. *Biblical Prophets in Byzantine Palestine: Reassessing the Lives of the Prophets*. SVTP 11. Leiden: Brill, 1995.

Schäfer, Peter. *The Hidden and Manifest God: Some Major Themes in Early Jewish Mysticism*. Trans. A. Pomerance. Albany: State University of New York Press, 1992.

Schäfer, Peter. *Synopse zur Hekhalot-Literatur*. TSAJ 2. Tübingen: Mohr Siebeck, 1981.

Schaff, P., and H. Wace, eds. *Nicene and Post-Nicene Fathers*. Second Series. 14 vols. Buffalo, N.Y.: Christian Literature, 1900.

Scharbach, Rebecca. "The Rebirth of a Book: Noachic Writing in Medieval and Renaissance Europe." In *Noah and His Book(s)*, ed. Michael E. Stone, Vered Hillel, and Aryeh Amihay, 113–33. Atlanta: Society of Biblical Literature, 2010.

Schechter, Solomon. "A Further Fragment of Ben Sira," *Jewish Quarterly Review* 12, o.s., (1900): 456–65.

Schechter, Solomon. "The Quotations from Ecclesiasticus in Rabbinic Literature," *Jewish Quarterly Review* 3 (1891): 682–706.

Schiffman, Lawrence H. "The Dead Sea Scrolls and the History of the Jewish Book," *Association of Jewish Studies Review* 34.2 (2010): 359–65.

Schiffman, Lawrence H. "Memory and Manuscript: Books, Scrolls, and the Tradition of the Dead Sea Scrolls." In *New Perspectives on Old Texts: Proceedings of the Tenth International Symposium of the Orion Center for the Study of the Dead Sea Scrolls and Associated Literature, 9-11 January 2005*, ed. Esther G. Chazon and Betsy Halpern Amaru, in collaboration with Ruth Clements, 133–50. STDJ 88. Leiden: Brill, 2010.

Schiffman, Lawrence H. "The Place of 4QMMT in the Corpus of Qumran Manuscripts." In *Reading 4QMMT*, eds John Kampen and Moshe J. Bernstein, 81–98. SBLSymS 2. Atlanta: Scholars Press, 1996.

Schiffman, Lawrence H. "Pseudepigrapha in the Pseudepigrapha: Mythical Books in Second Temple Literature," *Revue de Qumran* 21 (2004): 429–38.

Schiffman, Lawrence H. *Reclaiming the Dead Sea Scrolls: The History of Judaism, the Background of Christianity, the Lost Library of Qumran*. Philadelphia: Jewish Publication Society, 1994.

Schiffman, Lawrence H. *Understanding Second Temple and Rabbinic Judaism*, ed. Jon Bloomberg and Samuel Kapustin. Jersey City, N.J.: Ktav, 2003.

Schniedewind, William M. *How the Bible Became a Book: The Textualization of Ancient Israel*. New York: Cambridge University Press, 2004.

Schorch, Stefan. "The Libraries in 2 Macc 2:13–15." In *The Books of the Maccabees: History, Theology, Ideology: Papers of the Second International Conference on the Deuterocanonical Books, Pápa, Hungary, 9-11 June, 2005*, ed. Géza G. Xeravits and József Zsengellér, 169–80. JSJSup 118. Leiden: Brill, 2007.

Schorch, Stefan. "The Pre-eminence of the Hebrew Language and the Emerging Concept of the 'Ideal Text' in Late Second Temple Judaism." In *The Book of Ben Sira: Papers of the Third International Conference on the Deuterocanonical Books, Pápa, Hungary 2006*, ed. Géza G. Xeravits and József Zsengellér, 43–54. JSJS 127. Leiden: Brill, 2008.

Schorch, Stefan. "Which Kind of Authority? The Authority of the Torah during the Hellenistic and the Roman Periods." In *Scriptural Authority in Early Judaism and Ancient Christianity*, ed. Isaac Kalimi, Tobias Nicklas, and Geza G. Xeravits, 1–15. Berlin: de Gruyter, 2013.

Schrader, Lutz. *Leiden und Gerechtigkeit: Studien zu Theologie und Textgeschichte des Sirachbuches.* BBET 27. Frankfurt am Main: Peter Lang, 1994.

Schuller, Eileen M. "Some Reflections on the Function and Use of Poetical Texts among the Dead Sea Scrolls." In *Liturgical Perspectives: Prayer and Poetry in Light of the Dead Sea Scrolls. Proceedings of the Fifth International Symposium of the Orion Center, 19–23 January, 2000*, ed. Esther G. Chazon, 173–89. STDJ 48. Leiden: Brill, 2003.

Scott, J. M. "Geographic Aspects of Noachic Materials in the Scrolls at Qumran." In *The Scrolls and the Scriptures*, ed. Stanley E. Porter and Craig A. Evans, 368–81. Sheffield: Sheffield Academic Press, 1997.

Segal, Michael. *The Book of Jubilees: Rewritten Bible, Redaction, Ideology and Theology.* Leiden: Brill, 2007.

Segal, M. H. "The Evolution of the Hebrew Text of Ben Sira," *Jewish Quarterly Review* 25 (1934–35): 91–149.

Segal, M. H. *Sefer ben Sira ha-Shalem.* 2nd ed. Jerusalem: Mosad Byalik, 1958.

Seow, Choon-Leong. *Ecclesiastes: A New Translation with Introduction and Commentary.* Anchor Yale Bible Series. New Haven, Conn.: Yale University Press, 1997.

Shemesh, Aharon. "4Q265 and the Authoritative Status of Jubilees at Qumran." In *Enoch and the Mosaic Torah: The Evidence of Jubilees*, ed. Gabriele Boccaccini and Giovanni Ibba, 247–60. Grand Rapids, Mich.: Eerdmans, 2009.

Silverstein, Theodore, and Anthony Hilhorst, eds. *Apocalypse of Paul: A New Critical Edition of Three Long Latin Versions.* Geneva: P. Cramer, 1997.

Skehan, Patrick W. "The Acrostic Poem in Sirach 51:13-30," *Harvard Theological Review* 64 (1971): 387–400.

Skehan, Patrick W. "Gleanings from Psalms Texts from Qumrân." In *Mélanges bibliques et orientaux en l'honneur de M. Henri Cazelles*, ed. André Caquot and Mathias Delcor, 439–45. AOAT 212. Neukirchen-Vluyn: Neukirchener, 1981.

Skehan, Patrick W. "Qumran and Old Testament Criticism." In *Qumrân: Sa piété, sa théologie et son milieu*, ed. Mathias Delcor, 163–82. BETL 46. Leuven: Leuven University Press, 1978.

Skehan, Patrick W. and Alexander A. Di Lella. *The Wisdom of Ben Sira.* AB 39. New York: Doubleday, 1987.

Skehan, Patrick W., et al. "4QPsᵇ." In *Qumran Cave 4, XI: Psalms to Chronicles*, ed. Eugene Ulrich et al., 23–48. DJD 16. Oxford: Clarendon Press, 2000.

Skehan, Patrick W., Eugene Ulrich, and Peter W. Flint. "Two Manuscripts of Psalm 119 from Qumran Cave 4," *Revue de Qumran* 16 (1995): 477–86.

Slomovic, Elieser. "Toward an Understanding of the Formation of Historical Titles in the Book of Psalms," *Alttestamentliche Wissenschaft* 91 (1979): 352–80.

Smend, R. *Die Weisheit des Jesus Sirach erklärt.* Berlin: Reimer, 1906.

Smith, Jonathan Z. *Imagining Religion: From Babylon to Jonestown.* Chicago: University of Chicago Press, 1982.

Smith, Jonathan Z. "Prayer of Joseph." In *The Old Testament Pseudepigrapha*, vol. 2: *Expansions of the "Old Testament" and Legends, Wisdom and Philosophical Literature, Prayers, Psalms, and Odes, Fragments of Lost Judeo-Hellenistic Works*, ed. James A. Charlesworth, 699–714. Garden City, N.Y.: Doubleday, 1985.

Smith, Morton. "Pseudepigraphy in the Israelite Tradition." In *Pseudepigrapha I*, ed. Kurt von Fritz, 189–215. Geneva: Fondation Hardt, 1972.

Sommer, Benjamin D., ed. *Jewish Concepts of Scripture: A Comparative Introduction.* New York: New York University Press, 2012.

Sommer, Benjamin D. *A Prophet Reads Scripture: Allusion in Isaiah 40–66.* Stanford, Calif.: Stanford University Press, 1998.

Sparks, Hedley F. D. *The Apocryphal Old Testament.* Oxford: Clarendon Press, 1984.

Speyer, Wolfgang. *Die literarische Falschung in heidnischen und christlichen Altertum: Ein Versuch ihrer Deutung.* Munich: C. H. Beck, 1971.

Stackert, Jeffrey. *Rewriting the Torah: Literary Revision in Deuteronomy and the Holiness Code.* Tübingen: Mohr Siebeck, 2007.

Stadelmann, Helge. *Ben Sira als Schriftgelehrter.* Tübingen: Mohr Siebeck, 1980.

Stec, David M. *The Genizah Psalms.* Cambridge Genizah Studies Series 5. Leiden: Brill, 2013.

Stern, David. "The First Jewish Books and the Early History of Jewish Reading," *Jewish Quarterly Review* 98 (2008): 163–202.

Stone, Michael E. *Ancient Judaism: New Visions and Views.* Grand Rapids, Mich.: Eerdmans, 2011.

Stone, Michael E. "The Book of Enoch and Judaism in the Third Century B.C.E.," *Catholic Biblical Quarterly* 40 (1978): 479–92.

Stone, Michael E. "The Book(s) Attributed to Noah," *Dead Sea Discoveries* 13 (2006): 2–23.

Stone, Michael E. "The Dead Sea Scrolls and the Pseudepigrapha," *Dead Sea Discoveries* 3 (1996): 270–95.

Stone, Michael E. *Fourth Ezra: A Commentary on the Book of Fourth Ezra.* Minneapolis: Fortress Press, 1990.

Stone, Michael E., Vered Hillel, and Aryeh Amihay, eds. *Noah and His Book(s).* Atlanta: Society of Biblical Literature, 2010.

Strauss, Peter L., ed. *Fetha Nagast: The Law of the Kings,* 2nd ed. Trans. Paulos Tzadua. Durham, N.C.: Carolina Academic Press, 2009.

Strawn, Brent A. "David as One of the 'Perfect of (the) Way': On the Provenience of David's Compositions (and 11QPsᵃ as a Whole?)," *Revue de Qumran* 24 (2010): 607–27.

Strugnell, John. "Notes en marge du volume V des 'Discoveries in the Judaean Desert of Jordan,'" *Revue de Qumran* 7 (1970): 211–20.

Stuckenbruck, Loren T. "The Epistle of Enoch: Genre and Authorial Presentation," *Dead Sea Discoveries* 17 (2010): 387–417.

Stuckenbruck, Loren T. *1 Enoch 91–108.* Commentaries on Early Jewish Literature. Berlin: de Gruyter, 2007.

Stuckenbruck, Loren T. "Reflections on Sources behind the Epistle of Enoch and the Significance of 1 Enoch 104:9–13 for the Reception of Enochic Tradition." In *A Teacher for All Generations: Essays in Honor of James C. VanderKam,* 2 vols. ed. Eric F. Mason et al., 1: 704–14. Leiden: Brill, 2011.

Sulzbach, Carla. "The Function of the Sacred Geography in the Book of Jubilees," *Journal for Semitics* 14 (2005): 283–305.

Sutherland, Kathryn, ed. *Electronic Text: Investigations in Method and Theory.* Oxford: Clarendon Press, 1997.

Talmon, Shemaryahu. "Was the Book of Esther Known at Qumran?" *Dead Sea Discoveries* 2 (1995): 249–67.

Tanselle, G. Thomas. "The Editorial Problem of Final Authorial Intention," *Studies in Bibliography* 29 (1976): 167–211.

Tanselle, G. Thomas. "Historicism and Critical Editing," *Studies in Bibliography* 39 (1986): 1–46.

Tanselle, G. Thomas. "Recent Editorial Discussion and the Central Questions of Editing," *Studies in Bibliography* 34 (1981): 23–65.

Tanselle, G. Thomas. "The Varieties of Scholarly Editing." In *Scholarly Editing: A Guide to Research,* ed. D. C. Greetham, 9–32. New York: Modern Language Association, 1995.

Ta-Shma, Israel M. "The 'Open' Book in Medieval Hebrew Literature: The Problem of Authorized Editions," *Bulletin of the John Rylands University Library of Manchester* 75 (1993): 17–24.

Teeter, D. Andrew. "The Hebrew Bible and/as Second Temple Literature: Methodological Reflections," *Dead Sea Discoveries* 20 (2013): 349–77.

Teeter, D. Andrew. "On 'Exegetical Function' in Rewritten Scripture: Inner-Biblical Exegesis and the Abram/Ravens Narrative in Jubilees," *Harvard Theological Review* 106 (2013): 373–402.

Teeter, D. Andrew. "Torah, Wisdom, and the Composition of Rewritten Scripture: Jubilees and 11QPs^a in Comparative Perspective." In *Wisdom and Torah: The Reception of "Torah" in the Wisdom Literature of the Second Temple Period*, ed. Bernd U. Schipper and D. Andrew Teeter, 233–72. JSJSup 163. Leiden: Brill, 2013.

Teugels, Lieve. "Midrash in the Bible or Midrash on the Bible? Critical Remarks about the Uncritical Use of a Term." In *Bibel und Midrasch*, ed. Gerhard Bodendorfer and Matthias Millard, 43–63. FAT 22. Tübingen: Mohr Siebeck, 1998.

Thomas, Samuel I. "Eternal Writing and Immortal Writers: On the Non-Death of the Scribe in Early Judaism." In *A Teacher for All Generations: Essays in Honor of James C. VanderKam*, 2 vols. Ed. Eric F. Mason et al., 1: 573–88. Leiden: Brill, 2011.

Tigchelaar, Eibert J. C. "Classification of the Collection of Dead Sea Scrolls and the Case of Apocryphon of Jeremiah C," *Journal for the Study of Judaism* 43 (2012): 519–50.

Tigchelaar, Eibert J. C. "Editing the Hebrew Bible: An Overview of Some Problems." In *Editing the Bible: Assessing the Task Past and Present*, ed. John S. Kloppenborg and Judith H. Newman, 41–68. Atlanta: Society of Biblical Literature, 2012.

Tigchelaar, Eibert J. C. "Forms of Pseudepigraphy in the Dead Sea Scrolls." In *Pseudepigraphie und Verfasserfiktion in frühchristlichen Briefen*, ed. Jörg Frey, Jens Herzer, Martina Janßen, and Clare K. Rothschild, 85–101. WUNT 246. Tübingen: Mohr Siebeck, 2009.

Tigchelaar, Eibert J. C. "The Imaginal Context and the Visionary of the Aramaic *New Jerusalem*." In *Flores Florentino: Dead Sea Scrolls and Other Early Jewish Studies in Honour of Florentino García Martínez*, ed. Anthony Hilhorst, Émile Puech, and Eibert J. C. Tigchelaar, 257–70. JSJSup 122. Leiden: Brill, 2007.

Tigchelaar, Eibert J. C., ed. *Old Testament Pseudepigrapha and the Scriptures*. BETL 270. Leuven: Peeters, 2014.

Tov, Emanuel. "The Dimensions of the Qumran Scrolls," *Dead Sea Discoveries* 5 (1998): 69–91.

Tov, Emanuel. *Hebrew Bible, Greek Bible, and Qumran: Collected Essays*. TSAJ 121. Tübingen: Mohr Siebeck, 2008.

Tov, Emanuel. "From 4QReworked Pentateuch to 4QPentateuch (?)" In *Authoritative Scriptures in Ancient Judaism*, ed. Mladen Popović, 73–91. Leiden: Brill, 2010.

Tov, Emanuel. "The Rewritten Book of Joshua as Found at Qumran and Masada." In *Biblical Perspectives: Early Use and Interpretation of the Bible in the Light of the Dead Sea Scrolls: Proceedings of the First International Symposium of the Orion Center, 12–14 May 1996*, ed. Michael E. Stone and Esther G. Chazon, 233–56. STDJ 28. Leiden: Brill, 1998.

Tov, Emanuel. *Scribal Practices and Approaches Reflected in the Texts Found in the Judean Desert*. Leiden: Brill, 2004.

Tov, Emanuel. "The Text of Isaiah at Qumran." In *Writing and Reading the Scroll of Isaiah: Studies of an Interpretive Tradition*, ed. Craig C. Broyles and Craig A. Evans, 2.491–511. VTSup 70. Leiden: Brill, 1997.

Tzoref, Shani L. "Covenantal Election in 4Q252 and Jubilees' Heavenly Tablets," *Dead Sea Discoveries* 18 (2011): 74–89.

Tzoref, Shani L. (Berrin). " 'Heavenly Tablets' in the Book of Jubilees." In *Anafim: Proceedings of the Australian Jewish Studies Forum, University of Sydney, 8–9 February 2004*, ed. Suzanne Faigan, 29–47. Sydney: Mandelbaum, 2006.

Tzoref, Shani L. (Berrin). "The 'Hidden' and the 'Revealed': Progressive Revelation of Law and Esoterica" (Hebrew). In *Meghillot: Studies in the Dead Sea Scrolls 7*, ed. Moshe Bar-Asher and Devorah Dimant, 157–90. Jerusalem: Haifa University and Bialik Institute, 2009.

Ulrich, Eugene C. "The Bible in the Making: The Scriptures Found at Qumran." In *The Bible at Qumran: Text, Shape and Interpretation*, ed. Peter W. Flint, 51–66. Grand Rapids, Mich.: Eerdmans, 2001.

Ulrich, Eugene C. *The Dead Sea Scrolls and the Origins of the Bible*. Grand Rapids, Mich.: Eerdmans; Leiden: Brill, 1999.

Ulrich, Eugene C. "The Non-Attestation of a Tripartite Canon in 4QMMT," *Catholic Biblical Quarterly* 65 (2003): 202–14.

Ulrich, Eugene C. "The Text of the Hebrew Scriptures at the Time of Hillel and Jesus." In *Congress Volume: Basel 2001*, ed. André Lemaire, 85–108. VTSup 92. Leiden: Brill, 2002.

VanderKam, James C. "Authoritative Literature in the Dead Sea Scrolls," *Dead Sea Discoveries* 5 (1998): 396–401.

VanderKam, James C. *The Book of Jubilees: A Critical Text.* CSCO 510; Scriptores Aethiopici 87. Louvain: Peeters, 1989.

VanderKam, James C. *The Book of Jubilees: Translation.* CSCO 511; Scriptores Aethiopici 88. Louvain: Peeters, 1989.

VanderKam, James C. *The Dead Sea Scrolls Today.* Grand Rapids, Mich.: Eerdmans, 1994.

VanderKam, James C. "Enoch Traditions in Jubilees and Other Second-Century Sources." In *SBL Seminar Papers, 1978*, 2 vols. 1:229–51. SBLSP 13. Missoula, Mont.: Scholars Press, 1978.

VanderKam, James C. "Moses Trumping Moses." In *The Dead Sea Scrolls: Transmission of Traditions and Production of Texts*, ed. Sarianna Metso, Hindy Najman, and Eileen Schuller, 25–44. STDJ 92. Leiden: Brill, 2010.

VanderKam, James C. "Questions of Canon Viewed through the Dead Sea Scrolls," *Bulletin for Biblical Research* 11 (2001): 269–92.

VanderKam, James C. "Studies on 'David's Compositions,'" *Eretz Israel* 26 (1999): 212–20.

van der Kooij, Arie. "The Canonization of Ancient Books Kept in the Temple of Jerusalem." In *Canonization and Decanonization*, ed. Arie van der Kooij and Karel van der Toorn, 17–40. Studies in the History of Religions 82. Leiden: Brill, 1998.

Van der Ploeg, Johannes P. M. "Un petit rouleau de psaumes apocryphes (11QPsAp*)." In *Tradition und Glaube: Das frühe Christentum in seiner Umwelt: Festgabe für Karl Georg Kuhn zum 65. Geburtstag*, ed. Gert Jeremias et al., 128–39. Göttingen: Vandenhoeck & Ruprecht, 1971.

Van der Ploeg, Johannes P. M. "Le sens et un problème textuel du Ps LXXXIX." In *Mélanges bibliques et orientaux en l'honneur de M. Henri Cazelles*, ed. André Caquot and Matthias Delcor, 471–81. AOAT 212. Neukirchen-Vluyn: Neukirchener, 1981.

Van der Toorn, Karel. *Scribal Culture and the Making of the Hebrew Bible.* Cambridge, Mass.: Harvard University Press, 2007.

Van Peursen, Wido T. *Language and Interpretation in the Syriac Text of Ben Sira: A Comparative Linguistic and Literary Study.* Leiden: Brill, 2007.

Van Rooy, Herrie F. *Studies on the Syriac Apocryphal Psalms.* JSSSup 7. Oxford: Oxford University Press, 1999.

Van Ruiten, Jacques T. A. G. M. *Abraham in the Book of Jubilees: The Rewriting of Genesis 11:26–25:10 in the Book of Jubilees.* JSJSup 161. Leiden: Brill, 2012.

Van Ruiten, Jacques T. A. G. M. "Between Jacob's Death and Moses' Birth: The Intertextual Relationship between Genesis 50:15–Exodus 1:14 and Jubilees 46:1–16." In *Flores Florentino: Dead Sea Scrolls and Other Early Jewish Studies in Honour of Florentino García Martínez*, ed. Anthony Hilhorst, Émile Puech, and Eibert J. C. Tigchelaar, 467–89. JSJSup 122. Leiden: Brill, 2007.

Van Ruiten, Jacques T. A. G. M *Primeval History Interpreted: The Rewriting of Genesis 1–11 in the Book of Jubilees.* JSJS 66. Leiden: Brill, 2000.

Van Seters, John. "Creative Imitation in the Hebrew Bible," *Studies in Religion* 29 (2000): 395–409.

Vayntrub, Jacqueline. "The Book of Proverbs and the Idea of Ancient Israelite Education," *Zeitschrift für die Alttestamentliche Wissenschaft* (forthcoming).

Vayntrub, Jacqueline. "Proverbs and the Limits of Poetry." Ph.D. diss., University of Chicago, 2015.

Vermes, Geza. *Scripture and Tradition in Judaism: Haggadic Studies.* Leiden: Brill, 1961; 2nd ed., 1973.

Von Weissenberg, Hanne. *4QMMT: Reevaluating the Text, the Function, and the Meaning of the Epilogue.* STDJ 82. Leiden: Brill, 2009.

Von Weissenberg, Hanne. "4QMMT—Some New Readings." In *Northern Lights on the Dead Sea Scrolls: Proceedings of the Nordic Qumran Network, 2003–2006*, ed. Anders Klostergaard Petersen et al., 217–21. STDJ 80. Leiden: Brill, 2009.

Wacholder, Ben Zion. "David's Eschatological Psalter: 11QPsalmsᵃ," *Hebrew Union College Annual* 59 (1988): 23–72.

Wacholder, Ben Zion. "Jubilees as the Super Canon: Torah-Admonition versus Torah-Commandment." In *Legal Texts and Legal Issues: Proceedings of the Second Meeting of the International Organization for Qumran Studies, Cambridge 1995*, ed. Moshe J. Bernstein, Florentino García Martínez, and John Kampen, 195–211. STDJ 23. Leiden: Brill, 1997.

Weitzman, Steven P. "Absent but Accounted For: A New Approach to the Copper Scroll," *Harvard Theological Review* 108 (2015): 423–47.

Weitzman, Steven P. "David's Lament and the Poetics of Grief in 2 Samuel," *Jewish Quarterly Review* 85 (1995): 343–60.

Weitzman, Steven P. *Song and Story in Biblical Narrative: The History of a Literary Convention in Ancient Israel*. Bloomington: Indiana University Press, 1997.

Weiser, Arthur. *The Psalms: A Commentary*. Trans. H. Hartwell. OTL. Philadelphia: Westminster, 1962.

Wendland, P. *Philonis Alexandrini opera quae supersunt*, vol. 2. Berlin: Reimer, 1897; repr. Berlin: de Gruyter, 1962.

Werman, Cana. "Qumran and the Book of Noah." In *Pseudepigraphic Perspectives: The Apocrypha and Pseudepigrapha in Light of the Dead Sea Scrolls*, ed. Esther G. Chazon and Michael E. Stone, 171–81. STDJ 31. Leiden: Brill, 1999.

Werman, Cana. "The '[tôrâ] and the [tĕ'ûdâ]' Engraved on the Tablets," *Dead Sea Discoveries* 9 (2002): 75–103.

Wilson, Gerald H. *The Editing of the Hebrew Psalter*. SBLDS 76. Chico, Calif.: Scholars Press, 1985.

Wilson, Gerald H. "King, Messiah, and Reign of God: Revisiting the Royal Psalms and the Shape of the Psalter." In *The Book of Psalms: Composition and Reception*, ed. Peter W. Flint and Patrick D. Miller, 392–406. Leiden: Brill, 2005.

Wilson, Gerald H. "The Qumran Psalms Scroll (11QPsᵃ) and the Canonical Psalter: Comparison of Editorial Shaping," *Catholic Biblical Quarterly* 59 (1997): 448–64.

Wilson, Gerald H. "The Shape of the Book of Psalms," *Interpretation* 46 (1992): 129–42.

Winter, Michael M. "The Origins of Ben Sira in Syriac," *Vetus Testamentum* 27 (1977): 237–53, 494–507.

Wise, Michael O. *The First Messiah: Investigating the Savior before Jesus*. San Francisco: HarperCollins, 1999.

Wollenberg, Rebecca Scharbach. "The People of the Book without the Book: Jewish Ambivalence toward Biblical Text after the Rise of Christianity." PhD diss., University of Chicago, 2015.

Workineh, Habte-Mariam. *yeEthiopia Orthodox Tewahedo Bete Kristian Emnetna Timihirt (The Ethiopian Orthodox Tewahedo Church Faith and Doctrine)*. Addis Ababa: Berhanena Selam, 1969–70.

Wright, Benjamin G., III. "Ben Sira on the Sage as Exemplar." In *Praise Israel for Wisdom and Instruction: Essays on Ben Sira and Wisdom, the Letter of Aristeas and the Septuagint*, 165–82. Leiden: Brill, 2008.

Wright, Benjamin G., III. "B. Sanhedrin 100b and Rabbinic Knowledge of Ben Sira." In *Praise Israel for Wisdom and Instruction: Essays on Ben Sira and Wisdom, the Letter of Aristeas and the Septuagint*, 183–93. Leiden: Brill, 2008.

Wright, Benjamin G., III. "From Generation to Generation: The Sage as Father in Early Jewish Literature." In *Praise Israel for Wisdom and Instruction: Essays on Ben Sira and Wisdom, the Letter of Aristeas and the Septuagint*, 309–32. Leiden: Brill, 2008.

Wright, Benjamin G., III. *The Letter of Aristeas: 'Aristeas to Philocrates' or 'On the Translation of the Law of the Jews.'* Commentaries on Early Jewish Literature. Berlin: De Gruyter, 2015.

Wright, Benjamin G., III. "Moving beyond Translating a Translation: Reflections on A New English Translation of the Septuagint (NETS)." In *"Translation Is Required": The Septuagint in Retrospect and Prospect*, ed. R. Hiebert, 23–39. SBLSCS 30. Atlanta: Society of Biblical Literature, 2010.

Wright, Benjamin G., III. "Preliminary Thoughts about Preparing the Text of Ben Sira for a Commentary." In *Die Septuaginta: Text—Wirkung—Rezeption*, ed. Wolfgang Kraus and Martin Karrer, 89–109. Tübingen: Mohr Siebeck, 2014.

Wyrick, Jed. *The Ascension of Authorship: Attribution and Canon Formation in Jewish, Hellenistic, and Christian Traditions.* Cambridge, Mass.: Harvard University Press, 2004.

Yadin-Israel, Azzan. *Scripture and Tradition: Rabbi Akiva and the Triumph of Midrash.* Philadelphia: University of Pennsylvania Press, 2015.

Yadin [Yadin-Israel], Azzan. *Scripture as Logos: Rabbi Ishmael and the Origins of Midrash.* Philadelphia: University of Pennsylvania Press, 2004.

Yadin, Yigael. *The Ben Sira Scroll from Masada.* Jerusalem: Israel Exploration Society, 1965.

Yarchin, William. "Was 11Q5 a True Psalter?" Paper presented at the Society of Biblical Literature Annual Meeting, November 23, 2013. Published as "Were the Psalms Collections at Qumran True Psalters?" *Journal of Biblical Literature* 134 (2015): 775–89.

Zahn, Molly M. *Rethinking Rewritten Scripture: Composition and Exegesis in the 4QReworked Pentateuch Manuscripts.* STDJ 95. Leiden: Brill, 2011.

Zahn, Molly M. "Rewritten Scripture." In *The Oxford Handbook of the Dead Sea Scrolls*, ed. Timothy H. Lim and John J. Collins, 323–36. Oxford: Oxford University Press, 2010.

Zsengellér, József, ed. *Rewritten Bible after Fifty Years: Texts, Terms, or Techniques? A Last Dialogue with Geza Vermes.* JSJSupp 166. Leiden: Brill, 2014.

INDEX OF ANCIENT SOURCES

RABBINIC LITERATURE

Other Ancient Sources

INDEX OF MODERN AUTHORS

INDEX OF SUBJECTS

CPSIA information can be obtained
at www.ICGtesting.com
Printed in the USA
BVHW03s1620250318
511494BV00002B/19/P